A·N·N·U·A·L E·D·I·T

Social Problems 04/05

Thirty-Second Edition

EDITOR
Kurt Finsterbusch

University of Maryland, College Park

Kurt Finsterbusch received a bachelor's degree in history from Princeton University in 1957 and a bachelor of divinity degree from Grace Theological Seminary in 1960. His Ph.D. in sociology, from Columbia University, was conferred in 1969. Dr. Finsterbusch is the author of several books, including *Understanding Social Impacts* (Sage Publications, 1980), *Social Research for Policy Decisions* (Wadsworth Publishing, 1980, with Annabelle Bender Motz), and *Organizational Change as a Development Strategy* (Lynne Rienner Publishers, 1987, with Jerald Hage). He is currently teaching at the University of Maryland, College Park, and, in addition to serving as editor for *Annual Editions: Social Problems*, he is also editor of *Annual Editions: Sociology*, McGraw-Hill/Dushkin's *Taking Sides: Clashing Views on Controversial Social Issues*, and *Sources: Notable Selections in Sociology*.

McGraw-Hill/Dushkin

2460 Kerper Blvd., Dubuque, Iowa 52001

Visit us on the Internet
http://www.dushkin.com

Credits

1. **Introduction: The Nature of Social Problems and General Critiques of American Society**
   Unit photo—© 2003 by PhotoDisc, Inc.
2. **Problems of the Political Economy**
   Unit photo—Courtesy fo TRW, Inc.
3. **Problems of Poverty and Inequality**
   Unit photo—© 2003 by Sweet By & By/Cindy Brown.
4. **Institutional Problems**
   Unit photo—© 2003 by Cleo Freelance Photography.
5. **Crime, Violence, and Law Enforcement**
   Unit photo—© 2003 PhotoDisc, Inc.
6. **Problems of Population, Environment, Resources, and the Future**
   Unit photo—© 2003 by Sweet By & By/Cindy Brown.

Copyright

Cataloging in Publication Data
Main entry under title: Annual Editions: Social Problems. 2004/2005.
1. Social Problems—Periodicals. I. Finsterbusch, K, *comp*. II. Title: Social Problems.
ISBN 0–07–291729–6   658'.05   ISSN 0272–4464

Thirty-Second Edition

Cover image © D. Falconer/PhotoLink/Getty Images and Mel Curtis/Getty Images.
Printed in the United States of America   1234567890QPDQPD0987654

To the Reader

In publishing ANNUAL EDITIONS we recognize the enormous role played by the magazines, newspapers, and journals of the public press in providing current, first-rate educational information in a broad spectrum of interest areas. Many of these articles are appropriate for students, researchers, and professionals seeking accurate, current material to help bridge the gap between principles and theories and the real world. These articles, however, become more useful for study when those of lasting value are carefully collected, organized, indexed, and reproduced in a low-cost format, which provides easy and permanent access when the material is needed. That is the role played by ANNUAL EDITIONS.

The reason we study social problems is so that we can do something about them. Corrective action, however, is not taken until the situation is seen as a problem and the fire of concern is kindled in a number of citizens. A democratic country gives those citizens means for legally trying to change things, and this freedom and opportunity is a great pride for our country. In fact, most college students have already given some time or money to a cause in which they believe. This is necessary because each generation will face struggles for justice and rights. Daily forces operate to corrupt, distort, bias, exploit, and defraud as individuals and groups seek their own advantage at the expense of others and the public interest. Those dedicated to a good society, therefore, constantly struggle against these forces. Furthermore, the struggle is often complex and confusing. Not always are the defenders of the status quo in the wrong and the champions of change in the right. Important values will be championed by both sides. Today there is much debate about the best way to improve education. Opposing spokespersons think they are serving the good of the children and of America. In a similar manner, conscientious students in the same college class and reading the same material will hotly disagree. Therefore, solving problems is usually not a peaceful process. First it requires information and an understanding of the problem, and we can expect disagreements on both the facts and the interpretations. Second, it requires discussion, compromises, and a plan with majority support or at least the support of the powerful groups. Third, it requires action. In a democratic society this process should involve tolerance and even goodwill toward one's opponents as long as they act honestly, fairly, and democratically. Class discussions should involve respect for each others' opinions.

In some ways the study of social problems is easy and in some ways it is hard. The easy aspect is that most people know quite a lot about the problems that this book addresses; the hard part is that solving the problems is very difficult. If the solutions were easy, the problems would have been solved by now, and we would not be studying these particular issues. It may be easy to plan solutions, but it is hard to implement them. In general, however, Americans are optimistic and believe in progress; we learn by our mistakes and keep trying until conditions are acceptable. For instance, the members of Common Cause, including myself, have worked for campaign finance reform since 1970. Our efforts failed until Watergate created a huge public demand for it, and both campaign finance reform and public-right-to-know laws were passed. The reform, however, led to the formation of PACs (Political Action Committees) to get around the law and buy influence legally. Recently new campaign finance reform laws were passed. Nevertheless, I would speculate that while they will somewhat reduce the influence of money on politics, sooner or later moneyed interests will find a way to continue to have inordinate influence on policy decisions and eventually precipitate yet another reform effort. It could be that at the end of the twenty-first century Americans will be struggling with many of the same problems as today, but it is reasonable to believe that things will be somewhat better at that point because throughout this century people will mobilize again and again to improve our society; some will do this at considerable cost to themselves.

The articles presented here were selected for their attention to important issues, the value of the information and ideas that they present, and/or their ability to move the reader to concern and possibly even action toward correcting social problems. This edition of *Annual Editions: Social Problems* begins in unit 1 by defining social problems and presenting a general critique of American society. In unit 2 it examines some big issues in the political and economic systems that have society-wide impacts. Next, unit 3 examines issues of inequality and injustice that challenge basic American values. Unit 4 considers how well the various institutions of society work. Most are being heavily criticized. Why? Then, unit 5 studies the traditional problem of crime and law enforcement. Fortunately, there is some good news here. Finally, unit 6 confronts the issue of sustainability in a world experiencing serious environmental decline.

To assist the reader in identifying issues covered in the articles, the *topic guide* lists the topics in alphabetical order and the articles in which they are discussed. A reader doing research on a specific topic is advised to check this guide first. A valuable resource for users of this book is the *World Wide Web sites* that can be used to further explore article topics.

Annual Editions: Social Problems 04/05 depends upon reader response to develop and change. You are encouraged to return the postpaid *article rating form* at the back of the book with your opinions about existing articles, recommendations of articles for subsequent editions, and advice on how the anthology can be made more useful as a teaching and learning tool.

Kurt Finsterbusch

Kurt Finsterbu sch

Editor

Dedicated to my students who have taught me to be more concerned about many social problems.

Contents

UNIT 1
Introduction: The Nature of Social Problems and General Critiques of American Society

Three introductory articles summarize the three major theoretical approaches to studying social problems, the fragmentation of social life, and re-moralizing the United States.

The concepts in bold italics are developed in the article. For further expansion, please refer to the Topic Guide and the Index.

UNIT 2
Problems of the Political Economy

Six articles examine how the distribution of wealth, diplomacy, and the state of American workers have an impact on politics and the economy.

The concepts in bold italics are developed in the article. For further expansion, please refer to the Topic Guide and the Index.

UNIT 3
Problems of Poverty and Inequality

Eleven selections discuss how inequality affects the social structure. Topics include polarity of wealth, welfare, racial and ethnic inequality, gener inequality, and the vulnerability of the elderly.

The concepts in bold italics are developed in the article. For further expansion, please refer to the Topic Guide and the Index.

UNIT 4
Institutional Problems

Seven selections discuss problems with the institutions of family, education, and health.

Unit Overview   **112**

The concepts in bold italics are developed in the article. For further expansion, please refer to the Topic Guide and the Index.

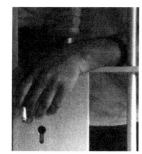

UNIT 5
Crime, Violence, and Law Enforcement

Six articles examine crime in today's society, how the law attempts to control this problem, and the dimension of violence and terrorism.

The concepts in bold italics are developed in the article. For further expansion, please refer to the Topic Guide and the Index.

UNIT 6
Problems of Population, Environment, Resources, and the Future

Six articles discuss the problems faced by our society with regard to the pressure of increasing population, environment degradation, and what our future may hold.

The concepts in bold italics are developed in the article. For further expansion, please refer to the Topic Guide and the Index.

The concepts in bold italics are developed in the article. For further expansion, please refer to the Topic Guide and the Index.

Topic Guide

This topic guide suggests how the selections in this book relate to the subjects covered in your course. You may want to use the topics listed on these pages to search the Web more easily.

On the following pages a number of Web sites have been gathered specifically for this book. They are arranged to reflect the units of this *Annual Edition.* You can link to these sites by going to the DUSHKIN ONLINE support site at *http://www.dushkin.com/online/.*

ALL THE ARTICLES THAT RELATE TO EACH TOPIC ARE LISTED BELOW THE BOLD-FACED TERM.

Abuse
17. Human Rights, Sex Trafficking, and Prostitution
20. When Baby Boomers Grow Old

African Americans
15. What's At Stake

Aggression
16. Why We Hate
17. Human Rights, Sex Trafficking, and Prostitution
28. Global Trends in Crime
32. Teaching Kids to Kill
33. The New Terrorism: Securing the Nation Against a Messianic Foe

AIDS
27. Death Stalks a Continent

Anxiety
22. We're Not in the Mood

Assisted living
20. When Baby Boomers Grow Old

Attachment
24. Should You Stay Together for the Kids?

Baby boomers
20. When Baby Boomers Grow Old

Beliefs
18. The War Over Gay Marriage
21. The American Family

Brain development
18. The War Over Gay Marriage
19. The New Gender Gap

Buffalo Commons
9. A Broken Heartland

Business
7. The End of Globalization
8. Where the Good Jobs Are Going
13. Corporate Welfare

22. We're Not in the Mood
26. The Doctor Won't See You Now

Campaign financing
6. How the Little Guy Gets Crunched

Capitalism
7. The End of Globalization
10. For Richer: How the Permissive Capitalism of the Boom Destroyed American Equality
13. Corporate Welfare

Career
22. We're Not in the Mood

Children and childhood
11. The Real Face of Homelessness
17. Human Rights, Sex Trafficking, and Prostitution
19. The New Gender Gap
21. The American Family
23. Divorce and Cohabitation: Why We Don't Marry
24. Should You Stay Together for the Kids?
32. Teaching Kids to Kill

Civil rights
5. Rights, Liberties, and Security: Recalibrating the Balance After September 11
15. What's At Stake
17. Human Rights, Sex Trafficking, and Prostitution
18. The War Over Gay Marriage
19. The New Gender Gap

Civil society
9. A Broken Heartland

Community
2. The Fragmentation of Social Life
3. How to Re-Moralize America
9. A Broken Heartland
16. Why We Hate
38. Community Building: Steps Toward a Good Society

Conflict
1. Social Problems: Definitions, Theories, and Analysis
6. How the Little Guy Gets Crunched
13. Corporate Welfare
15. What's At Stake
16. Why We Hate
18. The War Over Gay Marriage
33. The New Terrorism: Securing the Nation Against a Messianic Foe

World Wide Web Sites

The following World Wide Web sites have been carefully researched and selected to support the articles found in this reader. The easiest way to access these selected sites is to go to our DUSHKIN ONLINE support site at *http://www.dushkin.com/online/*.

AE: Social Problems 04/05

The following sites were available at the time of publication. Visit our Web site—we update DUSHKIN ONLINE regularly to reflect any changes.

General Sources

The Gallup Organization
http://www.gallup.com
Open this Gallup Organization home page for links to an extensive archive of public opinion poll results and special reports on a huge variety of topics related to American society.

Library of Congress
http://www.loc.gov
Examine this extensive Web site to learn about resource tools, library services/resources, exhibitions, and databases in many different fields related to social problems.

National Geographic Society
http://www.nationalgeographic.com
This site provides links to National Geographic's huge archive of maps, articles, and other documents. There is a great deal of material related to social and cultural topics that will be of great value to those interested in the study of cultural pluralism.

UNIT 1: Introduction: The Nature of Social Problems and General Critiques of American Society

American Studies Web
http://www.georgetown.edu/crossroads/asw/
This eclectic site provides links to a wealth of resources on the Internet related to social issues, from gender studies to education to race and ethnicity. It is of great help when doing research in demography and population studies.

Anthropology Resources Page
http://www.usd.edu/anth/
Many cultural topics can be accessed from this site from the University of South Dakota. Click on the links to find information about differences and similarities in values and lifestyles among the world's peoples.

Social Science Information Gateway
http://sosig.esrc.bris.ac.uk
SOSIG is an online catalog of Internet resources relevant to social science education and research. Every resource is selected by a librarian or subject specialist.

UNIT 2: Problems of the Political Economy

National Center for Policy Analysis
http://www.ncpa.org
Using these Policy Digest Archives, you can link to discussions on an array of topics that are of major interest in the study of American politics and government from a sociological perspective, from regulatory policy, to affirmative action, to income.

Penn Library: Sociology
http://www.library.upenn.edu/resources/subject/social/sociology/sociology. html
This site provides a number of indexes on culture and ethnic studies, population and demographics, and statistical sources that are of value in studying social problems.

Virtual Seminar in Global Political Economy/Global Cities & Social Movements
http://csf.colorado.edu/gpe/gpe95b/resources.html
The links at this site cover topics such as sustainable cities, megacities, and urban planning. The site also has links to many international nongovernmental organizations.

UNIT 3: Problems of Poverty and Inequality

grass-roots.org
http://www.grass-roots.org
Various resources and models for grassroots action and a summary and samples of Robin Garr's book, *Reinvesting in America,* are provided at this site.

Immigration Facts
http://www.immigrationforum.org
The pro-immigrant National Immigration Forum offers this page to examine the effects of immigration on the U.S. economy and society. Click on the links for discussion of underground economies, immigrant economies, and other topics.

Joint Center for Poverty Research
http://www.jcpr.org
Open this site to find research information related to poverty. The site provides working papers, answers to FAQs, and facts about who is poor in America. Welfare reform is also addressed.

SocioSite
http://www.pscw.uva.nl/sociosite/TOPICS/Women.html
This sociology site from the University of Amsterdam's Sociology Department provides links to affirmative action, family and children's issues, and much more.

William Davidson Institute
http://www.wdi.bus.umich.edu
Access the University of Michigan Business School's site for topics related to the changing global economy and the effects of globalization in general.

WWW Virtual Library: Demography & Population Studies
http://demography.anu.edu.au/VirtualLibrary/
Here is a definitive guide to demography and population studies. A multitude of important links to information about global poverty and hunger can be found here.

UNIT 4: Institutional Problems

The Center for Education Reform
http://edreform.com/school_choice/
Visit this site to view current opinions and concerns related to school choice and school reform.

Go Ask Alice!

http://www.goaskalice.columbia.edu

This interactive site provides discussion and insight into a number of personal issues of interest to college-age people and those younger and older. Questions about physical and emotional health and well-being in the modern world are answered.

The National Academy for Child Development (NACD)

http://www.nacd.org

This international organization is dedicated to helping children and adults to reach their full potential. Its home page presents links to various programs, research, and resources into topics related to the family and society.

National Council on Family Relations (NCFR)

http://www.ncfr.com

This NCFR home page will lead you to valuable links to articles, research, and other resources on important issues in family relations, such as stepfamilies, couples, and divorce.

National Institute on Aging (NIA)

http://www.nih.gov/nia/

The NIA presents this home page to lead you to a variety of resources on health, lifestyle, and social issues that are of concern to people as they grow older.

National Institute on Drug Abuse (NIDA)

http://165.112.78.61

Use this site index of the U.S. National Institute on Drug Abuse for access to NIDA publications, information on drugs of abuse, and links to other related Web sites.

National Institutes of Health (NIH)

http://www.nih.gov

Consult this site for links to extensive health information and scientific resources. Comprised of 24 institutes, centers, and divisions, including the Institute of Mental Health, the NIH is one of eight health agencies of the Public Health Service.

Parenting and Families

http://www.cyfc.umn.edu/features/index.html

The University of Minnesota's Children, Youth, and Family Consortium site leads to many organizations and other resources related to divorce, single parenting, and stepfamilies, and to information about other topics about the family.

A Sociological Tour Through Cyberspace

http://www.trinity.edu/~mkearl/index.html

This extensive site provides valuable essays, commentaries, data analyses, and links on every aspect of social problems, including such topics as death and dying, family, social gerontology, and social psychology.

World Health Organization (WHO)

http://www.who.int/home-page/

The World Health Organization will provide you with links to a wealth of statistical and analytical information about health and the environment in the developing world.

UNIT 5: Crime, Violence, and Law Enforcement

ACLU Criminal Justice Home Page

http://aclu.org/CriminalJustice/CriminalJusticeMain.cfm

This Criminal Justice page of the American Civil Liberties Union Web site highlights recent events in criminal justice, addresses police issues, lists important resources, and contains a search mechanism.

Terrorism Research Center

http://www.terrorism.com

The Terrorism Research Center features definitions and original research on terrorism, counterterrorism documents, a comprehensive list of Web links, and monthly profiles of terrorist and counterterrorist groups.

UNIT 6: Problems of Population, Environment, Resources, and the Future

Communications for a Sustainable Future

http://csf.colorado.edu

This site will lead you to information on topics in international environmental sustainability. It pays particular attention to the political economics of protecting the environment.

Human Rights and Humanitarian Assistance

http://www.etown.edu/vl/humrts.html

Through this part of the World Wide Web Virtual Library, you can conduct research into a number of human-rights concerns around the world. The site also provides links to many other subjects related to important social issues.

The Hunger Project

http://www.thp.org

Browse through this nonprofit organization's site to explore how it tries to achieve its goal: the end to global hunger through leadership at all levels of society. The Hunger Project contends that the persistence of hunger is at the heart of the major security issues threatening our planet.

We highly recommend that you review our Web site for expanded information and our other product lines. We are continually updating and adding links to our Web site in order to offer you the most usable and useful information that will support and expand the value of your Annual Editions. You can reach us at: *http://www.dushkin.com/annualeditions/*.

UNIT 1

Introduction: The Nature of Social Problems and General Critiques of American Society

Unit Selections

1. **Social Problems: Definitions, Theories, and Analysis**, Harold A. Widdison and H. Richard Delaney
2. **The Fragmentation of Social Life**, D. Stanley Eitzen
3. **How to Re-Moralize America**, Francis Fukuyama

Key Points to Consider

- What are your first five choices for the major social problems of America? In what ways does your list seem to reflect one of the three major approaches to social problems?

- How much distance do you feel from people with very different interests, values, lifestyles, religion, race or ethnicity, and class? What kinds of bonds do you feel with them?

- What signs of moral decay in America do you observe? What signs of moral strength do you observe?

- Describe what you imagine the re-moralization of society would be like?

 Links: www.dushkin.com/online/
These sites are annotated in the World Wide Web pages.

American Studies Web
http://www.georgetown.edu/crossroads/asw/

Anthropology Resources Page
http://www.usd.edu/anth/

Social Science Information Gateway
http://sosig.esrc.bris.ac.uk

What is a social problem? There are several different definitions of social problems and many different lists of serious social problems today. As editor of the 04/05 edition of *Annual Editions: Social Problems*, I have tried to provide valuable articles on all of the topics that are covered in most social problems textbooks.

Three articles are included in this introductory unit. The first deals with the issue of the definition of "social problems" and the major approaches to understanding these problems in a larger theoretical framework. The second is my selection for an article that provides a thoroughgoing broad critique of American society. It does not address one social problem but presents the author's view of what is wrong with America in general. Its main theme is that social life in America is extremely fragmented, so individual well-being suffers. The third accepts the moral decline thesis and analyzes how America could re-moralize.

Harold Widdison and H. Richard Delaney, in the first article, introduce the reader to sociology's three dominant theoretical positions and give examples of how those espousing each theory would look at specific issues. The three theories—symbolic interactionism, functionalism, and conflict theory—represent three radically different approaches to the study of social problems and their implications for individuals and societies. The perceived etiology of problems and their possible resolutions reflect the specific orientations of those studying them. As you read the subsequent articles, try to determine which of the three theoretical positions the various authors seem to be utilizing. Widdison and Delaney conclude this article by suggesting several approaches that students may wish to consider in defining conditions as "social" problems and how they can and should be analyzed.

In the second article, D. Stanley Eitzen admits that some social indicators are quite positive, such as low unemployment, but chooses to focus on some social problems. He cites several and then explores the fragmentation of social life. His question is, "Will society continue to cohere or will new crises pull us apart?" He discusses excessive individualism, heightened personal isolation, the widening income and wealth gaps, and the deepening racial/ethnic/religious/sexuality divide. He shows that these divisions are deep. The next issue is "whether the integrative societal mechanisms that have served us well in the past will save us again or whether we will continue to fragment." He does not answer this question, but he worries that the answer may be no.

Francis Fukuyama, in the third article, points out that recently many of the indicators of moral decline have started to improve. They are still far worse than three decades ago, but further decline does not seem likely. This raises an interesting sociological question: Can America re-moralize? And if so, how? Fukuyama tries to answer these questions. He must first explain the sources of value systems and then explain how they arise and change. Finally, he must extrapolate from these analyses a theory of value transformation that can explain the potential for moral regeneration in the 1990s. He sets for himself a daunting intellectual challenge and leads the reader through a sociological detective story as he takes on the task.

SOCIAL PROBLEMS:
Definitions, Theories, and Analysis

Harold A. Widdison and H. Richard Delaney

INTRODUCTION AND OVERVIEW

When asked, "What are the major social problems facing humanity today?" college students' responses tend to mirror those highlighted by the mass media—particularly AIDS, child abuse, poverty, war, famine, racism, sexism, crime, riots, the state of the economy, the environment, abortion, euthanasia, homosexuality, and affirmative action. These are all valid subjects for study in a social problems class, but some give rise to very great differences of opinion and even controversy. Dr. Jack Kevorkian in Michigan and his killing machine is one example that comes to mind. To some he evokes images of Nazi Germany with its policy of murdering the infirm and helpless. Others see Kevorkian's work as a merciful alternative to the slow and agonizing death of individuals with terminal illnesses. In the latter light, Kevorkian is not symbolic of a potentially devastating social issue, but of a solution to an escalating social problem.

The same controversy exists at the other end of life—specifically, what obligations do pregnant women have to themselves as opposed to the unborn? Some individuals see abortion as a solution to the problems of population, child abuse, disruption of careers, dangers to the physical and emotional health of women, as well as the prevention of the birth of damaged fetuses, and they regard it as a right to self-determination. Others look at abortion as attacking the sanctity of life, abrogating the rights of a whole category of people, and violating every sense of moral and ethical responsibility.

Affirmative action is another issue that can be viewed as both a problem and a solution. As a solution, affirmative action attempts to reverse the effects of hundreds of years of discrimination. Doors that have been closed to specific categories of people for many generations are, it is hoped, forced open; individuals, regardless of race, ethnicity, and gender, are able to get into professional schools, and secure good jobs, with the assurance of promotion. On the other hand, affirmative action forces employers, recruiting officers, and housing officials to give certain categories of individuals a preferred status. While affirmative action is promoted by some as a necessary policy to compensate for centuries of exclusion and discrimination, others claim that it is discrimination simply disguised under a new label but with different groups being discriminated against. If race, sex, age, ethnicity, or any other characteristic other than merit is used as the primary criterion for selection or promotion, then discrimination is occurring. Discrimination hurts both sides. William Wilson, an African American social scientist, argues that it is very damaging to the self-esteem of black individuals to know that the primary reason they were hired was to fill quotas.

Both sides to the debate of whether these issues themselves reflect a social problem or are solutions to a larger societal problem have valid facts and use societal-level values to support their claims. Robin William Jr. in 1970 identified a list of 15 dominant value orientations that represent the concept of the good life to many Americans:

1. Achievement and success as major personal goals.
2. Activity and work favored above leisure and laziness.
3. Moral orientation—that is, absolute judgments of good/bad, right/wrong.
4. Humanitarian motives as shown in charity and crisis aid.
5. Efficiency and practicality: a preference for the quickest and shortest way to achieve a goal at the least cost.
6. Process and progress: a belief that technology can solve all problems and that the future will be better than the past.
7. Material comfort as the "American dream."
8. Equality as an abstract ideal.
9. Freedom as a person's right against the state.
10. External conformity: the ideal of going along, joining, and not rocking the boat.
11. Science and rationality as the means of mastering the environment and securing more material comforts.

12. Nationalism: a belief that American values and institutions represent the best on earth.
13. Democracy based on personal equality and freedom.
14. Individualism, emphasizing personal rights and responsibilities.
15. Racism and group-superiority themes that periodically lead to prejudice and discrimination against those who are racially, religiously, and culturally different from the white northern Europeans who first settled the continent.

This list combines some political, economic, and personal traits that actually conflict with one another. This coexistence of opposing values helps explain why individuals hold contradictory views of the same behavior and why some issues generate such intensity of feelings. It is the intent of this article and the readings included in this book to attempt to help students see the complex nature of a social problem and the impact that various values, beliefs, and actions can have on them.

In the next segment of this article, the authors will look at specific examples of values in conflict and the problems created by this conflict. Subsequently the authors will look at the three major theoretical positions that sociologists use to study social problems. The article will conclude with an examination of various strategies and techniques used to identify, understand, and resolve various types of social problems and their implications for those involved.

As noted above, contemporary American society is typified by values that both complement and contradict each other. For example, the capitalistic free enterprise system of the United States stresses rugged individualism, self-actualization, individual rights, and self-expression. This economic philosophy meshes well with Christian theology, particularly that typified by many Protestant denominations. This fact was the basis of German sociologist Max Weber's "The Protestant Ethic and the Spirit of Capitalism" (1864). He showed that the concepts of grace (salvation is a gift—not something you can earn), predestination (the fact that some people have this gift while others do not), and a desire to know if the individual has grace gave rise to a new idea of what constitutes success. Whereas, with the communitarian emphasis of Catholicism where material success was seen as leading to selfishness and spiritual condemnation, Protestantism viewed material success as a sign of grace. In addition, it was each individual's efforts that resulted in both the economic success and the spiritual salvation of the individual. This religious philosophy also implied that the poor are poor because they lack the proper motivation, values, and beliefs (what is known as the "culture of poverty") and are therefore reaping the results of their own inadequacies. Attempts to reduce poverty have frequently included taking children from "impoverished" cultural environments and placing them in "enriched" environments to minimize the potentially negative effects

parents and a bad environment could have on their children. These enrichment programs attempt to produce attitudes and behaviors that assure success in the world but, in the process, cut children off from their parents. Children are forced to abandon the culture of their parents if they are to "succeed." Examples of this practice include the nurseries of the kibbutz in Israel and the Head Start programs in America. This practice is seen by some social scientists as a type of "cultural genocide." Entire cultures were targeted (sometimes explicitly, although often not intentionally) for extinction in this way.

This fact upsets a number of social scientists. They feel it is desirable to establish a pluralistic society where ethnic, racial, and cultural diversity exist and flourish. To them attempts to "Americanize" everyone are indicative of racism, bigotry, and prejudice. Others point to the lack of strong ethnic or racial identities as the unifying strength of the American system. When immigrants came to America, they put ethnic differences behind them, they learned the English language and democratic values, and they were assimilated into American life. In nations where immigrants have maintained their ethnic identities and held to unique cultural beliefs, their first loyalty is to their ethnic group. Examples of the destructive impact of strong ethnic loyalties can be seen in the conflict and fragmentation now occurring in the former Soviet Union, Czechoslovakia, and Yugoslavia.

James Q. Wilson (1994:54–55) noted in this regard:

> We have always been a nation of immigrants, but now the level of immigration has reached the point where we have become acutely conscious, to a degree not seen, I think, since the turn of the century, that we are a nation of many cultures. I believe that the vast majority of those who have come to this country came because they, too, want to share in the American Dream. But their presence here, and the unavoidable tensions that attend upon even well-intentioned efforts at mutual coexistence, makes some people—and alas, especially some intellectuals in our universities—question the American Dream, challenge the legitimacy of Western standards of life and politics, and demand that everybody be defined in terms of his or her group membership. The motto of this nation—*E pluribus unum*, out of the many, one—is in danger of being rewritten to read, *Ex uno plures*—out of the one, many.

THEORETICAL EXPLANATIONS: SYMBOLIC INTERACTION, FUNCTIONALISM, CONFLICT

In their attempts to understand social phenomena, researchers look for recurring patterns, relationships between observable acts, and unifying themes. The par-

4

ticular way in which researchers look at the world reflects not only their personal views and experiences, but their professional perspective as well. Sociologists focus on interactions between individuals, between individuals and groups, between groups, and between groups and the larger society in which they are located. They try to identify those things that facilitate or hinder interaction, and the consequences of each. But not all sociologists agree as to the most effective/appropriate approach to take, and they tend to divide into three major theoretical camps: symbolic interactionism, functionalism, and conflict theory. These three approaches are not mutually exclusive, but they do represent radically different perspectives of the nature of social reality and how it should be studied.

Symbolic Interaction

This theoretical perspective argues that no social condition, however unbearable it may seem to some, is inherently or objectively a social problem until a significant number of politically powerful people agree that it is contrary to the public good. Scientists, social philosophers, religious leaders, and medical people may "know" that a specific action or condition has or will eventually have a devastating effect on society or a specific group in society, but until they can convince those who are in a position to control and perhaps correct the condition, it is not considered a social problem. Therefore it is not the social condition, but how the condition is defined and by whom, that determines if it is or will become a social problem. The social process whereby a specific condition moves from the level of an individual concern to a societal-level issue can be long and arduous or very short. An example of the latter occurred in the 1960s when some physicians noticed a significant increase in infants born with severe physical deformities. Medical researchers looking into the cause made a connection between the deformities and the drug thalidomide. Pregnant women suffering from severe nausea and health-threatening dehydration were prescribed this drug, which dramatically eliminated the nausea and appeared to have no bad side effects. But their babies were born with terrible deformities. Once the medical researchers discovered the connection, they presented their findings to their colleagues. When the data were reviewed and found to be scientifically valid, the drug was banned immediately. Thus a small group's assessment of an issue as a serious problem quickly was legitimized by those in power as a societal-level social problem and measures were taken to eliminate it.

Most situations are not this clear-cut. In the mid-1960s various individuals began to question the real reason(s) why the United States was involved in the war in Southeast Asia. They discovered data indicating that the war was not about protecting the democratic rights of the Vietnamese. Those in power either ignored or rejected such claims as politically motivated and as militarily naive. Reports from the Vietcong about purported U.S. military atrocities were collected and used as supportive evidence. These claims were summarily dismissed by American authorities as Communistic propaganda. Convinced of the validity and importance of their cause, the protesters regrouped and collected still more evidence including data collected by the French government. This new information was difficult for the U.S. government to ignore. Nevertheless, these new claims were rejected as being somewhat self-serving since the Vietcong had defeated the French in Indochina and presumably the French government could justify its own failure if the United States also failed.

Over the years the amount of data continued to accumulate augmented by new information collected from disenchanted veterans. This growing pool of evidence began to bother legislators who demanded an accounting from the U.S. government and the Department of Defense, but none was forthcoming. More and more students joined the antiwar movement, but their protests were seen as unpatriotic and self-serving—that is, an attempt to avoid military service. The increasing numbers of protesters caused some legislators to look more closely at the claims of the antiwar faction. As the magnitude of the war and the numbers of American servicemen involved grew, the numbers of people affected by the war grew as well. Returning veterans' reports of the state of the war, questionable military practices (such as the wholesale destruction of entire villages), complaints of incompetent leadership in the military, and corrupt Vietnamese politicians gave greater credibility to the antiwar movement's earlier claims and convinced additional senators and representatives to support the stop-the-war movement, even though those in power still refused to acknowledge the legitimacy of the movement.

Unable to work within the system and convinced of the legitimacy of their cause, protesters resorted to unconventional and often illegal actions, such as burning their draft cards, refusing to register for the draft, seeking refuge in other countries, attacking ROTC (Reserve Officers' Training Corps) buildings on college campuses, and even bombing military research facilities. These actions were initially interpreted by government officials as criminal activities of self-serving individuals or activities inspired by those sympathetic with the Communist cause. The government engaged in increasingly repressive efforts to contain the movement. But public disaffection with the war was fueled by rising American casualties; this, coupled with the discontent within the ranks of the military, eventually forced those in power to acquiesce and accept the claims that the war was the problem and not the solution to the problem. Reaching this point took nearly 15 years.

For the symbolic interactionist, the fact that socially harmful conditions are thought to exist is not the criterion for what constitutes a social problem. Rather the real issue is to understand what goes into the assessment of a specific condition as being a social problem. To the symbolic interactionist, the appropriate questions are, (a) How is it that some conditions become defined as a social problem while others do not? (b) Who, in any society, can legitimate the designation of a condition as a social problem? (c) What solutions evolve and how do they evolve for specific social problems? (d) What factors exist in any specific society that inhibit or facilitate resolution of social problems?

In summary, symbolic interactionists stress that social problems do not exist independently of how people define their world. Social problems are socially constructed as people debate whether or not some social condition is a social problem and decide what to do about it. The focus is on the meanings the problem has for those who are affected by it and not on the impact it is having on them.

Functionalism

A second major theory sociologists use to study social problems is functionalism. Functionalists argue that society is a social system consisting of various integrated parts. Each of these parts fulfills a specific role that contributes to the overall functioning of society. In well-integrated systems, each part contributes to the stability of the whole. Functionalists examine each part in an attempt to determine the role it plays in the operation of the system as a whole. When any part fails, this creates a problem for the whole. These failures (dysfunctions) upset the equilibrium of the system and become social problems. To functionalists, anything that impedes the system's ability to achieve its goals is, by definition, a social problem. Unlike the symbolic interactionists, the functionalists argue that for itself that must necessarily be at the expense of other groups. It is this consistent conflict over limited resources that threatens societal peace and order.

Whereas the functionalists try to understand how different positions of power came into existence (Davis & Moore 1945), the conflictists show how those in power attempt to stay in power (Mills 1956). The conflict theorists see social problems as the natural and inevitable consequences of groups in society struggling to survive and gain control over those things that can affect their ability to survive. Those groups that are successful then attempt to use whatever means they must to control their environment and consolidate their position, thus increasing their chances of surviving. According to conflict theorists, those in power exploit their position and create poverty, discrimination, oppression, and crime in the process. The impact of these conditions on the exploited produces other pathological conditions such as alienation, alcoholism, drug abuse, mental illness, stress, health problems, and suicide. On occasions, such as that which occurred in Los Angeles in the summer of 1991 when policemen were found innocent of the use of excessive force in the beating of Rodney King, the feelings of helplessness and hopelessness can erupt as rage against the system in the form of violence and riots or as in Eastern Europe as rebellion and revolution against repressive governments.

The conflict theorists argue that drug abuse, mental illness, various criminal behaviors, and suicide are symptoms of a much larger societal malaise. To understand and eliminate these problems, society needs to understand the basic conflicts that are producing them. The real problems stem from the implications of being exploited. Being manipulated by the powerful and denied a sense of control tends (a) to produce a loss of control over one's life (powerlessness), (b) to lead to an inability to place one's productive efforts into some meaningful context (meaningless), (c) not to being involved in the process of change but only in experiencing the impact resulting from the changes (normlessness), and (d) to cause one to find oneself isolated from one's colleagues on the job (self-isolation). Conflictists see all of these problems as the product of a capitalistic system that alienates the worker from himself and from his or her fellow workers (Seeman 1959).

To protect their positions of power, privilege, prestige, and possessions, those in power use their wealth and influence to control organizations. For example, they manipulate the system to get key individuals into positions where they can influence legislation and decisions that are designed to protect their power and possessions. They might serve on or appoint others to school boards to assure that the skills and values needed by the economy are taught. They also assure that the laws are enforced internally (the police) or externally (the military) to protect their holdings. The war in the Persian Gulf is seen by many conflict theorists as having been fought for oil rather than for Kuwait's liberation. When the exploited attempt to do something about their condition by organizing, protesting, and rebelling, they threaten those in power. For example, they may go on a strike that might disrupt the entire nation. Under the pretext that it is for the best good of society, the government may step in and stop the strike. Examples are the air-traffic-controllers strike of 1987 and the railroad strike in 1991. In retaliation the workers may engage in work slow-down, stoppage, and even sabotage. They may stage protests and public demonstrations and cast protest votes at the ballot boxes. If these do not work, rebellions and revolutions may result. Those in power can respond very repressively as was the case in Tiananmen Square in China in 1989, threaten military force as the Soviet Union did with the Baltic countries in 1990, or back down completely as when the Berlin Wall came down. Thus reactions to exploitation may produce change but inevitably lead to other social problems. In Eastern Europe and the former Soviet Union, democracy has resulted in massive unemployment, spiraling inflation, hunger, crime, and homelessness.

Sometimes those in power make concessions to maintain power. Conflict theorists look for concessions and how they placate the poor while still protecting the privileged and powerful. The rich are viewed as sharing power only if forced to do so and only to the extent absolutely necessary.

Robert Michels (1949), a French social philosopher, looked at the inevitable process whereby the members of any group voluntarily give their rights, prerogatives, and power to a select few who then dominate the group. It may not be the conscious decision of those who end up in positions of power to dominate the group, but, in time, conscious decisions may be made to do whatever is necessary to stay in control of the group. The power, privilege, and wealth they acquire as part of the position alter their self-images. To give up the position would necessitate a complete revision of who they are, what they can do, and with whom they associate. Their "selves" have become fused/confused with the position they occupy, and in an attempt to protect their "selves," they resist efforts designed to undermine their control. They consider threats to themselves as threats to the organization and therefore feel justified in their vigorous resistance. According to Michels, no matter how democratic an organization starts out to be it will always become dominated and controlled by a few. The process whereby this occurs he labeled the "Iron Law of Oligarchy." For example, hospitals that were created to save lives, cure the sick, and provide for the chronically ill, now use the threat of closure to justify rate increases. The hospital gets its rate increase, the cost of health goes up, and the number of individuals able to afford health care declines, with the ultimate result being an increase in health problems for the community. Although not explicitly stated, the survival of the organization (and its administrators) becomes more important than the health of the community.

In summary, the conflict theoretical model stresses the fact that key resources such as power and privilege are limited and distributed unequally among the members/groups in a society. Conflict is therefore a natural and inevitable result of various groups pursuing their interests and values. To study the basis of social problems, researchers must look at the distribution of power and privilege because these two factors are always at the center of conflicting interests and values. Moreover, whenever social change occurs, social problems inevitably follow.

Conflict and Functionalism: A Synthesis

While conflict theorists' and functionalists' explanations of what constitutes the roots of social problems appear to be completely contradictory, Dahrendorf (1959) sees them as complementary. "Functionalism explains how highly talented people are motivated to spend twenty-five years of study to become surgeons; conflict theory explains how surgeons utilize their monopoly on their vital skills to obtain rewards that greatly exceed that necessary to ensure an adequate supply of talent." (See also Ossowski 1963; van de Berghe 1963; Williams 1966; Horowitz 1962; and Lenski 1966 for other attempts at a synthesis between these two theoretical models.)

SOCIAL PROBLEMS: DEFINITION AND ANALYSIS

Value Conflicts

It is convenient to characterize a social problem as a conflict of values, a conflict of values and duties, a conflict of rights (Hook, 1974), or a social condition that leads to or is thought to lead to harmful consequences. Harm may be defined as (a) the loss to a group, community, or society of something to which it is thought to be entitled, (b) an offense perceived to be an affront to our moral sensibilities, or (c) an impoverishment of the collective good or welfare. It is also convenient to define values as individual or collective desires that become attached to social objects. Private property, for example, is a valued social object for some while others disavow or reject its desirability; because of the public disagreement over its value, it presents a conflict of values. A conflict of values is also found in the current controversy surrounding abortion. Where pro-life supporters tend to see life itself as the ultimate value, supporters of pro-choice may, as some have, invoke the Fourteenth Amendment's right-to-privacy clause as the compelling value.

Values-versus-Duties Conflicts

A second format that students should be aware of in the analysis of social problems is the conflict between values and obligations or duties. This approach calls our attention to those situations in which a person, group, or community must pursue or realize a certain duty even though those participating may be convinced that doing so will not achieve the greater good. For example, educators, policemen, bureaucrats, and environmentalists may occupy organizational or social roles in which they are required to formulate policies and follow rules that, according to their understanding, will not contribute to the greater good of students, citizens, or the likelihood of a clean environment. On the other hand, there are situations in which we, as individuals, groups, or communities, do things that would not seem to be right in our pursuit of what we consider to be the higher value. Here students of social problems are faced with the familiar problem of using questionable, illogical, or immoral means to achieve what is perhaps generally recognized as a value of a higher order. Police officers, for example, are sometimes accused of employing questionable, immoral, or deceptive means (stings, scams, undercover operations) to achieve what are thought to be socially helpful ends and values such as removing a drug pusher from the streets. Familiar questions for this particular format are, Do the ends justify the means? Should ends be chosen according to the means available for their realization? What are the social processes by which means themselves become ends? These are questions to which students of social problems and social policy analysis should give attention since immoral, illegal, or deceptive means can themselves lead to harmful social consequences.

Max Weber anticipated and was quite skeptical of those modern bureaucratic processes whereby means are transformed into organizational ends and members of the bureaucracy become self-serving and lose sight of their original and earlier mission. The efforts of the Central Intelligence Agency (CIA) to maintain U.S. interests in Third World countries led to tolerance of various nations' involvement in illicit drugs. Thus the CIA actually contributed to the drug problem the police struggle to control. A second example is that of the American Association of Retired Persons (AARP). To help the elderly obtain affordable health care, life insurance, drugs, and so forth, the AARP established various organizations to provide or contract for services. But now the AARP seems to be more concerned about its corporate holdings than it is about the welfare of its elderly members.

RIGHTS IN CONFLICT

Finally, students of social problems should become aware of right-versus-right moral conflicts. With this particular format, one's attention is directed to the conflict of moral duties and obligations, the conflict of rights and, not least, the serious moral issue of divided loyalties. In divorce proceedings, for example, spouses must try to balance their personal lives and careers against the obligations and duties to each other and their children. Even those who sincerely want to meet their full obligations to both family and career often find this is not possible because of the real limits of time and means.

Wilson (1994:39, 54) observes that from the era of "Enlightenment" and its associated freedoms arose the potential for significant social problems. We are seeing all about us in the entire Western world the working out of the defining experience of the West, the Enlightenment. The Age of Enlightenment was the extraordinary period in the eighteenth century when individuals were emancipated from old tyrannies—from dead custom, hereditary monarchs, religious persecution, and ancient superstition. It is the period that gave us science and human rights, that attacked human slavery and political absolutism, that made possible capitalism and progress. The principal figures of the Enlightenment remain icons of social reform: Adam Smith, David Hume, Thomas Jefferson, Immanuel Kant, Isaac Newton, James Madison. The Enlightenment defined the West and set it apart from all of the other great cultures of the world. But in culture as in economics, there is no such thing as a free lunch. If you liberate a person from ancient tyrannies, you may also liberate him or her from familiar controls. If you enhance his or her freedom to create, you will enhance his or her freedom to destroy. If you cast out the dead hand of useless custom, you may also cast out the living hand of essential tradition. If you give an individual freedom of expres-

sion, he or she may write *The Marriage of Figaro* or he or she may sing "gangsta rap." If you enlarge the number of rights one has, you may shrink the number of responsibilities one feels.

There is a complex interaction between the rights an individual has and the consequences of exercising specific rights. For example, if an individual elects to exercise his or her right to consume alcoholic beverages, this act then nullifies many subsequent rights because of the potential harm that can occur. The right to drive, to engage in athletic events, or to work, is jeopardized by the debilitating effects of alcohol. Every citizen has rights assured him or her by membership in society. At the same time, rights can only be exercised to the degree to which they do not trample on the rights of other members of the group. If a woman elects to have a baby, must she abrogate her right to consume alcohol, smoke, consume caffeine, or take drugs? Because the effects of these substances on the developing fetus are potentially devastating, is it not reasonable to conclude that the rights of the child to a healthy body and mind are being threatened if the mother refuses to abstain during pregnancy? Fetal alcohol effect/syndrome, for instance, is the number-one cause of preventable mental retardation in the United States, and it could be completely eliminated if pregnant women never took an alcoholic drink. Caring for individuals with fetal alcohol effect/syndrome is taking increasingly greater resources that could well be directed toward other pressing issues.

Rights cannot be responsibly exercised without individuals' weighing their potential consequences. Thus a hierarchy of rights, consequences, and harms exists and the personal benefits resulting from any act must be weighed against the personal and social harms that could follow. The decision to use tobacco should be weighed against the possible consequences of a wide variety of harms such as personal health problems and the stress it places on society's resources to care for tobacco-related diseases. Tobacco-related diseases often have catastrophic consequences for their users that cannot be paid for by the individual, so the burden of payment is placed on society. Millions of dollars and countless health care personnel must be diverted away from other patients to care for these individuals with self-inflicted tobacco-related diseases. In addition to the costs in money, personnel, and medical resources, these diseases take tremendous emotional tolls on those closest to the diseased individuals. To focus only on one's rights without consideration of the consequences associated with those rights often deprives other individuals from exercising their rights.

The Constitution of the United States guarantees individuals rights without clearly specifying what the rights really entail. Logically one cannot have rights without others having corresponding obligations. But what obligations does each right assure and what limitations do these obligations and/or rights require? Rights for the collectivity are protected by limitations placed on each individual, but limits of collective rights are also mandated by laws assuring that individual rights are not infringed upon. Therefore, we have rights as a whole that often differ from those we have as individual members of that whole. For example, the right to free speech may impinge in a number of ways on a specific community. To the members of a small Catholic community, having non-Catholic missionaries preaching on street corners and proselytizing door-to-door could be viewed as a social problem. Attempts to control their actions such as the enactment and enforcements of "Green River" ordinances (laws against active solicitation), could eliminate the community's problem but in so doing would trample on the individual's constitutional rights or religious expression. To protect individual rights, the community may have to put up with individuals pushing their personal theological ideas in public places. From the perspective of the Catholic community, aggressive non-Catholic missionaries are not only a nuisance but a social problem that should be banned. To the proselytizing churches, restrictions on their actions are violations of their civil rights and hence a serious social problem.

Currently another conflict of interests/rights is dividing many communities, and that is cigarette smoking. Smokers argue that their rights are being seriously threatened by aggressive legislation restricting smoking. They argue that society should not and cannot legislate morality. Smokers point out how attempts to legislate alcohol consumption during the Prohibition of the 1920s and 1930s was an abject failure and, in fact, created more problems than it eliminated. They believe that the exact same process is being attempted today and will prove to be just as unsuccessful. Those who smoke then go on to say that smoking is protected by the Constitution's freedom of expression and that no one has the right to force others to adhere to his or her personal health policies, which are individual choices. They assert that if the "radicals" get away with imposing smoking restrictions, they can and will move on to other health-related behaviors such as overeating. Therefore, by protecting the constitutional rights of smokers, society is protecting the constitutional rights of everyone.

On the other hand, nonsmokers argue that their rights are being violated by smokers. They point to an increasing body of research data that shows that secondhand smoke leads to numerous health problems such as emphysema, heart disease, and throat and lung cancer. Not only do nonsmokers have a right not to have to breathe smoke-contaminated air, but society has an obligation to protect the health and well-being of its members from the known dangers of breathing smoke.

These are only a few examples of areas where rights come into conflict. Others include environmental issues, endangered species, forest management, enforcement of specific laws, homosexuality, mental illness, national health insurance, taxes, balance of trade, food labeling and packaging, genetic engineering, rape, sexual devia-

tion, political corruption, riots, public protests, zero population growth, the state of the economy, and on and on. It is notable that the degree to which any of these issues achieves widespread concern varies over time. Often, specific problems are given much fanfare by politicians and special interests groups for a time, and the media try to convince us that specific activities or behaviors have the greatest urgency and demand a total national commitment for a solution. However, after being in the limelight for a while, the importance of the problem seems to fade and new problems move into prominence. If you look back over previous editions of this book, you can see this trend. It would be useful to speculate why, in American society, some problems remain a national concern while others come and go.

The Consequences of Harm

To this point it had been argued that social problems can be defined and analyzed as (a) conflicts between values, (b) conflicts between values and duties, and (c) conflicts between rights. Consistent with the aims of this article, social problems can be further characterized and interpreted as social conditions that lead, or are generally thought to lead, to harmful consequences for the person, group, community, or society.

Harm—and here we follow Hyman Gross's (1979) conceptualization of the term—can be classified as (a) a loss, usually permanent, that deprives the person or group of a valued object or condition it is entitled to have, (b) offenses to sensibility—that is, harm that contributes to unpleasant experiences in the form of repugnance, embarrassment, disgust, alarm, or fear, and (c) impairment of the collective welfare—that is, violations of those values possessed by the group or society.

Harm can also be ranked as to the potential for good. Physicians, to help their patients, often have to harm them. The question they must ask is, "Will this specific procedure, drug, or operation, produce more good than the pain and suffering it causes?" For instance, will the additional time it affords the cancer patient be worth all the suffering associated with the chemotherapy? In Somalia, health care personnel are forced to make much harder decisions. They are surrounded by starvation, sickness, and death. If they treat one person, another cannot be treated and will die. They find themselves forced to allocate their time and resources, not according to who needs it the most, but according to who has the greatest chance of survival.

Judges must also balance the harms they are about to inflict on those they must sentence against the public good and the extent to which the sentence might help the individual reform. Justice must be served in that people must pay for their crimes, yet most judges also realize that prison time often does more harm than good. In times of recession employers must weigh harm when they are forced to cut back their workforce: Where should the cuts occur? Should they keep employees of long standing and cut those most recently hired (many of which are nonwhites hired through affirmative action programs)? Should they keep those with the most productive records, or those with the greatest need for employment? No matter what employers elect to do, harm will result to some. The harm produced by the need to reduce the workforce must be balanced by the potential good of the company's surviving and sustaining employment for the rest of the employees.

The notion of harm also figures into the public and social dialogue between those who are pro-choice and those who are pro-life. Most pro-lifers are inclined to see the greatest harm of abortion to be loss of life, while most pro-choicers argue that the compelling personal and social harm is the taking away of a value (the right to privacy) that everyone is entitled to. Further harmful consequences of abortion for most pro-lifers are that the value of life will be cheapened, the moral fabric of society will be weakened, and the taking of life could be extended to the elderly and disabled, for example. Most of those who are pro-choice, on the other hand, are inclined to argue that the necessary consequence of their position is that of keeping government out of their private lives and bedrooms. In a similar way this "conflict of values" format can be used to analyze, clarify, and enlarge our understanding of the competing values, harms, and consequences surrounding other social problems. We can, and should, search for the competing values underlying such social problems as, for example, income distribution, homelessness, divorce, education, and the environment.

Loss, then, as a societal harm consists in a rejection or violation of what a person or group feels entitled to have. American citizens, for example, tend to view life, freedom, equality, property, and physical security as ultimate values. Any rejection or violation of these values is thought to constitute a serious social problem since such a loss diminishes one's sense of personhood. Murder, violence, AIDS, homelessness, environmental degradation, the failure to provide adequate health care, and abortion can be conveniently classified as social problems within this class of harms.

Offenses to our sensibilities constitute a class of harm that, when serious enough, becomes a problem affecting moral issues and the common good of the members of a society. Issues surrounding pornography, prostitution, and the so-called victimless crimes are examples of behaviors that belong to this class of harm. Moreover some would argue that environmental degradation, the widening gap between the very rich and the very poor, and the condition of the homeless also should be considered within this class of harm.

A third class of harm—namely impairments to the collective welfare—is explained, in part, by Gross (1979:120) as follows:

> Social life, particularly in the complex forms of civilized societies, creates many dependencies among members of a community. The welfare of each member depends upon the exercise of restraint and precaution by others in the pursuit of their legitimate activities, as well as upon cooperation toward certain common objectives. These matters of collective welfare involve many kinds of interests that may be said to be possessed by the community.

In a pluralistic society, such as American society, matters of collective welfare are sometimes problematic in that there can be considerable conflict of values and rights between various segments of the society. There is likely to remain, however, a great deal of agreement that those social problems whose harmful consequences would involve impairments to the collective welfare would include poverty, poor education, mistreatment of the young and elderly, excessive disparities in income distribution, discrimination against ethnic and other minorities, drug abuse, health and medical care, the state of the economy, and environmental concerns.

BIBLIOGRAPHY

Dahrendorf, R. (1959). *Class and class conflict in industrial society*. Stanford, CA: Stanford University Press.

Davis, Kingsley, & Moore, Wilbert E. (1945). Some principles of stratification. *American Sociological Review*, 10, 242–249.

Gans, Herbert J. (1971). The uses of poverty: The poor pay all. *Social Policy*. New York: Social Policy Corporation.

Gross, Hyman. (1979). *A theory of criminal justice*. New York: Oxford University Press.

Hook, Sidney. (1974). *Pragmatism and the tragic sense of life*. New York: Basic Books.

Horowitz, M. A. (1962). Consensus, conflict, and cooperation. *Social Forces, 41*, 177–188.

Lenski, G. (1966). *Power and privilege*. New York: McGraw-Hill.

Michels, Robert. (1949). *Political parties: A sociological study of the oligarchical tendencies of modern democracy*. New York: Free Press.

Mills, C. Wright. (1956). *The power elite*. New York: Oxford University Press.

Ossowski, S. (1963). *Class structure in the social consciousness*. Translated by Sheila Patterson. New York: The Free Press.

Seeman, Melvin. (1959). On the meaning of alienation. *American Sociological Review, 24*, 783–791.

Van den Berghe, P. (1963). Dialectic and functionalism: Toward a theoretical synthesis. *American Sociological Review, 28*, 695–705.

Weber, Max. (1964). *The protestant ethic and the spirit of capitalism*. Translated by Talcott Parson. New York: Scribner's.

William, Robin, Jr. (1970). *American society: A sociological interpretation*, 3rd. ed. New York: Alfred A. Knopf.

Williams, Robin. (1966). Some further comments on chronic controversies. *American Journal of Sociology, 71,* 717–721.

Wilson, James Q. (1994, August). The moral life. *Brigham Young Magazine*, pp. 37–55.

Wilson, William. (1978). *The declining significance of race.* Chicago: University of Chicago Press.

CHALLENGE TO THE READER

As you read the articles that follow, try to determine which of the three major theoretical positions each of the authors seems to be using. Whatever approach the writer uses in his or her discussion suggests what he or she thinks is the primary cause of the social problem/issue under consideration.

Also ask yourself as you read each article, (1) What values are at stake or in conflict? (2) What rights are at issue or in conflict? (3) What is the nature of the harm in each case, and who is being hurt? (4) What do the authors suggest as possible resolutions for each social problem?

Written by Harold A. Widdison and H. Richard Delaney for *Annual Editions: Social Problems*. © 1995 by McGraw-Hill/Dushkin, Guilford, CT 06437.

The Fragmentation of Social Life

SOME CRITICAL SOCIETAL CONCERNS FOR THE NEW MILLENNIUM

Address by **D. STANLEY EITZEN,** *Emeritus Professor of Sociology, Colorado State University*
Delivered to the Life Enrichment Series, Bethel, North Newton, Kansas, April 12, 2000

D. STANLEY EITZEN

For many observers of American society this is the best of times. The current economic expansion is the longest in U.S. history. Unemployment is the lowest in three decades. Inflation is low and under control. The stock market has risen from 3500 to over 11,000 in eight years. The number of millionaires has more than doubled in the past five years to 7.1 million. The Cold War is over. The United States is the dominant player in the world both militarily and economically. Our society, obviously, is in good shape.

But every silver lining has a cloud. While basking in unprecedented wealth and economic growth, the U.S. has serious domestic problems. Personal bankruptcies are at a record level. The U.S. has the highest poverty rate and the highest child poverty rate in the Western world. We do not have a proper safety net for the disadvantaged that other countries take for granted. Hunger and homelessness are on the rise. Among the Western nations, the U.S. has the highest murder rate as well as the highest incarceration rate. Also, we are the only Western nation without a universal health care system, leaving 44 million Americans without health insurance.

I want to address another crucial problem that our society faces—the fragmentation of social life. Throughout U.S. history, despite a civil war, and actions separating people by religion, class, and race, the nation has somehow held together. Will society continue to cohere or will new crises pull us apart? That is the question of the morning. While there are many indicators of reduced societal cohesion, I will limit my discussion to four: (1) excessive individualism; (2) heightened personal isolation; (3) the widening income and wealth gap; and (4) the deepening racial/ethnic/religious/sexuality divide.

EXCESSIVE INDIVIDUALISM

We Americans celebrate individualism. It fits with our economic system of capitalism. We are self-reliant and responsible for our actions. We value individual freedom, including the right to choose our vocations, our mates, when and where to travel, and how to spend our money. At its extreme, the individualistic credo says that it is our duty to be selfish and in doing so, according to Adam Smith's notion of an "invisible hand," society benefits. Conservative radio commentator Rush Limbaugh said as much in his response to an initiative by President Clinton to encourage citizen volunteerism: "Citizen service is a repudiation of the principles upon which our country was based. We are here for ourselves."

While Rush Limbaugh may view rugged individualism as virtuous, I do not. It promotes inequality; it promotes the tolerance of inferior housing, schools, and services for "others"; and it encourages public policies that are punitive to the disadvantaged. For example, this emphasis on the individual has meant that, as a society, the United States has the lowest federal income tax rates in the Western world. Our politicians, especially Republicans, want to lower the rates even more so that individuals will have more and governments, with their presumed interest in the common good, will have less. As a result, the United States devotes relatively few resources to help the disadvantaged and this minimal redistribution system is shrinking.

In effect, our emphasis on individualism keeps us from feeling obligated to others.

Consider the way that we finance schools. Schools are financed primarily by the states through income taxes and local school districts through property taxes. This means that wealthy states and wealthy districts have more money to educate their children than the less advantaged states and districts. The prevailing view is that if my community or state is well-off, why should my taxes go to help children from other communities and other states?

The flaw in the individualistic credo is that we cannot go it alone—our fate depends on others. Paradoxically, it is in our individual interest to have a collective interest. We deny this at our peril for if we disregard those unlike ourselves, in fact doing violence to them, then we invite their hostility and violence, and, ultimately, a fractured society.

HEIGHTENED PERSONAL ISOLATION

There are some disturbing trends that indicate a growing isolation as individuals become increasingly isolated from their neighbors, their co-workers, and even their family members. To begin, because of computers and telecommunications there is a growing trend for workers to work at home. While home-based work allows flexibility and independence not found in most jobs, these workers are separated from social networks. Aside from not realizing the social benefits of personal interaction with colleagues, working from home means being cut off from pooled information and the collective power that might result in higher pay and better fringe benefits.

Our neighborhoods, too, are changing in ways that promote isolation. A recent study indicates that one in three Americans has never spent an evening with a neighbor. This isolation from neighbors is exacerbated in the suburbs. Not only do some people live in gated communities to physically wall themselves off from "others" but they wall themselves off from their neighbors behaviorally and symbolically within gated and nongated neighborhoods alike. Some people exercise on motorized treadmills and other home exercise equipment instead of running through their neighborhoods. Rather than walking to the corner grocery or nearby shop and visiting with the clerks and neighbors, suburbanites have to drive somewhere away from their immediate neighborhood to shop among strangers. Or they may not leave their home at all, shopping and banking by computer. Sociologist Philip Slater says that "a community life exists when one can go daily to a given location at a given time and see many of the people one knows." Suburban neighborhoods in particular are devoid of such meeting places for adults and children. For suburban teenagers almost everything is away—practice fields, music lessons, friends, jobs, school, and the malls. Thus, a disconnect from those nearby. For adults many go through their routines without sharing stories, gossip, and analyses of events with

friends on a regular basis at a coffee shop, neighborhood tavern, or at the local grain elevator.

Technology also encourages isolation. There was a major shift toward isolation with the advent of television as people spent more and more time within their homes rather than socializing with friends and neighbors. Now, we are undergoing a communications revolution that creates the illusion of intimacy but the reality is much different. Curt Suplee, science and technology writer for the Washington Post, says that we have seen "tenfold increases in 'communication' by electronic means, and tenfold reductions in person-to-person contact." In effect, as we are increasingly isolated before a computer screen, we risk what Warren Christopher has called "social malnutrition." John L. Locke, a professor [of] communications argues in The De-Voicing of Society that e-mail, voice mail, fax machines, beepers, and Internet chat rooms are robbing us of ordinary social talking. Talking, he says, like the grooming of apes and monkeys, is the way we build and maintain social relationships. In his view, it is only through intimate conversation that we can know others well enough to trust them and work with them harmoniously. In effect, Locke argues that we are becoming an autistic society, communicating messages electronically but without really connecting. Paradoxically, then, these incredible communication devices that combine to connect us in so many dazzling ways also separate us increasingly from intimate relationships.

Fragmentation is also occurring within many families, where the members are increasingly disconnected from each other. Many parents are either absent altogether or too self-absorbed to pay very much attention to their children or each other. On average, parents today spend 22 fewer hours a week with their children than parents did in the 1960s. Although living in the same house, parents or children may tune out each other by engaging in solitary activities. A survey by the Kaiser Family Foundation found that the average child between 2 and 18, spends 5 and one-half hours a day alone watching television, at a computer, playing video games, on the Internet, or reading. Many families rarely eat together in an actual sit-down meal. All too often material things are substituted for love and attention. Some children even have their own rooms equipped with a telephone, television, VCR, microwave, refrigerator, and computer, which while convenient, isolates them from other family members. Such homes may be full of people but they are really empty.

The consequences of this accelerating isolation of individuals are dire. More and more individuals are lonely, bitter, alienated, anomic, and disconnected. This situation is conducive to alcohol and drug abuse, depression, anxiety, and violence. The lonely and disaffected are ripe candidates for membership in cults, gangs, and militias where they find a sense of belonging and a cause to believe in but in the process they may become more paranoid and, perhaps, even become willing terrorists. At a less extreme level, the alienated will disengage from society by shunning voluntary associations, by home schooling their children, and by not participating in elections. In short, they will become increasingly individualistic, which compounds their problem and society's problem with unity.

THE WIDENING INEQUALITY GAP

There is an increasing gap between the rich and the rest of us, especially between the rich and the poor. Data from 1998 show that there were at least 268 billionaires in the United States, while 35 million were below the government official poverty line.

Timothy Koogle, CEO of Yahoo made $4.7 million a day in 1999, while the median household income in that year was $110 a day. Bill Gates, CEO of Microsoft is richer than Koogle by far. He is worth, depending on [the] stock market on a given day, around $90 billion or so. Together, eight Americans—Microsoft billionaires Bill Gates, Paul Allen, and Steve Ballmer plus the five Wal-Mart heirs—have a net worth of $233 billion, which is more than the gross domestic product of the very prosperous nation of Sweden. The Congressional Budget Office reports that in 1999, the richest 2.7 million Americans, the top 1 percent of the population, had as many aftertax dollars to spend as the bottom 100 million put together.

Compared to the other developed nations, the chasm between the rich and the poor in the U.S. is the widest and it is increasing. In 1979, average family income in the top 5 percent of the earnings distribution was 10 times that in the bottom 20 percent. Ten years later it had increased to 16:1, and in 1999 it was 19:1, the biggest gap since the Census Bureau began keeping track in 1947.

The average salary of a CEO in 1999 was 419 times the pay of a typical factory worker. In 1980 the difference was only 42 times as much. This inequality gap in the United States, as measured by the difference in pay between CEOs and workers, is by far the highest in the industrialized world. While ours stands at 419 to 1, the ratio in Japan is 25 to 1, and in France and Germany it is 35 to 1.

At the bottom end of wealth and income, about 35 million Americans live below the government's official poverty line. One out of four of those in poverty are children under the age of 18. Poor Americans are worse off than the poor in other western democracies. The safety net here is weak and getting weaker. We do not have universal health insurance. Funds for Head Start are so inadequate that only one in three poor children who are eligible actually are enrolled in the program. Welfare for single mothers is being abolished, resulting in many impoverished but working mothers being less well-off because their low-wage work is not enough to pay for child care, health care, housing costs, and other living expenses. Although the economy is soaring, a survey of 26 cities released by the U.S. Conference on Mayors shows that the numbers of homeless and hungry in the cities have risen for 15 consecutive years. The demand for emergency food is the highest since 1992 and the demand for emergency shelter is the largest since 1994. According to the U.S. Department of Agriculture, there were about 36 million, including 14 million children living in households afflicted with what they call "food insecurity," which is a euphemism for hunger.

Of the many reasons for the increase in homelessness and hunger amidst increasing affluence, three are crucial. First, the government's welfare system has been shrinking since the Reagan administration with the support of both Republicans and Democrats. Second, the cost of housing has risen dramatically causing many of the poor to spend over 50 percent of their meager incomes for rent. And, third, charitable giving has not filled the void, with less than 10 percent of contributions actually going to programs that help the poor. In effect, 90 percent of philanthropy is funneled to support the institutions of the already advantaged—churches (some of which trickles down to the poor), hospitals, colleges, museums, libraries, orchestras, and the arts.

The data on inequality show clearly, I believe, that we are moving toward a two-tiered society. Rather than "a rising tide lifting all boats," the justification for capitalism as postulated by President John Kennedy, the evidence is that "a rising tide lifts only the yachts." The increasing gap between the haves and the have-nots has crucial implications for our society. First, it divides people into the "deserving" and the "undeserving." If people are undeserving, then we are justified in not providing them with a safety net. As economist James K. Galbraith says: "A high degree of inequality causes the comfortable to disavow the needy. It increases the psychological distance separating these groups, making it easier to imagine that defects of character or differences of culture, rather than an unpleasant turn in the larger schemes of economic history, lie behind the separation." Since politicians represent the monied interests, the wealthy get their way as seen in the continuing decline in welfare programs for the poor and the demise of affirmative action. Most telling, the inequality gap is not part of the political debate in this, or any other, election cycle.

A second implication is that the larger the gap, the more destabilized society becomes.

In this regard economist Lester Thurow asks: "How much inequality can a democracy take? The income gap in America is eroding the social contract. If the promise of a higher standard of living is limited to a few at the top, the rest of the citizenry, as history shows, is likely to grow disaffected, or worse." Former Secretary of Labor, Robert Reich, has put it this way: "At some point, if the trends are not reversed, we cease being a society at all. The stability of the country eventually is threatened. No country can endure a massive gap between people at the top and people at the bottom." Or, as economist Galbraith puts it: "[Equality] is now so wide it threatens, as it did in the Great Depression, the social stability of the country. It has come to undermine our sense of ourselves as a nation of equals. Economic inequality, in this way, challenges the essential unifying myth of American national life."

THE DEEPENING RACIAL/ETHNIC/RELIGIOUS/SEXUALITY DIVIDE

The United States has always struggled with diversity. American history is stained by the enslavement of Africans and later the segregated and unequal "Jim Crow" south, the aggression toward native peoples based on the belief in "Manifest Destiny," the internment of Japanese Americans during World War II, episodes of intolerance against religious minorities, gays and lesbians, and immigrants. In each instance, the majority was not only intolerant of those labeled as "others," but they also used the law, religious doctrine, and other institutional forms of discrimination to keep minorities separate and unequal. Despite these ongoing societal wrongs against minorities, there has been progress culminating in the civil rights battles and victories of the 1950s, 1960s, and early 1970s.

But the civil rights gains of the previous generation are in jeopardy as U.S. society becomes more diverse. Currently, the racial composition of the U.S. is 72 percent white and 28 percent nonwhite. In 50 years it will be 50 percent nonwhite. The racial landscape is being transformed as approximately 1 million immigrants annually set up permanent residence in the United States and another 300,000 enter illegally and stay. These new residents are primarily Latino and Asian, not European as was the case of earlier waves of immigration. This "browning of America" has important implications including increased division.

An indicator of fragmentation along racial lines is the "White flight" from high immigration areas, which may lead to what demographer William Frey has called the "Balkanization of America." The trends toward gated neighborhoods, the rise of private schools and home schooling are manifestations of exclusiveness rather than inclusiveness and perhaps they are precursors to this "Balkanization."

Recent state and federal legislation has been aimed at reducing or limiting the civil rights gains of the 1970s. For example, in 1994 California passed Proposition 187 by a 3-to 2-popular vote margin, thereby denying public welfare to undocumented immigrants. Congress in 1996 voted to deny most federal benefits to legal immigrants who were not citizens. A number of states have made English the official state language. In 1997 California passed Proposition 209, which eliminated affirmative action (a policy aimed at leveling the playing field so that minorities would have a fair chance to succeed). Across the nation, Congress and various state legislatures, most recently Florida, have taken measures to weaken or eliminate affirmative action programs.

Without question racial and ethnic minorities in the U.S. are the targets of personal prejudicial acts as well as pervasive institutional racism. What will the situation be like by 2050 when the numbers of Latinos triple from their present population of 31.4 million, and the Asian population more than triples from the current 10.9 million, and the African American population increases 70 percent from their base of 34.9 million now?

Along with increasing racial and ethnic diversity, there is a greater variety of religious belief. Although Christians are the clear majority in the United States, there are also about 7 million Jews, 6 million Muslims (there are more Muslims than Presbyterians), and millions of other non-Christians, including Buddhists, and Hindus, as well as atheists.

While religion often promotes group integration, it also divides. Religious groups tend to emphasize separateness and superiority, thereby defining "others" as infidels, heathens, heretics, or nonbelievers. Strongly held religious ideas sometimes split groups within a denomination or congregation. Progressives and fundamentalists within the same religious tradition have difficulty finding common ground on various issues, resulting in division. This has always been the case to some degree, but this tendency seems to be accelerating now. Not only are there clashes within local congregations and denominational conferences but they spill out into political debates in legislatures and in local elections, most notably school board elections, as religious factions often push their narrow, divisive sectarian policies. These challenges to religious pluralism are increasing, thus promoting fragmentation rather than unity.

There is also widespread intolerance of and discrimination toward those whose sexual orientation differs from the majority. The behaviors of gay men and lesbian women are defined and stigmatized by many members of society as sinful; their activities are judged by the courts as illegal; and their jobs and advancement within those jobs are often restricted because of their being different sexually. As more and more homosexuals become public with their sexuality, their presence and their political agenda are viewed as ever more threatening and must be stopped.

My point is this: diversity and ever increasing diversity are facts of life in our society. If we do not find ways to accept the differences among us, we will fragment into class, race, ethnic, and sexual enclaves.

Two social scientists, John A. Hall and Charles Lindholm, in a recent book entitled Is America Breaking Apart? argue that throughout American history there has been remarkable societal unity because of its historically conditioned institutional patterns and shared cultural values. Columnist George Will picked up on this theme in a Newsweek essay, postulating that while the U.S. has pockets of problems, "American society is an amazing machine for homogenizing people." That has been the case but will this machine continue to pull us together? I believe, to the contrary, that while the U.S. historically has overcome great obstacles, a number of trends in contemporary society have enormous potential for pulling us apart. Our society is moving toward a two-tiered society with the gap between the haves and the have-nots, a withering bond among those of different social classes, and a growing racial, ethnic, and sexuality divide. The critical question is whether the integrative societal mechanisms that have served us well in the past will save us again or whether we will continue to fragment?

The challenge facing U.S. society as we enter the new millennium is to shift from building walls to building bridges. As our society is becoming more and more diverse, will Americans feel empathy for, and make sacrifices on behalf of, a wide variety of people who they define as different? The answer to this crucial question is negative at the present time. Social justice seems to be an outmoded concept in our individualistic society.

I shall close with a moral argument posed by one of the greatest social thinkers and social activists of the 20th century, the late Michael Harrington. Harrington, borrowing from philosopher John Rawls, provides an intuitive defi-nition of a justice. A just society is when I describe it to you and you accept it even if you do not know your place in it. Harrington then asks (I'm paraphrasing here): would you accept a society of 275 million where 44 million people do not have health insurance, where 35 million live in poverty including one-fifth of all children? Would you accept a society as just where discrimination against minorities is commonplace, even by the normal way society works? Would you accept a society where a sizable number of people live blighted lives in neighborhoods with a high concentration of poverty, with inferior schools, with too few good jobs? You'd be crazy to accept such a society but that is what we have. Harrington concludes: "If in your mind you could not accept a society in which we do unto you as we do unto them, then isn't it time for us to change the way we are acting towards them who are a part of us?" If, however, we accept an unjust society, then our society will move inexorably toward a divided and fortress society.

From *Vital Speeches of the Day*, July 1, 2000, pp. 563-566. © 2000 by City News Publishing Company, Inc. Reprinted by permission.

How to Re-Moralize America

by Francis Fukuyama

In 1994, William J. Bennett published a book called *The Index of Leading Cultural Indicators*, which brought together a variety of statistics about American social trends. Between the mid-1960s and the early 1990s, Bennett showed, there was a shocking deterioration of America's social health. By the 1990s, one American child out of three was being born to an unmarried mother, nearly a third of African American men between the ages of 20 and 29 were involved in some way with the criminal justice system, and scores on standardized tests of educational achievement had dropped America to the bottom of the pack among industrialized countries. While we were materially richer than at any time in history, Bennett argued, we were becoming morally poorer at an alarming rate.

In the brief period since Bennett's *Index* appeared, we have experienced what seems to be a remarkable turnaround. Crime, including violent crimes and those against property, has decreased by more than 15 percent nationally; the murder rate in New York City has declined to levels not seen since the mid-1960s. Divorce rates, which had already begun a downward trend in the 1980s, continue on that path. Starting in 1995, the illegitimacy rate ceased its upward climb and began to decline slightly. The teenage pregnancy rate dropped eight percent between 1991 and 1996; among black teenagers, it fell 21 percent. Welfare caseloads have dropped by as much as a quarter nationally, and states at the forefront of welfare reform, such as Wisconsin, have seen astonishing reductions of up to 75 percent. Americans' general level of

trust in their institutions and in one another, though difficult to gauge, has risen. In 1991, for example, only 15 to 20 percent of Americans said they trusted the federal government to do the right thing most of the time; by the end of the decade that percentage had rebounded to between 25 and 30 percent.

What are we to make of these improvements? Are Americans at century's end being blessed not only with a booming stock market and a near full-employment economy but a restoration of cultural health as well? Many conservatives, notably social scientist Charles Murray and historian Gertrude Himmelfarb, don't think so. The changes, they argue, are too shallow and recent; they may be the product of more jails and stiffer sentencing rather than any true improvement in moral behavior. One conservative activist, Paul Weyrich of the Free Congress Foundation, was thrown into such despair last summer by the public's refusal to repudiate President Bill Clinton despite a sex scandal and impeachment proceedings that he publicly declared that Americans have never been more degenerate than they are today.

But conservatives are wrong to dismiss the good news contained in the social statistics. In fact, there has been a shift back to more traditional social values, and they should take credit for helping to bring it about. It would be a mistake to become complacent, or to think that our social and cultural problems are now behind us. But there is good reason to think that American society is undergoing a degree of moral regeneration. There is still a great deal of confusion over the sources of moral decline, however, and over the nature of moral renewal. Liberals need to confront the reality of moral decline and the importance of socially beneficial, less self-centered values. Conservatives have to be realistic and recognize that many of the developments they dislike in contemporary society are driven by economic and technological change—change brought about by the same dynamic capitalist economy they so often celebrate.

Moral decline is not a myth or a figment of the nostalgic imagination. Perhaps the most important conservative achievement over the past couple of decades was to convince the rest of American society that these changes had occurred, that they reflected a disturbing shift in values, and that consequently not every social problem could be addressed by creating a new federal program and throwing money at it.

This reconception of social problems began with two large government-funded studies published in the mid-1960s: Daniel Patrick Moynihan's report, *The Negro Family: The Case for National Action* (1965), and James Coleman's *Equality of Educational Opportunity* (1966). Moynihan, then working for the U.S. Department of Labor, argued that family structure, and in particular the absence of fathers in many African American homes, was directly related to the incidence of crime, teenage pregnancy, low educational achievement, and other social pathologies. Coleman's study showed that student educational achievement was most strongly affected not by the tools of public policy, such as teacher salaries and classroom size, but by the environment a child's family and peers create. In the absence of a culture that emphasizes self-discipline, work, education, and other middle-class values, Coleman showed, public policy can achieve relatively little.

Once published, the Moynihan report was violently attacked. Moynihan was accused of "blaming the victim" and seeking to impose white values on a community that had different but not necessarily inferior cultural norms. Liberals at first denied the reality of massive changes in family structure, and then fell back on the argument that single-parent households are no worse from the standpoint of child welfare than traditional ones—the kind of argument Moynihan was later to label "defining deviancy down." By the early 1990s, however, conservatives had largely won the argument. In 1994, the publication of Sara McLanahan and Gary Sandefur's book *Growing Up with a Single Parent* (1994) made the social science community's shift more or less official. The two well-respected sociologists found that a generation's worth of empirical research supported Moynihan's basic conclusion: growing up in a single-parent family is correlated with a life of poverty and a host of other social ills.

Few Americans understand that they were not alone in experiencing these changes. All of the industrialized countries outside Asia experienced a massive increase in social disorder between the 1960s and '90s—a phenomenon that I have called the Great Disruption of Western social values. Indeed, by the 1990s Sweden, the United Kingdom, and New Zealand all had higher rates of property crime than the United States. More than half of all Scandinavian children are born to unmarried mothers, compared with one-third of American children. In Sweden, so few people bother to get married that the institution itself probably is in long-term decline.

While conservatives won their case that values had changed for the worse, they were on shakier ground in their interpretation of why this shift had occurred. There were two broad lines of argument. The first, advanced by Charles Murray in his landmark book *Losing Ground* (1984), argued that family breakdown, crime, and other social pathologies were ultimately the result of mistaken government policies. Chief among them was Aid to Families with Dependent Children (AFDC), which in effect subsidized illegitimacy by paying welfare benefits only to single mothers. But there were other causes, such as new court-imposed constraints on police departments won by civil libertarians. In this interpretation, any improvement in social indicators today must be the result of the unwinding of earlier social policies through measures such as the 1996 welfare reform bill.

The second conservative line of argument held that moral decline was the result of a broad cultural shift. Former federal judge Robert Bork, for example, blamed the 1960s counterculture for undermining traditional values and setting the young at war with authority. Others, such as philosopher John Gray, reached further back in time. They revived the arguments of Edmund Burke and Joseph de Maistre, tracing moral decay to an Enlightenment commitment to replacing tradition and religion with reason and secular humanism.

While there is more than a germ of truth in each of these interpretations, neither is adequate to explain the shift in values that occurred during the Great Disruption. Detailed econometric studies seeking to link AFDC to illegitimacy have shown that although there is some causal connection, the relationship is not terribly strong. More important, illegitimacy is only part of a much broader story of family breakdown that includes divorce, cohabitation in place of marriage, declining fertility, and the separation of cohabiting couples. These ills cut across the socioeconomic spectrum and can hardly be blamed on a federal poverty program.

The second line of argument, which sees moral breakdown as a consequence of a broad cultural shift, is not so much wrong as inadequate. No one who has lived through the last several decades can deny that there has been a huge shift in social values, a shift whose major theme has been the rise of individualism at the expense of communal sources of authority, from the family and neighborhood to churches, labor unions, companies, and the government. The problem with this kind of broad cultural explanation is that it cannot explain timing. Secular humanism, for example, has been in the works for the past four or five hundred years. Why all of a sudden in the last quarter of the 20th century has it produced social chaos?

The key to the timing of the Great Disruption, I believe, is to be found elsewhere, in changes that occurred in the economy and in technology. The most important social values that were shaken by the Great Disruption are those having to do with sex, reproduction, and the family. The reason the disruption happened when and where it did can be traced to two broad technological changes that began in the 1960s. One is the advent of birth control. The other is the shift from industrial to information-based economies and from physical to mental labor.

The nuclear family of the 1950s was based on a bargain that traded the husband's income for the wife's fertility: he worked, she stayed home to raise the family. With the economy's shift from manufacturing to services (or from brawn to brains), new opportunities arose for women. Women began entering the paid labor force in greater numbers throughout the West in the 1960s, which undid the old arrangement. Even as it liberated women from complete dependence on their husbands, it freed many men from responsibility for their families. Not surprisingly, women's participation in the labor force correlates strongly with divorce and family breakdown throughout the industrialized world.

The Pill reinforced this trend by shifting the burden of responsibility for the consequences of sex to women. No longer did men need to worry greatly if their adventures led to pregnancy. One sign of this change was found by economists Janet Yellen, George Akerlof, and Michael Katz. Between the 1960s and '90s, the number of brides who were pregnant at the altar declined significantly. The shotgun wedding, that ultimate symbol of male accountability, is increasingly a thing of the past.

Humans share a fundamental trait with other animal species: males are less selective in their choice of sexual partners than females, and less attached to their children. In humans, the role that fathers play in the care and nurture of their children tends to be socially constructed to a significant degree, shaped by a host of formal and informal controls that link men to their families. Human fatherhood is therefore more readily subject to disruption. The sexual revolution and the new economic and cultural independence of women provided that disruption. The perfectly reasonable desire of women to increase their autonomy became, for men, an excuse to indulge themselves. The vastly increased willingness of men to leave behind partners and children constitutes perhaps the single greatest change in moral values during the Great Disruption. It lies at the core of many of the period's social pathologies.

What are the chances of a moral renewal? What are its potential sources? Renewal must be possible. While conservatives may be right that moral decline occurred over the past generation, they cannot be right that it occurs in every generation. Unless we posit that all of human history has been a degeneration from some primordial golden age, periods of moral decline must be punctuated by periods of moral improvement.

Such cycles have occurred before. In both Britain and the United States, the period from the end of the 18th century until approximately the middle of the 19th century saw sharply increasing levels of social disorder. Crime rates in virtually all major cities increased. Illegitimacy rates rose, families dissolved, and social isolation increased. The rate of alcohol consumption, particularly in the United States, exploded. But then, from the middle of the century until its end, virtually all of these social indicators reversed direction. Crime rates fell. Families stabilized, and drunkards went on the wagon. New voluntary associations—from temperance and abolitionist societies to Sunday schools—gave people a fresh sense of communal belonging.

The possibility of re-moralization poses some large questions: Where do moral values come from, and what, in particular, are the sources of moral values in a postindustrial society? This is a subject that, strangely, has not received much attention. People have strong opinions about what moral values ought to be and where they ought to come from. If you are on the left, you are likely to believe in social equality guaranteed by a welfare state. If you are a cultural conservative, you may favor the authority of tradition and religion. But how values actually are formed in contemporary societies receives little empirical study. Most people would say that values are either passed along from previous generations through socialization (which fails to explain how change occurs) or are imposed by a church or other hierarchical authority. With the exception of a few discredited theories, sociologists and cultural anthropologists haven't had much to contribute. They have had much more success in describing value systems than in explaining their genesis.

Into this breach in the social sciences have stepped the economists, who have hardly been shy in recent years about applying their formidable methodological tools to matters beyond their usual realm. Economists tend to be opponents of hierarchy and proponents of bargaining—individuals, they say, act rationally on their own to achieve socially productive ends. This describes the market. But Friedrich A. Hayek (among others) suggested that moral rules—part of what he called the "extended order of human cooperation"—might also be the product of a similar decentralized evolutionary bargaining process.

Take the virtues of honesty and reliability, which are key to social cooperation and that intangible compound of mutual trust and engagement called "social capital." Many people have argued that such virtues have religious sources, and that contemporary capitalist societies are living off the cultural capital of previous ages—in America, chiefly its Puritan traditions. Modern capitalism, in this view, with its amoral emphasis on profits and efficiency, is steadily undermining its own moral basis.

Such an interpretation, while superficially plausible, is completely wrong. A decentralized group of individuals who have to deal with one another repeatedly will tend as a matter of self-interest to evolve norms of honesty and reliability. That is, reputation, whether for honesty or fair dealing or product quality, is an asset that self-interested individuals will seek to acquire. While religion may encourage them, a hierarchical source of rules is not necessary. Given the right background conditions—especially the need for repeated dealings with a particular group of people—order and rules will tend to emerge spontaneously from the ground up.

The study of how order emerges spontaneously from the interaction of individual agents is one of the most interesting and important intellectual developments of the late 20th century. One reason it is interesting is that the study is not limited to economists and other social scientists. Scientists since Charles Darwin have concluded that the high degree of order in the biological world was not the creation of God or some other creator but rather emerged out of the interaction of simpler units. The elaborate mounds of some species of African termites, taller than a human being and equipped with their own heating and air conditioning systems, were not designed by anyone, much less by the neurologically simple creatures that built them. And so on, throughout the natural world, order is created by the blind, irrational process of evolution and natural selection. (In the 1980s, the now famous Santa Fe Institute was created to support studies of just this type of phenomenon, so-called complex adaptive systems, in a wide variety of fields.)

Indeed, there is a good deal more social order in the world than even the economists' theories would suggest. Economists frequently express surprise at the extent to which supposedly self-interested, rational individuals do seemingly selfless things: vote, contribute to charities, give their loyalty to employers. People do these things because the ability to solve repeated dilemmas of social cooperation is genetically coded into the human brain, put there by an evolutionary process that rewarded those individuals best able to generate social rules for themselves. Human beings have innate capabilities that make them gravitate toward and reward cooperators who play by

the community's rules, and to ostracize and isolate opportunists who violate them. When we say that human beings are social creatures by nature, we mean not that they are cooperative angels with unlimited resources for altruism but that they have built-in capabilities for perceiving the moral qualities of their fellow humans. What James Q. Wilson calls the "moral sense" is put there by nature, and will operate in the absence of either a lawgiver or a prophet.

If we accept the fact that norms have spontaneous as well as hierarchical sources, we can place them along a continuum that extends from hierarchical and centralized types of authority at one end to the completely decentralized and spontaneous interactions of individuals at the other. But there is a second dimension. Norms and moral rules can be the product of rational bargaining and negotiation, or they can be socially inherited or otherwise a-rational in origin.

In order to clarify the origins of re-moralization, I have constructed a matrix (next page) that organizes these alternatives along two axes. Different types of moral rules fall into different quadrants. Formal laws handed down by governments belong in the rational/hierarchical quadrant; common law and spontaneously generated rules concerning, say, honesty in market relations, fall in the rational/spontaneous quadrant. Because, according to most recent research, incest taboos have biological origins, they are a spontaneous, a-rational norm. Revealed religion—Moses bringing the Ten Commandments down from Mount Sinai, for example—occupies the a-rational hierarchical quadrant. But folk religions—a cult of rock worshipers, for example–may be a species of spontaneous, a-rational order.

This taxonomy gives us a basis for at least beginning a discussion of where norms in a postindustrial society come from. Economists, following their rational, nonhierarchical bent, have been busy populating the upper-right quadrant with examples of spontaneously generated rules. A case in point is the database of more than 5,000 cases of so-called common pool resource problems compiled by Elinor Ostrom. Such problems confront communities with the need to determine rules for sharing common resources such as fisheries or pastureland. Contrary to the expectation that the self-interest of each individual will lead to the depletion of the resources—the famous "tragedy of the commons"—Ostrom finds many cases in which communities were able to spontaneously generate fair rules for sharing that avoided that result.

Max Weber, the founder of modern sociology, argued that as societies modernize, the two rational quadrants, and particularly the hierarchical quadrant, tend to play a strong role in the creation of norms. Rational bureaucracy was, for him, the essence of modernity. In postindustrial societies, however, all four quadrants continue to serve as

The Universe of Norms

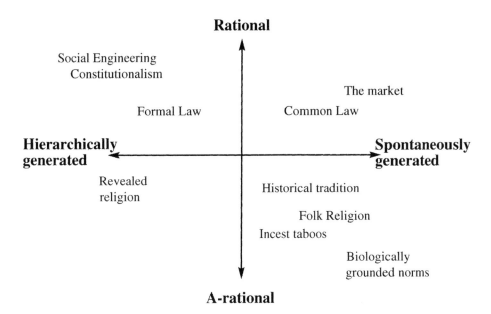

important sources of norms. Modern corporations, for example, have discovered that they cannot organize complex activities and highly skilled workers in a centralized, formal, top-down system of bureaucratic rules. The trend in management is to reduce formal bureaucracy in favor of informal norms that link a variety of firms and individuals in networks.

We now have a framework in which to discuss how the socially corrosive effects of the Great Disruption are being overcome, and what continuing possibilities for change there might be. In the quest for the source of authoritative new rules, one starting point is the rational-hierarchical quadrant, which is the sphere of public policy. Crime rates are down across the United States today in no small measure because government is embracing better policies, such as community policing, and spending more on law enforcement, prisons, and punishment.* But the fact that tougher policies have brought crime rates down would not be regarded by most people as evidence of moral renewal. We want people to behave better not because of a crackdown but because they have internalized certain standards. The question then becomes, Which of the three remaining quadrants can be the source of moral behavior?

Many cultural conservatives believe that religion is the sine qua non of moral values, and they blame the Great Disruption on a loss of religious values. Religion played a powerful role in the Victorian upsurge during

the second half of the 19th century, they note, and, therefore, any reversal of the Great Disruption must likewise depend on a religious revival. In this view, the cultural conservatives are supported (in a way) by Friedrich Nietzsche, who once denounced the English "flathead" John Stuart Mill for believing that one could have something approximating Christian values in the absence of a belief in the Christian God.

Nietzsche famously argued that God was on his deathbed and incapable, in Europe at least, of being resuscitated. There could be new religions, but they would be pagan ones that would provoke "immense wars" in the future. Religious conservatives can reply that, as an empirical matter, God is not dead anywhere but in Europe itself. A generation or two ago, social scientists generally believed that secularization was the inevitable byproduct of modernization, but in the United States and many other advanced societies, religion does not seem to be in danger of dying out.

Some religious conservatives hope, and many liberals fear, that the problem of moral decline will be resolved by a large-scale return to religious orthodoxy—a transformation as sudden as the one Ayatollah Khomeini wrought 20 years ago by returning to Iran on a jetliner. For a variety of reasons, this seems unlikely. Modern societies are so culturally diverse that it is not clear whose version of orthodoxy would prevail. Any true form of orthodoxy is likely to be seen as a threat to important groups and hence would neither get very far nor serve as a basis for widening the radius of trust. Instead of integrating society, a conservative religious revival might only increase social discord and fragmentation.

It is not clear, moreover, that the re-moralization of society need rely on the hierarchical authority of revealed religion. Against Nietzsche's view that moral behavior inevitably rests on dogmatic belief, we might counterpose Adam Smith, the Enlightenment philosopher with perhaps the most realistic and highly developed theory of moral action. Harking back to a kind of Aristotelian naturalism, Smith argued that human beings are social and moral creatures by nature, capable of being led to moral behavior both by their natural passions and by their reason. The Enlightenment has been justly criticized for its overemphasis on human reason. But reason does not have to take the form of a bureaucratic state seeking to engineer social outcomes through the wholesale rearrangement of society. It can also take the form of rational individuals interacting with one another to create workable moral rules, or, in Smith's language, being led from a narrowly selfish view of their interests to the view of an "impartial spectator" exercising reasoned moral judgment.

Religious conservatives, in other words, underestimate the innate ability of human beings to evolve reasonable moral rules for themselves. Western societies underwent an enormous shock during the mid-20th century, and it is not surprising that it has taken a long time to adjust. The process of reaching a rational set of norms is not easy or automatic. During the Great Disruption, for example, large numbers of men and women began to behave in ways that ended up hurting the interests of children. Men abandoned families, women conceived children out of wedlock, and couples divorced for what were often superficial and self-indulgent reasons. But parents also have a strong interest in the well-being of their children. If it can be demonstrated to them that their behavior is seriously injuring the life chances of their offspring, they are likely to react rationally and want to alter that behavior in ways that help their children.

During the Great Disruption, there were many intellectual and cultural currents at work obscuring from people the consequences of their personal behavior for people close to them. They were told by social scientists that growing up in a single-parent family was no worse than growing up in an intact one, reassured by family therapists that children were better off if the parents divorced, and bombarded by images from the popular culture that glamorized sex. Changing these perceptions requires discussion, argument, even "culture wars." And we have had them. Today Barbara Dafoe Whitehead's controversial 1993 assertion that "Dan Quayle was right" about the importance of families no longer seems radical.

W hat would the re-moralization of society look like? In some of its manifestations, it would represent a continuation of trends that have already occurred in the 1990s, such as the return of middle-class people from their gated suburban communities to downtown areas, where a renewed sense of order and civility once again makes them feel secure enough to live and work. It would show up in increasing levels of participation in civil associations and political engagement. And it would be manifest in more civil behavior on college campuses, where a greater emphasis on academics and more carefully codified rules of behavior are already apparent.

The kinds of changes we can expect in norms concerning sex, reproduction, and family life are likely to be more modest. Conservatives need to be realistic in understanding how thoroughly the moral and social landscapes have been altered by powerful technological and economic forces. Strict Victorian rules concerning sex are very unlikely to return. Unless someone can figure out a way to un-invent birth control, or move women out of the labor force, the nuclear family of the 1950s is not likely to be reconstituted in anything like its original form.

Yet the social role of fathers has proved very plastic from society to society and over time, and it is not unreasonable to think that the commitment of men to their families can be substantially strengthened. This was the message of two of the largest demonstrations in Washington during the 1990s, the Nation of Islam's Million Man March and the Promise Keepers' rally. People were rightly suspicious of the two sponsors, but the same message about male responsibility can and should be preached by more mainstream groups.

T here is also evidence that we are moving into a "postfeminist" age that will be friendlier to families and children. Feminism denigrated the work of raising children in favor of women's paid labor—an attitude epitomized by Hillary Clinton's dismissive response to questions about her Arkansas legal career that she could have just "stayed home and baked cookies." Many women are indeed now working—not as lawyers or policymakers but as waitresses and checkers at Wal-Mart, away from the children they are struggling to raise on their own after being abandoned by husbands or boyfriends. Many women like these might choose to stay at home with their children during their early years if the culture told them it was okay, and if they had the financial means to do so. I see anecdotal evidence all around me that the well-to-do are already making this choice. This does not represent a return of the housewife ideal of the 1950s, just a more sensible balancing of work and family.

Women might find it more palatable to make work and career sacrifices for the sake of children if men made similar sacrifices. The postindustrial economy, by undermining the notion of lifetime employment and steady movement up a career ladder for men, may be abetting just such a social change. In the industrial era, technology encouraged the separation of a male-dominated workplace from a female-dominated home; the information age may reintegrate the two.

Religion may serve a purpose in reestablishing norms, even without a sudden return to religious orthodoxy. Religion is frequently not so much the product of dogmatic belief as it is the provider of a convenient language that allows communities to express moral beliefs that they would hold on entirely secular grounds. A young woman I know does not want to have sex until she is married. She tells her suitors that she follows this rule out of religious conviction, not so much because she is a believer but because this is more convincing to them than a utilitarian explanation. In countless ways, modern, educated, skeptical people are drawn to religion because it offers them community, ritual, and support for values they otherwise hold. Religion in this sense is a form of a-rational, spontaneous order rather than a hierarchical alternative to it.

Re-moralizing a complex, diverse society such as the United States is not without pitfalls. If a return to broad orthodoxy is unlikely, re-moralization for many will mean dropping out of mainstream society—for example, by home-schooling one's children, withdrawing into an ethnic neighborhood or enclave, or creating one's own limited patch of social order. In his science fiction novel *The Diamond Age*, Neal Stephenson envisions a future world in which a group of computer programmers, realizing the importance of moral values for economic success, create a small community called New Atlantis. There they resurrect Victorian social values, complete with top hats and sexual prudery. The "Vickies" of New Atlantis do well for themselves but have nothing to say to the poor, disorganized communities that surround them. Re-moralization may thus go hand in hand with a sort of miniaturization of community, as it has in American civil society over the past generation. Conversely, if these small communities remain reasonably tolerant and open, they may light the way to a broader moral revival, just as Granges, Boy Scout troops, immigrant ethnic associations, and the other myriad small communities of the late 19th century did.

The reconstruction of values that has started in the 1990s, and any renorming of society that may happen in the future, has and will be the product of political, religious, self-organized, and natural norm building. The state is neither the source of all our troubles nor the instrument by which we can solve them. But its actions can both deplete and restore social capital in ways large and small. We have not become so modern and secularized that we can do without religion. But we are also not so bereft of innate moral resources that we need to wait for a messiah to save us. And nature, which we are constantly trying to evict with a pitchfork, always keeps running back.

Note

* A highly salient issue often is not what the government does, but what it refrains from doing, since an overly large and centralized state can rob individuals and communities of initiative and keep them from setting norms for themselves. During the 1960s and '70s, the American court system decriminalized many forms of petty deviance such as panhandling and public drunkenness. By limiting the ability of urban middle-class neighborhoods to set norms for social behavior, the state indirectly encouraged suburban flight and the retreat of the middle class into gated communities. To the extent that these kinds of policies can be limited or reversed, social order will increase.

FRANCIS FUKUYAMA *is Hirst Professor of Public Policy at George Mason University and former deputy director of the policy planning staff at the U.S. State Department. He is the author of* The End of History and the Last Man *(1992) and* Trust: The Social Virtues and the Creation of Prosperity *(1995). His new book, published by the Free Press, is* The Great Disruption: Human Nature and the Reconstitution of Social Order *(1999).*

UNIT 2

Problems of the Political Economy

Unit Selections

4. **Who Rules America?**, G. William Domhoff
5. **Rights, Liberties, and Security: Recalibrating the Balance After September 11**, Stuart Taylor Jr.
6. **How the Little Guy Gets Crunched**, Donald L. Barlett and James B. Steele
7. **The End of Globalization**, Michael Shuman
8. **Where the Good Jobs Are Going**, Jyoti Thottam
9. **A Broken Heartland**, Jeff Glasser

Key Points to Consider

- How could the political decision-making process be made more fair and democratic? How can the influence of money on politics be reduced?

- What is the proper role of the United States in the world today?

- What are the impacts of globalization that concern you the most?

- What are the strengths and weaknesses of American capitalism? What are some of the major problems that now face American businesses and how can they be solved?

- What are the factors that make communities succeed or fail?

 **Links: www.dushkin.com/online/**
These sites are annotated in the World Wide Web pages.

National Center for Policy Analysis
http://www.ncpa.org
Penn Library: Sociology
http://www.library.upenn.edu/resources/subject/social/sociology/sociology. html
Virtual Seminar in Global Political Economy/Global Cities & Social Movements
http://csf.colorado.edu/gpe/gpe95b/resources.html

Since the political system and the economy interpenetrate each other to a high degree, it is now common to study them together under the label *political economy*. Since the political economy is the most basic aspect of society, it should be studied first. The way it functions affects how problems in other areas can or cannot be addressed. Here we encounter issues of power, control, and influence. It is in this arena that society acts corporately to address the problems that are of concern. It is important, therefore, to ascertain the degree to which the economic elite controls the political system. The answer determines how democratic America is. Next we want to know how effective the American political economy is. Can government agencies be effective? Can government regulations be effective? Can the economy be effective? Can the economy make everyone prosper and not just the owners and top administrators?

The first subsection of unit 2 includes articles on the political system. In the first, G. William Domhoff examines the extent of the control that the economic elite has over the government. He concludes that its control is so great that it functions as a ruling class. Its control is decisive on policies concerning income, taxes, property rights, regulations, and other economic matters on which the economic elites are not deeply divided. It is in matters that do not concern them as a class that democratic processes work best. The second article reviews the political impact of 9/11. Stuart Taylor, Jr. points out that the extensive civil rights in the U.S. have to be curtailed to increase the investigative and detention powers of the government to assist it in protecting us from terrorism. But what is the right balance between civil rights and protection against terrorism? Taylor favors public protection over civil rights because of his dark assessment of out present situation. "Today we face dangers without precedent: a mass movement of militant Islamic terrorists who crave martyrdom, hide in shadows, are fanatically bent on slaughtering as many of us as possible and—if they can—using nuclear truck bombs to obliterate New York or Washington or both." The third article examines the campaign process and shows that the campaign contributions of powerful special interests bias the process. They provide gains for the contributor but losses for the little guy.

The next subsection deals with major problems and issues of the economy. The first article deals with globalization, which is often praised by many economists and politicians for stimulating economic growth and criticized by many on moral grounds for harming the poor and lower classes around the world. Both pro-

ponents and critics assume that global-scale corporations are the wave of the future. Michael Shuman takes issue with this assumption. Corporations are slimming down to be more competitive, not beefing up. Economies of scale reduce costs only up to a point. Thereafter, diseconomies of scale raise costs and Shuman explains why this is so under today's conditions. The next article on the economy documents the increasing foreign competition for American white-collar jobs. The loss of blue-collar jobs is ancient history. Now increasingly white-collar jobs are migrating overseas. The numbers are small today but increasing very rapidly.

The final subsection looks at issues of place. Cities have been the trouble spots of America. They are famous for crime, high unemployment for unskilled workers, poor government, failing schools, racial and ethnic tensions, and troubled neighborhoods. But the rural scene also has problems of its own. In "A Broken Heartland," Jeff Glasser grimly describes the decline of many Midwest rural counties. As manufacturing or other sources of economic activity decline or move, people drift away, making it hard for the remainder to survive economically. Public spirit, generous effort, and commitment cannot reverse the decline. Noble communities are dying.

Who Rules America?

G. William Domhoff

Power and Class in the United States

Power and *class* are terms that make Americans a little uneasy, and concepts like *power elite* and *dominant class* immediately put people on guard. The idea that a relatively fixed group of privileged people might shape the economy and government for their own benefit goes against the American grain. Nevertheless,... the owners and top-level managers in large income-producing properties are far and away the dominant power figures in the United States. Their corporations, banks, and agribusinesses come together as a *corporate community* that dominates the federal government in Washington. Their real estate, construction, and land development companies form *growth coalitions* that dominate most local governments. Granted, there is competition within both the corporate community and the local growth coalitions for profits and investment opportunities, and there are sometimes tensions between national corporations and local growth coalitions, but both are cohesive on policy issues affecting their general welfare, and in the face of demands by organized workers, liberals, environmentalists, and neighborhoods.

As a result of their ability to organize and defend their interests, the owners and managers of large income-producing properties have a very great share of all income and wealth in the United States, greater than in any other industrial democracy. Making up at best 1 percent of the total population, by the early 1990s they earned 15.7 percent of the nation's yearly income and owned 37.2 percent of all privately held wealth, including 49.6 percent of all corporate stocks and 62.4 percent of all bonds. Due to their wealth and the lifestyle it makes possible, these owners and managers draw closer as a common social group. They belong to the same exclusive social clubs, frequent the same summer and winter resorts, and send their children to a relative handful of private schools. Members of the corporate community thereby become a *corporate rich* who create a nationwide *social upper class* through their social interaction.... Members of the growth coalitions, on the other hand, are *place entrepreneurs,* people who sell locations and buildings. They come together as local upper classes in their respective cities

and sometimes mingle with the corporate rich in educational or resort settings.

The corporate rich and the growth entrepreneurs supplement their small numbers by developing and directing a wide variety of nonprofit organizations, the most important of which are a set of tax-free charitable foundations, think tanks, and policy-discussion groups. These specialized nonprofit groups constitute a *policy-formation network* at the national level. Chambers of commerce and policy groups affiliated with them form similar policy-formation networks at the local level, aided by a few national-level city development organizations that are available for local consulting.

Those corporate owners who have the interest and ability to take part in general governance join with top-level executives in the corporate community and the policy-formation network to form the *power elite,* which is the leadership group for the corporate rich as a whole. The concept of a power elite makes clear that not all members of the upper class are involved in governance; some of them simply enjoy the lifestyle that their great wealth affords them. At the same time, the focus on a leadership group allows for the fact that not all those in the power elite are members of the upper class; many of them are high-level employees in profit and nonprofit organizations controlled by the corporate rich....

The power elite is not united on all issues because it includes both moderate conservatives and ultraconservatives. Although both factions favor minimal reliance on government on all domestic issues, the moderate conservatives sometimes agree to legislation advocated by liberal elements of the society, especially in times of social upheaval like the Great Depression of the 1930s and the Civil Rights Movement of the early 1960s. Except on defense spending, ultraconservatives are characterized by a complete distaste for any kind of government programs under any circumstances—even to the point of opposing government support for corporations on some issues. Moderate conservatives often favor foreign aid, working through the United Nations, and making attempts to win over foreign enemies through patient diplomacy, treaties, and trade agreements. Historically, ultraconservatives have opposed most forms of foreign involvement, although they have become more tolerant of foreign trade agreements over the past thirty or forty years. At the same time, their hostility to the United Nations continues unabated.

Members of the power elite enter into the electoral arena as the leaders within a *corporate-conservative coalition,* where they are aided by a wide variety of patriotic, antitax, and other single-issue organizations. These conservative advocacy organizations are funded in varying degrees by the corporate rich, direct-mail appeals, and middle-class conservatives. This coalition has played a large role in both political parties at the presidential level and usually succeeds in electing a conservative majority to both houses of Congress. Historically, the conservative majority in Congress was made up of most Northern Republicans and most Southern Democrats, but that arrangement has been changing gradually since the 1960s as the conservative Democrats of the South are replaced by even more conservative Southern Republicans. The corporate-conservative coalition also has access to the federal government in Washington through lobbying and the appointment of its members to top positions in the executive branch.…

Despite their preponderant power within the federal government and the many useful policies it carries out for them, members of the power elite are constantly critical of government as an alleged enemy of freedom and economic growth. Although their wariness toward government is expressed in terms of a dislike for taxes and government regulations, I believe their underlying concern is that government could change the power relations in the private sphere by aiding average Americans through a number of different avenues: (1) creating government jobs for the unemployed; (2) making health, unemployment, and welfare benefits more generous; (3) helping employees gain greater workplace rights and protections; and (4) helping workers organize unions. All of these initiatives are opposed by members of the power elite because they would increase wages and taxes, but the deepest opposition is toward any government support for unions because unions are a potential organizational base for advocating the whole range of issues opposed by the corporate rich.…

Where Does Democracy Fit In?

…[T]o claim that the corporate rich have enough power to be considered a dominant class does not imply that lower social classes are totally powerless. *Domination* means the power to set the terms under which other groups and classes must operate, not total control. Highly trained professionals with an interest in environmental and consumer issues have been able to couple their technical information and their understanding of the legislative and judicial processes with well-timed publicity, lobbying, and lawsuits to win governmental restrictions on some corporate practices. Wage and salary employees, when they are organized into unions and have the right to strike, have been able to gain pay increases, shorter hours, better working conditions, and social benefits such as health insurance. Even the most powerless of people—the very poor and those discriminated against—sometimes develop the capacity to influence the power structure through sit-ins, demonstrations, social movements, and other forms of social disruption, and there is evidence that such activities do bring about some redress of grievances, at least for a short time.

More generally, the various challengers to the power elite sometimes work together on policy issues as a *liberal-labor coalition* that is based in unions, local environmental organizations, some minority group communities, university and arts communities, liberal churches, and small newspapers and magazines. Despite a decline in membership over the past twenty years, unions are the largest and best-financed part of the coalition, and the largest organized social force in the country (aside from churches). They also cut across racial and ethnic lines more than any other institutionalized sector of American society.…

The policy conflicts between the corporate-conservative and liberal-labor coalitions are best described as *class conflicts* because they primarily concern the distribution of profits and wages, the rate and progressivity of taxation, the usefulness of labor unions, and the degree to which business should be regulated by government. The liberal-labor coalition wants corporations to pay higher wages to employees and higher taxes to government. It wants government to regulate a wide range of business practices, including many that are related to the environment, and help employees to organize unions. The corporate-conservative coalition resists all these policy objectives to a greater or lesser degree, claiming they endanger the freedom of individuals and the efficient workings of the economic marketplace. The conflicts these disagreements generate can manifest themselves in many different ways: workplace protests, industrywide boycotts, massive demonstrations in cities, pressure on Congress, and the outcome of elections.

Neither the corporate-conservative nor the liberal-labor coalition includes a very large percentage of the American population, although each has the regular support of about 25–30 percent of the voters. Both coalitions are made up primarily of financial donors, policy experts, political consultants, and party activists.…

Pluralism. The main alternative theory [I] address…. claims that power is more widely dispersed among groups and classes than a class-dominance theory allows. This general perspective is usually called *pluralism,* meaning there is no one dominant power group. It is the theory most favored by social scientists. In its strongest version, pluralism holds that power is held by the general public through the pressure that public opinion and voting put on elected officials. According to this version, citizens form voluntary groups and pressure groups that shape public opinion, lobby elected officials, and back sympathetic political candidates in the electoral process.…

The second version of pluralism sees power as rooted in a wide range of well-organized "interest groups" that are often based in economic interests (e.g., industrialists, bankers, labor unions), but also in other interests as well (e.g., environmental, consumer, and civil rights groups). These interest groups join together in different coalitions depending on the specific issues. Proponents of this version of pluralism sometimes concede that public opinion and voting have only a minimal or indirect influence, but they see business groups as too fragmented and antagonistic to form a cohesive dominant class. They also claim that some business interest groups occasionally join coalitions with liberal or labor groups on specific issues, and that business-dominated coalitions sometimes lose. Furthermore, some proponents of this version of pluralism believe that the Democratic Party is responsive to the wishes of liberal and labor interest groups.

In contrast, I argue that the business interest groups are part of a tightly knit corporate community that is able to develop classwide cohesion on the issues of greatest concern to it: opposition to unions, high taxes, and government regulation. When a business group loses on a specific issue, it is often because other business groups have been opposed; in other words, there are arguments within the corporate community, and these arguments are usually settled within the governmental arena. I also claim that liberal and labor groups are rarely part of coalitions with business groups and that for most of its history the Democratic Party has been dominated by corporate and agribusiness interests in the Southern states, in partnership with the growth coalitions in large urban areas outside the South. Finally, I show that business interests rarely lose on labor and regulatory issues except in times of extreme social disruption like the 1930s and 1960s, when differences of opinion between Northern and Southern corporate leaders made victories for the liberal-labor coalition possible....

How the Power Elite Dominates Government

This [section] shows how the power elite builds on the ideas developed in the policy-formation process and its success in the electoral arena to dominate the federal government. Lobbyists from corporations, law firms, and trade associations play a key role in shaping government on narrow issues of concern to specific corporations or business sectors, but their importance should not be overestimated because a majority of those elected to Congress are predisposed to agree with them. The corporate community and the policy-formation network supply top-level governmental appointees and new policy directions on major issues.

Once again, as seen in the battles for public opinion and electoral success, the power elite faces opposition from a minority of elected officials and their supporters in labor unions and liberal advocacy groups. These opponents are sometimes successful in blocking ultra-conservative initiatives, but most of the victories for the liberal-labor coalition are the result of support from moderate conservatives....

Appointees to Government

The first way to test a class-dominance view of the federal government is to study the social and occupational backgrounds of the people who are appointed to manage the major departments of the executive branch, such as state, treasury, defense,

and justice. If pluralists are correct, these appointees should come from a wide range of interest groups. If the state autonomy theorists are correct, they should be disproportionately former elected officials or longtime government employees. If the class-dominance view is correct, they should come disproportionately from the upper class, the corporate community, and the policy-formation network.

There have been numerous studies over the years of major governmental appointees under both Republican and Democratic administrations, usually focusing on the top appointees in the departments that are represented in the president's cabinet. These studies are unanimous in their conclusion that most top appointees in both Republican and Democratic administrations are corporate executives and corporate lawyers—and hence members of the power elite....

Conclusion

This [section] has demonstrated the power elite's wide-ranging access to government through the interest-group and policy-formation processes, as well as through its ability to influence appointments to major government positions. When coupled with the several different kinds of power discussed in earlier [sections] this access and involvement add up to power elite domination of the federal government.

By *domination*, as stated in the first [section], social scientists mean the ability of a class or group to set the terms under which other classes or groups within a social system must operate. By this definition, domination does not mean control on each and every issue, and it does not rest solely on involvement in government. Influence over government is only the final and most visible aspect of power elite domination, which has its roots in the class structure, the corporate control of the investment function, and the operation of the policy-formation network. If government officials did not have to wait for corporate leaders to decide where and when they will invest, and if government officials were not further limited by the general public's acceptance of policy recommendations from the policy-formation network, then power elite involvement in elections and government would count for a lot less than they do under present conditions.

Domination by the power elite does not negate the reality of continuing conflict over government policies, but few conflicts, it has been shown, involve challenges to the rules that create privileges for the upper class and domination by the power elite. Most of the numerous battles within the interest-group process, for example, are only over specific spoils and favors; they often involve disagreements among competing business interests.

Similarly, conflicts within the policy-making process of government often involve differences between the moderate conservative and ultraconservative segments of the dominant class. At other times they involve issues in which the needs of the corporate community as a whole come into conflict with the needs of specific industries, which is what happens to some extent on tariff policies and also on some environmental legislation. In neither case does the nature of the conflict call into question the domination of government by the power elite.

…Contrary to what pluralists claim, there is not a single case study on any issue of any significance that shows a liberal-labor victory over a united corporate-conservative coalition, which is strong evidence for a class-domination theory on the "Who wins?" power indicator. The classic case studies frequently cited by pluralists have been shown to be gravely deficient as evidence for their views. Most of these studies reveal either conflicts among rival groups within the power elite or situations in which the moderate conservatives have decided for their own reasons to side with the liberal-labor coalition.…

More generally, it now can be concluded that all four indicators of power introduced in [the first section] point to the corporate rich and their power elite as the dominant organizational structure in American society. First, the wealth and income distributions are skewed in their favor more than in any other industrialized democracy. They are clearly the most powerful group in American society in terms of "Who benefits?" Second, the appointees to government come overwhelmingly from the corporate community and its associated policy-formation network. Thus, the power elite is clearly the most powerful in terms of "Who sits?"

Third, the power elite wins far more often than it loses on policy issues resolved in the federal government. Thus, it is the most powerful in terms of "Who wins?" Finally, as shown in reputational studies in the 1950s and 1970s,… corporate leaders are the most powerful group in terms of "Who shines?" By the usual rules of evidence in a social science investigation using multiple indicators, the owners and managers of large income-producing properties are the dominant class in the United States.

Still, as noted at the end of the first [section], power structures are not immutable. Societies change and power structures evolve or crumble from time to unpredictable time, especially in the face of challenge. When it is added that the liberal-labor coalition persists in the face of its numerous defeats, and that free speech and free elections are not at risk, there remains the possibility that class domination could be replaced by a greater sharing of power in the future.

Rights, Liberties, AND Security

Recalibrating the Balance after September 11

by Stuart Taylor, Jr.

When dangers increase, liberties shrink. That has been our history, especially in wartime. And today we face dangers without precedent: a mass movement of militant Islamic terrorists who crave martyrdom, hide in shadows, are fanatically bent on slaughtering as many of us as possible and—if they can—using nuclear truck bombs to obliterate New York or Washington or both, without leaving a clue as to the source of the attack.

How can we avert catastrophe and hold down the number of lesser mass murders? Our best hope is to prevent al-Qaida from getting nuclear, biological, or chemical weapons and smuggling them into this country. But we need be unlucky only once to fail in that. Ultimately we can hold down our casualties only by finding and locking up (or killing) as many as possible of the hundreds or thousands of possible al-Qaida terrorists whose strategy is to infiltrate our society and avoid attention until they strike.

The urgency of penetrating secret terrorist cells makes it imperative for Congress—and the nation—to undertake a candid, searching, and systematic reassessment of the civil liberties rules that restrict the government's core investigative and detention powers. Robust national debate and deliberate congressional action should replace what has so far been largely ad hoc presidential improvisation. While the USA-PATRIOT Act—no model of careful deliberation—changed many rules for the better (and some for the worse), it did not touch some others that should be changed.

Carefully crafted new legislation would be good not only for security but also for liberty. Stubborn adherence to the civil liberties status quo would probably damage our most fundamental freedoms far more in the long run than would judicious modifications of rules that are less fundamental. Considered congressional action based on open national debate is more likely to be sensitive to civil liberties and to the Constitution's checks and balances than unilateral expansion of executive power. Courts are more likely to check executive excesses if Congress sets limits for them to enforce. Government agents are more likely to respect civil liberties if freed from rules that create unwarranted obstacles to doing their jobs. And preventing terrorist mass murders is the best way of avoiding a panicky stampede into truly oppressive police statism, in which measures now unthinkable could suddenly become unstoppable.

This is not to advocate truly radical revisions of civil liberties. Nor is it to applaud all the revisions that have already been made, some of which seem unwarranted and even dangerous. But unlike most in-depth commentaries on the liberty-security balance since September 11—which argue (plausibly, on some issues) that we have gone too far in expanding government power—this article contends that in important respects we have not gone far enough. Civil libertarians have underestimated the need for broader investigative powers and exaggerated the dangers to our fundamental liberties. Judicious expansion of the government's powers to find suspected terrorists would be less dangerous to freedom than either risking possibly preventable attacks or resorting to incarceration without due process of law—as the Bush administration has begun to do. We should worry less about being wiretapped or searched or spied upon or interrogated and more about seeing innocent people put behind bars—or about being blown to bits.

Recalibrating the Liberty-Security Balance

The courts, Congress, the president, and the public have from the beginning of this nation's history demarcated the scope of protected rights "by a weighing of competing interests... the public-safety interest and the liberty interest," in the words of Judge Richard A. Posner of the U.S. Court of Appeals for the Seventh Circuit. "The safer the nation feels, the more weight judges will be willing to give to the liberty interest."

During the 1960s and 1970s, the weight on the public safety side of the scales seemed relatively modest. The isolated acts of violence by groups like the Weather Underground and Black Panthers—which had largely run their course by the mid-1970s—were a minor threat compared with our enemies today. Suicide bombers were virtually unheard of. By contrast, the threat to civil liberties posed by broad governmental investigative and detention powers and an imperial presidency had been dramatized by Watergate and by disclosures of such ugly abuses of power as FBI Director J. Edgar Hoover's spying on politicians, his wiretapping and harassment of the Rev. Martin Luther King, Jr., and the government's disruption and harassment of antiwar and radical groups.

To curb such abuses, the Supreme Court, Congress, and the Ford and Carter administrations placed tight limits on law enforcement and intelligence agencies. The Court consolidated and in some ways extended the Warren Court's revolutionary restrictions on government powers to search, seize, wiretap, interrogate, and detain suspected criminals (and terrorists). It also barred warrantless wiretaps and searches of domestic radicals. Congress barred warrantless wiretaps and searches of suspected foreign spies and terrorists—a previously untrammeled presidential power—in the 1978 Foreign Intelligence Surveillance Act. And Edward Levi, President Ford's attorney general, clamped down on domestic surveillance by the FBI.

We are stuck in habits of mind that have not yet fully processed how dangerous our world has become or how ill-prepared our legal regime is to meet the new dangers.

As a result, today many of the investigative powers that government could use to penetrate al-Qaida cells—surveillance, informants, searches, seizures, wiretaps, arrests, interrogations, detentions—are tightly restricted by a web of laws, judicial precedents, and administrative rules. Stalked in our homeland by the deadliest terrorists in history, we are armed with investigative powers calibrated largely for dealing with drug dealers, bank robbers, burglars, and ordinary murderers. We are also stuck in habits of mind that have not yet fully processed how dangerous our world has become or how ill-prepared our legal regime is to meet the new dangers.

Rethinking Government's Powers

Only a handful of the standard law-enforcement investigative techniques have much chance of penetrating and defanging groups like al-Qaida. The four most promising are: infiltrating them through informants and undercover agents; finding them and learning their plans through surveillance, searches, and wiretapping; detaining them before they can launch terrorist attacks; and interrogating those detained. All but the first (infiltration) are now so tightly restricted by Supreme Court precedents (sometimes by mistaken or debatable readings of them), statutes, and administrative rules as to seriously impede terrorism investigators. Careful new legislation could make these powers more flexible and useful while simultaneously setting boundaries to minimize overuse and abuse.

Searches and Surveillance

The Supreme Court's case law involving the Fourth Amendment's ban on "unreasonable searches and seizures" does not distinguish clearly between a routine search for stolen goods or marijuana and a preventive search for a bomb or a vial of anthrax. To search a dwelling, obtain a wiretap, or do a thorough search of a car or truck, the government must generally have "probable cause"—often (if incorrectly) interpreted in the more-probable-than-not sense—to believe that the proposed search will uncover evidence of crime. These rules make little sense when the purpose of the search is to prevent mass murder.

Federal agents and local police alike need more specific guidance than the Supreme Court can quickly supply. Congress should provide it, in the form of legislation relaxing for terrorism investigations the restrictions on searching, seizing, and wiretapping, including the undue stringency of the burden of proof to obtain a search warrant in a terrorism investigation.

Search and seizure restrictions were the main (if widely unrecognized) cause of the FBI's famous failure to seek a warrant during the weeks before September 11 to search the computer and

other possessions of Zacarias Moussaoui, the alleged "20th hijacker." He had been locked up since August 16, technically for overstaying his visa, based on a tip about his strange behavior at a Minnesota flight school. The FBI had ample reason to suspect that Moussaoui—who has since admitted to being a member of al-Qaida—was a dangerous Islamic militant plotting airline terrorism.

Congressional and journalistic investigations of the Moussaoui episode have focused on the intelligence agencies' failure to put together the Moussaoui evidence with other intelligence reports that should have alerted them that a broad plot to hijack airliners might be afoot. Investigators have virtually ignored the undue stringency of the legal restraints on the government's powers to investigate suspected terrorists. Until these are fixed, they will seriously hobble our intelligence agencies no matter how smart they are.

From the time of FDR until 1978, the government could have searched Moussaoui's possessions without judicial permission, by invoking the president's inherent power to collect intelligence about foreign enemies. But the 1978 Foreign Intelligence Security Act (FISA) bars searches of suspected foreign spies and terrorists unless the attorney general could obtain a warrant from a special national security court (the FISA court). The warrant application has to show not only that the target is a foreign terrorist, but also that he is a member of some international terrorist "group."

Coleen Rowley, a lawyer in the FBI's Minneapolis office, argued passionately in a widely publicized letter last May 21 to FBI Director Robert S. Mueller III that the information about Moussaoui satisfied this FISA requirement. Congressional investigators have said the same. FBI headquarters officials have disagreed, because before September 11 no evidence linked Moussaoui to al-Qaida or any other identifiable terrorist group. Unlike their critics, the FBI headquarters officials were privy to any relevant prior decisions by the FISA court, which cloaks its proceedings and decisions in secrecy. In addition, they were understandably gun-shy about going forward with a legally shaky warrant application in the wake of the FISA court's excoriation of an FBI supervisor in the fall of 2000 for perceived improprieties in his warrant applications. In any event, even if the FBI had done everything right, it was and is at least debatable whether its information about Moussaoui was enough to support a FISA warrant.

More important for future cases, it is clear that FISA—even as amended by the USA-PATRIOT Act—would not authorize a warrant in any case in which the FBI cannot tie a suspected foreign terrorist to one or more confederates, whether because his confederates have escaped detection or cannot be identified or because the suspect is a lone wolf.

Congress could strengthen the hand of FBI terrorism investigators by amending FISA to include the commonsense presumption that any foreign terrorist who comes to the United States is probably acting for (or at least inspired by) some international terrorist group. Another option would be to lower the burden of proof from "probable cause" to "reasonable suspicion." A third option—which could be extended to domestic as well as international terrorism investigations—would be to authorize a warrantless "preventive" search or wiretap of anyone the government has reasonable grounds to suspect of preparing or helping others prepare for a terrorist attack. To minimize any temptation for government agents to use this new power in pursuit of ordinary criminal suspects, Congress could prohibit the use in any prosecution unrelated to terrorism of any evidence obtained by such a preventive search or wiretap.

The Supreme Court seems likely to uphold any such statute as consistent with the ban on "unreasonable searches and seizures." While the Fourth Amendment says that "no warrants shall issue, but upon probable cause," warrants are not required for many types of searches, are issued for administrative searches of commercial property without probable cause in the traditional sense, and arguably should never be required. Even in the absence of a warrant or probable cause, the justices have upheld searches based on "reasonable suspicion" of criminal activities, including brief "stop-and-frisk" encounters on the streets and car stops. They have also upheld mandatory drug-testing of certain government employees and transportation workers whose work affects the public safety even when there is no particularized suspicion at all. In the latter two cases, the Court suggested that searches designed to prevent harm to the public safety should be easier to justify than searches seeking evidence for criminal cases.

Exaggerated Fear of Big Brother

Proposals to increase the government's wiretapping powers awaken fears of unleashing Orwellian thought police to spy on, harass, blackmail, and smear political dissenters and others. Libertarians point out that most conversations overheard and e-mails intercepted in the war on terrorism will be innocent and that the tappers and buggers will overhear intimacies and embarrassing disclosures that are none of the government's business.

Such concerns argue for taking care to broaden wiretapping and surveillance powers only as much as seems reasonable to prevent terrorist acts. But broader wiretapping authority is not all bad for civil liberties. It is a more accurate and benign method of penetrating terrorist cells than the main alternative, which is planting and recruiting informers—a dangerous, ugly, and unreliable business in which the government is already free to engage without limit. The narrower the government's surveillance powers, the more it will rely on informants.

Moreover, curbing the government's power to collect information through wiretapping is not the only way to protect against misuse of the information. Numerous other safeguards less damaging to the counterterrorism effort—inspectors general, the Justice Department's Office of Professional Responsibility, congressional investigators, a gaggle of liberal and conservative civil liberties groups, and the news media—have become extremely potent. The FBI has very little incentive to waste time and resources on unwarranted snooping.

To keep the specter of Big Brother in perspective, it's worth recalling that the president had unlimited power to wiretap suspected foreign spies and terrorists until 1978 (when FISA was adopted); if this devastated privacy or liberty, hardly anyone noticed. It's also worth noting that despite the government's already-vast power to comb through computerized records of our banking and commercial transactions and much else that we do in the computer age, the vast majority of the people who have seen their privacy or reputations shredded have not been wronged by rogue officials. They have been wronged by media organizations, which do far greater damage to far more people with far less accountability.

Nineteen years ago, in *The Rise of the Computer State*, David Burnham wrote: "The question looms before us: Can the United States continue to flourish and grow in an age when the physical movements, individual purchases, conversations and meetings of every citizen are constantly under surveillance by private companies and government agencies?" It can. It has. And now that the computer state has risen indeed, the threat of being watched by Big Brother or smeared by the FBI seems a lot smaller than the threat of being blown to bits or poisoned by terrorists.

The Case for Coercive Interrogation

The same Zacarias Moussaoui whose possessions would have been searched but for FISA's undue stringency also epitomizes another problem: the perverse impact of the rules—or what are widely assumed to be the rules—restricting interrogations of suspected terrorists.

"We were prevented from even attempting to question Moussaoui on the day of the attacks when, in theory, he could have possessed further information about other co-conspirators," Coleen Rowley complained in a little-noticed portion of her May 21 letter to Mueller. The reason was that Moussaoui had requested a lawyer. To the FBI that meant that any further interrogation would violate the Fifth Amendment "*Miranda* rules" laid down by the Supreme Court in 1966 and subsequent cases.

It's not hard to imagine such rules (or such an interpretation) leading to the loss of countless lives. While interrogating Moussaoui on September 11 might not have yielded any useful information, suppose that he had been part of a team planning a second wave of hijackings later in September and that his resistance could have been cracked. Or suppose that the FBI learns tomorrow, from a wiretap, that another al-Qaida team is planning an imminent attack and arrests an occupant of the wiretapped apartment.

We all know the drill. Before asking any questions, FBI agents (and police) must warn the suspect: "You have a right to remain silent." And if the suspect asks for a lawyer, all interrogation must cease until the lawyer arrives (and tells the suspect to keep quiet). This seems impossible to justify when dealing with people suspected of planning mass murder. But it's the law, isn't it?

Actually, it's not the law, though many judges think it is, along with most lawyers, federal agents, police, and cop-show mavens. You do *not* have a right to remain silent. The most persuasive interpretation of the Constitution and the Supreme Court's precedents is that agents and police are free to interrogate any suspect without *Miranda* warnings; to spurn requests for a lawyer; to press hard for answers; and—at least in a terrorism investigation—perhaps even to use hours of interrogation, verbal abuse, isolation, blindfolds, polygraph tests, death-penalty threats, and other forms of psychological coercion short of torture or physical brutality. Maybe even truth serum.

The Fifth Amendment self-incrimination clause says only that no person "shall be compelled in any criminal case to be a witness against himself." The clause prohibits forcing a defendant to testify at his trial and also making him a witness against himself indirectly by using compelled pretrial statements. It does not prohibit compelling a suspect to talk. *Miranda* held only that in determining whether a defendant's statements (and information derived from them) may be used against him at his trial, courts must treat all interrogations of arrested suspects as inherently coercive unless the warnings are given.

Courts typically ignore this distinction because in almost every litigated case the issue is whether a criminal defendant's incriminating statements should be suppressed at his trial; there is no need to focus on whether the constitutional problem is the conduct of the interrogation, or the use at trial of evidence obtained, or both. And as a matter of verbal shorthand, it's a lot easier to say "the police violated *Miranda*" than to say "the judge would be violating *Miranda* if he or she were to admit the defendant's statements into evidence at his trial."

You do *not* have a right to remain silent. The Fifth Amendment self-incrimination clause does not prohibit compelling a suspect to talk; it limits what can be used at trial.

But the war against terrorism has suddenly increased the significance of this previously academic question. In terrorism investigations, it will often be more important to get potentially life-saving information from a suspect than to get incriminating statements for use in court.

Fortunately for terrorism investigators, the Supreme Court said in 1990 that "a constitutional violation [of the Fifth Amendment's self-incrimination clause] occurs only at trial." It cited an earlier ruling that the government can obtain court orders compelling reluctant witnesses to talk and can imprison them for contempt of court if they refuse, if it first guarantees them immunity from prosecution on the basis of their statements or any derivative evidence. These decisions support the conclusion that the self-incrimination clause "does not forbid the forcible extraction of information but only the use of information so extracted as evidence in a criminal case," as a federal appeals court ruled in 1992.

Of course, even when the primary reason for questioning a suspected terrorist is prevention, the government could pay a heavy cost for ignoring *Miranda* and using coercive interrogation techniques, because it would sometimes find it difficult or impossible to prosecute extremely dangerous terrorists. But terrorism investigators may be able to get their evidence and use it too, if the Court—or Congress, which unlike the Court would not have to wait for a proper case to come along—extends a 1984 precedent creating what the justices called a "public safety" exception to *Miranda*. That decision allowed use at trial of a defendant's incriminating answer to a policeman's demand (before any *Miranda* warnings) to know where his gun was hidden.

Those facts are not a perfect parallel for most terrorism investigations, because of the immediate nature of the danger (an accomplice might pick up the gun) and the spontaneity of the officer's question. And as Rowley testified, "In order to give timely advice" about what an agent can legally do, "you've got to run to a computer and pull it up, and I think that many people have kind of forgotten that case, and many courts have actually limited it to its facts."

But when the main purpose of the interrogation is to prevent terrorist attacks, the magnitude of the danger argues for a broader public safety exception, as Rowley implied in her letter.

Congress should neither wait for the justices to clarify the law nor assume that they will reach the right conclusions without prodding. It should make the rules as clear as possible as soon as possible. Officials like Rowley need to know that they are free to interrogate suspected terrorists more aggressively than they suppose. While a law expanding the public safety exception to *Miranda* would be challenged as unconstitutional, it would contradict no existing Supreme Court precedent and—if carefully calibrated to apply only when the immediate purpose is to save lives—would probably be upheld.

Would investigators routinely ignore *Miranda* and engage in coercive interrogation—perhaps extorting false confessions—if told that the legal restraints are far looser than has been supposed? The risk would not be significantly greater than it is now. Police would still need to comply with *Miranda* in almost all cases for fear of jeopardizing any prosecution. While that would not be true in terrorism investigations if the public safety exception were broadened, extreme abuses such as beatings and torture would violate the due process clause of the Fifth Amendment (and of the Fourteenth Amendment as well), which has been construed as barring interrogation techniques that "shock the conscience," and is backed up by administrative penalties and the threat of civil lawsuits.

Bringing Preventive Detention inside the Law

Of all the erosions of civil liberties that must be considered after September 11, preventive detention—incarcerating people because of their perceived dangerousness even when they are neither convicted nor charged with any crime—would represent the sharpest departure from centuries of Anglo-American jurisprudence and come closest to police statism.

But the case for some kind of preventive detention has never been as strong. Al-Qaida's capacity to inflict catastrophic carnage dwarfs any previous domestic security threat. Its "sleeper" agents are trained to avoid criminal activities that might arouse suspicion. So the careful ones cannot be arrested on criminal charges until it is too late. And their lust for martyrdom renders criminal punishment ineffective as a deterrent.

Without preventive detention, the Bush administration would apparently have no solid legal basis for holding the two U.S. citizens in military brigs in this country as suspected "enemy combatants"—or for holding the more than 500 noncitizens at Guantanamo Bay. Nor would it have had a solid legal basis for detaining any of the 19 September 11 hijackers if it had suspected them of links to al-Qaida before they struck. Nor could it legally have detained Moussaoui—who was suspected of terrorist intent but was implicated in no provable crime or conspiracy—had he had not overstayed his visa.

What should the government do when it is convinced of a suspect's terrorist intent but lacks admissible evidence of any crime? Or when a criminal trial would blow vital intelligence secrets? Or when ambiguous evidence makes it a tossup whether a suspect is harmless or an al-Qaidan? What should it do with suspects like Jose Padilla, who was arrested in Chicago and is now in military detention because he is suspected of (but not

charged with) plotting a radioactive "dirty-bomb" attack on Washington, D.C.? Or with a (hypothetical) Pakistani graduate student in chemistry, otherwise unremarkable, who has downloaded articles about how terrorists might use small planes to start an anthrax epidemic and shown an intense but unexplained interest in crop-dusters?

Only four options exist. Let such suspects go about their business unmonitored until (perhaps) they commit mass murders; assign agents to tail them until (perhaps) they give the agents the slip; bring prosecutions without solid evidence and risk acquittals; and preventive detention. The latter could theoretically include not only incarceration but milder restraints such as house arrest or restriction to certain areas combined with agreement to carry (or to be implanted with) a device enabling the government to track the suspect's movements at all times.

As an alternative to preventive detention, Congress could seek to facilitate prosecutions of suspected "sleepers" by allowing use of now-inadmissible and secret evidence and stretching the already broad concept of criminal conspiracy so far as to make it almost a thought crime. But that would have a harsher effect on innocent terrorism suspects than would preventive detention and could weaken protections for all criminal defendants.

As Alan Dershowitz notes, "[N]o civilized nation confronting serious danger has ever relied exclusively on criminal convictions for past offenses. Every country has introduced, by one means or another, a system of preventive or administrative detention for persons who are thought to be dangerous but who might not be convictable under the conventional criminal law."

The best argument against preventive detention of suspected international terrorists is history's warning that the system will be abused, could expand inexorably—especially in the panic that might follow future attacks—and has such terrifying potential for infecting the entire criminal justice system and undermining our Bill of Rights that we should never start down that road. What is terrorist intent, and how may it be proved? Through a suspect's advocacy of a ter-

rorist group's cause? Association with its members or sympathizers? If preventive detention is okay for people suspected of (but not charged with) terrorist intent, what about people suspected of homicidal intent, or violent proclivities, or dealing drugs?

These are serious concerns. But the dangers of punishing dissident speech, guilt by association, and overuse of preventive detention could be controlled by careful legislation. This would not be the first exception to the general rule against preventive detention. The others have worked fairly well. They include pretrial detention without bail of criminal defendants found to be dangerous, civil commitment of people found dangerous by reason of mental illness, and medical quarantines, a practice that may once again be necessary in the event of bioterrorism. All in all, the danger that a preventive detention regime for suspected terrorists would take us too far down the slippery slope toward police statism is simply not as bad as the danger of letting would-be mass murderers roam the country.

In any event, we already have a preventive detention regime for suspected international terrorists—three regimes, in fact, all created and controlled by the Bush administration without congressional input. First, two U.S. citizens—Jose Padilla, the suspected would-be dirty bomber arrested in Chicago, and Yaser Esam Hamdi, a Louisiana-born Saudi Arabian captured in Afghanistan and taken first to Guantanamo—have been in military brigs in this country for many months without being charged with any crime or allowed to see any lawyer or any judge. The administration claims that it never has to prove anything to anyone. It says that even U.S. citizens arrested in this country—who may have far stronger grounds than battlefield detainees for denying that they are enemy combatants—are entitled to no due process whatever once the government puts that label on them. This argument is virtually unprecedented, wrong as a matter of law, and indefensible as a matter of policy.

Second, Attorney General John Ashcroft rounded up more than 1,100 mostly Muslim noncitizens in the fall of 2001, which involved preventive detention in many cases although they were charged with immigration violations or crimes (mostly minor) or held under the material witness statute. This when-in-doubt-detain approach effectively reversed the presumption of innocence in the hope of disrupting any planned followup attacks. We may never know whether it succeeded in this vital objective. But the legal and moral bases for holding hundreds of apparently harmless detainees, sometimes without access to legal counsel, in conditions of unprecedented secrecy, seemed less and less plausible as weeks and months went by. Worse, the administration treated many (if not most) of the detainees shabbily and some abusively. (By mid-2002, the vast majority had been deported or released.)

Third, the Pentagon has incarcerated hundreds of Arab and other prisoners captured in Afghanistan at Guantanamo, apparently to avoid the jurisdiction of all courts—and has refused to create a fair, credible process for determining which are in fact enemy combatants and which of those are "unlawful."

These three regimes have been implemented with little regard for the law, for the rights of the many (mostly former) detainees who are probably innocent, or for international opinion. It is time for Congress to step in—to authorize a regime of temporary preventive detention for suspected international terrorists, while circumscribing that regime and specifying strong safeguards against abuse.

Civil Liberties for a New Era

It is senseless to adhere to overly broad restrictions imposed by decades-old civil-liberties rules when confronting the threat of unprecedented carnage at the hands of modern terrorists. In the words of Harvard Law School's Laurence H. Tribe, "The old adage that it is better to free 100 guilty men than to imprison one innocent describes a calculus that our Constitution—which is no suicide pact—does not impose on government when the 100 who are freed belong to terrorist cells that slaughter innocent civilians, and may well have access to chemical, biological, or nuclear weapons." The question is not whether we should increase governmental power to meet such dangers. The question is how much.

Stuart Taylor, Jr., is a senior writer for National Journal.

HOW THE LITTLE GUY GETS CRUNCHED

When powerful interests shower Washington with millions in campaign contributions, they often get what they want. But it's ordinary citizens and firms that pay the price—and most of them never see it coming

By Donald L. Barlett and James B. Steele

IT WAS JUST YOUR TYPICAL PIECE OF congressional dirty work. As 1999 wound down, the House and Senate passed the District of Columbia Appropriations Act. You might think that would be a boring piece of legislation. You would be wrong. For buried in the endless clauses authorizing such spending items as $867 million for education and $5 million to promote the adoption of foster children was Section 6001: Superfund Recycling Equity. It had nothing to do with the District of Columbia, nor appropriations, nor "equity" as it is commonly defined.

Instead Section 6001 was inserted in the appropriations bill by Senator Trent Lott of Mississippi, the Senate majority leader, to take the nation's scrap-metal dealers off the hook for millions of dollars in potential Superfund liabilities at toxic-waste sites. In doing so, Lott had the support of colleagues in both parties.

This early Christmas present to the scrap-metal dealers—who contributed more than $300,000 to political candidates and committees during the 1990s—made them very happy. Others in the recycling chain were not so happy. All of a sudden, they were potentially responsible for millions of dollars in damages the junkmen might otherwise have had to pay.

While clever in its obscurity, Section 6001 is not an especially big giveaway by Capitol Hill standards. Rather, it is typical among the growing litany of examples of how Washington extends favorable treatment to one set of citizens at the expense of another. It's a process that frequently causes serious, sometimes fatal economic harm to unwary individuals and businesses that are in the way.

How do you get that favorable treatment? If you know the right people in Congress and in the White House, you can often get anything you want. And there are two surefire ways to get close to those people:

- Contribute to their political campaigns.
- Spend generously on lobbying.

If you do both of these things, success will maul you like groupies at a rock concert. If you do neither—and this is the case with about 200 million individuals of voting age and several million corporations—those people in Washington will treat you accordingly. In essence, campaign spending in America has divided all of us into two groups: first- and second-class citi-

zens. This is what happens if you are in the latter group:

You pick up a disproportionate share of America's tax bill.

You pay higher prices for a broad range of products, from peanuts to prescription drugs.

You pay taxes that others in a similar situation have been excused from paying.

You are compelled to abide by laws while others are granted immunity from them.

You must pay debts that you incur while others do not.

You are barred from writing off on your tax return some of the money spent on necessities while others deduct the cost of their entertainment.

You must run your business by one set of rules while the government creates another set for your competitors.

In contrast, first-class citizens—the fortunate few who contribute to the right politicians and hire the right lobbyists—enjoy all the benefits of their special status. Among them:

If they make a bad business decision, the government bails them out.

If they want to hire workers at below-market wage rates, the government provides the means to do so.

If they want more time to pay their debts, the government gives them an extension.

If they want immunity from certain laws, the government gives it.

If they want to ignore rules their competitors must comply with, the government gives its approval.

If they want to kill legislation that is intended for the public good, it gets killed.

Call it government for the few at the expense of the many. Looked at another way, almost any time a citizen or a business gets what it wants through campaign contributions and lobbying, someone else pays the price for it. Sometimes it's a few people, sometimes millions. Sometimes it's one business, sometimes many. In short, through a process often obscured from public view, Washington anoints winners and creates losers. Among the recent winners and the wannabes, who collectively have contributed millions of dollars to candidates and their parties and spent generously on lobbying:

• **TAX-FREE PROFITS** Last December, President Clinton signed into law the Ticket to Work and Work Incentives Improvement Act, hailing the legislation as providing "the most significant advancement for people with disabilities since the Americans with Disabilities Act almost a decade ago." He called it "a genuinely American bill."

Indeed so. For it also provided something quite unrelated to disabilities: a lucrative tax break for banks, insurers and financial-service companies. A provision woven into the legislation allowed the foreign subsidiaries of these businesses to extend the income-tax-free status of foreign earnings from the sale of securities, annuities and other financial holdings. Among the big winners: American International Group Inc., an insurance giant, as well as the recently formed Citigroup. Overall, the tax break will cost the U.S. Treasury $1.5 billion in the next two years, just as it did

in the past two years. The amount is equivalent to all the income taxes paid over four years by 300,000 individuals and families that earn between $25,000 and $30,000 a year.

• **THE GREAT S&L GIVEBACK** Owners of savings and loan associations, many of whom are suing the Federal Government for clamping down on them during the S&L crisis in the 1980s, will benefit from a one-paragraph clause that was slipped into legislation that will hold the U.S. government liable for billions of dollars in damage claims because federal regulators nixed certain accounting practices. As is typical with special-interest measures, there were no hearings or estimates of the cost before the clause mysteriously showed up in the Omnibus Consolidated and Emergency Supplemental Appropriations Act of 1998. Among the potential beneficiaries: billionaires Ron Perelman and the Pritzker and Bass families. The losers: all other taxpayers, who will have to pick up the tab.

THE FUTURE PROMISES MUCH MORE OF THE same. In this presidential election year, companies and industries that hope for special treatment in the new decade are busy making their political contributions and their connections. Examples:

• **A LONGER LIFE FOR GOLDEN DRUGS** Major pharmaceutical companies will seek legislation to extend the patent life on their most valuable drugs. In the past, such giveaways were often inserted into unrelated legislation and covered a single drug or two. But this year, watch for heavy lobbying for the grand-daddy of all patent extenders. It would protect pharmaceutical company sales of $3 billion annually and add years to the profitable life of at least seven expensive drugs, such as Schering-Plough's Claritin for allergies and Eulexin for prostate cancer, SmithKline Beecham's Relafen for arthritis and G.D. Searle's Daypro for arthritis. The big losers: patients, especially senior citizens on fixed incomes, who must buy expensive prescription drugs instead of cheaper generic versions. Estimates of the added cost run from $1 billion to $11 billion over the next decade.

• **CARS WITH A CHECKERED PAST** The National Automobile Dealers Association is pushing for a federal law regulating the sale of rebuilt wrecked cars. Like a lot of special-interest legislation, the Na-

tional Salvage Motor Vehicle Consumer Protection Act, as it's called, sounds good. No one is likely to argue with its call for federal standards to govern the sale of "nonrepairable and rebuilt vehicles." But look closely. The fine print actually provides minimal standards, gives states the option of ignoring these, applies to only half the cars on the road and keeps secret the history of near totaled vehicles. Sponsored by majority leader Lott, the bill has cleared the Senate Commerce Committee, whose chairman, presidential candidate John McCain, is a co-sponsor. Losers: consumers who unknowingly buy rebuilt wrecks at inflated prices.

Over and over, Washington extends favored treatment to those who pay up—at the expense of those who don't.

BOTH THE RECIPIENTS OF CAMPAIGN CONtributions and the givers insist that no public official is for sale, that no favors are granted in exchange for cash. Few people believe that; U.S. Supreme Court Justice David Souter summed up the prevailing public attitude during arguments in a case that led the Justices last week to uphold the current $1,000 limit on individual campaign contributions. (Donations to parties are still unlimited.) Said Souter:

"I think most people assume—I do, certainly—that someone making an extraordinarily large contribution is going to get some kind of an extraordinary return for it. I think that is a pervasive assumption. And… there is certainly an appearance of, call it an attenuated corruption, if you will, that large contributors are simply going to get better service, whatever that service may be, from a politician than the average contributor, let alone no contributor."

Campaign-finance reform has emerged as an issue during the budding presidential race. Three of the four leading candidates are for it; one is against. McCain has made limiting campaign contributions his defining issue, although the Arizona Republican has accepted contributions from corporations seeking favors from his Commerce committee. Bill Bradley has also spoken out for reform, calling for public financing of elections. Vice President Gore, although involved in the Clinton Administration's 1996 fund-raising scandals, also advocates publicly funded campaigns. Only Texas Governor George W. Bush favors the status quo.

Just how obsessed with raking in cash are the 535 members of Congress?

A veteran Washington lawyer who once served an apprenticeship with a prominent U.S. Senator relates a telling experience. The lawyer, who represents an agency of a state government, visited the home office of a Congressman in that state to discuss a national issue affecting the agency and, indirectly, the Congressman's constituents. After an effusive greeting, the Congressman's next words were brief and to the point:

"How much money can you contribute?"

The stunned lawyer explained that he represented a state agency and that state governments do not contribute to political candidates. As if in response to hearing some programmed words that altered his brain circuitry, the Congressman changed his tone and demeanor instantly. Suddenly, he had more pressing obligations. He would be unable to meet with the lawyer. Rather, he said, an aide would listen to whatever it was the lawyer had to say.

Of course, those who give money to political candidates or their parties don't necessarily get everything they seek. Often the reason is that their opponents are just as well connected. But they do get access—to the Representative or Senator, the White House aide or Executive Branch official—to make their case.

Try it yourself. You won't get it.

Bits and pieces of the story of those who give the money and what they get in return have been told, here and elsewhere. But who gets hurt—the citizens and businesses that do not play the game—remains an untold story.

Over the next nine months, continuing until the presidential election in November, TIME will publish periodic reports examining the anonymous victims of big money and politics.

Editor's note: In early 2002, Congress considered the Shays-Meehan campaign finance reform bill. It passed in the House, but it was delayed in the Senate.

The End of Globalization?

Multinational corporations are more vulnerable than you think

BY MICHAEL SHUMAN

Globalization, argues *New York Times* columnist Tom Friedman, is "making it possible for... corporations to reach farther, faster, cheaper, and deeper around the world" and is fostering "a flowering of both wealth and technological innovation the likes of which the world has never before seen." To David Korten, a former Ford Foundation official and now a prominent globalization critic, it is "market tyranny... extending its reach across the planet like a cancer, colonizing ever more of the planet's living spaces, destroying livelihoods, displacing people, rendering democratic institutes impotent, and feeding on life in an insatiable quest for money." The careful listener to this by-now-familiar debate can actually discern a striking point of agreement: Both sides assume, one with euphoria and the other with fear, that global-scale business is the wave of the future. Yet there's mounting evidence that multinational firms may be *less* capable of delivering competitive products than national or local firms.

AT&T stunned financial analysts in October 2000 when it announced that it was carving itself up into four, more versa-

tile companies. In May 2001, British Telecom unveiled a plan to spin off its wholesale arm, part of its wireless business, and numerous assets in Asia. Other self-initiated split-ups and slim-downs seem likely to follow. These developments are important reminders of a point all but forgotten in the globalization debate: Scale matters.

Any first-year economics student learns that firms can lower average costs by expanding, *but only up to a point.* Beyond that point (according to the law of diminishing returns to scale), complexities, breakdowns, and inefficiencies begin to drive average costs back up. The collapse of massive state-owned enterprises in the old Soviet Union and the bankruptcies of Chrysler and New York City are notable reminders of a lesson we should have absorbed from the dinosaur: Bigger is not always better.

A telling example in economic life is commercial banking. Despite all the headlines about mergers, researchers at the Federal Reserve in Minneapolis have concluded that "after banks reach a fairly modest size [about $100 million in assets],

there is no cost advantage to further expansion. Some evidence even suggests diseconomies of scale for very large banks." The Financial Markets Center, a financial research and education organization, has found that, compared to banks with far-flung portfolios, those that concentrate lending in a geographic region were typically twice as profitable and wind up with fewer bad loans. While the press has diligently reported national and global mergers, it has largely ignored the recent proliferation of community banks, credit unions, and microloan funds.

Banking, it turns out, is not the only exception to the rules of globalization. Five factors are playing a significant role in shrinking the economies of scale for a wide range of industries.

1. First, it turns out that global-scale industry is surprisingly inefficient at distribution. In 1910, for every dollar Americans spent for food, 50 cents went to farmers and 50 cents to marketers and providers of inputs like seeds, energy, and fertilizer; now 9 cents goes to farmers, 24 cents to input providers, and 67 cents to marketers. The marketers' 67 cents are largely unrelated to the end product that consumers really want. They're wasted on packaging, refrigeration, spoilage, advertising, trucking, supermarket fees, and middlemen.

When farmers can link more directly with nearby consumers, they can cut out these inefficiencies. This explains the spread of community-supported agriculture (CSA), pioneered initially in Japan and then Switzerland, now growing by leaps and bounds across North America. It works like this: A farmer is supported by 60 or 70 households, each of which pays a fee to receive a weekly supply of vegetables. More than 600 community-supported agricultural or horticultural operations now operate in 42 states, with 100,000 members.

Local is Logical

Many companies are finding it makes more economic sense to get smaller, not larger. According to Michael Shuman, here's why:

- Global industries are inefficient at distribution.
- Shipping costs seem destined to get higher.
- Local and regional companies make better use of market research.
- The growing service-related industries are local by nature.
- The information revolution gives smaller businesses a new edge.

2. A second factor exacerbating the inefficiency of global-scale distribution is the rising cost of shipping. In the past two years the per-barrel price of oil has quadrupled. And with expected increases in global population and per capita consumption, the U.S. Energy Information Administration projects that demand for oil worldwide will grow by 20 million barrels a day, a third more than current consumption levels. Improving technologies for petroleum recovery may ease upward pressures on oil prices a bit. But political pressures, including attempts to levy "green taxes" and political instability in oil regions like the Middle East and Central Asia could drive up prices. Until other fuels are substituted for oil, global shipping probably will become more expensive.

"The real work of planet-saving will be small, humble, and humbling."

Wendell Berry

---

3. A third challenge facing global businesses is the difficulty of managing information. Conservative economist Friedrich Hayek once argued convincingly against state socialism by noting that knowledge is too complex, too subjective, and too dependent on particular circumstances of time and place for even the best-intentioned national-scale bureaucracies to grasp it. The exact same problem afflicts multinational corporations.

In principle, a global producer can wield its resources to produce different products for different local tastes. But in practice, a local producer is better situated to intuit, design, manufacture flexibly, and deliver just-in-time products. Consumers can better communicate their needs to local producers, either directly or through local retailers. General Foods probably will never be able to convince New Yorkers to replace their locally baked bagels with Minnesota-made generics. Microbrewers have flourished throughout the United States and the United Kingdom because each of them caters to highly specialized tastes. The desires of Bay Area food shoppers wanting more varieties of locally grown fruits and vegetables, have expanded the region's agricultural economy by 61 percent over the past decade, which translates into $915 million of additional agricultural income in the local economy each year.

4. A fourth trend is the transformation of the U.S. economy from manufacturing goods to providing services. The main reason for this shift, according to MIT's Paul Krugman and Harvard's Robert Lawrence, is that technological advances have brought down the prices of many manufactured goods. As Americans spend less to acquire the same refrigerators and toasters, they spend more on services. These changes, Krugman argues in *Pop Internationalism* (MIT Press, 1997), are moving the U.S. economy inexorably toward what he calls localization: "A steadily rising share of the workforce produces services that are sold only within that same metropolitan area." For most services—whether it is health care, teaching, legal representa-

tion, accounting, or massage—consumers demand a personal, trusting relationship.

5. A fifth difficulty facing large-scale business is the information revolution. Global corporations are still amassing huge networks of factories, technology centers, and experts at a time when profitability is increasingly uncoupled from size. Small companies can now fit what used to be busy departments overseeing accounting, management, taxes, communications, and publications neatly onto a desktop computer. The Internet has given even home-based businesses the ability to compete against established, large-scale players in practically everything, including books and CDs, stocks and bonds, airline travel, and hotel rooms.

Even for industries like automobiles, where large economies of scale still make sense, the communications revolution is making it possible for small firms to achieve the same advantages through collaborations and partnerships. In northern Italy, locally owned firms involved in flexible manufacturing networks have become world-class exporters of high-tech products like robotic arms. A network typically forms temporarily to create a specific project for a well-defined niche market. Once the project is complete, the network disbands. Following successful models in Europe, more than 50 flexible manufacturing networks have been set up in the United States.

These five trends do not mean that all goods and services can be produced cost-effectively in every community. (The economics of any company or industry depend on how the new diseconomies of large scale balance against the old economies of scale.) At a minimum, however, they suggest that much of the hype from globalization's fans—and its enemies too—is overblown. If smaller businesses wind up being the most efficient producers and suppliers of many goods and services to nearby markets, then neither the utopian nor the nightmare scenarios of globalization will come to pass. Indeed, global trade may simply become a relatively minor part of most economies, as it is for ours right now (exports are responsible for less than 10 percent of our national income)—provided, of course, that politicians resist the temptation to bail out global businesses doomed by inappropriate scale.

The next wave of economic development—local, national, and global—may turn not on the rise or fall of any grand concepts like globalization, but on the slow, steady creation of appropriately scaled businesses. As the poet Wendell Berry once remarked, "The real work of planet-saving will be small, humble, and humbling.... Its jobs will be too many to count, too many to report, too many to be publicly noticed or rewarded, too small to make anyone rich or famous."

Michael H. Shuman, an attorney and economist, is co-director of the Institute for Economics and Entrepreneurship for the Village Foundation, a Washington, D.C.-based organization that works with African American men and boys on community-based economic solutions. He is the author of Going Local: Creating Self-Reliant Communities in a Global Age *(Routledge, 2000), which is available form www.progressivepubs.com. The former director of the Institute for Policy Studies, Shuman's wide-ranging interests include North-South development cooperation, citizen diplomacy, and the devolving of federal power to state and local governments. He lives in Washington, D.C.*

From *Utne Reader*, July/August 2002, pp. 51-53. © 2002 by Michael Schuman.

WHERE THE GOOD JOBS ARE GOING

Forget sweatshops. U.S. companies are now shifting high-wage work overseas, especially to India

By JYOTI THOTTAM

LITTLE BY LITTLE, SAB MAGLIONE could feel his job slipping away. He worked for a large insurance firm in northern New Jersey, developing the software it uses to keep track of its agents. But in mid-2001, his employer introduced him to Tata Consultancy Services, India's largest software company. About 120 Tata employees were brought in to help on a platform-conversion project. Maglione, 44, trained and managed a five-person Tata team. When one of them was named manager, he started to worry. By the end of last year, 70% of the project had been shifted to India and nearly all 20 U.S. workers, including Maglione, were laid off.

Since then, Maglione has been able to find only temporary work in his field, taking a pay cut of nearly 30% from his former salary of $77,000. For a family and mortgage, he says, "that doesn't pay the bills." Worried about utility costs, he runs after his two children, 11 and 7, to turn off the lights. And he has considered a new career as a house painter. "It doesn't require that much skill, and I don't have to go to school for it," Maglione says. And houses, at least, can't be painted from overseas.

Jobs that stay put are becoming a lot harder to find these days. U.S. companies are expected to send 3.3 million jobs overseas in the next 12 years, primarily to India, according to a study by Forrester Research. If you've ever called Dell about a sick PC or American Express about an error on your bill, you have already bumped the tip of this "offshore outsourcing" iceberg. The friendly voice that answered your questions was probably a customer-service rep

in Bangalore or New Delhi. Those relatively low-skilled jobs were the first to go, starting in 1997.

But more and more of the jobs that are moving abroad today are highly skilled and highly paid—the type that U.S. workers assumed would always remain at home. Instead Maglione is one of thousands of Americans adjusting to the unsettling new reality of work. "If I can get another three years in this industry, I'll be fortunate," he says. Businesses are embracing offshore outsourcing in their drive to stay competitive, and almost any company, whether in manufacturing or services, can find some part of its work that can be done off site. By taking advantage of lower wages overseas, U.S. managers believe they can cut their overall costs 25% to 40% while building a more secure, more focused work force in the U.S. Labor leaders—and nonunion workers, who make up most of those being displaced—aren't buying that rationale. "How can America be competitive in the long run sending over the very best jobs?" asks Marcus Courtney, president of the Seattle-based Washington Alliance of Technology Workers. "I don't see how that helps the middle class."

On the other side of the world, though, educated Indian workers are quickly adjusting to their new status as the world's most sought-after employees. They have never been more confident and optimistic—as Americans usually like to think of themselves. For now, at least, in ways both tangible and

emotional, educated Americans and Indians are trading places.

INCOMING
Uma Satheesh
Bangalore, India

Satheesh, 32, manages 38 Wipro employees who work on networking software for Hewlett-Packard in Bangalore—in jobs that were once done mainly in the U.S.

Uma Satheesh, 32, an employee of Wipro, one of India's leading outsourcing companies, is among her country's new elite. She manages 38 people who work for Hewlett-Packard's enterprise-servers group doing maintenance, fixing defects and enhancing the networking software developed by HP for its clients. Her unit includes more than 300 people who work for HP, about 90 of whom were added last November when HP went through a round of cost-cutting.

"We've been associated with HP for a long time, so it was an emotional thing," Satheesh says. "It was kind of a mixed feeling. But that is happening at all the companies, and it's going to continue." Satheesh says that five years ago, computer-science graduates had one career option in India: routine, mind-numbing computer programming. Anything more rewarding required emigrating. "Until three years ago, the first preference was to go overseas," she says. Nowadays her colleagues are interested only in business trips to the U.S. "People are pretty comfortable with the

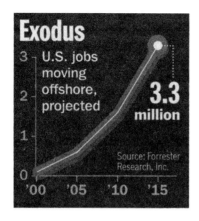

Exodus

U.S. jobs moving offshore, projected

3.3 million

Source: Forrester Research, Inc.

and analysis or market research for developing new business. Evalueserve, a niche outsourcing company in Delhi, already performs research for patent attorneys and consulting firms in the U.S. In April, J.P. Morgan Chase said it would hire about 40 stock-research analysts in Bombay—about 5% of its total research staff. Novartis employs 40 statisticians in Bombay who process data from the drug company's clinical research.

OUTSOURCED
Bernie Lantz
Logan, Utah

Lantz, 58, says offshore hirings made his troubleshooting job with a Texas software firm obsolete. He left the tech business to teach computer science at Utah State University

Playing the Savings Game
As these average-salary figures show, outsourcing lowers costs
SOFTWARE PROGRAMMER U.S. $66,100 INDIA $10,000
MECHANICAL ENGINEER U.S. $55,600 INDIA $5,900
IT MANAGER U.S. $55,000 INDIA $8,500
ACCOUNTANT U.S. $41,000 INDIA $5,000
FINANCIAL OPERATIONS U.S. $37,625 INDIA $5,500
Sources: PayScale Inc; the Paàras Group

jobs here and the pay here"—not to mention the cars and houses that once seemed out of reach. Employees in her group earn from $5,200 a year to $36,000 for the most experienced managers.

And as American companies have grown more familiar with their Indian outsourcing partners, they have steadily increased the complexity of work they are willing to hand over. Rajeshwari Rangarajan, 28, leads a team of seven Wipro workers enhancing the intranet site on which Lehman Brothers employees manage personal benefits like their 401(k) accounts. "I see myself growing with every project that I do here," Rangarajan says. "I really don't have any doubts about the growth of my career."

Her experience with a leading brokerage will probably help. Financial-services companies in the U.S. are expected to move more than 500,000 jobs overseas in the next five years, according to a survey by management consultant A.T. Kearney, and India is by far the top destination. U.S. banks, insurance firms and mortgage companies have been using outsourcing to handle tech support for years. Now these firms are using Indian workers to handle the business operations—say, assessing loan applications and credit checks—that the technology supports. Kumar Mahadeva, CEO of the thriving outsourcing firm Cognizant, explains the appeal: "It becomes logical for them to say, 'Hey, you know everything about the way we do claims processing. Why not take a piece of it?'"

The next logical step, says Andrea Bierce, a co-author of the A.T. Kearney study, is jobs that require more complex financial skills such as equity research

But as educated workers in India are finding new opportunities, those in the U.S. feel the doors closing. Last week Bernie Lantz drove 1,400 miles from his home in Plano, Texas, to begin a new life in Utah. He is 58 years old, a bachelor, and had lived in the Dallas area for 24 years. "I'm leaving all my friends," he says with a sigh. "It's quite an upheaval." Lantz used to earn $80,000 a year as a troubleshooter for Sabre, a company based in Southlake, Texas, whose software powers airline-reservations systems. But over the past two years, Sabre has gradually standardized and has centralized its software service. As Sabre began to outsource its internal IT services, Lantz says, he became convinced that jobs like his were becoming endangered. He was laid off in December. (A company spokesman denies that Lantz's firing was related to outsourcing.)

Discouraged by a depressed job market in Dallas, Lantz realized he would have to do something else. In the fall he will begin teaching computer science at Utah State University in Logan, and in the meantime he has learned a lesson of his own: "Find a job that requires direct hands-on work on site," Lantz advises. "Anything that can be sent overseas is going to be sent overseas."

Pat Fluno, 53, of Orlando, Fla., says she, like Maglione, had to train her replacement—a common practice in the

domestic outsourcing industry—when her data-processing unit at Germany-based Siemens was outsourced to India's Tata last year. "It's extremely insulting," she says. "The guy's sitting there doing my old job." After 10 months of looking, she is working again, but she had to take a $10,000 pay cut.

BYPASSED
Pat Fluno
Orlando, Fla.

Fluno's 12-person data-processing unit at the local Siemens operation was replaced by a team from Tata Consultancy Services in India. It took her 10 months—and a $10,000 cut in pay—to find a new job.

To protect domestic jobs, U.S. labor activists are pushing to limit the number of H-1B and L-1 visas granted to foreign workers. That would make it harder for offshore companies to have their employees working on site in the U.S. "Those programs were designed for a booming high-tech economy, not a busting high-tech economy," says Courtney of the Washington Alliance of Technology Workers. Courtney and his allies are starting to get the attention of lawmakers. Several congressional committees have held hearings on the impact of offshore outsourcing on the U.S. economy, and lawmakers in five states have introduced bills that would limit or forbid filling government contracts through offshore outsourcing.

Stephanie Moore, a vice president of Forrester Research, says companies are concerned about the backlash but mainly because of the negative publicity. "The retail industry is very hush-hush about its offshoring," she says. But within the boardroom, such outsourcing enjoys wide support. In a June survey of 1,000 firms by Gartner Research, 80% said the backlash would have no effect on their plans.

The advantages, businesses say, are just too great to ignore. They begin with cost but don't end there. Jennifer Cotteleer, vice president of Phase Forward, a Waltham, Mass., company that designs software for measuring clinical-trials data for drug companies, has for the past two years used offshore employees from Cognizant to customize the application for specific drug trials. Lately she has been relying on their expertise to develop even more-tailored programming. "I certainly couldn't have grown this fast without them," Cotteleer says. Her company is growing 30% annually, on track to reach $65 million in revenue this year. "What I've been able to do in very tough economic times is manage very directly to my margins," she says. "I'm providing job security for the workers I do have."

Creative use of offshore outsourcing, says Debashish Sinha of Gartner Research, offers benefits that outweigh the direct loss of jobs. In an economy that has shed 2 million jobs over two years, he contends, the 200,000 that have moved overseas are less significant than the potential for cost savings and strategic growth. But he concedes that "when you're a laid-off employee who can't find a job, that's hard to understand."

Perhaps some will follow the example of Dick Taggart, 41, of Old Greenwich, Conn. After 18 years in financial services, most recently at J.P. Morgan Chase, he now works for Progeon, an affiliate of the Indian outsourcing giant Infosys, as its man on Wall Street. One week out of every six or seven, he takes securities firms to India to show them the savings that are possible. He knows the transition is painful for the workers left behind, but he has seen it before. "It was the same thing when we moved from Wall Street to New Jersey and then to Dallas," he says. "Guess what? This is next."

—*With reporting by Sean Gregory/ New York City*

A broken heartland

Nothing manifest about the destiny
of small towns on the Great Plains

BY JEFF GLASSER

LARSON, N.D.—The white steeple of St. John's German Lutheran Church lists from the weight of its rusted, half-ton church bell. The 93-year-old church's pews, pulpit, baptismal font, and, most important, congregants have vanished. At the end of a deserted Main Street, tumbleweeds obscure the Great Northern Railroad tracks where trains once routinely carried the world's finest durum wheat to the trade centers of the Midwest.

Across from the tracks stands the Larson Hotel, its paint peeling, its roof about to be patched with discarded aluminum newspaper printing plates. It is now home to a disabled construction worker and his family who moved here from Pennsylvania last fall, saying they could only afford to live in the middle of nowhere. An empty lot away sits the X-treme North Bar and Barely South Restaurant, a last-chance saloon with a rich history of bourbon and burlesque.

Welcome to Larson, population 17, the least populated place in one of the nation's fastest-declining counties. Burke County, N.D., lost 25.3 percent of its population in the past 10 years, falling from 3,002 to 2,242, according to 2000 census figures released this spring. Its neighbor, Divide

County, shrank by 21 percent, from 2,899 to 2,283, during the same period. The two counties are littered with dozens of Larsons, Northgates, and Alkabos—virtual ghost towns that grew up as stops for steam trains and died along with the railroads. Larson has withered to the point where none of its residents—including the candidate—bothered to vote in last June's election for alderman. Four miles down state Highway 5 in Columbus, all that remains of the 74-year-old brick high school are 700 commemorative letter openers hand carved by the town elder out of its maple floors and given away as mementos. To the north, dozens of Canadian oil rigs, coal mines, and a SaskPower plant loom in the distance, a mirage of economic activity 25 miles away but a country apart. To the west, past forgotten little houses on the prairie, Crosby's cemeteries have so many fresh mounds that it looks like badgers have dug there all winter. "We're going to have to start importing pallbearers," jokes Crosby farmer Ole Svangstu, 55, noting there were 48 more deaths than births last year.

Ghost towns. Up and down the Great Plains, the country's spine, from the Sandhills of western Nebraska to the sea of prairie grass in eastern Montana, small towns

are decaying, and in some cases, literally dying out. The remarkable prosperity of the last decade never reached this far. Nearly 60 percent (250 of 429) of the counties on the Great Plains lost population in the 1990s, according to a *U.S. News* analysis of the new census data.

The emptying out of the nation's rural breadbasket was all the more surprising considering the population resurgence in cities and suburbs. The nation as a whole grew at a robust 13 percent. The 10 states of the Plains, too, expanded by 10 percent overall, a 672,554-person increase fueled by the growth of cities like Billings, Mont., and the tremendous urban sprawl that swallowed the countryside adjacent to Denver, Austin, and San Antonio. Some larger rural areas in the Plains also blossomed from their natural beauty as recreation areas, but the picture was bleak in counties with fewer than 15,000 people, where 228 of 334 (nearly 70 percent) of the counties regressed. "It's like the parting of the Red Sea," says Fannie Mae demographer Robert Lang, a census expert. "There are rivers of people flowing out of the [rural] Plains."

The degeneration of a large swath of this country's midsection—covering a

317,320-square-mile area spread over parts of the 10 states—has not seeped into the conscience of urban America. City dwellers might still perceive small towns as refuges from society's maddening stew of gridlock, smog, and crime. Where else can a visitor leave a car unlocked, not to mention *running*, on a quick trip to the post office? Farmers in small towns are considered the ultimate entrepreneurs, "our national icon of autonomy," as Yale Prof. Kathryn Marie Dudley writes in *Debt and Dispossession: Farm Loss in America's Heartland*. But, as Dudley points out, the contemporary ideal collides with a harsh economic reality.

The problem is seemingly intractable. Once thriving mining and railroad commerce are distant memories. The farm economy has been in a state of contraction for at least 30 years. Forty-two percent of Midwestern farmers, the dominant economic group, earn less than $20,000 annually. A lack of Plains industry limits other opportunities for professionals. Jeff Peterson, 53, Burke County's sole lawyer, sighs wistfully as he explains why he's packing it in after 26 years. "There just aren't so many people for clients now," says Peterson. There aren't even enough people to justify having county judges. Nearly everyone else has already left Burke County, bailing out when their farming and oil and gas jobs dried up in the late 1980s and early 1990s. Peterson says he will have to write off his $120,000 office building. So far, he has found no takers for his $135,000 house. "This wasn't a smart place to invest in," he says.

Manifest destiny. That wasn't always the case. From Thomas Jefferson's stewardship of the Louisiana Purchase, which included present day Burke and Divide counties, sprang forth the concept of America's "Manifest Destiny" to inhabit all the nation's land. In 1862, Congress passed the Homestead Act, giving immigrants free 160-acre parcels called "quarters." Northwestern North Dakota was one of the final places homesteaded. At the turn of the 20th century, the region filled with Norwegians, Swedes, Danes, Belgians, and a few Germans. The territory was so forbidding that it had no trees, so the pioneers built sod homes on a virgin landscape described by novelist Willa Cather as "nothing but land, not a country at all, but the material out of which countries are made."

Postmaster Columbus Larson's settlement on the western tip of Burke County split in two with the coming of the railroads. Half set up in front of the Great Northern tracks at "Larson," half 4 miles to the northeast next to the Soo Line at "Columbus." By 1930, every quarter in Burke and Divide was inhabited, with what would be a peak 19,634 people on the land. Crowds gathered on Saturday nights at the Opera House in Larson to dance the polka and listen to traditional Norwegian yodeling. Colorful vaudeville troops headlined the marquee at Columbus Theater. Lawrence Welk and his dance band played his signature "champagne music" there. Bootleggers peddled liquor during Prohibition, and the Larson Opera House was the place for bawdy pantomime. Occasionally the townspeople gathered on Main Street and fearfully watched local young men test their strength against that of bears for cash prizes (provided they won).

In the "dirty Thirties," pioneer women placed wet bedsheets over windows to keep out dust. The perseverance and courage of the settlers—lionized by Cather in her novel *O Pioneers!*—were tested as the soil crumbled in a series of crop disasters. Most of Larson's 114 residents left the Dust Bowl behind in search of an easier life. Columbus continued to boom in the immediate post-World War II period, though, with coal miners, power-plant workers, farmers, and a few oil roughnecks keeping the place full. The town peaked with nearly 700 people in the early 1950s. Then the coal mines closed, and the local power plant shut down. Advances in technology improved crop yields, so far fewer people were needed to farm the land. A series of government conservation programs prompted hundreds of local farmers to retire to Arizona, exacerbating the exodus.

In 1972, Columbus still had 20 businesses. Larson was hanging on with six shops, including Witty's grocery store and Ole Johnson's gas station. Virtually all are gone today. Columbus, with just 151 residents, has one cafe and a farm tool supplier, both set to close later this year. The only eatery left in Larson is the X-treme North Bar and Barely South Restaurant, which may also close. "The handwriting's on the wall," says Harold Pasche, 80, a retired farmer from Larson who now lives in Columbus. "Every little town in this whole area here is going down." The collapse of the retail trade in Columbus and Larson mirrors a national decline. From 1977 to 1997, the number of American grocery stores fell by 61.2 percent, men's clothing stores dropped by 46.6 percent, and hardware stores slipped by 40.6 percent, according to the Census

of Retail Trade. Ken Stone, an Iowa State University economist specializing in rural development, says small-town Main Streets are going the way of the railroads. "There's very little way to bring [them] back," he says.

On the farm, net income is projected to decline 20 percent in the next two years because of a worldwide depression in commodity prices and higher energy costs. Without government intervention, 10 percent of farmers could not survive one year, says former Agriculture Secretary Dan Glickman. He calls federal farm subsidies "rural support" programs and fears "economic devastation in large parts of rural America" if the government nixes them. Yet President Bush's budget package does not allocate any disaster money for farmers, who in the past three years received $25 billion in extra federal relief. Despite Glickman's warnings, there is little room in today's debate for Jeffersonian programs to resettle the Plains. People simply do not want to deal with harsh winters and broiling summers. "It's still a loser in [Plains] politics to say, 'Let them die,'" says Frank Popper, a Rutgers University land-use expert. "You've got an ongoing aversion, a denial of what's going on. But every year there are fewer farmers and ranchers. Every year they are losing their kids." In 1988, Popper and his wife, Deborah, also a professor, dreamed up a radical alternative for the rural Plains: a vast "Buffalo Commons," in which the federal government would return the territory to its pristine state before white settlement, when the buffalo roamed and the prairie grasses grew undisturbed.

Where the buffalo roam? Farmers hated the idea. But in the decade that followed, thousands of miles on the Northern Plains have reverted to "wilderness" areas with buffalo herds and fewer than two people per square mile. "I actually think this is the last American frontier," says Larson's town treasurer, Debra Watterud, 53.

That leaves places like Larson and Columbus with even fewer totems of their town histories. The latter held its final Columbus Day Parade in 1992, when Pasche drove his treasured 1932 Chevrolet Roadster down Main one last time. At the last major civic gathering in 1994, residents scooped up bricks and floor planks from the soon-to-be-demolished high school. Doug Graupe, 56, a Divide County farmer, argues that the remaining residents have an obligation to their ancestors to persevere.

"Economics shouldn't drive every decision," he says. "Do you have to have money to have a good quality of life?... People in small towns are always there to help others, to raise kids. You have a sense of community." Graupe and others in the region are excited about a $2.5 million pasta processing plant that they're planning to build in nearby Crosby, but not everyone's confident it will succeed, given the perilous demographics and the area's previous failed attempts at renewal.

In Larson, Debra Watterud proposed shutting down the town after the no-show election because the level of interest was so low. Her father-in-law, retired farmer Myron Watterud, 76, opposed the idea. If Larson deincorporated, he said, who would pay for the lights (which consumes half the $3,000 town budget)? The town would disappear from maps. No one would ever bring it back, a possibility that's hard to fathom for a man who has spent his life here. His daughter-in-law agreed to table her suggestion, but Myron Watterud says he's "scared" to watch the town in the approaching darkness of its final demise. "If the leaders of this town saw what happened," he says, "they'd turn over in their graves."

UNIT 3
Problems of Poverty and Inequality

Unit Selections

Key Points to Consider

- Why has inequality increased over the past two decades? How might increased inequality have adverse impacts on American society?

- How is corporate capitalism organized to protect or advance its own interests at the expense of others?

- How different are the worlds of men and women in American society today? Compare the treatment of women in America with their treatment around the world.

- Americans believe in tolerance, but what should be tolerated and what should not be tolerated? Explain.

 **Links: www.dushkin.com/online/**
These sites are annotated in the World Wide Web pages.

grass-roots.org
   http://www.grass-roots.org
Immigration Facts
   http://www.immigrationforum.org
Joint Center for Poverty Research
   http://www.jcpr.org
SocioSite
   http://www.pscw.uva.nl/sociosite/TOPICS/Women.html
William Davidson Institute
   http://www.wdi.bus.umich.edu
WWW Virtual Library: Demography & Population Studies
   http://demography.anu.edu.au/VirtualLibrary/

America is famous as the land of opportunity, and people from around the world have come to these shores in pursuit of the American dream. But how is America living up to this dream today? It is still a place for people to get rich, but it is also a place where people are trapped in poverty. This unit tells a number of stories of Americans dealing with advantages and disadvantages, opportunities and barriers, power and powerlessness.

The first subsection of this unit deals with income inequality and the hardship of the poor. In his article, "For Richer," Paul Krugman describes the great increase in the inequality of income in the past three decades and explains its causes. He also discusses some rather unpleasant political and social consequences of these inequalities. In the next article, Joel Stein shows some of the underside of the inequality that Krugman describes. He discusses homelessness but not the homelessness that is imaged in our minds by the drunk sleeping on the park bench. Increasingly the homeless are mothers with children and Joel Stein tells some of their stories. He also points out why this is the case. The next article examines an aspect of inequality that is seldom analyzed. Rodney Ward argues that the costs in deaths and injuries of the war in Iraq are born mainly by working class American soldiers. In addition the war is being used as an excuse to strip the working class and the poor of programs that

benefit them. It is also imposing other economic hardships on these groups.

The American welfare system is addressed in the second subsection of unit 3. The first article describes the generous welfare system for the rich, and the next describes the effects of the 1996 welfare reform on the poor. First, Donald Barlett and James Steele explain how corporations milk federal, state, and local governments of billions of dollars. It comes as no surprise to a student of society that the political economy is set up to benefit the upper class and the powerful but the extent of that bias, when pointed out, can shock us anyway. The next article evaluates the results of the 1996 welfare reform. It begins by providing facts which show that it was not as bad as it was made out to be. For example, it was not very costly, being less than 5% of the costs of social security. Nevertheless, it needed to be reformed and the reform lowered caseloads 57 percent through 2001, and the majority of leavers are working (much of this change was due to the good economy). On the negative side, the jobs generally are bad jobs that pay little and are unsteady. Finally, on several counts the new welfare system is more punitive.

The next subsection examines racial and ethnic inequality and conflict issues. The most poignant inequality in America is the gap between blacks and whites. Recently there has been considerable good news that the gap has been closing and many indicators that quality of life has improved for blacks. In the next article Barbara Kantrowitz and Pat Wingert clarify where affirmative action is today. It had a glorious history in the past when it pushed the nation toward fairness. However, what is its proper role today? Is it needed now and is it unfair now? This article clarifies what affirmative action is, where it stands legally today, and how universities should handle the issue. In the next article in this section, the authors demonstrate the prevalence of prejudice and hatred in America and how quickly hatred toward a group can evolve. Since September 11, 2001, hatred toward Muslims has erupted despite calls for tolerance from President George W. Bush and other public leaders. One explanation of hatred and prejudice against entire groups is social identity theory. People have a powerful drive to classify people into groups, identify with one group, and develop negative views of some of the out groups. Fortunately, "people who are concerned about their prejudices have the power to correct them."

The next subsection focuses on gender inequality and issues. In its first article, Alice Leuchtag describes one of the great evils that is haunting the world today which is sex slavery. The sex trade system grows out of poverty and profits. Extreme poverty forces parents to sell their girls into servitude often not knowing that they will become sex slaves and considerable prof-

its drive the system. The exploitation involved is horrendous so this is a worldwide human rights issue. In the next article, Evan Thomas reviews the current hot issue of gay marriages. Gay people have demanded and gradually obtained equal rights as citizens. Now they seek to gain the right to officially marry members of the same sex, and two states have made gay marriages legal. According to many straight people, however, this is contrary to the true meaning of marriage as an institution so their resistance is strong. Thomas explains the current situation on this issue. In the next article, Michelle Conlin examines a very different sex inequality issue, boys are not equal to girls. The new gender gap is the educational superiority of females over males. Conlin shows that from kindergarten to grad school girls outperform boys and have higher graduation rates. How can this be explained and what should be done about it if anything?

In the last subsection Elizabeth Benedict discusses a disadvantaged group: the elderly. Theirs is not a pretty picture. The plight of the elderly will get worse when the baby boomers grow old. The costs of assisted-living arrangements are exorbitant and deplete even sizeable savings and assets quickly. In some nursing homes the care is so bad that it is nearly criminal. The elderly prefer to stay at home and often refuse the invitations of their children to live with them. When their capacities decline, however, the options are usually not good.

For Richer

How the permissive capitalism of the boom
destroyed American equality.

By Paul Krugman

I. The Disappearing Middle

When I was a teenager growing up on Long Island, one of my
favorite excursions was a trip to see the great Gilded Age mansions of the North Shore. Those mansions weren't just pieces of
architectural history. They were monuments to a bygone social
era, one in which the rich could afford the armies of servants
needed to maintain a house the size of a European palace. By
the time I saw them, of course, that era was long past. Almost
none of the Long Island mansions were still private residences.
Those that hadn't been turned into museums were occupied by
nursing homes or private schools.

For the America I grew up in—the America of the 1950's
and 1960's—was a middle-class society, both in reality and in
feel. The vast income and wealth inequalities of the Gilded Age
had disappeared. Yes, of course, there was the poverty of the
underclass—but the conventional wisdom of the time viewed
that as a social rather than an economic problem. Yes, of course,
some wealthy businessmen and heirs to large fortunes lived far
better than the average American. But they weren't rich the way
the robber barons who built the mansions had been rich, and
there weren't that many of them. The days when plutocrats were
a force to be reckoned with in American society, economically
or politically, seemed long past.

Daily experience confirmed the sense of a fairly equal society. The economic disparities you were conscious of were
quite muted. Highly educated professionals—middle managers,
college teachers, even lawyers—often claimed that they earned
less than unionized blue-collar workers. Those considered very
well off lived in split-levels, had a housecleaner come in once a
week and took summer vacations in Europe. But they sent their
kids to public schools and drove themselves to work, just like
everyone else.

But that was long ago. The middle-class America of my
youth was another country.

We are now living in a new Gilded Age, as extravagant as the
original. Mansions have made a comeback. Back in 1999 this
magazine profiled Thierry Despont, the "eminence of excess,"
an architect who specializes in designing houses for the super-
rich. His creations typically range from 20,000 to 60,000 square
feet; houses at the upper end of his range are not much smaller
than the White House. Needless to say, the armies of servants
are back, too. So are the yachts. Still, even J.P. Morgan didn't
have a Gulfstream.

As the story about Despont suggests, it's not fair to say that
the fact of widening inequality in America has gone unreported.
Yet glimpses of the lifestyles of the rich and tasteless don't necessarily add up in people's minds to a clear picture of the tec-
tonic shifts that have taken place in the distribution of income
and wealth in this country. My sense is that few people are
aware of just how much the gap between the very rich and the
rest has widened over a relatively short period of time. In fact,
even bringing up the subject exposes you to charges of "class
warfare," the "politics of envy" and so on. And very few people
indeed are willing to talk about the profound effects—economic, social and political—of that widening gap.

Yet you can't understand what's happening in America
today without understanding the extent, causes and consequences of the vast increase in inequality that has taken place
over the last three decades, and in particular the astonishing
concentration of income and wealth in just a few hands. To
make sense of the current wave of corporate scandal, you need
to understand how the man in the gray flannel suit has been replaced by the imperial C.E.O. The concentration of income at
the top is a key reason that the United States, for all its economic
achievements, has more poverty and lower life expectancy than

any other major advanced nation. Above all, the growing concentration of wealth has reshaped our political system: it is at the root both of a general shift to the right and of an extreme polarization of our politics.

But before we get to all that, let's take a look at who gets what.

II. The New Gilded Age

The Securities and Exchange Commission hath no fury like a woman scorned. The messy divorce proceedings of Jack Welch, the legendary former C.E.O. of General Electric, have had one unintended benefit: they have given us a peek at the perks of the corporate elite, which are normally hidden from public view. For it turns out that when Welch retired, he was granted for life the use of a Manhattan apartment (including food, wine and laundry), access to corporate jets and a variety of other in-kind benefits, worth at least $2 million a year. The perks were revealing: they illustrated the extent to which corporate leaders now expect to be treated like *ancien régime* royalty. In monetary terms, however, the perks must have meant little to Welch. In 2000, his last full year running G.E., Welch was paid $123 million, mainly in stock and stock options.

The 13,000 richest families in America now have almost as much income as the 20 million poorest. And those 13,000 families have incomes 300 times that of average families.

Is it news that C.E.O.'s of large American corporations make a lot of money? Actually, it is. They were always well paid compared with the average worker, but there is simply no comparison between what executives got a generation ago and what they are paid today.

Over the past 30 years most people have seen only modest salary increases: the average annual salary in America, expressed in 1998 dollars (that is, adjusted for inflation), rose from $32,522 in 1970 to $35,864 in 1999. That's about a 10 percent increase over 29 years—progress, but not much. Over the same period, however, according to Fortune magazine, the average real annual compensation of the top 100 C.E.O.'s went from $1.3 million—39 times the pay of an average worker—to $37.5 million, more than 1,000 times the pay of ordinary workers.

The explosion in C.E.O. pay over the past 30 years is an amazing story in its own right, and an important one. But it is only the most spectacular indicator of a broader story, the reconcentration of income and wealth in the U.S. The rich have always been different from you and me, but they are far more different now than they were not long ago—indeed, they are as different now as they were when F. Scott Fitzgerald made his famous remark.

That's a controversial statement, though it shouldn't be. For at least the past 15 years it has been hard to deny the evidence for growing inequality in the United States. Census data clearly show a rising share of income going to the top 20 percent of families, and within that top 20 percent to the top 5 percent, with a declining share going to families in the middle. Nonetheless, denial of that evidence is a sizable, well-financed industry. Conservative think tanks have produced scores of studies that try to discredit the data, the methodology and, not least, the motives of those who report the obvious. Studies that appear to refute claims of increasing inequality receive prominent endorsements on editorial pages and are eagerly cited by right-leaning government officials. Four years ago Alan Greenspan (why did anyone ever think that he was nonpartisan?) gave a keynote speech at the Federal Reserve's annual Jackson Hole conference that amounted to an attempt to deny that there has been any real increase in inequality in America.

The concerted effort to deny that inequality is increasing is itself a symptom of the growing influence of our emerging plutocracy (more on this later). So is the fierce defense of the backup position, that inequality doesn't matter—or maybe even that, to use Martha Stewart's signature phrase, it's a good thing. Meanwhile, politically motivated smoke screens aside, the reality of increasing inequality is not in doubt. In fact, the census data understate the case, because for technical reasons those data tend to undercount very high incomes—for example, it's unlikely that they reflect the explosion in C.E.O. compensation. And other evidence makes it clear not only that inequality is increasing but that the action gets bigger the closer you get to the top. That is, it's not simply that the top 20 percent of families have had bigger percentage gains than families near the middle: the top 5 percent have done better than the next 15, the top 1 percent better than the next 4, and so on up to Bill Gates.

Studies that try to do a better job of tracking high incomes have found startling results. For example, a recent study by the nonpartisan Congressional Budget Office used income tax data and other sources to improve on the census estimates. The C.B.O. study found that between 1979 and 1997, the after-tax incomes of the top 1 percent of families rose 157 percent, compared with only a 10 percent gain for families near the middle of the income distribution. Even more startling results come from a new study by Thomas Piketty, at the French research institute Cepremap, and Emmanuel Saez, who is now at the University of California at Berkeley. Using income tax data, Piketty and Saez have produced estimates of the incomes of the well-to-do, the rich and the very rich back to 1913.

The first point you learn from these new estimates is that the middle-class America of my youth is best thought of not as the normal state of our society, but as an interregnum between Gilded Ages. America before 1930 was a society in which a small number of very rich people controlled a large share of the nation's wealth. We became a middle-class society only after the concentration of income at the top dropped sharply during the New Deal, and especially during World War II. The economic historians Claudia Goldin and Robert Margo have dubbed the narrowing of income gaps during those years the Great Compression. Incomes then stayed fairly equally distributed until the 1970's: the rapid rise in incomes during the first postwar generation was very evenly spread across the population.

Since the 1970's, however, income gaps have been rapidly widening. Piketty and Saez confirm what I suspected: by most measures we are, in fact, back to the days of "The Great Gatsby." After 30 years in which the income shares of the top 10 percent of taxpayers, the top 1 percent and so on were far below their levels in the 1920's, all are very nearly back where they were.

And the big winners are the very, very rich. One ploy often used to play down growing inequality is to rely on rather coarse statistical breakdowns—dividing the population into five "quintiles," each containing 20 percent of families, or at most 10 "deciles." Indeed, Greenspan's speech at Jackson Hole relied mainly on decile data. From there it's a short step to denying that we're really talking about the rich at all. For example, a conservative commentator might concede, grudgingly, that there has been some increase in the share of national income going to the top 10 percent of taxpayers, but then point out that anyone with an income over $81,000 is in that top 10 percent. So we're just talking about shifts within the middle class, right?

Wrong: the top 10 percent contains a lot of people whom we would still consider middle class, but they weren't the big winners. Most of the gains in the share of the top 10 percent of taxpayers over the past 30 years were actually gains to the top 1 percent, rather than the next 9 percent. In 1998 the top 1 percent started at $230,000. In turn, 60 percent of the gains of that top 1 percent went to the top 0.1 percent, those with incomes of more than $790,000. And almost half of those gains went to a mere 13,000 taxpayers, the top 0.01 percent, who had an income of at least $3.6 million and an average income of $17 million.

A stickler for detail might point out that the Piketty-Saez estimates end in 1998 and that the C.B.O. numbers end a year earlier. Have the trends shown in the data reversed? Almost surely not. In fact, all indications are that the explosion of incomes at the top continued through 2000. Since then the plunge in stock prices must have put some crimp in high incomes—but census data show inequality continuing to increase in 2001, mainly because of the severe effects of the recession on the working poor and near poor. When the recession ends, we can be sure that we will find ourselves a society in which income inequality is even higher than it was in the late 90's.

So claims that we've entered a second Gilded Age aren't exaggerated. In America's middle-class era, the mansion-building, yacht-owning classes had pretty much disappeared. According to Piketty and Saez, in 1970 the top 0.01 percent of taxpayers had 0.7 percent of total income—that is, they earned "only" 70 times as much as the average, not enough to buy or maintain a mega-residence. But in 1998 the top 0.01 percent received more than 3 percent of all income. That meant that the 13,000 richest families in America had almost as much income as the 20 million poorest households; those 13,000 families had incomes 300 times that of average families.

And let me repeat: this transformation has happened very quickly, and it is still going on. You might think that 1987, the year Tom Wolfe published his novel "The Bonfire of the Vani-

ties" and Oliver Stone released his movie "Wall Street," marked the high tide of America's new money culture. But in 1987 the top 0.01 percent earned only about 40 percent of what they do today, and top executives less than a fifth as much. The America of "Wall Street" and "The Bonfire of the Vanities" was positively egalitarian compared with the country we live in today.

III. Undoing the New Deal

In the middle of the 1980's, as economists became aware that something important was happening to the distribution of income in America, they formulated three main hypotheses about its causes.

The "globalization" hypothesis tied America's changing income distribution to the growth of world trade, and especially the growing imports of manufactured goods from the third world. Its basic message was that blue-collar workers—the sort of people who in my youth often made as much money as college-educated middle managers—were losing ground in the face of competition from low-wage workers in Asia. A result was stagnation or decline in the wages of ordinary people, with a growing share of national income going to the highly educated.

A second hypothesis, "skill-biased technological change," situated the cause of growing inequality not in foreign trade but in domestic innovation. The torrid pace of progress in information technology, so the story went, had increased the demand for the highly skilled and educated. And so the income distribution increasingly favored brains rather than brawn.

> Some economists think the New Deal imposed norms of relative equality in pay that persisted for more than 30 years, creating a broadly middle-class society. Those norms have unraveled.

Finally, the "superstar" hypothesis—named by the Chicago economist Sherwin Rosen—offered a variant on the technological story. It argued that modern technologies of communication often turn competition into a tournament in which the winner is richly rewarded, while the runners-up get far less. The classic example—which gives the theory its name—is the entertainment business. As Rosen pointed out, in bygone days there were hundreds of comedians making a modest living at live shows in the borscht belt and other places. Now they are mostly gone; what is left is a handful of superstar TV comedians.

The debates among these hypotheses—particularly the debate between those who attributed growing inequality to globalization and those who attributed it to technology—were many and bitter. I was a participant in those debates myself. But I won't dwell on them, because in the last few years there has been a growing sense among economists that none of these hypotheses work.

I don't mean to say that there was nothing to these stories. Yet as more evidence has accumulated, each of the hypotheses has seemed increasingly inadequate. Globalization can explain part of the relative decline in blue-collar wages, but it can't explain the 2,500 percent rise in C.E.O. incomes. Technology may explain why the salary premium associated with a college education has risen, but it's hard to match up with the huge increase in inequality among the college-educated, with little progress for many but gigantic gains at the top. The superstar theory works for Jay Leno, but not for the thousands of people who have become awesomely rich without going on TV.

The Great Compression—the substantial reduction in inequality during the New Deal and the Second World War—also seems hard to understand in terms of the usual theories. During World War II Franklin Roosevelt used government control over wages to compress wage gaps. But if the middle-class society that emerged from the war was an artificial creation, why did it persist for another 30 years?

Some—by no means all—economists trying to understand growing inequality have begun to take seriously a hypothesis that would have been considered irredeemably fuzzy-minded not long ago. This view stresses the role of social norms in setting limits to inequality. According to this view, the New Deal had a more profound impact on American society than even its most ardent admirers have suggested: it imposed norms of relative equality in pay that persisted for more than 30 years, creating the broadly middle-class society we came to take for granted. But those norms began to unravel in the 1970's and have done so at an accelerating pace.

Exhibit A for this view is the story of executive compensation. In the 1960's, America's great corporations behaved more like socialist republics than like cutthroat capitalist enterprises, and top executives behaved more like public-spirited bureaucrats than like captains of industry. I'm not exaggerating. Consider the description of executive behavior offered by John Kenneth Galbraith in his 1967 book, "The New Industrial State": "Management does not go out ruthlessly to reward itself—a sound management is expected to exercise restraint." Managerial self-dealing was a thing of the past: "With the power of decision goes opportunity for making money.... Were everyone to seek to do so... the corporation would be a chaos of competitive avarice. But these are not the sort of thing that a good company man does; a remarkably effective code bans such behavior. Group decision-making insures, moreover, that almost everyone's actions and even thoughts are known to others. This acts to enforce the code and, more than incidentally, a high standard of personal honesty as well."

Thirty-five years on, a cover article in *Fortune* is titled "You Bought. They Sold." "All over corporate America," reads the blurb, "top execs were cashing in stocks even as their companies were tanking. Who was left holding the bag? You." As I said, we've become a different country.

Let's leave actual malfeasance on one side for a moment, and ask how the relatively modest salaries of top executives 30 years ago became the gigantic pay packages of today. There are two main stories, both of which emphasize changing norms rather than pure economics. The more optimistic story draws an analogy between the explosion of C.E.O. pay and the explosion of baseball salaries with the introduction of free agency. According to this story, highly paid C.E.O.'s really are worth it, because having the right man in that job makes a huge difference. The more pessimistic view—which I find more plausible—is that competition for talent is a minor factor. Yes, a great executive can make a big difference—but those huge pay packages have been going as often as not to executives whose performance is mediocre at best. The key reason executives are paid so much now is that they appoint the members of the corporate board that determines their compensation and control many of the perks that board members count on. So it's not the invisible hand of the market that leads to those monumental executive incomes; it's the invisible handshake in the boardroom.

But then why weren't executives paid lavishly 30 years ago? Again, it's a matter of corporate culture. For a generation after World War II, fear of outrage kept executive salaries in check. Now the outrage is gone. That is, the explosion of executive pay represents a social change rather than the purely economic forces of supply and demand. We should think of it not as a market trend like the rising value of waterfront property, but as something more like the sexual revolution of the 1960's—a relaxation of old strictures, a new permissiveness, but in this case the permissiveness is financial rather than sexual. Sure enough, John Kenneth Galbraith described the honest executive of 1967 as being one who "eschews the lovely, available and even naked woman by whom he is intimately surrounded." By the end of the 1990's, the executive motto might as well have been "If it feels good, do it."

How did this change in corporate culture happen? Economists and management theorists are only beginning to explore that question, but it's easy to suggest a few factors. One was the changing structure of financial markets. In his new book, "Searching for a Corporate Savior," Rakesh Khurana of Harvard Business School suggests that during the 1980's and 1990's, "managerial capitalism"—the world of the man in the gray flannel suit—was replaced by "investor capitalism." Institutional investors weren't willing to let a C.E.O. choose his own successor from inside the corporation; they wanted heroic leaders, often outsiders, and were willing to pay immense sums to get them. The subtitle of Khurana's book, by the way, is "The Irrational Quest for Charismatic C.E.O.'s."

But fashionable management theorists didn't think it was irrational. Since the 1980's there has been ever more emphasis on the importance of "leadership"—meaning personal, charismatic leadership. When Lee Iacocca of Chrysler became a business celebrity in the early 1980's, he was practically alone: Khurana reports that in 1980 only one issue of Business Week featured a C.E.O. on its cover. By 1999 the number was up to 19. And once it was considered normal, even necessary, for a C.E.O. to be famous, it also became easier to make him rich.

Economists also did their bit to legitimize previously unthinkable levels of executive pay. During the 1980's and 1990's a torrent of academic papers—popularized in business magazines and incorporated into consultants' recommendations—argued that Gordon Gekko was right: greed is good; greed works. In order to get the best performance out of executives, these papers argued, it was necessary to align their interests with those of stockholders. And the way to do that was with large grants of stock or stock options.

It's hard to escape the suspicion that these new intellectual justifications for soaring executive pay were as much effect as cause. I'm not suggesting that management theorists and economists were personally corrupt. It would have been a subtle, unconscious process: the ideas that were taken up by business schools, that led to nice speaking and consulting fees, tended to be the ones that ratified an existing trend, and thereby gave it legitimacy.

What economists like Piketty and Saez are now suggesting is that the story of executive compensation is representative of a broader story. Much more than economists and free-market advocates like to imagine, wages—particularly at the top—are determined by social norms. What happened during the 1930's and 1940's was that new norms of equality were established, largely through the political process. What happened in the 1980's and 1990's was that those norms unraveled, replaced by an ethos of "anything goes." And a result was an explosion of income at the top of the scale.

IV. The Price of Inequality

It was one of those revealing moments. Responding to an e-mail message from a Canadian viewer, Robert Novak of "Crossfire" delivered a little speech: "Marg, like most Canadians, you're ill informed and wrong. The U.S. has the longest standard of living—longest life expectancy of any country in the world, including Canada. That's the truth."

But it was Novak who had his facts wrong. Canadians can expect to live about two years longer than Americans. In fact, life expectancy in the U.S. is well below that in Canada, Japan and every major nation in Western Europe. On average, we can expect lives a bit shorter than those of Greeks, a bit longer than those of Portuguese. Male life expectancy is lower in the U.S. than it is in Costa Rica.

Still, you can understand why Novak assumed that we were No. 1. After all, we really are the richest major nation, with real G.D.P. per capita about 20 percent higher than Canada's. And it has been an article of faith in this country that a rising tide lifts all boats. Doesn't our high and rising national wealth translate into a high standard of living—including good medical care—for all Americans?

Well, no. Although America has higher per capita income than other advanced countries, it turns out that that's mainly because our rich are much richer. And here's a radical thought: if the rich get more, that leaves less for everyone else.

That statement—which is simply a matter of arithmetic—is guaranteed to bring accusations of "class warfare." If the accuser gets more specific, he'll probably offer two reasons that it's foolish to make a fuss over the high incomes of a few people at the top of the income distribution. First, he'll tell you that what the elite get may look like a lot of money, but it's still a small share of the total—that is, when all is said and done the rich aren't getting that big a piece of the pie. Second, he'll tell you that trying to do anything to reduce incomes at the top will hurt, not help, people further down the distribution, because attempts to redistribute income damage incentives.

These arguments for lack of concern are plausible. And they were entirely correct, once upon a time—namely, back when we had a middle-class society. But there's a lot less truth to them now.

First, the share of the rich in total income is no longer trivial. These days 1 percent of families receive about 16 percent of total pretax income, and have about 14 percent of after-tax income. That share has roughly doubled over the past 30 years, and is now about as large as the share of the bottom 40 percent of the population. That's a big shift of income to the top; as a matter of pure arithmetic, it must mean that the incomes of less well off families grew considerably more slowly than average income. And they did. Adjusting for inflation, average family income—total income divided by the number of families—grew 28 percent from 1979 to 1997. But median family income—the income of a family in the middle of the distribution, a better indicator of how typical American families are doing—grew only 10 percent. And the incomes of the bottom fifth of families actually fell slightly.

Let me belabor this point for a bit. We pride ourselves, with considerable justification, on our record of economic growth. But over the last few decades it's remarkable how little of that growth has trickled down to ordinary families. Median family income has risen only about 0.5 percent per year—and as far as we can tell from somewhat unreliable data, just about all of that increase was due to wives working longer hours, with little or no gain in real wages. Furthermore, numbers about income don't reflect the growing riskiness of life for ordinary workers. In the days when General Motors was known in-house as Generous Motors, many workers felt that they had considerable job security—the company wouldn't fire them except in extremis. Many had contracts that guaranteed health insurance, even if they were laid off; they had pension benefits that did not depend on the stock market. Now mass firings from long-established companies are commonplace; losing your job means losing your insurance; and as millions of people have been learning, a 401(k) plan is no guarantee of a comfortable retirement.

Still, many people will say that while the U.S. economic system may generate a lot of inequality, it also generates much higher incomes than any alternative, so that everyone is better off. That was the moral Business Week tried to convey in its recent special issue with "25 Ideas for a Changing World." One of those ideas was "the rich get richer, and that's O.K." High incomes at the top, the conventional wisdom declares, are the result of a free-market system that provides huge incentives for performance. And the system delivers that performance, which means that wealth at the top doesn't come at the expense of the rest of us.

A skeptic might point out that the explosion in executive compensation seems at best loosely related to actual performance. Jack Welch was one of the 10 highest-paid executives in the United States in 2000, and you could argue that he earned it. But did Dennis Kozlowski of Tyco, or Gerald Levin of Time Warner, who were also in the top 10? A skeptic might also point out that even during the economic boom of the late

1990's, U.S. productivity growth was no better than it was during the great postwar expansion, which corresponds to the era when America was truly middle class and C.E.O.'s were modestly paid technocrats.

But can we produce any direct evidence about the effects of inequality? We can't rerun our own history and ask what would have happened if the social norms of middle-class America had continued to limit incomes at the top, and if government policy had leaned against rising inequality instead of reinforcing it, which is what actually happened. But we can compare ourselves with other advanced countries. And the results are somewhat surprising.

Many Americans assume that because we are the richest country in the world, with real G.D.P. per capita higher than that of other major advanced countries, Americans must be better off across the board—that it's not just our rich who are richer than their counterparts abroad, but that the typical American family is much better off than the typical family elsewhere, and that even our poor are well off by foreign standards.

But it's not true. Let me use the example of Sweden, that great conservative *bête noire*.

A few months ago the conservative cyberpundit Glenn Reynolds made a splash when he pointed out that Sweden's G.D.P. per capita is roughly comparable with that of Mississippi—see, those foolish believers in the welfare state have impoverished themselves! Presumably he assumed that this means that the typical Swede is as poor as the typical resident of Mississippi, and therefore much worse off than the typical American.

As the rich get richer, they can buy a lot besides goods and services. Money buys political influence; used cleverly, it also buys intellectual influence.

But life expectancy in Sweden is about three years higher than that of the U.S. Infant mortality is half the U.S. level, and less than a third the rate in Mississippi. Functional illiteracy is much less common than in the U.S.

How is this possible? One answer is that G.D.P. per capita is in some ways a misleading measure. Swedes take longer vacations than Americans, so they work fewer hours per year. That's a choice, not a failure of economic performance. Real G.D.P. per hour worked is 16 percent lower than in the United States, which makes Swedish productivity about the same as Canada's.

But the main point is that though Sweden may have lower average income than the United States, that's mainly because our rich are so much richer. The median Swedish family has a standard of living roughly comparable with that of the median U.S. family: wages are if anything higher in Sweden, and a higher tax burden is offset by public provision of health care and generally better public services. And as you move further down the income distribution, Swedish living standards are way ahead of those in the U.S. Swedish families with children that are at the 10th percentile—poorer than 90 percent of the population—

have incomes 60 percent higher than their U.S. counterparts. And very few people in Sweden experience the deep poverty that is all too common in the United States. One measure: in 1994 only 6 percent of Swedes lived on less than $11 per day, compared with 14 percent in the U.S.

The moral of this comparison is that even if you think that America's high levels of inequality are the price of our high level of national income, it's not at all clear that this price is worth paying. The reason conservatives engage in bouts of Sweden-bashing is that they want to convince us that there is no tradeoff between economic efficiency and equity—that if you try to take from the rich and give to the poor, you actually make everyone worse off. But the comparison between the U.S. and other advanced countries doesn't support this conclusion at all. Yes, we are the richest major nation. But because so much of our national income is concentrated in relatively few hands, large numbers of Americans are worse off economically than their counterparts in other advanced countries.

And we might even offer a challenge from the other side: inequality in the United States has arguably reached levels where it is counterproductive. That is, you can make a case that our society would be richer if its richest members didn't get quite so much.

I could make this argument on historical grounds. The most impressive economic growth in U.S. history coincided with the middle-class interregnum, the post-World War II generation, when incomes were most evenly distributed. But let's focus on a specific case, the extraordinary pay packages of today's top executives. Are these good for the economy?

Until recently it was almost unchallenged conventional wisdom that, whatever else you might say, the new imperial C.E.O.'s had delivered results that dwarfed the expense of their compensation. But now that the stock bubble has burst, it has become increasingly clear that there was a price to those big pay packages, after all. In fact, the price paid by shareholders and society at large may have been many times larger than the amount actually paid to the executives.

It's easy to get boggled by the details of corporate scandal—insider loans, stock options, special-purpose entities, mark-to-market, round-tripping. But there's a simple reason that the details are so complicated. All of these schemes were designed to benefit corporate insiders—to inflate the pay of the C.E.O. and his inner circle. That is, they were all about the "chaos of competitive avarice" that, according to John Kenneth Galbraith, had been ruled out in the corporation of the 1960's. But while all restraint has vanished within the American corporation, the outside world—including stockholders—is still prudish, and open looting by executives is still not acceptable. So the looting has to be camouflaged, taking place through complicated schemes that can be rationalized to outsiders as clever corporate strategies.

Economists who study crime tell us that crime is inefficient—that is, the costs of crime to the economy are much larger than the amount stolen. Crime, and the fear of crime, divert resources away from productive uses: criminals spend their time stealing rather than producing, and potential victims spend time and money trying to protect their property. Also, the things people do to avoid becoming victims—like avoiding dangerous districts—have a cost even if they succeed in averting an actual crime.

The same holds true of corporate malfeasance, whether or not it actually involves breaking the law. Executives who devote their time to creating innovative ways to divert shareholder money into their own pockets probably aren't running the real business very well (think Enron, WorldCom, Tyco, Global Crossing, Adelphia…). Investments chosen because they create the illusion of profitability while insiders cash in their stock options are a waste of scarce resources. And if the supply of funds from lenders and shareholders dries up because of a lack of trust, the economy as a whole suffers. Just ask Indonesia.

The argument for a system in which some people get very rich has always been that the lure of wealth provides powerful incentives. But the question is, incentives to do what? As we learn more about what has actually been going on in corporate America, it's becoming less and less clear whether those incentives have actually made executives work on behalf of the rest of us.

V. Inequality and Politics

In September the Senate debated a proposed measure that would impose a one-time capital gains tax on Americans who renounce their citizenship in order to avoid paying U.S. taxes. Senator Phil Gramm was not pleased, declaring that the proposal was "right out of Nazi Germany." Pretty strong language, but no stronger than the metaphor Daniel Mitchell of the Heritage Foundation used, in an op-ed article in The Washington Times, to describe a bill designed to prevent corporations from rechartering abroad for tax purposes: Mitchell described this legislation as the "Dred Scott tax bill," referring to the infamous 1857 Supreme Court ruling that required free states to return escaped slaves.

Twenty years ago, would a prominent senator have likened those who want wealthy people to pay taxes to Nazis? Would a member of a think tank with close ties to the administration have drawn a parallel between corporate taxation and slavery? I don't think so. The remarks by Gramm and Mitchell, while stronger than usual, were indicators of two huge changes in American politics. One is the growing polarization of our politics—our politicians are less and less inclined to offer even the appearance of moderation. The other is the growing tendency of policy and policy makers to cater to the interests of the wealthy. And I mean the wealthy, not the merely well-off: only someone with a net worth of at least several million dollars is likely to find it worthwhile to become a tax exile.

You don't need a political scientist to tell you that modern American politics is bitterly polarized. But wasn't it always thus? No, it wasn't. From World War II until the 1970's—the same era during which income inequality was historically low—political partisanship was much more muted than it is today. That's not just a subjective assessment. My Princeton political science colleagues Nolan McCarty and Howard Rosenthal, together with Keith Poole at the University of Houston, have done a statistical analysis showing that the voting behavior of a congressman is much better predicted by his party affiliation today than it was twenty-five years ago. In fact, the division between the parties is sharper now than it has been since the 1920's.

What are the parties divided about? The answer is simple: economics. McCarty, Rosenthal and Poole write that "voting in Congress is highly ideological—one-dimensional left/right, liberal versus conservative." It may sound simplistic to describe Democrats as the party that wants to tax the rich and help the poor, and Republicans as the party that wants to keep taxes and social spending as low as possible. And during the era of middle-class America that would indeed have been simplistic: politics wasn't defined by economic issues. But that was a different country; as McCarty, Rosenthal and Poole put it, "If income and wealth are distributed in a fairly equitable way, little is to be gained for politicians to organize politics around nonexistent conflicts." Now the conflicts are real, and our politics is organized around them. In other words, the growing inequality of our incomes probably lies behind the growing divisiveness of our politics.

But the politics of rich and poor hasn't played out the way you might think. Since the incomes of America's wealthy have soared while ordinary families have seen at best small gains, you might have expected politicians to seek votes by proposing to soak the rich. In fact, however, the polarization of politics has occurred because the Republicans have moved to the right, not because the Democrats have moved to the left. And actual economic policy has moved steadily in favor of the wealthy. The major tax cuts of the past twenty-five years, the Reagan cuts in the 1980's and the recent Bush cuts, were both heavily tilted toward the very well off. (Despite obfuscations, it remains true that more than half the Bush tax cut will eventually go to the top 1 percent of families.) The major tax increase over that period, the increase in payroll taxes in the 1980's, fell most heavily on working-class families.

The most remarkable example of how politics has shifted in favor of the wealthy—an example that helps us understand why economic policy has reinforced, not countered, the movement toward greater inequality—is the drive to repeal the estate tax. The estate tax is, overwhelmingly, a tax on the wealthy. In 1999, only the top 2 percent of estates paid any tax at all, and half the estate tax was paid by only 3,300 estates, 0.16 percent of the total, with a minimum value of $5 million and an average value of $17 million. A quarter of the tax was paid by just 467 estates worth more than $20 million. Tales of family farms and businesses broken up to pay the estate tax are basically rural legends; hardly any real examples have been found, despite diligent searching.

You might have thought that a tax that falls on so few people yet yields a significant amount of revenue would be politically popular; you certainly wouldn't expect widespread opposition. Moreover, there has long been an argument that the estate tax promotes democratic values, precisely because it limits the ability of the wealthy to form dynasties. So why has there been a powerful political drive to repeal the estate tax, and why was such a repeal a centerpiece of the Bush tax cut?

There is an economic argument for repealing the estate tax, but it's hard to believe that many people take it seriously. More significant for members of Congress, surely, is the question of who would benefit from repeal: while those who will actually benefit from estate tax repeal are few in number, they have a lot of money and control even more (corporate C.E.O.'s can now count on leaving taxable estates behind). That is, they are the sort of people who command the attention of politicians in search of campaign funds.

But it's not just about campaign contributions: much of the general public has been convinced that the estate tax is a bad thing. If you try talking about the tax to a group of moderately prosperous retirees, you get some interesting reactions. They refer to it as the "death tax"; many of them believe that their estates will face punitive taxation, even though most of them will pay little or nothing; they are convinced that small businesses and family farms bear the brunt of the tax.

These misconceptions don't arise by accident. They have, instead, been deliberately promoted. For example, a Heritage Foundation document titled "Time to Repeal Federal Death Taxes: The Nightmare of the American Dream" emphasizes stories that rarely, if ever, happen in real life: "Small-business owners, particularly minority owners, suffer anxious moments wondering whether the businesses they hope to hand down to their children will be destroyed by the death tax bill,... Women whose children are grown struggle to find ways to re-enter the work force without upsetting the family's estate tax avoidance plan." And who finances the Heritage Foundation? Why, foundations created by wealthy families, of course.

The point is that it is no accident that strongly conservative views, views that militate against taxes on the rich, have spread even as the rich get richer compared with the rest of us: in addition to directly buying influence, money can be used to shape public perceptions. The liberal group People for the American Way's report on how conservative foundations have deployed vast sums to support think tanks, friendly media and other institutions that promote right-wing causes is titled "Buying a Movement."

Not to put too fine a point on it: as the rich get richer, they can buy a lot of things besides goods and services. Money buys political influence; used cleverly, it also buys intellectual influence. A result is that growing income disparities in the United States, far from leading to demands to soak the rich, have been accompanied by a growing movement to let them keep more of their earnings and to pass their wealth on to their children.

This obviously raises the possibility of a self-reinforcing process. As the gap between the rich and the rest of the population grows, economic policy increasingly caters to the interests of the elite, while public services for the population at large—above all, public education—are starved of resources. As policy increasingly favors the interests of the rich and neglects the interests of the general population, income disparities grow even wider.

VI. Plutocracy?

In 1924, the mansions of Long Island's North Shore were still in their full glory, as was the political power of the class that owned them. When Gov. Al Smith of New York proposed building a system of parks on Long Island, the mansion owners were bitterly opposed. One baron—Horace Havemeyer, the "sultan of sugar"—warned that North Shore towns would be "overrun with rabble from the city." "Rabble?" Smith said. "That's me you're talking about." In the end New Yorkers got their parks, but it was close: the interests of a few hundred wealthy families nearly prevailed over those of New York City's middle class.

America in the 1920's wasn't a feudal society. But it was a nation in which vast privilege—often inherited privilege—stood in contrast to vast misery. It was also a nation in which the government, more often than not, served the interests of the privileged and ignored the aspirations of ordinary people.

Those days are past—or are they? Income inequality in America has now returned to the levels of the 1920's. Inherited wealth doesn't yet play a big part in our society, but given time—and the repeal of the estate tax—we will grow ourselves a hereditary elite just as set apart from the concerns of ordinary Americans as old Horace Havemeyer. And the new elite, like the old, will have enormous political power.

Kevin Phillips concludes his book "Wealth and Democracy" with a grim warning: "Either democracy must be renewed, with politics brought back to life, or wealth is likely to cement a new and less democratic regime—plutocracy by some other name." It's a pretty extreme line, but we live in extreme times. Even if the forms of democracy remain, they may become meaningless. It's all too easy to see how we may become a country in which the big rewards are reserved for people with the right connections; in which ordinary people see little hope of advancement; in which political involvement seems pointless, because in the end the interests of the elite always get served.

Am I being too pessimistic? Even my liberal friends tell me not to worry, that our system has great resilience, that the center will hold. I hope they're right, but they may be looking in the rearview mirror. Our optimism about America, our belief that in the end our nation always finds its way, comes from the past—a past in which we were a middle-class society. But that was another country.

Paul Krugman is a Times columnist and a professor at Princeton.

THE REAL FACE OF Homelessness

More than ever, it is mothers with kids who are ending up on the streets. Bush has a plan, but will it help?

By JOEL STEIN

THE LIBERALS TRIED. THEY gave money. They watched boring news specials. They held hands all the way across America. They even pretended to laugh at sketches with Robin Williams, Billy Crystal and Whoopi Goldberg. But at some point in every one-way relationship, pity turns to resentment, and now even the liberals are turning on the homeless: San Francisco has voted to reduce their benefits 85%; Santa Monica, Calif., passed laws preventing them from sleeping in the doors of shops or receiving food from unlicensed providers; Madison, Wis., is handing them a record number of tickets; Seattle banned the sale of malt liquor and Thunderbird in Pioneer Square as its initiative to shoo away the alcoholics.

THE YOUNG MOM

LOCATION Falls Church, Va.

NAMES Jessica Lampman, 22; Destinee, 2

HOW THEY BECAME HOMELESS

After dropping out of ninth grade, Jessica fled her mom's home because her brother was using drugs. Looking for stability for her daughter, she pitched a tent at a campground. She got into a shelter and found a job, but a low salary and bad credit kept her from getting an apartment

Sensing an opening, the Bush Administration has decided to make the homeless problem a target of compassionate conservatism, which got pushed back after Sept. 11, when conservatism was everywhere but compassion was available only for the attack victims. And it's putting its central domestic doctrine to the test on an issue on which the Democrats have been unable to show much progress. It's a good choice, not only because the expectations are so low after decades of failure but also because it is unassailable in its immediate need.

With a freak-show economy in which unemployment has reached 60%—a 50% increase since November 2000—but housing prices have stayed at or near historic highs, the number of homeless appears to be at its highest in at least a decade in a wide range of places across the U.S., according to Bush's own

homelessness czar. "It's embarrassing to say that they're up," says czar Philip Mangano of the number, "but it's better to face the truth than to try to obfuscate."

THE PRICED-OUT

LOCATION Harlem, N.Y.

NAMES Kim Berrios, 26; Julius Cabrera, 22; Jonathan, 8; Sunsarei, 5; Jerimiah, 2

HOW THEY BECAME HOMELESS

Kim and Julius had to leave their Staten Island apartment when the landlord renovated and raised the rent. Kim's family is in Florida, and Julius' mother has five other kids in a three-bedroom apartment. "We couldn't go stay with anybody," says Kim, who is pregnant. After moving to a Harlem shelter, she quit work to take care of Jonathan, who has attention-deficit disorder; Julius had to quit a nighttime supermarket job owing to the shelter's curfew. They are waiting for an apartment in the projects

You don't see homeless people as much as you did in the '80s because the one great policy initiative of the past 20 years has been to move them from grates into the newest form of the poorhouse, the shelter. Even though cities are building shelters as fast as they can, the homeless are pouring out of them again, returning to the grates. Homeless numbers are notoriously unreliable (many people may be counted twice or not at all, and some homeless advocates include people who move in with family members), but a TIME survey of the eight jurisdictions that have good statistics shows that this population has grown significantly and that its fastest-growing segment is composed of families. Homeless parents and their kids made up roughly 15% of the case load in 1999—or, if you count every head, about 35% of all homeless people, according to the Urban Institute, a liberal D.C. think tank. The TIME survey suggests that population has since increased—registering year-over-year jumps in either 2001 or 2002 (*see graphic for individual cities*). These families mainly consist of single women with kids, whose greater housing needs, compared with those of single people, make them more vulnerable to rental increases than are single people.

Even as the problem worsens, there's little appetite in Washington for the large-scale solutions the Democrats have been advocating for 40 years: creating affordable housing and strengthening programs that attack the causes of poverty by finding people jobs, teaching them skills, giving them transportation to jobs, getting them off drugs, providing medical care— essentially trying to fix entire lives. Some homeless experts are beginning to wonder whether building shelters only exaggerates the numbers: they argue that poor people who wouldn't otherwise be homeless are attracted to shelters as a way of quickly tapping into government assistance. "It didn't take long for people to figure out that this was a way to scam the system," admits Andrew Cuomo, the Secretary of Housing and Urban Development (HUD) under President Bill Clinton. Given all this failure and disgust, Republicans could deal with this problem however they wanted.

The first G.O.P. member to pick up on this was Susan Baker, who had the ability to get the White House's attention because she's the wife of James Baker, chief of staff to Ronald Reagan, Secretary of State to Bush's father and, more important, the guy who ran W.'s election-after-the-election campaign in Florida. Baker is co-chairwoman of the National Alliance to End Homelessness, a cause in which she became interested in the early '80s, when she got involved in organizing D.C. food banks.

Baker read a 1998 study by University of Pennsylvania professor of social work Dennis Culhane that suggested that the most efficient solution to homelessness was to provide permanent housing to the "chronic homeless"—those helpless cases, usually the mentally ill, substance abusers or very sick—who will probably be homeless for life. The study found the chronic homeless make temporary shelters their long-term home; they take up 50% of the beds each year, even though they make up 10% of the homeless population. Culhane's idea appeals to conservatives: it has had proved results in 20-year-old projects across the country; it gets the really hard-to-look-at people off the street; and it saves money, because administrative costs make it more expensive to put up people at a shelter than to give them their own apartment (sheltering a homeless person on a cot in a New York City shelter, for example, costs on average $1,800 a month). It's similar to the problem faced by hospitals, where the uninsured use ambulances and emergency rooms as a very expensive version of primary care. Culhane's finding is also attractive in its simple if unspoken logic: because the mentally ill were put out into the street after the public discovered the abuses in mental hospitals and J.F.K. passed the 1963 Community Health Center Act, which deinsitutionalized 430,000 people, the plan really amounts to building much nicer, voluntary mental hospitals.

Three weeks after Bush named Mel Martinez his HUD Secretary, Baker landed a meeting with him. She sold him Culhane's research, arguing that with just 200,000 apartments, the Administration could end chronic homelessness in 10 years. The meeting went so well that the plan became Bush's official stance on homelessness: the 2003 budget has four paragraphs promising to end chronic homelessness in a decade.

THE LARGE FAMILY

LOCATION Dallas
NAMES Gina Christian, 36; David, 34; Alex, 14; Martin, 11; Thalia, 6; Tatiana, 4
HOW THEY BECAME HOMELESS

David worked as a mechanic in Austin, Texas, for a company that fixed Hertz cars. When the business went under, Gina's income as a nursing-home temp wasn't enough to cover rent and food for six. They hocked their belongings, and Gina resorted to begging. David still wasn't able to find work, so they moved to Dallas' Interfaith House, a private shelter for needy families. "We went from doing fine to one day being homeless," says Gina

Bush reinstated last spring the office of homeless czar, a position that had been dormant for six years, tapping Mangano to be head of the Interagency Council on Homelessness. He is liked by members of both parties and fits Bush's theme of faith-based compassion. A former rock manager who represented members of Buffalo Springfield and Peter, Paul and Mary, Mangano says his life changed in 1972 when he saw Franco Zeffirelli's *Brother Sun, Sister Moon,* a movie about the life of St. Francis. For Mangano, who calls himself a homeless abolitionist, ending chronic homeless is a moral call. "Is there any manifestation of homelessness more tragic or more visible than chronic homelessness experienced by those who are suffering from mental illness, addiction or physical disability?" he asks.

Building permanent housing for the chronically ill is in fact a long-standing Democratic initiative. In 1990 New York Governor Mario Cuomo began building "supportive housing" projects with attached mental-health services; there are now more than 60,000 such units across the country, funded by a combination of government and private organizations. While the buildings are not licensed like mental hospitals, nurses, social workers and psychologists keep office hours. In midtown Manhattan's Prince George Hotel, which has a ballroom, a restored lobby and salon, former street dwellers bake cookies, use the computer lab and take Pilates and yoga classes. Director Nancy Porcaro says the surroundings give the homeless enough help and pride to better themselves. "People do rise to the occasion, despite what the mainstream may think. They want more," she says.

That's the compassionate part. Here's the conservatives side: Bush isn't spending any money on this. While HUD already spends 30% of its homeless dollars on permanent housing, all the administration has added so far for its new push is $35 million, scraped together from within the existing budgets of three departments. To give a sense of how much that means in Washington budgetary terms, $35 million is equal to the money set aside to help keep insects from crossing the border. Although last month HUD touted the $1.1 billion in the budget for homeless services as the largest amount of homeless assistance in history, it's about the same as the amount set aside before Newt Gingrich's Congress made major cuts. And the Administration, more quietly, also announced a 30% cut in operating funds for public housing last week.

Congressman Barney Frank, ranking Democrat on the House Financial Services Committee (which oversees government housing agencies), is not kind about the Bush Administration's intentions. "They are just lying when they say they have a housing program," he says. And of the additional $35 million pledged to end chronic homelessness, Frank says, "it's not only peanuts; it's taking the peanuts from one dish and putting them in another." In fact, in October the House Appropriations Committee approved a bill that, if it becomes law, will cut $938 million from the President's budget for rental vouchers, one of the government's main methods of paying to house the homeless.

THE WANDERER

LOCATION Los Angeles
NAMES Debra Rollins, 35; two daughters, 11 and 16
HOW THEY BECAME HOMELESS

Having lived in 19 places in the past 30 years, including a stint as a teen-age runaway, Rollins spent the past five years in a one-bedroom flat with her two daughters, two friends and one of their kids. She moved to a hotel after falling out with her roommates. "I didn't have family or any friends around, so I didn't have anybody to help," she says. When her money ran out, she landed in a shelter. A high school dropout, Rollins is trying to obtain a GED and is working part time as a cashier so she can get a place of her own.

The old-school Democrats are also upset at the philosophy behind Bush's plan, which they argue is more interested in getting the homeless out of view than in solving their problems. "The largest-growing sector is actually women and children," says Donald Whitehead, the executive director of the National Coalition for the Homeless, the oldest and largest advocacy group on this issue. "A true strategy needs to include the entire population."

Andrew Cuomo, founder of HELP USA, a national, non-profit shelter provider, says the Administration is merely redefining the issue so as to appear to be doing something. "What makes you say that a guy who has been on the street for five years and is a heroin addict is any more needy than a woman who is being beaten nightly in front of her children?" he asks. For his part, Senator John Kerry, a Democrat running for President, has proposed legislation that would add 1.5 million units of affordable housing to address the fact that America's population has grown 11% in the past decade while rental stock has shrunk. According to the National Low Income Housing Coalition, which lobbies for government housing, for the fourth year in a row there isn't a single jurisdiction in the U.S., with the exception of places in Puerto Rico, where a person working full time for minimum wage can afford to rent a one-bedroom home at fair-market value.

Without a federal plan that has worked, cities have lost patience, concentrating on getting the homeless out of sight. In New York City, where shelter space can't be created fast enough, Mayor Mike Bloomberg has proposed using old cruise ships for housing. New Orleans removed park benches in Jackson Square to discourage the homeless; Philadelphia launched an ad campaign asking people not to give to panhandlers; and in Orlando, Fla., a new law makes it a jailable offense to lie down on the sidewalk.

THE LAID-OFF WORKER

LOCATION Dallas
NAME Gary Jones, 36
HOW HE BECAME HOMELESS

Jones was pulling in $12 an hour as a welder who often dangled from skyscrapers. Then he got laid off and started drinking heavily and doing drugs. "My self-esteem kind of left me," he says. "I've thought about trying to get back out there and find work, get myself off these here mean streets, but you have to be in the right frame of mind to do that."

Polls in San Francisco, where the streets are clogged with the homeless who lose the nightly lottery for limited shelter beds, indicate that homelessness is a major concern. Billboards show resident holding cardboard signs that read, I DON'T WANT TO HOLD MY BREATH PAST EVERY ALLEY. Voters last November overwhelmingly passed Proposition N, which cuts handouts from $395 a month to $59, providing food and shelter instead. The proposition was proposed by Gavin Newsom, 35, a member of the city's Board of Supervisors who describes himself as a liberal. Newsom's proposal was supported by a $1 million campaign and was so controversial that Newsom felt compelled to travel with police protection as Election Day approached. To his critics who contend that Proposition N doesn't do much to help the people whose assistance he's taking away, Newsom says, "We never said N is going to solve homelessness." Two weeks after the proposal became law, Newsom announced a mayoral bid.

Even in Miami, where homelessness has been reduced because of a 1997 court settlement that forced the city to decriminalize it and develop an elaborate system for dealing with it, citizens are demanding that the streets be cleared. New laws prevent sleeping on the beach and building shelters too close to one another. "They want to hide us with all kind of zoning tricks and such," says Steve Silva, 50, who makes $7 and a 5% commission selling Miami Heat tickets and lives in a shelter. "But it's a Band-Aid on a sucking chest wound, man."

Likewise in Dallas, where the problem continues to worsen, the homeless complain of cops delivering wake-up calls from their car loudspeakers by blaring "Wake up, crackheads!" and handing out vagrancy tickets. "It doesn't make you want to go and rejoin society," says Gary Jones, 36, a laid-off welder. "What's lower than writing a man a ticket for sleeping on the street? If he had somewhere else to go, don't you think he'd be there?"

Neither cracking down on vagrancy nor Bush's plan to end chronic homelessness is going to help the growing number of families without housing. David and Gina Christian and their four children have avoided the streets by staying in a 600-sq.-ft. apartment

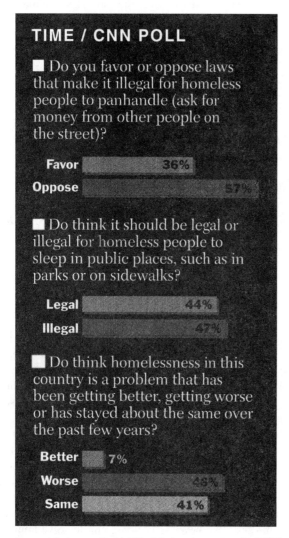

TIME / CNN POLL

■ Do you favor or oppose laws that make it illegal for homeless people to panhandle (ask for money from other people on the street)?

Favor	36%
Oppose	57%

■ Do think it should be legal or illegal for homeless people to sleep in public places, such as in parks or on sidewalks?

Legal	44%
Illegal	47%

■ Do think homelessness in this country is a problem that has been getting better, getting worse or has stayed about the same over the past few years?

Better	7%
Worse	48%
Same	41%

From a telephone poll of 1,006 adult Americans taken for TIME/CNN on Nov. 13-14 by Harris Interactive. Margin of error is ±3.1%. "Not sures" omitted

found David an $8-an-hour job as a mechanic at a Texaco station, and now that the Christians are not paying rent, they are able to save a little money. But time at Interfaith is running out. The program already broke its own rule by letting the family back for a second stay.

Given that so many are without a home but have temporary shelter, the real policy debate is no longer about whether society is responsible for keeping people out of the cold—we have agreed it is—but whether it is obligated to give them somewhere permanent to live. By fighting to end chronic homelessness, the Bush Administration argues that we need to give houses to those who are incapable of providing for themselves. The others will have to weather the storm in a shelter, if it can be built fast enough.

RHODE ISLAND
Number of families, 700, topped singles for the first time, up 17% over '01

COLUMBUS, OHIO
Families jumped 11% in '02 to 340. The number has grown 20% in two years

ANCHORAGE
Families accounted for 1,700 people seeking shelter, up 17% from '00 to '01

PHILADELPHIA
After a decline in '01, the number of families rose 5% last year to 400

SPOKANE, WASH.
It sheltered 1,500 families in '01, up 35%, and numbers still grow

BOSTON
A city report in '01 found 1,692 family members, up 9%, as singles rose just 1%

KANSAS CITY, MO.
It counted 960 families in '01 in the area, up 18% from '00

NEW YORK CITY
Its system now harbors 9,000 families, up 40% in the past year

---

—Reported by Simon Crittle and Jyoti Thottam/New York, Laura A. Locke/San Francisco, Deborah Edler Brown and Margot Roosevelt/Los Angles, Tim Padgett/Miami, Melissa August/Washington, Adam Pitluk/Dallas, Greg Land/Atlanta and Matt Baron/Chicago

at the Interfaith House in Dallas, which provides three months' housing to 100 needy families each year. David, 34, lost his job fixing rental cars in Austin after Sept. 11 when the tourism industry fell apart. Gina, 36, wasn't making enough as a nursing-home temp to cover the family's expenses. The Christians hocked everything they owned—their TV, the kids' PlayStation, Dad's tools—to follow David's old boss to a new job in Dallas. When that business fell apart too, David sold the tires from their two cars to pay for their nightly meals of rice and beans. "I was reduced to begging. I felt degraded, like I was less than human," Gina says. "When I was a child growing up in Watts, there was a 10-month period where we were homeless. I didn't want that for my family." Interfaith has

IN HARM'S WAY

The Working Class on the
War Front and the Home Front

BY RODNEY WARD

"Old man Bush wasn't half the president his son is. When the father was president, I only took a 15% pay cut. Now that his idiot son is president, I get to take a 40% pay cut. Way to go, George!"

—*a US Airways Fleet Services union activist*

"I've had enough of being fired at from all directions. I just want to go home."

—*a U.S. Marine, speaking to BBC News*

First, the obvious: In Iraq, a U.S. and allied military made up of working-class soldiers has fought against a working-class Iraqi military. But the war tears at the lives of working people in the United States as well. As Martin Luther King observed about an earlier war, the bombs raining down on the "enemy" also jeopardize the futures and livelihoods of people in poor and working-class communities in the United States.

On any number of dimensions, the war in Iraq is hurting working people back home. The U.S. soldiers who return will find their benefits slashed by Congress and their prospects limited by continuing economic stagnation. The massive cost of the war and occupation robs resources from those who can least afford it and exacerbates federal and state budget crises. In turn, the social safety

net is unraveling further just as wartime anxiety pushes the economy back toward recession.

The Bush administration is using wartime insecurity as a pretext to strip union rights from many federal workers and to intensify the criminalization of immigrant communities. In the private sector, entire industries—most notably, the airlines—are using the moment as an opportunity to bludgeon unions and savagely restructure their workplaces. As the shooting in Iraq winds down, an unwelcome occupation begins that will drain more resources away from meeting urgent human needs; just as important, it will prolong an atmosphere of crisis that gives cover for those whose agenda is to weaken the union movement and workers' rights.

WORKING WARRIORS

The modern U.S. military is vaunted as an all-volunteer force, but the truth is more complex. Conscription was ended in 1973 as a result of antiwar protest at home and, more important, among soldiers. Since then, the Department of Defense has built a voluntary military, primarily on a system of economic incentives. The military targets communities that have been devastated by disinvestment for recruitment, and military service has become a primary economic opportunity structure for working-class communities, disproportionately so for people of color.

Oskar Castro of the Youth and Militarism Project of the American Friends Service Committee (AFSC) points out that "most people didn't sign up because they were gung-ho warriors. Most people signed up for the college money and wonderful career opportunities, leadership skills and respect" that military recruiters offer—attractive promises to a young person whose alternatives are a dead-end job or unemployment. Researchers at the Rand Corporation found that low personal or family income and unemployment (particularly long term) increase the chances that someone will enlist. Not surprisingly, the military "seems to resemble the makeup of a two-year commuter or trade school outside Birmingham or Biloxi," note *New York Times* reporters David Halbfinger and Steven Holmes. As a result, close observers of military enlistment like the Central Committee for Conscientious Objectors refer to today's recruitment strategy as a "poverty draft."

Half of the 3.2 million soldiers in the U.S. military are reservists. In addition to the emotional trauma soldiers and their loved ones experience during a wartime mobilization, reservists also endure significant economic hardships. As they are activated from civilian jobs, many face dramatic pay cuts and disruption of health benefits. Tod Ensign of Citizen Soldier, an advocacy group for soldiers, explains, "Take an EMT making $42K driving an ambulance, enough to support a wife and two or three kids in a working-class suburb of New York City. They will earn $18K–22K once activated. Setting aside the risk of war, these people are taking heavy hits, often 30% to 50% cuts in pay!" Though some unionized workers have contractual pay protections in the event of reserve call-up, most reservists are out of luck. Civilian bills at best stay the same; with one parent absent, child care costs may go up. One New York City reservist explained that activation would mean his family would lose their home.

And when the war is over, the GIs will return home to find that politicians—many of whom used privilege to avoid military service themselves—are mouthing support while actually pulling the rug out from under soldiers' futures. On March 20, the Congress overwhelmingly passed a resolution to "express the gratitude of the Nation to all members of the United States Armed Forces." Then, early the next morning, the House of Representatives voted to cut funding for veterans' health care and benefit programs by nearly $25 billion over the next ten years. The cuts are designed to accommodate the massive tax cuts the Bush administration has been pursuing—while the war diverts the public's attention. The government track record on ignoring postwar problems like Agent Orange, post-traumatic stress disorder, and

Gulf War Syndrome does not bode well for the soldiers fighting the current war. Says the AFSC's Castro, "Even the military doesn't support the troops. Families are not supported. When it comes to dollars and cents, the military doesn't put its money where its mouth is."

Speaking of money, Defense Secretary Donald Rumsfeld's strategy for the Iraq war was based on the cost-cutting lean, just-in-time production model favored by corporate restructuring consultants. Rumsfeld apparently quashed the logistics plans of experienced officers, pressuring them to stage far fewer personnel and much less hardware in the Gulf than they considered adequate. Observers of the impact of lean restructuring in the corporate world report that increased workplace injuries are a major result. One wonders what impact importing this model into the battlefield will have on soldiers and civilians.

UNION BUSTING AS HOMELAND SECURITY

Meanwhile, on the home front, both public- and private-sector workers are suffering a savage assault. The fiscal crisis brought about by war spending, recession, and tax cuts for the wealthy is squeezing public workers at all levels, resulting in wage freezes and elimination of entire departments. Thousands of public-sector workers are losing their jobs. Treasury Department worker Renee Toback reports that her department was told their budget would be "taxed" to pay for the war in Iraq.

> "Northwest is using the Iraq conflict as an excuse to justify mass layoffs planned before the conflict started."

At the same time, the Bush administration has stripped thousands of federal workers in the hastily cobbled-together Department of Homeland Security of union rights in the name of national security. The Department of Defense is developing plans to do the same. Are fearful employees with no voice on the job in the best position to protect national security? No. But it's no surprise that the administration's agenda prioritizes union busting over public safety. AFL-CIO Organizing Director Stewart Acuff says, "The most outrageous thing they [the Bush administration] said was that they had to remove union rights from the Department of Homeland Security when all of the people who answered the call on September 11, all of the firefighters and cops who died trying to save people, were union members! And 90% of the people who cleaned up in the aftermath were union members as well."

Against this backdrop, the administration has also called for the privatization of as many as 800,000 non-postal federal jobs. If Bush succeeds, this move would replace large numbers of union jobs with non-union ones at lower pay and with less accountability; it would strike a huge blow at the strength of public-sector unions. (Naturally, Bush also plans to privatize Iraqi health care and education.)

Diane Witiak, an American Federation of Government Employees (AFGE) spokeswoman, describes the current atmosphere: "If you dare to oppose the administration, you're almost considered a traitor. We resent that the administration considers unionization and patriotism incompatible. In fact, [unionization is] essential. [The administration] will go back to the old cronyism and favoritism that the Civil Service Act corrected. It's only a matter of time before Bush starts with the private sector!"

Much as Witiak predicted, the administration is using the national-security pretext to erode the rights of some private-sector workers as well. Last year, Homeland Security director Tom Ridge called the president of the west coast longshore union. He claimed a strike would harm national security and threatened dockworkers with replacement by military personnel. Ultimately, it was management that locked out the dockworkers, but Bush invoked the Taft-Hartley Act and threatened to prosecute International Longshore and Warehouse Union members who engaged in any kind of work slowdown or other industrial action.

More broadly, efforts are under way in Congress to ban strikes by airline workers and to pass a number of other anti-worker measures. Among these are expansion of the restrictive Railway Labor Act's jurisdiction to include certain industries now under the umbrella of the National Labor Relations Act, making it harder for workers in these sectors to win union recognition and severely limiting their right to strike. Another legislative initiative would eliminate "card-check," the system of conducting a union recognition election once a certain number of representation petition cards have been signed by workers at a particular facility. In recent years, card-check has been the chief mechanism of successful union organizing drives. The AFL-CIO's Acuff points out that "the direction the government is moving in will indeed have a chilling effect on mobilizations, collective activity, demonstrations and direct action, all necessary parts of contract and bargaining campaigns and union strength. This administration, by law and by culture, is trying to stigmatize or make illegal the kinds of activity that are necessary to build union workplace strength."

WHAT DOES A TERRORIST LOOK LIKE?

Wartime is always dangerous for immigrant communities. When the towers collapsed on September 11, they crushed the movement to give undocumented immigrants amnesty. Since then, immigrants have been subject to a dramatically stepped-up campaign by the federal government to find and deport them. Rachael Kamel, AFSC education director, points to "growing attempts to criminalize immigrant workers—all now justified in the name of security." As the next episode in the now-permanent war on terror, the war in Iraq only serves to extend the period in which such policies appear legitimate.

For example, the Social Security Administration (SSA) sends so-called no-match letters to employers when it finds that a worker's Social Security number does not match SSA records. These letters serve to intimidate workers, since employers can threaten to turn them in to the Immigration and Naturalization Service (INS). The number of no-match letters has increased 800% since 9/11. Similarly, special registration of immigrants from a select list of countries, mostly in the Middle East and Southern Asia, has snared thousands of people with minor visa infractions, many of whom face deportation. (Of bizarre note is the case of Iraqi exile Katrin Michael. She met with President Bush on March 14 to recount the gas attack she survived, and then found herself on the INS deportation list the next week, according to a *Washington Post* story.)

All of this has a powerful impact on worker organization because, for the past decade, immigrant workers have been the bedrock of aggressive labor organizing campaigns in economically strategic states like California, Texas and New York. Last year in Los Angeles, 60 workers active in organizing the Koreatown Assi Supermarket were placed on indefinite suspension after their names appeared on no-match letters. And the same Homeland Security rules that stripped newly-federalized airport screeners of union rights also banned immigrant workers in those positions. As a result, 7,000 immigrant airport security screeners—some of whom had just succeeded in winning union representation—have been fired. (See "Immigrant Workers in the Crosshairs," *D&S*, January/February 2003.)

SHOCK AND AWE FOR AIRLINE WORKERS?

Amid official and unofficial repression against public sector workers and immigrant communities, the economy appears stalled and is likely heading for a double-dip recession. The World Bank is already estimating that the Iraq war will reduce worldwide economic growth by one-half of a percentage point during the first six months of this year.

When the economy is weak, the industries most affected make cuts wherever they can, and workers bear the brunt of industry restructuring. The airline industry continues to be the crucible of this restructuring; as such, it provides an instructive case study. Before the war, the industry's Air Transport Association predicted 70,000 layoffs (100,000 if a terrorist attack accompanied the war) in addition to the thousands already cut since September 11, as well as $4 billion in additional losses. Editorials intoned about "Airline Apocalypse."

True to their word, airlines began shedding employees by the thousands as soon as the bombs started to fall on Baghdad. Continental laid off 1,200, with more to come, Northwest, 4,900, while United and American (possibly in Chapter 11 bankruptcy reorganization by the time you read this) plan to get rid of thousands more. Jeff Matthews, the Aircraft Mechanics Fraternal Association's national contract coordinator at Northwest, told Reuters: "Northwest is using the Iraq conflict as an excuse to justify mass layoffs planned before the conflict started. The number of planned layoffs is far larger than would be justified based on the number of planes Northwest is removing from service." One United employee and Marines veteran describes wartime layoffs as United's own campaign of "shock and awe."

All of these airlines have succeeded in, or are in the process of, extracting concessions on levels unheard of in the history of the industry. Of particular importance has been US Airways' use of the war as leverage to terminate the defined-benefit pension plan for its pilots. At a time when defined-benefit plans are underfunded by about $300 billion in the United States, this is alarming. Representative Bernie Sanders (I-Vt.) warned in the *Wall Street Journal* that "this could set a horrible precedent by making it easier for companies to renege on the retirement promises they made to their workers." Nomi Prins, author of the forthcoming book *Money for Nothing*, points out, "The poor stock market is offering a convenient excuse for companies that already desired to reduce future plan benefits."

The airlines cite the war as a major reason for the concessions they demand. United mechanic Jennifer Salazar-Biddle remarked, "The crisis is real, but the graft is unbelievable." In fact, executive compensation in the midst of the industry's crisis has shocked and awed even Republicans. Responding to reports of the doubling of Delta CEO Leo Mullin's compensation package, Sen. John McCain (who champions eliminating airline workers' right to strike) exclaimed, "You ought to be ashamed of yourself." Nonetheless, a new bailout is in the works for the airline industry. The bailout bill does include a cap on executive compensation, but at 2002 levels—a good example of closing the barn doors after the escape. It also requires the airline companies to reduce operating costs, a provision that will primarily bleed workers. The only bone the bill offers airline workers is a meager extension of their unemployment benefits.

CHAIN OF CHANGE

Wars have always had a deep impact on working people. In addition to the slaughter of war, wars have often undermined the strength of working class organization. Government repression tied to World War I all but destroyed the Industrial Workers of the World and the Socialist Party. Workplace regimentation in World War II played an important role in the long-term bureaucratization of unions, replacing militant shop floor activity with safer routinized grievance and arbitration procedures.

On the other hand, soldiers returning from war have also played an important role in reviving struggles at home. At the end of World War II and during the Vietnam War, opposition to the war surfaced among GIs, along with discussions of soldiers' rights to free speech and even to unions. Soldiers returning from Vietnam played an important role in the antiwar movement as well as rebellions within a variety of unions, most notably the wave of auto-worker wildcat strikes from 1969 to 1972. African-American soldiers returning from both of these wars parlayed their wartime experiences into civil-rights activism.

There are some hopeful signs that workers will fight back against the current wave of assaults on their rights. Transportation Security Administration (TSA) employees are continuing to organize themselves with AFGE in spite of TSA director James Loy's directives to the contrary. AFGE succeeded in securing a one-year moratorium on the de-unionization of the Department of Homeland Security. Federal workers in Seattle and dozens of other localities have begun a campaign of public rallies to protest privatization.

Time will tell how working people in the military will respond to what they are enduring today. One thing is clear, though: The immediate impact of the war has been to strengthen the hands of corporations and weaken unions and other worker organizations while placing thousands of working people in harm's way. In the long term, whether grassroots activists can turn this tide will depend on how they understand and address the class dimensions of this and future wars.

RESOURCES

Soldiers & Veterans: Citizen Soldier, www.citizen-soldier. org; Military Families Speak Out, www.mfso.org; Veterans for Common Sense, www.veteransforcommonsense. org; National Gulf War Resource Center, www.ngwrc. org; *Immigrant Rights*: National Network for Immigrant and Refugee Rights, www.nnirr.org; *Labor*: US Labor Against War, www.uslaboragainstwar.org; Dept. of Homeland Security Workers, wwwdhsworkers.org; Association of Flight Attendants, www.afanet.org; Airline Mechanics Fraternal Association, www.amfanatl.org; *See also*: David Cortright, *Soldiers in Revolt: The American Military Today* (Anchor Press/Doubleday, 1976); Kim Moody, *An Injury To All* (Routledge, 1997).

Rodney Ward is a longtime labor and peace activist, laid-off flight attendant, and staff member at Dollars & Sense. *Rodney writes extensively about the experience of workers in the airline industry and is also working to form a Flight Attendants for Peace Network. He can be reached at rodney@dollarsandsense.org.*

CORPORATE WELFARE

A TIME investigation uncovers how hundreds of companies get on the dole—and why it costs every working American the equivalent of two weeks' pay every year

By Donald L. Barlett and James B. Steele

HOW WOULD YOU LIKE TO PAY ONLY A QUARTER OF THE REAL ESTATE TAXES you owe on your home? And buy everything for the next 10 years without spending a single penny in sales tax? Keep a chunk of your paycheck free of income taxes? Have the city in which you live lend you money at rates cheaper than any bank charges? Then have the same city install free water and sewer lines to your house, offer you a perpetual discount on utility bills—and top it all off by landscaping your front yard at no charge?

Fat chance. You can't get any of that, of course. But if you live almost anywhere in America, all around you are taxpayers getting deals like this. These taxpayers are called corporations, and their deals are usually trumpeted as "economic development" or "public-private partnerships." But a better name is corporate welfare. It's a game in which governments large and small subsidize corporations large and small, usually at the expense of another state or town and almost always at the expense of individual and other corporate taxpayers.

Two years after Congress reduced welfare for individuals and families, this other kind of welfare continues to expand, penetrating every corner of the American economy. It has turned politicians into bribery specialists, and smart business people into con artists. And most surprising of all, it has rarely created any new jobs.

While corporate welfare has attracted critics from both the left and the right, there is no uniform definition. By TIME's definition, it is this: any action by local, state or federal government that gives a corporation or an entire industry a benefit not offered to others. It can be an outright subsidy, a grant, real estate, a low-interest loan or a government service. It can also be a tax break—a credit, exemption, deferral or deduction, or a tax rate lower than the one others pay.

The rationale to curtail traditional welfare programs, such as Aid to Families with Dependent Children and food stamps, and to impose a lifetime limit on the amount of aid received, was compelling: the old system didn't work. It was unfair, destroyed incentive, perpetuated dependence and distorted the economy. An 18-month TIME investigation has found that the same indictment, almost to the word, applies to corporate welfare. In some ways, it represents pork-barrel legislation of the worst order. The difference, of course, is that instead of rewarding the poor, it rewards the powerful.

And it rewards them handsomely. The Federal Government alone shells out $125 billion a year in corporate welfare, this in the midst of one of the more robust economic periods in the nation's history. Indeed, thus far in the 1990s, corporate profits have totaled $4.5 trillion—a sum equal to the cumulative paychecks of 50 million working Americans who earned less than $25,000 a year, for those eight years.

> **During one of the most robust economic periods in our nation's history, the Federal Government has shelled out $125 billion in corporate welfare, equivalent to all the income tax paid by 60 million individuals and families.**

That makes the Federal Government America's biggest sugar daddy, dispensing a range of giveaways from tax abatements to price supports for sugar itself. Companies get government money to advertise their products; to help build new plants, offices and stores; and to train their workers. They sell their goods to foreign buyers that make the acquisitions with tax dollars supplied by the U.S. government; engage in foreign transactions that are insured by the government; and are excused from paying a portion of their income tax if they sell products overseas. They pocket lucrative government contracts to carry out ordinary business operations, and government grants to conduct research that will improve their profit margins. They are extended partial tax immunity if they locate in certain geographical areas, and they may write off as business expenses some of the perks enjoyed by their top executives.

The justification for much of this welfare is that the U.S. government is creating jobs. Over the past six years, Congress appropriated $5 billion to run the Export-Import Bank of the United States, which subsidizes companies that sell goods abroad. James A. Harmon, president and chairman, puts it this way: "American workers... have higher-quality, better-paying jobs, thanks to Eximbank's financing." But the numbers at the bank's five biggest beneficiaries—AT&T, Bechtel, Boeing, General Electric and McDonnell Douglas (now a part of Boeing)—tell another story. At these companies, which have accounted for about 40% of all loans, grants and long-term guarantees in this decade, overall employment has fallen 38%, as more than a third of a million jobs have disappeared.

The picture is much the same at the state and local level, where a different kind of feeding frenzy is taking place. Politicians stumble over one another in the rush to arrange special deals for select corporations, fueling a growing economic war among the states. The result is that states keep throwing money at companies that in many cases are not serious about moving anyway. The companies are certainly not reluctant to take the money, though, which is available if they simply utter the word relocation. And why not? Corporate executives, after all, have a fiduciary duty to squeeze every dollar they can from every locality waving blandishments in their face.

State and local governments now give corporations money to move from one city to another—even from one building to another—and tax credits for hiring new employees. They supply funds to train workers or pay part of their wages while they are in training, and provide scientific and engineering assistance to solve workplace technical problems. They repave existing roads and build new ones. They lend money at bargain-basement interest rates to erect plants or buy equipment. They excuse corporations from paying sales and property taxes and relieve them from taxes on investment income.

There are no reasonably accurate estimates on the amount of money states shovel out. That's because few want you to know. Some say they maintain no records. Some say they don't know where the files are. Some say the information is not public. All that's certain is that the figure is in the many billions of dollars each year—and it is growing, when measured against the subsidy per job.

In 1989 Illinois gave $240 million in economic incentives to Sears, Roebuck & Co. to keep its corporate headquarters and 5,400 workers in the state by moving from Chicago to suburban Hoffman Estates. That amounted to a subsidy of $44,000 for each job.

In 1991 Indiana gave $451 million in economic incentives to United Airlines to build an aircraft-maintenance facility that would employ as many as 6,300 people. Subsidy: $72,000 for each job.

In 1993 Alabama gave $253 million in economic incentives to Mercedes-Benz to build an automobile-assembly plant near Tuscaloosa and employ 1,500 workers. Subsidy: $169,000 for each job.

And in 1997 Pennsylvania gave $307 million in economic incentives to Kvaerner ASA, a Norwegian global engineering and construction company, to open a shipyard at the former Philadelphia Naval Shipyard and employ 950 people. Subsidy: $323,000 for each job.

This kind of arithmetic seldom adds up. Let's say the Philadelphia job pays $50,000. And each new worker pays $6,700 in local and state taxes. That means it will take nearly a half-century of tax collections from each individual to earn back the money granted to create his or her job. And that assumes all 950 workers will be recruited from outside Philadelphia and will relocate in the city, rather than move from existing jobs within the city, where they are already paying taxes.

All this is in service of a system that may produce jobs in one city or state, thus fostering the illusion of an uptick in employment. But it does not create more jobs in the nation as a whole. Market forces do that, and that's why 10 million jobs have been created since 1990. But most of those jobs have been created by small- and medium-size companies, from high-tech start-ups to franchised cleaning services. FORTUNE 500 companies, on the other

hand, have erased more jobs than they have created this past decade, and yet they are the biggest beneficiaries of corporate welfare.

To be sure, some economic incentives are handed out for a seemingly worthwhile public purpose. The tax breaks that companies receive to locate in inner cities come to mind. Without them, companies might not invest in those neighborhoods. However well intended, these subsidies rarely produce lasting results. They may provide short-term jobs but not long-term employment. And in the end, the costs outweigh any benefits.

And what are those costs? The equivalent of nearly two weekly paychecks from every working man and woman in America—extra money that would stay in their pockets if it didn't go to support some business venture or another.

If corporate welfare is an unproductive end game, why does it keep growing in a period of intensive government cost cutting? For starters, it has good p.r. and an army of bureaucrats working to expand it. A corporate-welfare bureaucracy of an estimated 11,000 organizations and agencies has grown up, with access to city halls, statehouses, the Capitol and the White House. They conduct seminars, conferences and training sessions. They have their own trade associations. They publish their own journals and newsletters. They create attractive websites on the Internet. And they never call it "welfare." They call it "economic incentives" or "empowerment zones" or "enterprise zones."

Whatever the name, the result is the same. Some companies receive public services at reduced rates, while all others pay the full cost. Some companies are excused from paying all or a portion of their taxes due, while all others must pay the full amount imposed by law. Some companies receive grants, low-interest loans and other subsidies, while all others must fend for themselves.

In the end, that's corporate welfare's greatest flaw. It's unfair. One role of government is to help ensure a level playing field for people and businesses. Corporate welfare does just the opposite. It tilts the playing field in favor of the largest or the most politically influential or most aggressive businesses....

Requiem for Welfare

Evelyn Z. Brodkin

THERE WERE few mourners at welfare's funeral. In fact, its demise was widely celebrated when congressional Republicans teamed up with a majority of their Democratic colleagues and then-president Bill Clinton to enact a new welfare law in 1996. The law ended the sixty-one-year old federal commitment to aid poor families and ushered in a commitment to lower welfare rolls and put recipients to work.

To many politicians and the public, anything seemed preferable to the widely discredited program known as Aid to Families with Dependent Children (AFDC). Conservatives were sure that the new welfare would pull up the poor by their bootstraps and redeem them through the virtues of work. Liberals set aside their misgivings, hoping that work would redeem the poor politically and open opportunities to advance economic equality.

More than six years later, the demise of the old welfare remains largely unlamented. But what to make of the changes that have occurred in the name of reform? Often, laws produce more smoke than fire, intimating big change, but producing little. Not this time. In ways both apparent and not fully appreciated, welfare reform has reconfigured both the policy and political landscape. Some of these changes can evoke nostalgia for the bad old days of welfare unreformed.

Reconsidering Welfare's Fate

An immediate consequence of the new law was to defuse welfare as a hot political issue. There's little attention to it these days—apart from some five million parents and children who rely on welfare to alleviate their poverty (and the policy analysts who pore over mountains of data to calculate how it "works"). Legislators have shown no appetite for restarting the welfare wars of prior years. And is it any wonder? The news about welfare has looked good—at least, superficially. Caseloads have plummeted since implementation of the new welfare, dropping 57 percent between 1997 and 2001. Some smaller states essentially cleared their caseloads, with Wyoming and Idaho proudly announcing reductions of 88.9 percent and 85.1 percent, respectively. Even states with large, urban populations have cut caseloads by one-half to three-quarters.

As an issue, welfare ranked among the top five items of interest to the public in 1995 and 1996. But in recent years, it has almost dropped off the Gallup charts. Other polls show that, among respondents who are aware of welfare reform, more than 60 percent think it's working well. Meanwhile, the nation has moved on to other concerns: terrorism, Iraq, the economy. Why reopen the welfare issue now?

In part, the 1996 law itself spurred reassessment. The law was designed to expire in 2002 unless reauthorized by Congress. With Congress unable to reach agreement before the 2002 election, welfare's reauthorization became one of the many measures to get a temporary extension and a handoff to the 108th Congress.

Beyond reauthorization, welfare merits a close look because battles over welfare policy have often been a bellwether of broader political developments. Welfare policy was near the forefront of sixties social activism, one of the banners under which the urban poor, minorities, and other disaffected groups successfully pressed for greater government intervention on behalf of social and economic equality. For the national Democratic Party, the politics of poverty fit an electoral strategy aimed at mobilizing urban and minority voters. Although the expansion of welfare proved to be temporary and limited, the politics of poverty produced federal initiatives that had broad and lasting impact, among them Medicaid, food stamps, earned income tax credits, and programs to aid schools in poor communities.

Attacks on welfare marked the beginning of a conservative mobilization against the welfare state in the late 1970s. Lurid accounts in George Gilder's *Wealth and Poverty* and Mickey Kaus's *The End of Equality* portrayed welfare and the poor as enemies of the democratic marketplace. President Ronald Reagan picked up these themes and contributed his own colorful anecdotes about welfare cheats and fraud, as he pushed forward cuts in taxes and social welfare programs. These forays into the politics of personal piety fit a Republican electoral strategy aimed at mobilizing the religious right and bringing the white working class into the party fold.

Out with the "Old" Welfare

Reforming welfare assumed new urgency in the 1990s, an urgency grounded less in policy realities than in electoral politics. Alarms were sounded about a crisis of cost, although for three decades, spending on AFDC amounted to less than 2 percent of the federal budget. The $16 billion the federal government allocated to AFDC was dwarfed by spending on Social Security and defense, each costing more than $300 billion per year. Public opinion polls, however, indicated a different perception. Forty percent of respondents believed that welfare was one of the most expensive national programs, even larger than Social Security or defense.

Polls also indicated that much of the public believed welfare recipients had it too easy, although few knew what welfare really provided. In fact, AFDC gave only meager support to poor families. In 1996, the median monthly benefit for a family of three was $366. Even when combined with food stamps, welfare lifted few poor families above the federal poverty line. Even the much-touted crisis of dependency ("dependent" being a term loosely applied to anyone receiving welfare) was not reflected in the evidence. The share of families receiving welfare for extended periods declined between 1970 and 1985 and leveled off after that. Families that received welfare for more than six years constituted only a small minority of the welfare caseload at any point in time.

Although the hue and cry over a supposed welfare crisis was greatly overblown, Bill Clinton clearly appreciated welfare's potent political symbolism. As a presidential candidate, he famously pledged to "end welfare as we know it," a turn of phrase useful in demonstrating that he was a "new Democrat" unburdened by the liberalism of his predecessors. His proposals for reform emphasized neoliberal themes of work and individual responsibility, but coupled demands for work with provision of social services intended to improve individual employment prospects. The Clinton administration's plans also assumed the enactment of universal health insurance that would help underwrite the well-being of the working poor. But that did not happen.

After the Republicans took over Congress in 1994, and Clinton began his fateful descent into personal irresponsibility, the initiative shifted decidedly toward the right. House Majority Leader Newt Gingrich seized the opportunity to turn Clinton's pledge against him, sending the president two welfare measures then thought to be so harsh that they almost begged for a veto. The measures ended the federal guarantee of income support, imposed strict work rules, and set time limits on the provision of benefits. Clinton vetoed them.

But on the eve of his renomination at the 1996 Democratic convention, Clinton signed a measure much like those he had vetoed. There followed a few highly public resignations among indignant staff and a rebuke from the Congressional Black Caucus. But Clinton's decision (advocated by strategist Dick Morris and running mate Al Gore, among others) effectively took the welfare issue away from the Republicans and highlighted Clinton's "new Democratic" appeal to critical swing suburban and blue-collar, crossover voters.

Clinton became the first elected Democratic President since Franklin Roosevelt to win a second term. But Clinton was no Roosevelt. In fact, he redeemed his pledge to "end welfare" by presiding over the destruction of a pillar of the New Deal welfare state.

Enter the "New" Welfare

The Personal Responsibility and Work Opportunity Reconciliation Act of 1996 replaced AFDC with a program aptly named Temporary Assistance to Needy Families (TANF). AFDC had provided an open-ended entitlement of federal funds to states based on the amount of benefits they distributed to poor families. TANF ended that entitlement, establishing a five-year block grant fixed at $16.5 billion annually (based on the amount allocated to AFDC in its last year) that states could draw down to subsidize welfare and related expenditures.

Mistrusting the states' willingness to be tough enough on work, Congress incorporated detailed and coercive provisions. First, it set time limits for assistance, restricting federal aid to a lifetime maximum of sixty months. If states wanted to exceed those limits, they would have to pay for most of it themselves. Second, parents were required to work or participate in so-called work activities after a maximum of two years of welfare receipt. Third, TANF established escalating work quotas. States that wanted to collect their full portion of federal dollars would have to show, by 2002, that 50 percent of adults heading single-parent households were working thirty hours per week. Fourth, it meticulously specified those work "activities" that would enable states to meet their quotas, among them paid work, job search, and unpaid workfare (in which recipients "worked off" their welfare benefits at minimum wage or provided child care for other welfare recipients). It limited the use of education and vocational training as countable activities.

Although the "work" side of TANF was clearly pre-eminent, there were some modest provisions on the "opportunity" side, with Congress providing $2.3 billion to help subsidize child care for working mothers and $3 billion in a block grant for welfare-to-work programs.

Beyond these prominent features, the new welfare also packed some hidden punches. It rewarded states for cutting welfare caseloads, largely without regard to how they did it. States that reduced their caseloads (whether those losing welfare found work or not) received credit against officially mandated quotas. If Congress was worried about states' slacking off from its tough work demands, the law indicated no concern that they might go too far in restricting access to benefits or pushing people off the welfare rolls. Only caseload reductions counted.

Under the banner of devolution, the law also gave states new authority to design their own welfare programs. While the welfare debate highlighted the professed virtues of innovation, less obvious was the license it gave states to craft policies even tougher and more restrictive than those allowed by federal law.

Pushing welfare decision making to the state and local level has never been good for the poor. In many states, poor families and their allies have little political influence. Moreover, constitutional balanced-budget requirements make states structurally unsuited to the task of protecting vulnerable residents against economic slumps. When unemployment goes up and state tax revenue goes down, the downward pressure on social spending intensifies.

The secret triumph of devolution lay, not in the opportunities for innovation, but in the opportunity for a quiet unraveling of the safety net.

The Unfolding Story of Welfare Transformed[1]

What has happened since 1996? For one thing, the new welfare changed a national program of income assistance to an array of state programs, each with its own assortment of benefits, services, restrictions, and requirements. There has always been wide variation in the amount of cash aid states provided, and federal waivers allowed states to deviate from some national rules. But devolution spurred far greater policy inconsistency by allowing states, essentially, to make their own rules. Consequently, what you get (or whether you get anything at all) depends on where you live.

In addition, devolution set off a state "race to the bottom," not by reducing benefit levels as some had predicted, but by imposing new restrictions that limited access to benefits. States across the nation have taken advantage of devolution to impose restrictions tougher than those required by federal law.

For example, although federal law required recipients to work within two years, most states require work within one year, some require immediate work, and others demand a month of job search before they even begin to process an application for assistance. No longer required to exempt mothers with children under three years old from work requirements, most states permit an exemption only for mothers with babies under one year old, and some have eliminated exemptions altogether. In nineteen states, lifetime limits for welfare receipt are set below the federal maximum of sixty months. Other states have imposed so-called family caps that preclude benefits for babies born to mothers already receiving welfare. If federal policymakers secretly hoped that states would do part of the dirty work of cutting welfare for them, they must be pleased with these results.

However, the picture from the states is anything but consistent or uniformly punitive. Many help those recipients accepting low-wage jobs by subsidizing the costs of transportation, child care, and medical insurance (although often only for one year). Twenty-two states try to keep low-wage workers afloat by using welfare benefits to supplement their incomes, "stopping the clock" on time limits for working parents. Significantly, the federal clock keeps ticking, and states adopting this strategy must use their own funds to support working families reaching the five-year lifetime limit. With state budgets increasingly squeezed by recession, it is hard to predict how strong the state commitment to preserve these supports will be.

Many state and local agencies have already cut back work preparation and placement programs funded under a $3 billion federal welfare-to-work block grant. Those funds spurred a short-term boom in contracting to private agencies. But the block grant expired leaving little evidence that states were able to build new systems for supporting work over the long term. In fact, no one knows exactly what all of this contracting produced, as state and local agencies kept limited records and conducted few careful evaluations. A close look at contracting in Illinois, for example, revealed the creation of a diffuse array of short-term programs operating under contract requirements that left many agencies unable to build anything of lasting value.

There is another strange twist to the convoluted welfare story: in their zest for services over support, states actually shifted government funds from the pockets of poor families to the pockets of private service providers. They distributed 76 percent of their AFDC funds in cash aid to the poor in 1996, but gave poor families only 41 percent of their TANF funds in 2000. Substantial portions of the TANF budget were consumed by child care costs, although it is difficult to say exactly how all the TANF funds were used. The General Accounting Office suggests that there is a fair amount of "supplantation" of services previously funded from other budget lines but now paid for by TANF.

Beyond the Caseload Count

The picture becomes still more complicated when one attempts to peer behind the head count in order to assess what actually happened in the purge of welfare caseloads. Exactly how did states push those caseloads down? What has happened to poor families that no longer have recourse to welfare? What kind of opportunities does the lower wage labor market really offer? Research has only begun to illuminate these crucial questions, but the evidence is disheartening.

Finding Good Jobs: There are three ways to lower welfare caseloads. One is by successfully moving recipients into good jobs with stable employment where they can earn enough to maintain their families above poverty (or, at least, above what they could get on welfare). Recipients may find jobs on their own, which many do, or with connections facilitated by welfare agencies and service providers.

Financial supports provided by TANF have allowed some recipients to take jobs where they earn too little to make ends meet on their own. Child-care and transportation subsidies make a difference for those workers. They also benefit from federally funded food stamps that stretch the grocery budget. But food stamp use fell off 40 percent after 1994, although fewer families were receiving welfare and more had joined the ranks of the working poor. Absent external pressures, most states made no effort to assure access to food stamps for those losing welfare. In fact, government studies indicate that administrative hassles and misinformation discouraged low-income families from obtaining benefits.

Taking Bad Jobs: A second way to lower welfare caseloads is to pressure recipients into taking bad jobs. Not all lower wage jobs are bad, but many of those most readily available to former recipients undermine their best efforts to make it as working parents. These jobs are characterized by unstable schedules, limited access to health insurance or pensions, no sick leave, and job insecurity. Because high turnover is a feature of these jobs, at any given moment, many are apt to be available. Indeed, employers seeking to fill these undesirable "high-velocity" jobs, where there is continuous churning of the workforce, are all too eager to use welfare agencies as a hiring hall.

This may partially explain why more than a fifth of those leaving welfare for work return within a year or two. Proponents of the new welfare conveniently blame individual work behavior or attitudes for job churning, but ignore the role of employers who structure jobs in ways that make job loss inevitable. What's a supermarket clerk to do when her manager makes frequent schedule changes, periodically shortens her hours, or asks her to work in a store across town? What happens is that carefully constructed child care arrangements break down, lost pay days break the family budget, and the hours it takes to commute on public transportation become unmanageable. The family-friendly workplace that more sought-after workers demand couldn't be farther from the hard reality of lower wage jobs.

One of the little appreciated virtues of the old welfare is that it served as a sort of unemployment insurance for these lower wage workers excluded from regular unemployment insurance by their irregular jobs. Welfare cushioned the layoffs, turnover, and contingencies that go with the territory. Under the new welfare, these workers face a hard landing because welfare is more difficult to get and offers little leeway to acquire either the time or skills that might yield a job with a future. Over the longer term, low-wage workers may find their access to welfare blocked by time limits. Although the five-year lifetime limit ostensibly targets sustained reliance on welfare, this limit could come back to bite those who cycle in and out of the lower wage labor force. At this point, no one knows how this will play out.

Creating Barriers to Access: A third way to reduce welfare caseloads is by reducing access—making benefits harder to acquire and keep. Some states explicitly try to divert applicants by imposing advance job-search requirements, demanding multiple trips to the welfare office in order to complete the application process, or informally advising applicants that it may not be worth the hassle. In some welfare offices, caseworkers routinely encourage applicants to forgo cash aid and apply only for Medicaid and food stamps.

Benefits are also harder to keep, as caseworkers require recipients to attend frequent meetings either to discuss seemingly endless demands for documentation or to press them on issues involving work. Everyday life in an urban welfare office is difficult to describe and, for many, even harder to believe. There are the hours of waiting in rows of plastic chairs, the repeated requests for paperwork, the ritualized weekly job club lectures about how to smile, shake hands, and show a good attitude to employers. As inspiration, caseworkers leading job club sessions often tell stories from their own lives of rising from poverty to become welfare workers (positions likely to be cut back as caseloads decline). When clients tell their own tales of cycling from bad jobs to worse and ask for help getting a good job, caseworkers are apt to admonish them for indulging in a "pity party."

Access to welfare may also be constrained through a profoundly mundane array of administrative barriers that simply make benefits harder to keep. A missed appointment, misplaced documents (often lost by the agency), delayed entry of personal data—these common and otherwise trivial mishaps can result in a loss of benefits for "non-cooperation."

The Public Benefits Hotline, a call-in center that provides both advice and intervention for Chicago residents, received some ten thousand calls in the four years after welfare reform, most of them involving hassles of this sort.[2] In other parts of the country, these types of problems show up in administrative hearing records and court cases, where judges have criticized welfare agencies for making "excessive" demands for verification documents, conducting "sham assessments" leading to inappropriate imposition of work requirements, and sanctioning clients for missing appointments when they should have helped them deal with child care or medical difficulties.

Is There a Bottom Line?

The new welfare has produced neither the immediate cataclysm its opponents threatened nor the economic and social redemption its proponents anticipated. Opponents had warned that welfare reform would plunge one million children into poverty. In the midst of an unprecedented economic boom, that didn't happen. But, even in the best of times, prospects were not auspicious for those leaving welfare.

According to the Urban Institute, about half of those leaving welfare for work between 1997 and 1999 obtained jobs where they earned a median hourly wage of only $7.15. If the jobs offered a steady forty hours of work a week (which lower wage jobs usually don't), that would provide a gross annual income of $14,872. That places a mother with two children a precarious $1,000 above the formal poverty line for the year 2000 and a two-parent family with two children nearly $3,000 *below* that line. But more than one-fifth of those leaving welfare for work didn't make it through the year—either because they lost their jobs, got sick, or just couldn't make ends meet. The only thing surprising about these figures is that the numbers weren't higher. Others left or lost welfare, but did not find work, with one in seven adults losing welfare reporting no alternative means of support. Their specific fate is unknown, but most big cities have been reporting worrisome increases in homelessness and hunger.

If there is any bottom line, it is that caseloads have been purged. But neither the market for lower wage workers nor the policies put into practice in the name of welfare reform have purged poverty from the lives of the poor. Even in the last years of the economic boom, between 1996 and 1998, the Urban Institute found that three hundred thousand more individuals in single-parent families slipped into extreme poverty. Although they qualified for food stamps that might have stretched their resources a bit further, many did not get them. Government figures indicate that families leaving welfare for work often lose access to other benefits, which states do not automatically continue irrespective of eligibility.

More recently, census figures have begun to show the effects of recession coupled with an eroded safety net. The nation's poverty rate rose to 11.7 percent in 2001, up from 11.3 percent the prior year. More troubling still, inequality is growing and poverty is deepening. In 2001, the "poverty gap," the gap between the official poverty line and the income of poor individuals, reached its highest level since measurements were first taken in 1979. In California, often a harbinger of larger social trends, a startling two in three poor children now live in families where at least one adult is employed. Can the families of lower wage workers live without access to welfare and other government supports? Apparently, they can live, but not very well.

Slouching Toward Reauthorization

"We have to remember that the goal of the reform program was not to get people out of poverty, but to achieve financial independence, to get off welfare." This statement by a senior Connecticut welfare official quoted in the *New York Times* is more candid than most. But it illustrates the kind of political rationale that policymakers use to inoculate themselves against factual evidence of the new welfare's failure to relieve poverty.

With TANF facing reauthorization in the fall of 2002, it was clear that reconsideration of welfare policy would take place on a new playing field. Tough work rules, time limits, and devolution were just the starting point. The Bush administration advanced a reauthorization plan that increased work requirements, cut opportunities for education and training, added new doses of moralism, and extended devolution.

The Republican-controlled House passed a TANF reauthorization bill (later deferred by the Senate) requiring recipients to work forty hours a week and demanding that states enforce these requirements for 70 percent of families receiving welfare by 2007. The bill also created incentives for states to require work within a month of granting welfare benefits and continued to credit states for caseload reductions, regardless of whether families losing welfare had jobs that could sustain them.

Families would face harsh new penalties, simply for running afoul of administrative rules. The House-passed measure required states to impose full family sanctions if caseworkers find a recipient in violation of those rules for sixty days. This makes entire families vulnerable to losing aid if a parent misses a couple of appointments or gets tangled in demands to supply documents verifying eligibility, just the type of problem that crops up routinely in states with complicated rules and outdated record-keeping systems.

One of the least mentioned but most dangerous features of the House bill was a "superwaiver" that would allow the executive branch to release states from social welfare obligations contained in more than a dozen federal poverty programs, including not only TANF, but also food stamps and Medicaid. This stealth provision would allow the Bush administration to override existing legislation by fiat. The nominal justification for the superwaiver is that it would ease the path of state innovation and experimentation. It would also ease the path for state cuts in social programs beyond all previous experience.

A more visibly contentious feature of the House bill was a provision to spend $300 million dollars per year on programs to induce welfare recipients to marry. This provision is one of the favorites of the religious right, along with the administration's funding for faith-based social services. These moral redemption provisions may be more important for what they signify to the Republican Party's conservative base than for what they do, as many states have resisted these types of things in the past. However, on this point, it is irresistible to quote America's favorite president, the fictional President Josiah Bartlet of the television series *West Wing*, who quipped: "When did the government get into the yenta business?"

Of Poverty, Democracy, and Welfare

The demise of the old welfare marked more than an end to a policy that many believed had outlived its usefulness. It also marked the end of welfare *politics* as we knew it. In the tepid debate over reauthorization in the fall of 2002, the bitter conflicts of earlier years over government's role in addressing poverty were replaced by half-hearted tinkering. Even provisions with the potential to induce hand-to-hand combat—such as those on marriage or the superwaiver—elicited relatively low-intensity challenges.

Is this because the new welfare yielded the benefits that liberals had hoped for, removing a contentious issue from the table and conferring legitimation on the poor, not as recipients, but as workers? Did it satisfy conservatives by clearing caseloads and demanding work? That does not seem to be the case.

If the poor have benefited from a new legitimacy, it is hard to see the rewards. Congress has not rushed to offer extensive new work supports. In fact, the House bill contained $8 to $10 billion less for work supports than the Congressional Budget Office estimated would be needed. In 2002, Congress couldn't even agree to extend unemployment insurance for those outside the welfare system who were felled by recession, corporate collapses, and the high-tech slide. While conservatives celebrated the caseload count, they also savored the opportunity to raise the ante with more onerous work requirements and marriage inducements, and even made a bid to eliminate other social protections through the superwaiver.

In the aftermath of the November 2002 election, a conservative consolidation of power was in the air. In a televised interview with Jim Lehrer, Republican spokesman Grover Norquist dared Democrats to take on the welfare issue. "If the Democrats want to stand up against welfare reform, let them! Two years from now, they'll be in even worse shape in the Senate elections."

Some congressional Democrats did take tentative steps against the tide, suggesting provisions that would fund new welfare-to-work services, provide additional job subsidies, increase the child care allotment, provide alternatives to work for recipients categorized as having work "barriers," and restore benefits to legal immigrants who were cut from welfare in 1996. Maryland Representative Benjamin Cardin was chief sponsor of a bill suggesting that states should be held accountable, not only for caseload reduction, but for poverty reduction. This notion had little traction in the 107th Congress and is likely to have even less in the next. Without the foundation of a politics of poverty to build on, such laudable ideas seem strangely irrelevant, even to the Democrats' agenda.

If welfare is a bellwether of broader political developments, there's little mistaking which way the wind is blowing. It has a decidedly Dickensian chill. The politics of poverty that gave birth to the old welfare has been supplanted by the politics of personal piety that gave birth to the new. This reflects a convergence between a neoliberal agenda of market dominance and a neoconservative agenda of middle-class moralism. In this reconfigured politics, personal responsibility is code for enforcement of the market. The new Calvinism advanced by welfare policy treats inequality as a natural consequence of personal behavior and attitude in an impartial marketplace. It is consistent with a shift in the role of the state from defender of the vulnerable and buffer against the market to one of protector-in-chief of both market and morals. This shift does not favor a small state, but a different state, one capable of enforcing market demands on workers, responding to corporate demands for capital (through public subsidies, bailouts, and tax breaks), and, perhaps more symbolically, regulating morality.

Welfare policy neither created, nor could prevent, these developments. Nor is it a foregone conclusion that government will shirk its social responsibilities. After all, America's growing economic inequality is fundamentally at odds with its commitment to political equality.

In contrast to the United States, the policies of Western European countries suggest that there need not be an absolute conflict between the welfare state and the market. Despite their allegiance to the latter, other nations continue to offer greater social protection to their citizens and worry about the democratic consequences of excluding the disadvantaged from the economy and the polity. U.S. policymakers need to move past stale debates pitting work against welfare and the poor against the nonpoor, if they are to advance policies that promote both social inclusion and economic opportunity.

Welfare, though small in scope, is large in relevance because it is a place where economic, social, and political issues converge. The old welfare acknowledged, in principle, a political commitment to relieve poverty and lessen inequality, even if, in practice, that commitment was limited, benefits were ungenerous, and access uneven. The new welfare dramatically changed the terms of the relationship between disadvantaged citizens and their state. It devolved choices about social protection from the State to the states, and it placed the value of work over the values of family well-being and social equity. As bad as the old welfare may have been, there is reason to lament its demise after all.

Notes

1. The discussion in this section draws, in part, on research conducted for the Project on the Public Economy of Work at the University of Chicago, supported by the Ford Foundation, the National Science Foundation, and the Open Society Institute. The author and Susan Lambert are co-directors.

2. The Hotline is a collaborative effort of the Legal Assistance Foundation of Chicago and community antipoverty advocates.

EVELYN Z. BRODKIN is associate professor at the School of Social Service Administration and lecturer in the Law School of the University of Chicago. She writes widely on poverty and politics.

What's At Stake

In the competitive world of college admissions, 'fairness' is often in the eye of the beholder. Here are the facts about affirmative action.

BY BARBARA KANTROWITZ AND PAT WINGERT

IN 1978, THE SUPREME COURT opened the doors of America's elite campuses to a generation of minority students when it ruled that universities' admissions policies could take applicants' race into account. But the decision, by a narrowly divided court drawing a hairsplitting distinction between race as a "plus factor" (allowed) and numerical quotas (forbidden), did not end an often bitter and emotional debate. A quarter of a century after the ruling in *Regents of the University of California v. Bakke*, affirmative action is still being challenged by disappointed applicants to selective colleges and graduate schools, and still hotly defended by civil-rights groups. Now that two such cases, both involving the University of Michigan, have reached the Supreme Court, the issue can no longer be evaded: when, if ever, should schools give preferential treatment to minorities, based solely on their race?

4.3%
THE PERCENTAGE OF BLACK PLAYERS ON THE UNIVERSITY OF MICHIGAN FOOTBALL TEAM, 1941

45%
THE PERCENTAGE OF BLACK PLAYERS ON THE UNIVERSITY OF MICHIGAN FOOTBALL TEAM, 2002

7%
THE PERCENTAGE OF YALE UNIVERSITY STUDENTS WHOM ARE BLACK

It's a measure of how far we've come that the desirability of improving opportunities for black and Hispanic students is a given in the debate. But the fundamental question of where "fairness" lies hasn't changed, and the competition keeps growing. Each year, more students apply to the top universities, which by and large have not increased the sizes of their classes in the past 50 years. The court will have to decide who deserves first crack at those scarce resources. (Right now, about one sixth of blacks get college degrees, compared with 30 percent of whites and 40 percent of Asians.) And if the court allows affirmative action to continue in some form, it will only set the stage for future debate over even more perplexing questions. Do all minorities deserve an edge or just those from disadvantaged backgrounds? What about white students from poor families? And how do you balance the academic records of students from the suburbs and the inner cities? As the controversy heats up, here's a 10-step guide to sorting out the issues at stake:

1 What is affirmative action?

When President Kennedy first used the term in the early 1960s, "affirmative action" simply meant taking extra measures to ensure integration in federally funded jobs. Forty years later, a wide range of programs fall under this rubric, although all are meant to encourage enrollment of underrepresented minorities—generally blacks, Hispanics and Native Americans. Schools vary in how much weight they assign to the student's race. For some, it's a decisive consideration; for others, it's jut one among a number of factors such as test scores, grades, family background, talents and extracurricular activities. After the *Bakke* decision emphasized the importance of campus diversity as a "compelling" benefit to society, colleges quickly responded with efforts not just to attract minorities but to create a broader geographic and socioeconomic mix, along with a range of academic, athletic or artistic talent.

In 2003, the debate over the merits of affirmative action essentially boils down to questions of fairness for both black and white applicants. Critics say it results in "reverse discrimination" against white applicants who are passed over in favor of less well-qualified black students, some of whom suffer when they attend schools they're not prepared for. But Gary Orfield, director of Harvard University's Civil Rights Project, argues that emphasizing diversity has not meant admitting unqualified students. "I have been on the admissions committees of five different

Diversity Is Essential...
He knew he was in for a fight. But it's a battle the former University of Michigan president believes must be won.

BY LEE C. BOLLINGER

When I became president of the University of Michigan in 1997, affirmative action in higher education was under siege from the right. Buoyed by a successful lawsuit against the University of Texas Law School's admissions policy and by ballot initiatives such as California's Proposition 209, which outlawed race as a factor in college admissions, the opponents set their sights on affirmative-action programs at colleges across the country.

The rumor that Michigan would be the next target in this campaign turned out to be correct. I believed strongly that we had no choice but to mount the best legal defense ever for diversity in higher education and take special efforts to explain this complex issue, in simple and direct language, to the American public. There are many misperceptions about how race and ethnicity are considered in college admissions. Competitive colleges and universities are always looking for a mix of students with different experiences and backgrounds—academic, geographic, international, socioeconomic, athletic, public-service oriented and, yes, racial and ethnic.

It is true that in sorting the initial rush of applications, large universities will give "points" for various factors in the selection process in order to ensure fairness as various officers review applicants. Opponents of Michigan's undergraduate system complain that an applicant is assigned more points for being black, Hispanic or Native American than for having a perfect SAT score. This is true, but it trivializes the real issue: whether, in principle, race and ethnicity are appropriate considerations.

The simple fact about the Michigan undergraduate policy is that it gives overwhelming weight to traditional academic factors—some 110 out of a total of 150 points. After that, there are some 40 points left for other factors, of which 20 can be allocated for race or socioeconomic status.

Race has been a defining element of the American experience. The historic *Brown v. Board of Education* decision is almost 50 years old, yet metropolitan Detroit is more segregated now than it was in 1960. The majority of students who each year arrive on a campus like Michigan's graduated from virtually all-white or all-black high schools. The campus is their first experience living in an integrated environment.

This is vital. Diversity is not merely a desirable addition to a well-rounded education. It is as essential as the study of the Middle Ages, of international politics and of Shakespeare. For our students to better understand the diverse country and world they inhabit, they must be immersed in a campus culture that allows them to study with, argue with and become friends with students who may be different from them. It broadens the mind, and the intellect—essential goals of education.

Reasonable people can disagree about affirmative action. But it is important that we do not lose the sense of history, the compassion and the largeness of vision that defined the best of the civil-rights era, which has given rise to so much of what is good about America today.

BOLLINGER is president of Columbia University.

... But Not at This Cost
Admissions policies like Michigan's focus not on who, but what, you are—perpetuating a culture of victimhood

BY ARMSTRONG WILLIAMS

Back in 1977, when I was a senior in high school, I received scholarship offers to attend prestigious colleges. The schools wanted me in part because of my good academic record—but also because affirmative action mandates required them to encourage more black students to enroll. My father wouldn't let me take any of the enticements. His reasoning was straightforward: scholarship money should go to the economically deprived. And since he could pay for my schooling, he would. In the end, I chose a historically black college—South Carolina State.

What I think my father meant, but was perhaps too stern to say, was that one should always rely on hard work and personal achievement to carry the day—every day. Sadly, this rousing point seems lost on the admissions board at the University of Michigan, which wrongly and unapologetically discriminates on the basis of skin color. The university ranks applicants on a scale that awards points for SAT scores, highschool grades and race. For example, a perfect SAT score is worth 12 points. Being black gets you 20 points. Is there anyone who can look at those two numbers and think they are fair?

Supporters maintain that the quota system is essential to creating a diverse student body. And, indeed, there is some validity to this sort of thinking. A shared history of slavery and discrimination has ingrained racial hierarchies into our national identity, divisions that need to be erased. There is, however, a very real danger that we are merely reinforcing the idea that minorities are first and foremost victims. Because of this victim status, the logic goes, they are owed special treatment. But that isn't progress, it's inertia.

If the goal of affirmative action is to create a more equitable society, it should be need-based. Instead, affirmative action is defined by its tendency to reduce people to fixed categories: at many universities, it seems, admissions officers look less at who you are than *what* you are. As a result, affirmative-action programs rarely help the least among us. Instead, they often benefit the children of middle- and upper-class black Americans who have been conditioned to feel they are owed something.

This is alarming. We have finally, after far too long, reached a point where black Americans have pushed into the mainstream—and not just in entertainment and sports. From politics to corporate finance, blacks succeed. Yet many of us still feel entitled to special benefits—in school, in jobs, in government contracts.

It is time to stop. We must reach a point where we expect to rise or fall on our own merits. We just can't continue to base opportunities on race while the needs of the poor fall by the wayside. As a child growing up on a farm, I was taught that personal responsibility was the lever that moved the world. That is why it pains me to see my peers rest their heads upon the warm pillow of victim status.

WILLIAMS is a syndicated columnist.

universities," he says, "and I have never seen a student admitted just on the basis of race. [Committees] think about what the class will be like, what kind of educational experience the class will provide." Opponents also say that with the expansion of the black middle class in the past 20 years, these programs should be refocused on kids from low-income homes. "It just doesn't make sense to give preference to the children of a wealthy black businessman, but not to the child of a Vietnamese boat person or an Arab-American who is suffering discrimination," says Curt Levey, director of legal affairs at the Center for Individual Rights, which is representing the white applicants who were turned down by the University of Michigan.

Despite the public perception that affirmative action is rampant on campuses, these programs really only affect a very small number of minority students. It's a legal issue mainly on highly selective public campuses, such as Michigan, Berkeley or Texas. Even at these schools, the actual numbers of minority students are still small—which is why supporters of affirmative action say race should still matter. Blacks account for 11 percent of undergraduates nationally; at the most elite schools the percentage is often smaller. For example, fewer than 7 percent of Harvard's current freshman class is black, compared with 12.9 percent of the overall population.

2 How did the University of Michigan become the test case?

Both sides say it was really a matter of chance more than anything else. "It's not like we studied 1,000 schools and picked them out," says Levey. To have the makings of a test case, the suit had to involve a public university whose admissions information could be obtained under the Freedom of Information Act. It also had to be a very large school that relied on some kind of numerical admissions formula—unlike the more individualized approach generally used by private colleges with large admissions staffs.

In fact, Michigan is just one of a number of public universities that have faced legal challenges in recent years. In 1996, the U.S. Court of Appeals for the Fifth Circuit banned the use of race in admissions at the University of Texas Law School. The Supreme Court declined to hear the law school's appeal, but by that time, the university had changed its admissions procedures anyway. The University of Georgia dropped race as a factor after a similar suit. But when Michigan's admissions policy came under challenge in the mid-1990s, university officials decided to fight back—all the way to the Supreme Court.

3 How does the Michigan system work?

Although President George W. Bush reduced Michigan's complex admissions process to a single sound bite—comparing the relative values given to SAT scores and race—a student's academic record is actually the most important factor. For undergraduate applicants, decisions are made on a point system. Out of a total of 150 possible points, a student can get up to 110 for academics. That includes a

possible 80 points for grades and 12 points for standardized test scores. Admissions counselors then add or subtract points for the rigor of the high school (up to 10) and the difficulty of the curriculum (up to 8 for students who take the toughest courses). Applicants can get up to 40 more points for such factors as residency in underrepresented states (2 points) or Michigan residency (10 points, with a 6-point bonus for living in an underrepresented county). Being from an underrepresented minority group or from a predominantly minority high school is worth 20 points. So is being from a low-income family—even for white students. The same 20 points are awarded to athletes. Students also earn points for being related to an alumnus (up to 4 points), writing a good personal essay (up to 3 points) and participating in extracurricular activities (up to 5 points). Admissions officials say the scale is only a guide; there's no target number that automatically determines whether a student is admitted or rejected. Michigan also has a "rolling" admissions policy, which means that students hear a few months after they apply. The number of spaces available depends on when in this cycle a student applies.

At the law school, there's no point system, but the admissions officers say higher grades and standardized test scores do increase an applicant's chances. Those factors are considered along with the rigor of an applicant's courses, recommendations and essays. The school also says that race "sometimes makes the difference in whether or not a student is admitted."

4 Does the Michigan system create quotas?

This is an issue the court will probably have to decide. Awarding points could amount to a quota if it resulted in routinely filling a fixed number of places. Levey claims that the fact that the number of minority students admitted is relatively stable from year to year proves there is a target Michigan tries to hit. Michigan's president, Mary Sue Coleman, is adamant that that's not the case. "We do not have, and never have had, quotas or numerical targets in either the undergraduate or Law School admissions programs," she said in a statement issued after Bush's speech last week. At the law school, the most recent entering class of 352 students included 21 African-Americans, 24 Latinos and 8 Native Americans. The year before, there were 26 African-Americans, 16 Latinos and 3 Native Americans. The university says that over the past nine years, the number of blacks in the entering class has ranged from 21 to 37. On the undergraduate level, the university says that blacks generally make up between 7 and 9 percent of the entering class.

In general, few outright quota systems exist anymore. "The only legal way to have quotas today is to address a proven constitutional violation," says Orfield. "For instance, if you can prove that a police or fire department intentionally did not hire any blacks for 25 years, and you can prove discrimination, a judge can rule that there can be a quota for the next five years."

Affirmative Action, 25 Years Later

Lawsuits are prompting the Supreme Court to revisit a landmark 1978 decision in favor of race-based college admissions. Affirmative action's legacy, and its uncertain future.

SAT Scores

SAT1: 2002 NAT'L AVERAGE	
White	1060
Black	857
Hispanic	910
Asian/Pac. Islander	1070
Native American	962
SAT1: 2002 UNIV. AVERAGE	
UC Berkeley	1180–1440*
Univ. of Florida (2001)	1229
Univ. of Michigan	1180–1390*
UT Austin	1222

The Case Against Michigan

Plaintiff Barbara Grutter claims she lost her spot at Michigan Law School to less qualified minorities; 100% of blacks with Grutter's ranking were accepted the year she applied, but only 9% of whites.

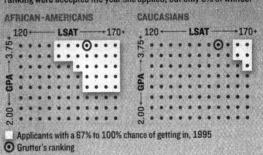

☐ Applicants with a 67% to 100% chance of getting in, 1995
⊙ Grutter's ranking

Univ. of Mich. Point System

The university uses a point scale to rate prospective students. Its policy of awarding minorities an extra 20 has stirred protest. Here's how a fictional applicant would score a promising 130:

GPA Score	Points
2.0	40
2.1	42
2.2	44
2.3	46
2.4	48
2.5	50
2.6	52
2.7	54
2.8	56
2.9	58
3.0	60
3.1	62
3.2	64
3.3	66
3.4	68
3.5	(70)
3.6	72
3.7	74
3.8	76
3.9	78
4.0	80

HIGH-SCHOOL QUALITY
Score	Points
0	0
1	2
2	4
3	(6)
4	8
5	10

DIFFICULTY OF CURRICULUM
Score	Points
-2	-4
-1	-2
0	0
1	2
2	(4)
3	6
4	8

Points (maximum of 40)
GEOGRAPHY
(10) Michigan resident
6 Underrepresented Michigan county
2 Underrepresented state

ALUMNI
4 Legacy (parents, stepparents)
1 Other (grandparents, siblings)

ESSAY
1 Very good
(2) Excellent
3 Outstanding

PERSONAL ACHIEVEMENT
1 State
(3) Regional
5 National

LEADERSHIP AND SERVICE
1 State
2 Regional
(5) National

MISCELLANEOUS (choose one)
20 Socioeconomic disadvantage
(20) Underrepresented racial/ethnic minority identification or education
5 Men in nursing
20 Scholarship athlete
20 Provost's discretion

TEST SCORES
ACT	SAT1	Points
1–19	400–920	0
20–21	930–1000	6
22–26	1010–1190	(10)
27–30	1200–1350	11
31–36	1360–1600	12

Race and Higher Education

The number of minorities attending four-year colleges has risen about 85% since the Supreme Court OK'd affirmative action in admissions.

Race/ethnicity
☒ White
■ Black
■ Hispanic
■ Asian/Pac. Islander
■ Native American
☐ Other/Did not answer

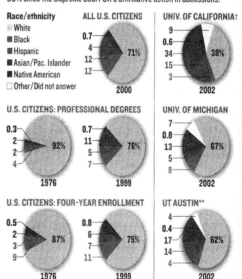

ALL RACES ARE NON-HISPANIC EXCEPT "HISPANIC." NUMBERS DO NOT ADD TO 100 DUE TO ROUNDING. "25TH TO 75TH PERCENTILES. †FRESHMAN ADMITS ONLY. **UNDERGRADUATES. SOURCES: U.S. CENSUS BUREAU, UC BERKELEY, UNIV. OF MICHIGAN, UT AUSTIN, UNIV. OF FLORIDA, THE CENTER FOR INDIVIDUAL RIGHTS, THE COLLEGE BOARD. RESEARCH AND TEXT BY JOSH ULICK. GRAPHIC BY BONNIE SCRANTON.

New Options for Diversity?

Several states have enacted the alternatives to affirmative action that Bush favors. But do they reach an equal number of minorities?

• **CALIFORNIA**: Voters passed Proposition 209 in **1996.** It bans affirmative action in university admissions. The plan promises a state-university spot for the top **4%** of students from every high school, including the most disadvantaged ones. Other factors may be involved, but Berkeley's black undergraduate enrollment has dropped **33%** from **1996** to **2001.**

• **TEXAS:** A **1997** plan ended affirmative action in admissions. High-school students in the top **10%** of their class are guaranteed slots at state schools. Since then, black enrollment has remained relatively stable at UT Austin.

• **FLORIDA:** As of **2000**, state universities no longer consider race in admissions, but promise slots for students in the top **20%** of classes.

Making the Grade
Bush wants admissions policies to look like his home state's. But in Texas, his plan gets middling marks.

BY LEIF STRICKLAND

Natalie Fogiel, an 18-year-old high-school senior in Dallas, has SAT scores higher than the Ivy League's collective average—she scored 1490 out of 1600. She's a National Merit Scholar semifinalist, and she's active in Student Congress. Fogiel doesn't want to go to Harvard or Yale. She wants to go to the business school at her state university's flagship campus, the University of Texas at Austin. But under Texas's five-year-old "affirmative access" policy—which guarantees admission to any state university for all seniors graduating in the top 10 percent of their classes—Fogiel isn't sure she'll get in. Because she goes to Highland Park High School in Dallas—one of the most competitive public schools in the country—she's only in the top 15 percent.

As the Supreme Court prepares to review the constitutionality of affirmative-action programs, President Bush has been championing programs such as Texas's, which passed when he was governor. But at some of the state's best schools, the policy has been attacked with the same words—"unfair" and "divisive"—that Bush uses to describe affirmative action. "If I had gone anywhere else, I probably would be in the top 1 percent," Fogiel says. While Texas's program prohibits using race as a factor, Texas's many segregated high schools mean the result is much the same. Since the 10 percent plan was implemented, minority enrollment at UT Austin has returned to roughly the same levels as when affirmative action was in effect.

The problem with the 10 percent policy, some Highland Park students say, is that it assumes all high schools are alike. And Highland Park High—with its 97 percent white student population—is clearly unique. Even a student who scores all A's in regular classes for four straight years wouldn't be guaranteed a place in the top quarter of his class. (You'd need to add honors classes to the mix.)

But elsewhere, the policy is playing well. Israel Hernandez is in the top 10 percent of W. H. Adamson High School, which is overwhelmingly Hispanic. He's the first member of his family to go to college; he'll be attending Texas A&M in the fall. "It's like everyone has their hopes and dreams on me," he says. Texas A&M has been to Adamson (average SAT score: 838) more than a dozen times this year touting its Century Scholars program, which specifically targets promising inner-city students like Hernandez.

Texas's plan doesn't just help traditional minorities. "The 10 percent diversifies economically," says Harvard Law professor Lani Guinier. "It benefits rural west Texas, which is primarily white but also very poor."

The policy isn't causing Highland Park students too much hardship—98 percent of its graduates went to college last year. Most of those who applied to UT and didn't get into their preferred programs were admitted to the university nonetheless—either into another school or to a provisional program. For her part, Fogiel says she probably won't go to UT if she isn't accepted to Austin's business program. She'll opt for one of her safeties: Georgetown or Boston College.

With MARK MILLER in Dallas

On campuses, some education experts say that what appear to be quotas may actually just reflect a relatively steady number of minority applicants within a certain state. "I don't know of a public or private institution that uses quotas," says Alexander Astin, director of the Higher Education Research Institute at UCLA. "That's a red herring. There is always a consideration of merit given." Nonetheless, admissions officers at public and private universities admit that they are always very conscious of demography—and work hard to make sure that the number of minority students does not decline precipitously from one year to the next.

5 How can the court rule?

The short answer is: the Supreme Court can do whatever it wants. The options range from leaving the *Bakke* decision intact to barring any use of race in college admissions. Or the court could issue a narrowly tailored opinion, one that would affect only Michigan's point system and perhaps only the number of points the university assigns to race. "I think it's a good guess that they may say that they cannot give minorities a specific number of points, or say points are fine, but they can only award 10," says Levey.

The experts agree that the key vote will belong to Justice Sandra Day O'Connor. Some court watchers predict that she will try to find a very specific solution that will leave affirmative action largely intact. "She probably won't buy anything that's open-ended," says Sheldon Steinbach, general counsel of the American Council on Education, a consortium of the nation's leading research universities. "Maybe she will say that it can be done in some narrowly defined way." Steinbach doesn't think the court will order schools to disregard everything but the supposedly objective criteria of grades and test scores. Such a ruling "would tie the hands of admissions officers from shaping the kind of class they want to fulfill the academic mission of the institution," Steinbach says. Another possibility is that the court will order schools to give preference to students who are economically disadvantaged, which would cover many minority applicants.

6 Will the decision affect private universities and colleges?

The answer really depends on what the justices rule, but legal experts generally agree that private institutions would have to follow the court's guidelines because virtually all receive some federal funding. However, the ruling would have a noticeable impact only at elite institutions since most colleges in this country accept the vast majority of applicants. And the elite schools—no more than several dozen around the country—generally employ multistep admissions procedures that leave plenty of room for subjective judgments. Unlike the numerical formulas used by large public universities, these would be difficult to challenge in court.

Already, several landmark state cases have pushed private schools to make changes. In the wake of the Texas decision, officials at highly selective Rice University in Houston, on the advice of the state attorney general, banned the use of race in all admissions decisions. Clerks were told to strip any reference to a student's race or ethnicity from admissions and financial-aid applications before they were forwarded to the admission committee. Although the proportion of minorities dropped right after the change, it's now back up to the levels before the ruling, officials say—about 7 percent black and 10.5 percent Hispanic. That was accomplished through "significant" recruiting, a Rice spokesman said.

7 How would an anti-affirmative-action ruling affect other preferences for legacies and athletes?

Some educators think legacies (the children or grandchildren of alumni) could become unintended victims of an anti-affirmative-action ruling. On the face of it, providing preferential treatment to these applicants does not violate the Constitution, but as a matter of fairness—and politics—legacies would be hard to defend, since they are usually white and middle class. However, many colleges would probably resist the change because legacies bring a sense of tradition and continuity to the school. (They also are a powerful inducement to alumni donations.) Athletic preferences are a different story. They don't disproportionately favor whites so they're probably not as vulnerable.

8 Whom does affirmative action hurt and whom does it help?

Opponents of affirmative action claim it actually hurts some minority students, particularly those who end up struggling to compete in schools they're not prepared for. And, they say, it unfairly tars well-qualified minority students with the suspicion that they were admitted because of their race. Supporters say that's a spurious argument because race may sometimes be the deciding factor between qualified applicants, but it is never the only reason a student is admitted.

The more obvious potential victims, of course, are white students who have been denied admission—like the plaintiffs in the Michigan suit. But there's no guarantee that these students would have been admitted even if there were no black applicants. In their 1998 book "The Shape of the River," William Bowen and Derek Bok (former presidents of Princeton and Harvard, respectively) analyzed the records of 45,000 students at elite uni-

versities and found that without race-sensitive admissions, white applicants' chances of being admitted to selective universities would have increased only slightly, from 25 to 26.2 percent. But Bowen and Bok also found that black applicants' chances were greatly enhanced by affirmative action, and the vast majority of black students went on to graduate within six years—even at the most selective institutions. The black graduates were more likely to go to graduate or professional school than their white counterparts and more likely to be leaders of community, social service or professional organizations after college.

Supporters of affirmative action say both white and black students benefit from living in a diverse academic environment, one that closely resembles the increasingly diverse workplace. Opponents say schools don't need affirmative action to create a diverse campus; instead they say that other admissions strategies, such as "affirmative access," can accomplish the same goals.

9 What is "affirmative access"?

In the wake of lawsuits, several states have adopted alternative ways to bring minority students to campus. Modern political marketing seems to require a label for everything, and "affirmative access" has emerged as the label for these plans. Each operates differently. In California, the top 4 percent of students at each in-state high school is guaranteed admission to the University of California (although not necessarily to the most prestigious campuses, Berkeley and UCLA). For the University of Texas, it's the top 10 percent, and in Florida, the top 20 percent. The success of these new initiatives varies. California's plan was enacted after the passage of Proposition 209, which forbids using race in admissions. In 1997, the last year before the use of race was banned, 18.8 percent of the class consisted of underrepresented minorities. Last year that number was 19.1 percent systemwide. But some individual campuses, like Berkeley and UCLA, have not returned to pre-1997 levels. At the University of Texas, the percentage of black and Hispanic entering freshmen has remained fairly steady, but officials say the 10 percent law alone isn't enough. "You have to add some targeted procedures that work in tandem with the law," says University of Texas president Larry Faulkner. "And for us that's been pretty aggressive recruiting programs aimed at top 10 percent students in areas where minority students live, and carefully tailored scholarship programs aimed at students in areas or schools that have not historically attended UT."

Opponents of affirmative access like lawyer Martin Michaelson, who specializes in higher-education cases, say these programs rest on the dubious premise that "residential segregation patterns are a better method for choosing a college class than the judgment of educators" and create, in effect, a built-in constituency for continued segregation. Critics also worry that a program that mixes schools of widely different qualities may reward less-

What Merit Really Means

JONATHAN ALTER

ANYONE WITH HALF A BRAIN KNOWS THAT GRADES AND TEST scores aren't the only way to define "merit" in college admissions. Sometimes a good jump shot or batting average is "merit." Or a commitment to a soup kitchen. Or the ability to overcome an obstacle in life. Conscientious admissions officers take a wide variety of factors into account and make rounded, subtle judgments about the composition of the incoming class. The debate over affirmative action in education boils down to whether universities should be free to make that judgment or be told by the government how to choose.

The problem with affirmative action is not, as some conservatives suggest, that it has eroded standards and dumbed down elite institutions. The level of academic achievement among freshmen at, say, Yale is far higher than it was when George W. Bush entered in 1964. With his highschool record, he probably wouldn't be admitted today, even if he were black. No, what's wrong with affirmative action is that it has too often been routinized and mechanized, and has thus begun to resemble the very thinking it was supposed to replace.

Conservatives, trying to stand on principle, argue that affirmative action is simply reverse discrimination. In certain realms, like the awarding of federal contracts, that may be true. But college is different. The college experience is partly about preparing students for adult life, which increasingly means learning to deal with people of many different backgrounds. To hear the Bill Bennetts of the world, whites and Asian-Americans rejected by the colleges of their choice are like blacks rejected by the lunch counters of their choice in the Jim Crow South. It's a lame analogy. Lunch counters (and other public facilities) have no right to discriminate; neither do nonselective colleges, about 80 percent of the total. But exclusive institutions, by definition, must exclude.

The basis on which they do so should at least be consistent. You either favor weighing immutable nonacademic "preferences" or you don't. Some conservatives want to continue preferences for alumni children and end those for minorities. Some liberals want the reverse—to keep affirmative action but end legacies. Both sides ace their hypocrisy boards. Personally, I go for preferences, within limits, because I want the smart alumni kid from Pacific Palisades to sit in the dining hall and get to know the smart poor kid from Camden. Neither the University of Michigan policy nor the Bush administration challenge to it are likely to take us closer to that end.

The larger problem is that exclusive colleges too often use that worn-out crutch of a word—"diversity"—to cover for their lack of genuine integration (in dorms, for instance), and a lack of progress on socioeconomic affirmative action. Only 3 percent of students in top universities come from the poorest quarter of the American population. A Harvard study last year found that colleges are too often "recyclers of privilege" instead of "engines of upward mobility." Harvard itself falls short on this score, with fewer than 9 percent of its students coming from families eligible for Pell grants (i.e., the modest means). Princeton and Notre Dame are among those that don't do discernibly better.

Ironically, colleges like these with nice-sounding "needs-blind admission" policies consistently admit fewer poorer kids because, as a James Irvine Foundation report discovered, "they feel like they're off the hook." They're so proud of themselves for not calculating students' ability to pay in making admissions decisions that they do less than they could to recruit poorer students—and thus fail to take enough "affirmative action" (in its original, beating-the-bushes sense) to redress socioeconomic disparities. It's easier to go with familiar, relatively affluent high schools they know will produce kids more likely to succeed.

Recently, Berkeley, UCLA and USC have done twice or three times better than every other elite school in enrolling economically disadvantaged students. Why? Because California has abolished racial preferences, which forced these schools to adopt economic affirmative action. Richard Kahlenberg of The Century Foundation says that's the only way to get more poor kids admitted. A forthcoming study from that foundation will show that substituting economic preferences for race at the top 146 schools would lessen the black and Hispanic representation only two percentage points (from 12 percent currently to 10 percent).

But I still think it makes sense to allow both class and race to be considered—and to let 1,000 other factors bloom, as good colleges do. Just don't make it mechanical. The anti-affirmative-action forces have to abandon the notion that GPAs and SATs add up to some numerical right to admission; the advocates for the status quo have to give up the numerical awarding of points for things like race, because sometimes being African American or Hispanic or Native American should be a big plus, and sometimes it shouldn't. It depends on the kid. All of which means that no matter what happens in the Supreme Court, the University of Michigan and other large schools should spend the money needed for a more subtle and subjective quest for true merit.

---

qualified students than more-traditional programs. At the University of Texas, Faulkner says no; he believes that class rank is a better predictor of collegiate success than test scores, even at high schools with large numbers of disadvantaged students. But Orfield, who is in the final stages of completing a formal study of these programs, disagrees; he says that less-qualified students are being admitted under the percentage programs. Often, Orfield says, 60 percent of kids at suburban high schools have better credentials than the top 10 percent of kids at inner-city schools (sidebar). The affirmative-access approach would also be hard to apply in nonstate colleges and graduate schools that draw students from all over the country.

Another approach would be to target students from low-income homes, regardless of race. That would eliminate the problem of giving middle-class blacks an edge. But Orfield says that being middle class does not protect black students from the effects of racism, and they are still often at a disadvantage in the admissions process. "Race still matters," he says. "It's fine with me if we apply affirmative action to poor people, but I think we need it for middle-class blacks as well."

10 So what is the most equitable way to select the best-qualified applicants?

In judging admissions policies, it's important to remember that schools aren't just looking to reward past achievement. They want to attract students who will create the richest academic and social communities, and who have the best odds of success in college and later life. As a result, admissions officers say, what they really look for are signs of intellectual energy and personal enthusiasm—qualities that can show up in grades, scores, essays, recommendations, extracurricular activities, or a mix of all these. "Merit" has become particularly difficult to define in an era when elite colleges are getting many more well-qualified applicants than they can possibly accept, and when distrust of standardized admissions tests is growing. And making hard and fast distinctions based on race isn't going to get any easier as the growing trend toward racial mixing increases over the next century and people choose to identify with more than one group. The only thing educators who have struggled with these issues agree on is that there is no magic formula, not even for the Supreme Court.

With VANESSA JUAREZ
and ANA FIGUEROA

WHY WE HATE

We may not admit it, but we are plagued with xenophobic tendencies. Our hidden prejudices run so deep, we are quick to judge, fear and even hate the unknown.

By Margo Monteith, Ph.D. and Jeffrey Winters

BALBIR SINGH SODHI WAS SHOT TO DEATH ON September 15 in Mesa, Arizona. His killer claimed to be exacting revenge for the terrorist attacks of September 11. Upon his arrest, the murderer shouted, "I stand for America all the way." Though Sodhi wore a turban and could trace his ancestry to South Asia, he shared neither ethnicity nor religion with the suicide hijackers. Sodhi—who was killed at the gas station where he worked—died just for being different in a nation gripped with fear.

For Arab and Muslim Americans, the months after the terrorist attacks have been trying. They have been harassed at work and their property has been vandalized. An Arab San Francisco shop owner recalled with anger that his five-year-old daughter was taunted by name-callers. Classmates would yell "terrorist" as she walked by.

Public leaders from President George W. Bush on down have called for tolerance. But the Center for American-Islamic Relations in Washington, D.C., has tallied some 1,700 incidents of abuse against Muslims in the five months following September 11. Despite our better nature, it seems, fear of foreigners or other strange-seeming people comes out when we are under stress. That fear, known as xenophobia, seems almost hardwired into the human psyche.

Researchers are discovering the extent to which xenophobia can be easily—even arbitrarily—turned on. In just hours, we can be conditioned to fear or discriminate against those who differ from ourselves by characteristics as superficial as eye color. Even ideas we believe are just common sense can have deep xenophobic underpinnings. Research conducted this winter at Harvard reveals that even among people who claim to have no bias, the more strongly one supports the ethnic profiling of Arabs

at airport-security checkpoints, the more hidden prejudice one has against Muslims.

But other research shows that when it comes to whom we fear and how we react, we do have a choice. We can, it seems, choose not to give in to our xenophobic tendencies.

THE MELTING POT

America prides itself on being a melting pot of cultures, but how we react to newcomers is often at odds with that self-image. A few years ago, psychologist Markus Kemmelmeier, Ph.D., now at the University of Nevada at Reno, stuck stamped letters under the windshield wipers of parked cars in a suburb of Detroit. Half were addressed to a fictitious Christian organization, half to a made-up Muslim group. Of all the letters, half had little stickers of the American flag.

Would the addresses and stickers affect the rate at which the letters would be mailed? Kemmelmeier wondered. Without the flag stickers, both sets of letters were mailed at the same rate, about 75 percent of the time. With the stickers, however, the rates changed: Almost all the Christian letters were forwarded, but only half of the Muslim letters were mailed. "The flag is seen as a sacred object," Kemmelmeier says. "And it made people think about what it means to be a good American."

In short, the Muslims didn't make the cut.

Not mailing a letter seems like a small slight. Yet in the last century, there have been shocking examples of xenophobia in our own back yard. Perhaps the most famous in American history was the fear of the Japanese during World War II. This particular wave of hysteria lead to the rise of slurs and bigoted depictions in the media, and more alarmingly, the mass internment of 120,000 people of Japanese ancestry beginning in 1942. The internments have become a national embarrassment: Most of the Japanese held were American citizens, and there is little evidence that the imprisonments had any real strategic impact.

Today the targets of xenophobia—derived from the Greek word for *stranger*—aren't the Japanese. Instead, they are Muslim immigrants. Or Mexicans. Or Chinese. Or whichever group we have come to fear.

Just how arbitrary are these xenophobic feelings? Two famous public-school experiments show how easy it is to turn one "group" against another. In the late 1960s, California high school history teacher Ron Jones recruited students to participate in an exclusive new cultural program called "the Wave." Within weeks, these students were separating themselves from others and aggressively intimidating critics. Eventually, Jones confronted the students with the reality that they were unwitting participants in an experiment demonstrating the power of nationalist movements.

Sonam Wangmo:
"Am I fearful of Arab men in turbans? No, I am not. I was born and raised in India, and I am familiar with other races. I have learned to be attuned to different cultures. I find that there are always new, positive things to be learned from other people; it brings out the best in us."

A few years later, a teacher in Iowa discovered how quickly group distinctions are made. The teacher, Jane Elliott, divided her class into two groups—those with blue eyes and those with brown or green eyes. The brown-eyed group received privileges and treats, while the blue-eyed students were denied rewards and told they were inferior. Within hours, the once-harmonious classroom became two camps, full of mutual fear and resentment. Yet, what is especially shocking is that the students were only in the third grade.

SOCIAL IDENTITY

The drive to completely and quickly divide the world into "us" and "them" is so powerful that it must surely come from some deep-seated need. The exact identity of that need, however, has been subject to debate. In the 1970s, the late Henri Tajfel, Ph.D., of the University of Bristol in England, and John Turner, Ph.D., now of the Australian National University, devised a theory to explain the psy-

chology behind a range of prejudices and biases, not just xenophobia. Their theory was based, in part, on the desire to think highly of oneself. One way to lift your self-esteem is to be part of a distinctive group, like a winning team; another is to play up the qualities of your own group and denigrate the attributes of others so that you feel your group is better.

Terry Kalish:
"I am planning a trip to Florida, and I'm nervous about flying with my kids; I'm scared. If an Arab man sat next to me, I would feel nervous. I would wonder, 'Does he have explosives?' But then I feel ashamed to think this way. These poor people must get so scrutinized. It's wrong."

Tajfel and Turner called their insight "social identity theory," which has proved valuable for understanding how prejudices develop. Given even the slenderest of criteria, we naturally split people into two groups—an "in-group" and an "out-group." The categories can be of geopolitical importance—nationality, religion, race, language—or they can be as seemingly inconsequential as handedness, hair color or even height.

Once the division is made, the inferences and projections begin to occur. For one, we tend to think more highly of people in the in-group than those in the out-group, a belief based only on group identity. Also, a person tends to feel that others in the in-group are similar to one's self in ways that—although stereotypical—may have little to do with the original criteria used to split the groups. Someone with glasses may believe that other people who wear glasses are more voracious readers—even more intelligent—than those who don't, in spite of the fact that all he really knows is that they don't see very well. On the other hand, people in the out-group are believed to be less distinct and less complex than are cohorts in the in-group.

Although Tajfel and Turner found that identity and categorization were the root cause of social bias, other researchers have tried to find evolutionary explanations for discrimination. After all, in the distant past, people who shared cultural similarities were found to be more genetically related than those who did not. Therefore, favoring the in-group was a way of helping perpetuate one's genes. Evolutionary explanations seem appealing, since they rely on the simplest biological urges to drive complicated behavior. But this fact also makes them hard to prove. Ironically, there is ample evidence backing up the "softer" science behind social identity theory.

HIDDEN BIAS

Not many of us will admit to having strong racist or xenophobic biases. Even in cases where bias becomes public debate—such as the profiling of Arab Muslims at airport-security screenings—proponents of prejudice claim that they are merely promoting common sense. That reluctance to admit to bias makes the issue tricky to study.

To get around this problem, psychologists Anthony Greenwald, Ph.D., of the University of Washington in Seattle, and Mahzarin Banaji, Ph.D., of Harvard, developed the Implicit Association Test. The IAT is a simple test that measures reaction time: The subject sees various words or images projected on a screen, then classifies the images into one of two groups by pressing buttons. The words and images need not be racial or ethnic in nature—one group of researchers tested attitudes toward presidential candidates. The string of images is interspersed with words having either pleasant or unpleasant connotations, then the participant must group the words and images in various ways—Democrats are placed with unpleasant words, for instance.

Rangr:

"For the months following 9/11, I had to endure my daily walk to work along New York City's Sixth Avenue. It seemed that half the people stared at me with accusation. It became unbearable. Yet others showed tremendous empathy. Friends, co-workers and neighbors, even people I had never met, stopped to say, 'I hope your turban has not caused you any trouble.' At heart, this is a great country."

The differences in reaction time are small but telling. Again and again, researchers found that subjects readily tie in-group images with pleasant words and out-group images with unpleasant words. One study compares such groups as whites and blacks, Jews and Christians, and young people and old people. And researchers found that if you identify yourself in one group, it's easier to pair images of that group with pleasant words—and easier to pair the opposite group with unpleasant imagery. This reveals the underlying biases and enables us to study how quickly they can form.

Really though, we need to know very little about a person to discriminate against him. One of the authors of this story, psychologist Margo Monteith, Ph.D., performed an IAT experiment comparing attitudes toward two sets of made-up names; one set was supposedly "American,"

the other from the fictitious country of Marisat. Even though the subjects knew nothing about Marisat, they showed a consistent bias against it.

While this type of research may seem out in left field, other work may have more "real-world" applications. The Southern Poverty Law Center runs a Web version of the IAT that measures biases based on race, age and gender. Its survey has, for instance, found that respondents are far more likely to associate European faces, rather than Asian faces, with so-called American images. The implication being that Asians are seen as less "American" than Caucasians.

Similarly, Harvard's Banaji has studied the attitudes of people who favor the racial profiling of Arab Muslims to deter terrorism, and her results run contrary to the belief that such profiling is not driven by xenophobic fears. "We show that those who endorse racial profiling also score high on both explicit and implicit measures of prejudice toward Arab Muslims," Banaji says. "Endorsement of profiling is an indicator of level of prejudice."

BEYOND XENOPHOBIA

If categorization and bias come so easily, are people doomed to xenophobia and racism? It's pretty clear that we are susceptible to prejudice and that there is an unconscious desire to divide the world into "us" and "them." Fortunately, however, new research also shows that prejudices are fluid and that when we become conscious of our biases we can take active—and successful—steps to combat them.

Researchers have long known that when observing racially mixed groups, people are more likely to confuse the identity of two black individuals or two white ones, rather than a white with a black. But Leda Cosmides, Ph.D., and John Tooby, Ph.D., of the Center for Evolutionary Psychology at the University of California at Santa Barbara, and anthropologist Robert Kurzban, Ph.D., of the University of California at Los Angeles, wanted to test whether this was innate or whether it was just an artifact of how society groups individuals by race.

To do this, Cosmides and her colleagues made a video of two racially integrated basketball teams locked in conversation, then they showed it to study participants. As reported in the *Proceedings of the National Academy of Sciences*, the researchers discovered that subjects were more likely to confuse two players on the same team, regardless of race, rather than two players of the same race on opposite teams.

Cosmides says that this points to one way of attacking racism and xenophobia: changing the way society imposes group labels. American society divides people by race and by ethnicity; that's how lines of prejudice form. But simple steps, such as integrating the basketball teams, can reset mental divisions, rendering race and ethnicity less important.

This finding supports earlier research by psychologists Samuel Gaertner, Ph.D., of the University of Delaware in Newark, and John Dovidio, Ph.D., of Colgate University in Hamilton, New York. Gaertner and Dovidio have studied how bias changes when members of racially mixed groups must cooperate to accomplish shared goals. In situations where team members had to work together, bias could be reduced by significant amounts.

Monteith has also found that people who are concerned about their prejudices have the power to correct them. In experiments, she told subjects that they had performed poorly on tests that measured belief in stereotypes. She discovered that the worse a subject felt about her performance, the better she scored on subsequent tests. The guilt behind learning about their own prejudices made the subjects try harder not to be biased.

This suggests that the guilt of mistaking individuals for their group stereotype—such as falsely believing an Arab is a terrorist—can lead to the breakdown of the belief in that stereotype. Unfortunately, such stereotypes are reinforced so often that they can become ingrained. It is difficult to escape conventional wisdom and treat all people as individuals, rather than members of a group. But that seems to be the best way to avoid the trap of dividing the world in two—and discriminating against one part of humanity.

READ MORE ABOUT IT:

Nobody Left to Hate: Teaching Compassion After Columbine, Elliot Aronson (W.H. Freeman and Company, 2000)
The Racist Mind: Portraits of American Neo-Nazis and Klansmen, Madonna Kolbenschlag (Penguin Books, 1996)

Margo Monteith, Ph.D., is an associate professor of psychology at the University of Kentucky. Jeffrey Winters is a New York-based science writer.

Human Rights, Sex Trafficking, and Prostitution

by Alice Leuchtag

Despite laws against slavery in practically every country, an estimated twenty-seven million people live as slaves. Kevin Bales, in his book *Disposable People: New Slavery in the Global Economy* (University of California Press, Berkeley, 1999), describes those who endure modern forms of slavery. These include indentured servants, persons held in hereditary bondage, child slaves who pick plantation crops, child soldiers, and adults and children trafficked and sold into sex slavery.

A Life Narrative

Of all forms of slavery, sex slavery is one of the most exploitative and lucrative with some 200,000 sex slaves worldwide bringing their slaveholders an annual profit of $10.5 billion. Although the great preponderance of sex slaves are women and girls, a smaller but significant number of males—both adult and children—are enslaved for homosexual prostitution.

The life narrative of a Thai girl named Siri, as told to Bales, illustrates how sex slavery happens to vulnerable girls and women. Siri is born in northeastern Thailand to a poor family that farms a small plot of land, barely eking out a living. Economic policies of structural adjustment pursued by the Thai government under the aegis of the World Bank and the International Monetary Fund have taken former government subsidies away from rice farmers, leaving them to compete against imported, subsidized rice that keeps the market price artificially depressed.

Siri attends four years of school, then is kept at home to help care for her three younger siblings. When Siri is fourteen, a well-dressed woman visits her village. She offers to find Siri a

"good job," advancing her parents $2,000 against future earnings. This represents at least a year's income for the family. In a town in another province the woman, a trafficker, "sells" Siri to a brothel for $4,000. Owned by an "investment club" whose members are business and professional men—government bureaucrats and local politicians—the brothel is extremely profitable. In a typical thirty-day period it nets its investors $88,000.

To maintain the appearance that their hands are clean, members of the club's board of directors leave the management of the brothel to a pimp and a bookkeeper. Siri is initiated into prostitution by the pimp who rapes her. After being abused by her first "customer," Siri escapes, but a policeman—who gets a percentage of the brothel profits—brings her back, whereupon the pimp beats her up. As further punishment, her "debt" is doubled from $4,000 to $8,000. She must now repay this, along with her monthly rent and food, all from her earnings of $4 per customer. She will have to have sex with three hundred men a month just to pay her rent. Realizing she will never be able to get out of debt, Siri tries to build a relationship with the pimp simply in order to survive.

The pimp uses culture and religion to reinforce his control over Siri. He tells her she must have committed terrible sins in a past life to have been born a female; she must have accumulated a karmic debt to deserve the enslavement and abuse to which she must reconcile herself. Gradually Siri begins to see herself from the point of view of the slaveholder—as someone unworthy and deserving of punishment. By age fifteen she no longer protests or runs away. Her physical enslavement has become psychological as well, a common occurrence in chronic abuse.

Siri is administered regular injections of the contraceptive drug Depo-Provera for which she is charged. As the same needle is used for all the girls, there is a high risk of HIV and other sexual diseases from the injections. Siri knows that a serious illness threatens her and she prays to Buddha at the little shrine in her room, hoping to earn merit so he will protect her from dreaded disease. Once a month she and the others, at their own expense, are tested for HIV. So far Siri's tests have been negative. When Siri tries to get the male customers to wear condoms—distributed free to brothels by the Thai Ministry of Health—some resist wearing them and she can't make them do so.

As one of an estimated 35,000 women working as brothel slaves in Thailand—a country where 500,000 to one million prostituted women and girls work in conditions of degradation and exploitation short of brothel slavery—Siri faces at least a 40 percent chance of contracting the HIV virus. If she is lucky, she can look forward to live more years before she becomes too ill to work and is pushed out into the street.

Thailand's Sex Tourism

Though the Thai government denies it, the World Health Organization finds that HIV is epidemic in Thailand, with the largest segment of new cases among wives and girlfriends of men who buy prostitute sex. Viewing its women as a cash crop to be exploited, and depending on sex tourism for foreign exchange dollars to help pay interest on the foreign debt, the Thai government can't acknowledge the epidemic without contradicting the continued promotion of sex tourism and prostitution.

By encouraging investment in the sex industry, sex tourism creates a business climate conducive to the trafficking and enslavement of vulnerable girls such as Siri. In 1996 nearly five million sex tourists from the United States, Western Europe, Australia, and Japan visited Thailand. These transactions brought in about $26.2 billion—thirteen times more than Thailand earned by building and exporting computers.

In her 1999 report *Pimps and Predators on the Internet: Globalizing the Sexual Exploitation of Women and Children,* published by the Coalition Against Trafficking in Women (CATW), Donna Hughes quotes from postings on an Internet site where sex tourists share experiences and advise one another. The following is one man's description of having sex with a fourteen-year-old prostituted girl in Bangkok:

> "Even though I've had a lot of better massages… after fifteen minutes, I was much more relaxed… Then I asked for a condom and I fucked her for another thirty minutes. Her face looked like she was feeling a lot of pain.… She blocked my way when I wanted to leave the room and she asked for a tip. I gave her 600 bath. Altogether, not a good experience."

Hughes says, "To the men who buy sex, a 'bad experience' evidently means not getting their money's worth, or that the prostituted woman or girl didn't keep up the act of enjoying

what she had to do… one glimpses the humiliation and physical pain most girls and women in prostitution endure."

Nor are the men oblivious to the existence of sexual slavery. One customer states, "Girls in Bangkok virtually get sold by their families into the industry; they work against their will." His knowledge of their sexual slavery and lack of sensitivity thereof is evident in that he then names the hotels in which girls are kept and describes how much they cost!

As Hughes observes, sex tourists apparently feel they have a right to prostitute sex, perceiving prostitution only from a self-interested perspective in which they commodify and objectify women of other cultures, nationalities, and ethnic groups. Their awareness of racism, colonialism, global economic inequalities, and sexism seems limited to the way these realities benefit them as sex consumers.

Sex Traffickers Cast Their Nets

According to the *Guide to the New UN Trafficking Protocol* by Janice Raymond, published by the CATW in 2001, the United Nations estimates that sex trafficking in human beings is a $5 billion to $7 billion operation annually. Four million persons are moved illegally from one country to another and within countries each year, a large proportion of them women and girls being trafficked into prostitution. The United Nations International Children's Emergency Fund (UNICEF) estimates that some 30 percent of women being trafficked are minors, many under age thirteen. The International Organization on Migration estimates that some 500,000 women per year are trafficked into Western Europe from poorer regions of the world. According to *Sex Trafficking of Women in the United States: International and Domestic Trends,* also published by the CATW in 2001, some 50,000 women and children are trafficked into the United States each year, mainly from Asia and Latin America.

Because prostitution as a system of organized sexual exploitation depends on a continuous supply of new "recruits," trafficking is essential to its continued existence. When the pool of available women and girls dries up, new women must be procured. Traffickers cast their nets ever wide and become ever more sophisticated. The Italian Camorra, Chinese Triads, Russian Mafia, and Japanese Yakuza are powerful criminal syndicates consisting of traffickers, pimps, brothel keepers, forced labor lords, and gangs which operate globally.

After the breakdown of the Soviet Union, an estimated five thousand criminal groups formed the Russian Mafia, which operates in thirty countries. The Russian Mafia traffics women from African countries, the Ukraine, the Russian Federation, and Eastern Europe into Western Europe, the United States, and Israel. The Triads traffic women from China, Korea, Thailand, and other Southeast Asian countries into the United States and Europe. The Camorra traffics women from Latin America into Europe. The Yakuza traffics women from the Philipines, Thailand, Burma, Cambodia, Korea, Nepal, and Laos into Japan.

A Global Problem Meets a Global Response

Despite these appalling facts, until recently no generally agreed upon definition of trafficking in human beings was written into international law. In Vienna, Austria, during 1999 and 2000, 120 countries participated in debates over a definition of trafficking. A few nongovernmental organizations (NGOs) and a minority of governments—including Australia, Canada, Denmark, Germany, Ireland, Japan, the Netherlands, Spain, Switzerland, Thailand, and the United Kingdom—wanted to separate issues of trafficking from issues of prostitution. They argued that persons being trafficked should be divided into those who are forced and those who give their consent, with the burden of proof being placed on persons being trafficked. They also urged that the less explicit means of control over trafficked persons—such as abuse of a victim's vulnerability—not be included in the definition of trafficking and that the word *exploitation* not be used. Generally supporters of this position were wealthier countries where large numbers of women were being trafficked and countries in which prostitution was legalized or sex tourism encouraged.

People being trafficked shouldn't be divided into those who are forced and those who give their consent because trafficked persons are in no position to give meaningful consent.

The CATW—140 other NGOs that make up the International Human Rights Network plus many governments (including those of Algeria, Bangladesh, Belgium, China, Columbia, Cuba, Egypt, Finland, France, India, Mexico, Norway, Pakistan, the Philippines, Sweden, Syria, Venezuela, and Vietnam)—maintains that trafficking can't be separated from prostitution. Persons being trafficked shouldn't be divided into those who are forced and those who give their consent because trafficked persons are in no position to give meaningful consent. The subtler methods used by traffickers, such as abuse of a victim's vulnerability, should be included in the definition of trafficking and the word *exploitation* be an essential part of the definition. Generally supporters of this majority view were poorer countries from which large numbers of women were being trafficked or countries in which strong feminist, anti-colonialist, or socialist influences existed. The United States, though initially critical of the majority position, agreed to support a definition of trafficking that would be agreed upon by consensus.

The struggle—led by the CATW to create a definition of trafficking that would penalize traffickers while ensuring that all victims of trafficking would be protected—succeeded when a compromise proposal by Sweden was agreed to. A strongly worded and inclusive *UN Protocol to Prevent, Suppress, and Punish Trafficking in Persons*—especially women and children—was drafted by an ad hoc committee of the UN as a supplement to the Convention Against Transnational Organized Crime. The UN protocol specifically addresses the trade in human beings for purposes of prostitution and other forms of sexual exploitation, forced labor or services, slavery or practices similar to slavery, servitude, and the removal of organs. The protocol defines trafficking as:

> The recruitment, transportation, transfer, harboring or receipt of persons, by means of the threat or use of force or other forms of coercion, of abduction, of fraud, of deception, of the abuse of power or of a position of vulnerability or of the giving or receiving of payments or benefits to achieve the consent of a person having control over another person, for the purpose of exploitation.

While recognizing that the largest amount of trafficking involves women and children, the wording of the UN protocol clearly is gender and age neutral, inclusive of trafficking in both males and females, adults and children.

In 2000 the UN General Assembly adopted this convention and its supplementary protocol; 121 countries signed the convention and eighty countries signed the protocol. For the convention and protocol to become international law, forty countries must ratify them.

Highlights

Some highlights of the new convention and protocol are:

For the first time there is an accepted international definition of trafficking and an agreed-upon set of prosecution, protection, and prevention mechanisms on which countries can base their national legislation.

- The various criminal means by which trafficking takes place, including indirect and subtle forms of coercion, are covered.
- Trafficked persons, especially women in prostitution and child laborers, are no longer viewed as illegal migrants but as victims of a crime.

For the first time there is an accepted international definition of trafficking and an agreed-upon set of prosecution, protection, and prevention mechanisms on which countries can base their national legislation.

- The convention doesn't limit its scope to criminal syndicates but defines an organized criminal group as "any structured group of three or more persons which engages in criminal activities such as trafficking and pimping."

- All victims of trafficking in persons are protected, not just those who can prove that force was used against them.
- The consent of a victim of trafficking is meaningless and irrelevant.
- Victims of trafficking won't have to bear the burden of proof.
- Trafficking and sexual exploitation are intrinsically connected and not to be separated.
- Because women trafficked domestically into local sex industries suffer harmful effects similar to those experienced by women trafficked transnationally, these women also come under the protections of the protocol.
- The key element in trafficking is the exploitative purpose rather than the movement across a border.

The protocol is the first UN instrument to address the demand for prostitution sex, a demand that results in the human rights abuses of women and children being trafficked. The protocol recognizes an urgent need for governments to put the buyers of prostitution sex on their policy and legislative agendas, and it calls upon countries to take or strengthen legislative or other measures to discourage demand, which fosters all the forms of sexual exploitation of women and children.

As Raymond says in the *Guide to the New UN Trafficking Protocol*:

"The least discussed part of the prostitution and trafficking chain has been the men who buy women for sexual exploitation in prostitution.... If we are to find a permanent path to ending these human rights abuses, then we cannot just shrug our shoulders and say, "men are like this," or "boys will be boys," or "prostitution has always been around." Or tell women and girls in prostitution that they must continue to do what they do because prostitution is inevitable. Rather, our responsibility is to make men change their behavior, by all means available—educational, cultural and legal."

Two U.S. feminist, human rights organizations—Captive Daughters and Equality Now—have been working toward that goal. Surita Sandosham of Equality Now says that when her organization asked women's groups in Thailand and the Philippines how it could assist them, the answer came back, "Do something about the demand." Since then the two organizations have legally challenged sex tours originating in the United States and have succeeded in closing down at least one operation.

Refugees, Not Illegal Aliens

In October 2000 the U.S. Congress passed a bill, the Victims of Trafficking and Violence Protection Act of 2000, introduced by New Jersey republican representative Chris Smith. Under this law penalties for traffickers are raised and protections for victims increased. Reasoning that desperate women are unable to give meaningful consent to their own sexual exploitation, the law adopts a broad definition of sex trafficking so as not to exclude so-called consensual prostitution or trafficking that occurs solely within the United States. In these respects the new federal law conforms to the UN protocol.

Two features of the law are particularly noteworthy:

- In order to pressure other countries to end sex trafficking, the U.S. State Department is to make a yearly assessment of other countries' anti-trafficking efforts and to rank them according to how well they discourage trafficking. After two years of failing to meet even minimal standards, countries are subject to sanctions, although not sanctions on humanitarian aid. "Tier 3" countries—those failing to meet even minimal standards—include Greece, Indonesia, Israel, Pakistan, Russia, Saudi Arabia, South Korea, and Thailand.
- Among persons being trafficked into the United States, special T-visas will be provided to those who meet the criteria for having suffered the most serious trafficking abuses. These visas will protect them from deportation so they can testify against their traffickers. T-non immigrant status allows eligible aliens to remain in the United States temporarily and grants specific non-immigrant benefits. Those acquiring T-1 non-immigrant status will be able to remain for a period of three years and will be eligible to receive certain kinds of public assistance—to the same extent as refugees. They will also be issued employment authorization to "assist them in finding safe, legal employment while they attempt to retake control of their lives."

A Debate Rages

A worldwide debate rages about legalization of prostitution fueled by a 1998 International Labor Organization (ILO) report entitled *The Sex Sector: The Economic and Social Bases of Prostitution in Southeast Asia.* The report follows years of lobbying by the sex industry for recognition of prostitution as "sex work." Citing the sex industry's unrecognized contribution to the gross domestic product of four countries in Southeast Asia, the ILO urges governments to officially recognize the "sex sector" and "extend taxation nets to cover many of the lucrative activities connected with it." Though the ILO report says it stops short of calling for legalization of prostitution, official recognition of the sex industry would be impossible without it.

Raymond points out that the ILO's push to redefine prostitution as sex work ignores legislation demonstrating that countries can reduce organized sexual exploitation rather than capitulate to it. For example, Sweden prohibits the purchase of sexual services with punishments of still fines or imprisonment, thus declaring that prostitution isn't a desirable economic and labor sector. The government also helps women getting out of prostitution to rebuild their lives. Venezuela's Ministry of Labor has ruled that prostitution can't be considered work because it lacks the basic elements of dignity and social justice. The Socialist Republic of Vietnam punishes pimps, traffickers, brothel owners, and buyers—sometimes publishing buyer's names in the mass media. For women in prostitution, the government finances medical, educational, and economic rehabilitation.

Instead of transforming the male buyer into a legitmate customer, the ILO should give thought to innovative programs that make the buyer accountable for his sexual exploitation.

Raymond suggests that instead of transforming the male buyer into a legitimate customer, the ILO should give thought to innovative programs that make the buyer accountable for his sexual exploitation. She cites the Sage Project, Inc. (SAGE) program in San Francisco, California, which educates men arrested for soliciting women in prostitution about the risks and impacts of their behavior.

Legalization advocates argue that the violence, exploitation, and health effects suffered by women in prostitution aren't inherent to prostitution but simply result from the random behaviors of bad pimps or buyers, and that if prostitution were regulated by the state these harms would diminish. But examples show these arguments to be false.

Prostituted women are even more marginalized and tightly locked into the system of organized sexual exploitation while the state, now an official party to the exploitation, has become the biggest pimp of all.

In the pamphlet entitled *Legalizing Prostitution Is Not the Answer: The Example of Victoria, Australia,* published by the CATW in 2001, Mary Sullivan and Sheila Jeffreys describe the way legalization in Australia has perpetuated and strengthened the culture of violence and exploitation inherent in prostitution. Under legalization, legal and illegal brothels have proliferated, and trafficking in women has accelerated to meet the increased demand. Pimps, having even more power, continue threatening and brutalizing the women they control. Buyers continue to abuse women, refuse to wear condoms, and spread the HIV virus—and other sexually transmitted diseases—to their wives and girlfriends. Stigmatized by identity cards and medial inspections, prostituted women are even more marginalized and tightly locked into the system of organized sexual exploitation while the state, now an official party to the exploitation, has become the biggest pimp of all.

The government of the Netherlands has legalized prostitution, doesn't enforce laws against pimping, and virtually lives off taxes from the earnings of prostituted women. In the book *Making the Harm Visible* (published by the CATW in 1999), Marie-Victoire Louis describes the effects on prostituted women of municipal regulation of brothels in Amsterdam and other Dutch cities. Her article entitled "Legalizing Pimping, Dutch Style" explains the way immigration policies in the Netherlands are shaped to fit the needs of the prostitution industry so that traffickers are seldom prosecuted and a continuous supply of women is guaranteed. In Amsterdam's 250 officially listed brothels, 80 percent of the prostitutes have been trafficked in from other countries and 70 percent possess no legal papers. Without money, papers, or contact with the outside world, these immigrant women live in terror instead of being protected by the regulations governing brothels, prostituted women are frequently beaten up and raped by pimps. These "prostitution managers" have practically been given a free hand by the state and by buyers who, as "consumers of prostitution," feel themselves entitled to abuse the women they buy. Sadly and ironically the "Amsterdam model" of legalization and regulation is touted by the Netherlands and Germany as "self-determination and empowerment for women." In reality it simply legitimizes the "right" to buy, sexually use, and profit from the sexual exploitation of someone else's body.

A Human Rights Approach

As part of a system of organized sexual exploitation, prostitution can be visualized along a continuum of abuse with brothel slavery at the furthest extreme. All along the continuum, fine lines divide the degrees of harm done to those caught up in the system. At the core lies a great social injustice no cosmetic reforms can right: the setting aside of a segment of people whose bodies can be purchased for sexual use by others. When this basic injustice is legitimized and regulated by the state and when the state profits from it, that injustice is compounded.

In her book *The Prostitution of Sexuality* (New York University Press, 1995), Kathleen Barry details a feminist human rights approach to prostitution that points the way to the future. Ethically it recognizes prostitution, sex trafficking, and the globalized industrialization of sex as massive violations of women's human rights. Sociologically it considers how and to what extent prostitution promotes sex discrimination against individual women, against different racial categories of women, and against women as a group. Politically it calls for decriminalizing prostitutes while penalizing pimps, traffickers, brothel owners, and buyers.

Understanding that human rights and restorative justice go hand in hand, the feminist human rights approach to prostitution addresses the harm and the need to repair the damage. As Barry says:

> "Legal proposals to criminalize customers, based on the recognition that prostitution violates and harms women, must... include social-service, health and counseling and job retraining programs. Where states would be closing down brothels if customers were criminalized, the economic resources poured into the

former prostitution areas could be turned toward producing gainful employment for women."

With the help of women's projects in many countries—such as Buklod in the Philippines and the Council for Prostitution Alternatives in the United States—some women have begun to confront their condition by leaving prostitution, speaking out against it, revealing their experiences, and helping other women leave the sex industry.

Ending the sexual exploitation of trafficking and prostitution will mean the beginning of a new chapter in building, a hu-manist future—a more peaceful and just future in which men and women can join together in love and respect, recognizing one another's essential dignity and humanity. Humanity's sexuality then will no longer be hijacked and distorted.

Freelance writer Alice Leuchtag has worked as a social worker, counselor, college instructor, and researcher. Active in the civil rights, peace, socialist, feminist, and humanist movements, she has helped organize women in Houston to oppose sex trafficking.

The War Over Gay Marriage

In a landmark decision, the Supreme Court affirms gay privacy and opens the way to a revolution in family life

IT WAS A HOMEY SCENE. STANDING in their warm kitchen on a winter's day in 2001, Julie and Hillary Goodridge, a couple for 16 years, played the old Beatles song "All You Need Is Love" for their young daughter, Annie. Hillary asked Annie if she knew any people who loved each other. The little girl rattled off the names of her mothers' married friends, heterosexuals all. "What about Mommy and Ma?" asked Hillary. "Well," the child replied, "if you loved each other you'd get married."

That did it. "My heart just dropped," said Hillary. The gay couple headed for the Massachusetts Department of Public Health to get a marriage license. Julie was optimistic, Hillary less so. "I thought we'd be led away in handcuffs," Hillary recalled. Blood tests and $30 in hand, they anxiously asked for an application. "No, you're not allowed to," responded the woman behind the counter. "I'll need two grooms first." Hillary and Julie asked to speak to the department's director. The woman politely told them, "No, you can't get married, and there's nothing you can do about it."

Actually, there was. With the help of the Gay & Lesbian Advocates & Defenders (GLAD), Hillary and Julie sued for the right to be legally wed. Any day now, the Massachusetts Supreme Judicial Court is expected to decide their case. No court in America has ever recognized gay marital vows. But last week Hillary and Julie—and every gay person who wants to be married or adopt a child or hold a job or receive a government benefit or simply enjoy the right to be respected—received a tremendous boost from the highest court in the land.

The outcome of *Lawrence et al. v. Texas*, handed down on the final day of the Supreme Court's 2002–2003 term, was not unexpected. In a Houston apartment five years ago, Tyron Garner and John Geddes Lawrence had been arrested by police for performing a homosexual act and fined $200. By a 6–3 vote, the high court struck down the Texas anti-sodomy law. In some ways, the Supreme Court was just catching up to public opinion. In 1986, in

Bowers v. Hardwick, a decision that lived in infamy among gays in America, the court had upheld a Georgia anti-sodomy law. At the time, 25 states had such laws. Some 17 years later, only four states banned sodomy between homosexuals (an additional nine states had laws, on the books but rarely enforced, barring sodomy between any sexual partners).

Advocates have had to deal with what one called 'the ick factor'—the revulsion some heterosexuals feel about homosexuals.

What stunned court watchers—and what promises to change forever the status of homosexuals in America—was the far reach of the court's reasoning. Gays "are entitled to respect for their private lives," said Justice Anthony Kennedy, reading from his majority opinion from the high court's mahogany bench. His voice was quiet and he seemed a little nervous, but his words rang with lasting meaning. Under the due-process clause of the 14th Amendment of the Constitution, Kennedy ruled, gays were entitled to a right of privacy. "The state cannot demean their existence or control their destiny by making their private sexual conduct a crime," said Kennedy. In the crowded courtroom, some of the gay activists and lawyers silently but visibly wept as they listened.

Justice Kennedy's ruling in the *Lawrence* case "may be one of the two most important opinions of the last 100 years," says David Garrow, legal scholar at Emory University and Pulitzer Prize-winning biographer of Martin Luther King Jr. "It's the most libertarian majority opinion ever issued by the Supreme Court. It's arguably bigger than *Roe v. Wade*," said Garrow, referring to the 1973 Supreme Court decision giving women a right to abortion. At least in symbolic terms, Garrow put the decision on a par with *Brown v. Board of Education*, the landmark 1954

A Winding Road
A look back at the highs and lows of gay rights:

1895 The writer Oscar Wilde is convicted for "gross indecency between males."

1924 The first formal U.S. gay-activist group is founded in Chicago.

1969 Patrons of Stonewall Inn resist a police raid in what's considered birth of the gay-rights movement.

1975 Former NFL player Dave Kopay announces he's gay—the first pro athlete to do so.

1977 Anita Bryant mounts national crusade to block gay rights.

1986 Supreme Court rules in *Bowers* that sodomy is a crime.

1987 ACT UP is born, taking up the fight against AIDS.

1993 Military adopts "don't ask, don't tell" policy for gays.

1993 Thousands of gay-rights supporters march on Washington.

1996 High court: gays enjoy equal rights under the Constitution.

1997 Ellen DeGeneres's TV-show character comes out.

2000 Vermont allows gay couples to form civil unions.

2001 Federal judge upholds law banning gay adoption.

2003 An openly gay Episcopal bishop is elected in N.H.

ruling declaring that separate was not equal in the nation's public schools.

But it may be years before the ripple effects of *Lawrence* are felt. Just as schools were still segregated in parts of the South a decade after the *Brown* decision, it is likely that attempts to give gays true legal equality with heterosexuals

will encounter fierce resistance from people and institutions that still regard homosexuality as morally deviant. The battle—over gay marriage, gay adoption, gays in the military and gays in the workplace—will be fought out court to court, state to state for years to come. Nonetheless, there is no question that the *Lawrence* case represents a sea change, not just in the Supreme Court, a normally cautious institution, but also in society as a whole.

In 1986, when the court had ruled in the *Bowers* case, Justice Byron White curtly dismissed the argument that the Constitution protected the right of homosexuals to have sex in their own homes. Writing for the majority of justices, White had called such an assertion "facetious." But social norms have been transformed over the past two decades. How mainstream is the idea of "gay rights"? Of the six justices who voted to strike down laws against homosexual sodomy, four were appointed by Republican presidents. (Kennedy, David Souter and John Paul Stevens all subscribed to a right of privacy for gays; Justice Sandra Day O'Connor stuck to the narrower ground that it was unfair to punish gays but not heterosexuals for sodomy.) Polls showed that the justices have public opinion behind them: some six out of 10 Americans believe that homosexual sex between consenting adults should be legal.

One veteran gay activist could sense the change in the attitudes of the justices. Kevin Cathcart, executive director of the Lambda Legal Defense and Education Fund, has been part of a small but determined circle of lawyers plotting gay-rights strategy since 1984. In the past, he had to deal with what he called the "ick factor"—the revulsion some heterosexuals feel about homosexual acts. "The Kennedy opinion not only does not have an ick factor," says Cathcart, "but is almost an apology for the ick factor 17 years ago."

One justice was still full of disgust. In a biting, sarcastic voice, Justice Antonin Scalia read his dissent from the bench. He denounced his colleagues for "taking sides in the culture war." He accused the court's majority of having "largely signed on to the so-called homosexual agenda." Most Americans, Scalia warned, "do not want persons who openly engage in homosexual conduct as partners in their business, as scout-masters for their children, as teachers in their children's schools, or as boarders in their homes." Scalia predicted that the court's decision would cause "a massive disruption of the current social order" by calling into question the government's right to legislate morality. While noting the majority's statement that the case did not involve gay marriage, Scalia scoffed, "Do not believe it."

Scalia's fulmination was impressive, but (as even he might privately concede) it was also an overstatement of the legal and political reality, at least for the immediate future. While gays can now claim some constitutional protection—their new right to privacy under the *Lawrence* decision—the federal government and the states can override those rights if they have a good enough reason, a "legitimate state interest." Thus, national security could trump privacy in the military and preserve the Pentagon's "don't ask, don't tell" policy on gays. Or the state's interest in preserving "traditional institutions"—like marriage between different-sex couples—might overcome a homosexual's right to not be "demeaned," as Justice Kennedy put it. After *Lawrence*, gays can no longer be branded as criminals. But that does not mean they will enjoy all the rights of "straight" citizens. The current Supreme Court has shown, albeit erratically, a federalist streak: it will not lightly trample "states' rights"—that is, second-guess the power of states to make up their own rules, especially if popular opinion is running strong.

Inevitably, politics will play a role. Some conservative groups were apoplectic. "People of faith are not going to lie down and allow their faith to be trampled because a politically correct court has run amok," promised the Rev. Lou Sheldon, president of the Traditional Values Coalition. He offered a hint of the battles that lie ahead when a vacancy opens up on the high court. "In this court, you do not have friends of the Judeo-Christian standard. We know who our friends are. And we know who needs to be replaced," said Sheldon. Sandy Rios, president of the Concerned Women for America, predicted moral Armageddon. "We're opening up a complete Pandora's box," she said. Some conservatives, including Justice Scalia, warned that the court's decision would undermine laws barring bigamy, incest and prostitution.

> Blood tests and $30 in hand, the Goodridges asked for a license. 'No,' the clerk told the women. 'I'll need two grooms first.'

Maybe. But states will still be able to ban sexual practices that are obviously hurtful or exploitative of women or minors. Nonetheless, the fear of legalized wantonness will quickly become a campaign issue. Last week the White House—which decided not to file a brief in the case—was taking cover; White House spokesman Ari Fleischer defensively mumbled that gay rights were a matter for the states to decide. Bush's political handlers were fearful of alienating either gay voters or the legion of Christian conservatives who provided Bush with his electoral base in 2000. "Bush officials apparently think homosexual activists make better leaders than the conservative activists who delivered millions of votes," taunted Bob Knight, director of the conservative Culture and Family Institute.

The fight over gay rights could easily become a "wedge issue" in the 2004 presidential campaign, though Democrats, too, will be wary of getting ahead of public opinion. For the most part, gay rights will be fought out at the local and state level. The struggle will be protracted

and there may be a real backlash. An overview of the main battlegrounds:

Gay Marriage. Although gay couples routinely have commitment ceremonies and The New York Times wedding pages now run photos of gay and lesbian pairings, no state in the country recognizes or grants gay marriages. (Churches are badly split, with some denominations honoring same-sex unions and others vehemently opposing them.) Vermont comes the closest of any state with "civil unions" that bestow many of the same rights and responsibilities as marriage, but give it a different name—for purely political reasons. A few other states, most notably Massachusetts and California, seem to be edging toward the recognition of gay marriage, either by legislation or judicial fiat. But the stronger movement, at least for now, appears to be in the other direction. Some 37 states—and the federal government—have adopted "Defense of Marriage Acts," which define marriage as applying only to a man and a woman, and—significantly—bar recognition of same-sex marriage from other states.

These laws will inevitably be challenged in the courts under the *Lawrence* decision. On June 11, a court in Ontario, Canada, ruled that same-sex marriages are legal (they are also legal in the Netherlands and Belgium). Last weekend in Toronto, during the city's Gay Pride celebration, the city's marriage office stayed open for extended hours. A dozen of the first 200 customers were Americans who had driven across the border. Legal experts are divided over whether a gay couple with a Canadian marriage license will be recognized back in the States, but they are sure that sooner or later the issue of gay marriage will wind up in the Supreme Court, though probably not for several years.

By then the court may be, as the saying goes, following the election returns. Gary Bauer, the president of American Values and a former presidential candidate, warned that if the Republicans do not take a stand against gay marriage in the 2004 election, then GOP "family values" activists might just sit home rather than work for the party. On the other hand, Bush may pick up votes from libertarians and Republican moderates (the "soccer moms") if he is seen as being compassionate or tolerant of different sexual orientations.

Adoption and Custody. Most states now permit single gays to adopt children. Resistance to gay adoption has waned as studies show that children raised by gays look a lot like those raised by straights—and are no more or less likely to be gay. Still, only 11 states permit same-sex couples to adopt children. The rest of the states are a patchwork of conflicting rules. Florida, swayed by Anita Bryant's 1977 "Save the Children" campaign, is the most restrictive, banning adoption by any gay or lesbian individuals. That law, based largely on moral disapproval, seems vulnerable after *Lawrence*.

The most immediate impact of *Lawrence* will be on custody battles. One Virginia judge, for instance, asked a lesbian to detail her homosexual acts in court testimony and

THE NEXT FRONT

Marriage is one thing. But what happens when partners part? For gay couples splitting up, it's still a legal 'no man's land.'

Breaking Up Is Hard to Do

BY DEBRA ROSENBERG

When Texans Russell Smith and John Anthony traveled to Vermont to join in a civil union in February 2002, they had all the romantic intentions of any couple exchanging "I do's." But like the 50 percent of Americans whose marriages end in divorce, Smith and Anthony later decided to call it quits. Because the two had shared business deals, Smith worried he might one day face financial obligations from his ex. So he filed for divorce in a Texas court. Though a district judge initially agreed to grant one, Texas Attorney General Greg Abbott intervened. He feared granting a divorce would signal that the state recognized the union in the first place—a step Texas and other states aren't yet willing to take. "A judge cannot grant a divorce where no marriage existed," Abbott argued. The judge reversed the divorce and the couple was forced to hash things out on their own. "They were just wanting to legally terminate this relationship," says Anthony's lawyer, Tommy Gunn. "Obviously the divorce route did not work."

If gay couples think it's tough to get married, they may find it's even harder to split up. Few want to think about it on the way to the altar, but "we're not immune to relationship problems," says David Buckel, an attorney who directs the marriage project at Lambda Legal. Though all it takes is a romantic weekend to tie the knot under Canada's just-passed same-sex marriage law or get linked by civil union in Vermont, both places require at least one member of the couple to establish residency for a year before granting a divorce or official dissolution. Of the roughly 5,000 civil unions performed so far in Vermont, the only state that legally recognizes the same-sex commitments, 85 percent went to out-of-staters.

That has left other states grappling with what to do when civil unions sour—and whether standard divorce laws can apply. A West Virginia family-court judge agreed to use divorce laws to dissolve a civil union there last year. But Connecticut courts dismissed the divorce case filed by Glen Rosengarten, who decided to end his 15-year relationship shortly after he and his partner got a civil union in Vermont. Dying of AIDS, Rosengarten wanted to preserve his estate for children from an earlier marriage, says his lawyer Gary I. Cohen. "He had incredible anxiety about it—he really wanted closure in his life," Cohen says. Rosengarten appealed to the state Supreme Court, but died before the case was heard. Medical bills ate up his estate, so inheritance became a moot point too.

Without access to divorce, all the benefits gay couples get with a civil union—shared property, adoption rights, insurance—must be undone one by one. If they can't dissolve the union, they may not be free to enter into a new union or marriage, either. "It shoves gay people into a no man's land where they have to fight it out for themselves," says Evan Wolfson, director of Freedom to Marry. "Because it's not marriage, people don't have one of the automatic protections that comes with marriage." Gay couples can't hope to erase the pain that comes with parting. But after last week, there's at least a chance they may one day get a little more help when things fall apart.

With PAT WINGERT

---

then told her she would lose her child because her behavior was immoral. That sort of reasoning will likely no longer pass constitutional muster.

Gays in the Workplace, Schools and the Military. Big employers have already gotten the message. In 1992 only one of the Fortune 500 companies offered benefits to gay partners. Today the number is 197, including 27 of the top 50. Unfounded worries about getting tagged with massive AIDS bills have been replaced by top companies' desire to compete for gay workers.

Schools and the military will be slower going. Teachers fear harassment or retribution if they support student efforts to form "gay-straight alliances" (even so, there are some 1,700 pro-tolerance clubs in 50 states). The Pentagon will argue that "unit cohesion" will suffer if gays are openly tolerated in the military. Part of the underlying legal basis for the armed services' restrictive "don't ask, don't tell" policy, a federal anti-sodomy law, is likely to

be struck down. Still, the courts are very reluctant to interfere with the military.

PRAYERFUL PROTEST AT THE HIGH COURT
Critics share Scalia's view that the decision hurts the state's right to legislate morality

Despite the challenges ahead, the alliance of gay lawyers who have been working for two decades to overturn discriminatory laws can feel the ground shifting beneath their feet. Last week Susan Sommer, the supervising attorney at the Lambda Legal Defense and Education Fund, went to an early court hearing in a case aimed at overturning New Jersey's ban on gay marriages. The U.S. Supreme Court's ruling in *Lawrence* "didn't come up," she noted. "But now I feel like when I walk in the courtroom I've got a powerful symbol on our side, the ringing words of Justice Kennedy that *Bowers v. Hardwick* had demeaned gay people."

Lambda is trying to soften up public opinion with town-hall meetings designed to show that gay families are good for the community. "The town halls we're doing tell people, 'Hey, we're just like anyone else—a middle-class, hometown suburban couple that's been called boring'," says Cindy Meneghin, 45, who with her partner, Maureen Kilian, also 45, and their two children, Joshua, 10, and Sarah, 8, are suing to be recognized as a legal family in New Jersey. "You can't look at our beautiful, charming kids and not notice that we're a family, and the myths start tumbling down. What we've found is that people get to know us as people with families and kids, that I coach soccer and take pictures, and Maureen is the best dessert maker in town, and, oh yes, Maureen and Cindy are a gay couple."

At their home in the liberal Boston enclave of Jamaica Plain, Julie and Hillary Goodridge (who adopted the common last name from Hillary's grandmother because it sounded "positive") have found acceptance—except for the time a bunch of high-school kids urinated on their car and yelled "Dyke!" Last week Julie sat down with their daughter, Annie, to explain the *Lawrence* decision. "I had to do it without talking about sodomy," said Julie. "I mean, she's only 7 and three quarters!" "The Supreme Court made an important decision yesterday," Julie told Annie. "They said it was OK for lesbians and gays to love each other." "That's good," said Annie. But she still wants her parents to be married.

This story was reported by T. TRENT GEGAX, DEBRA ROSENBERG, PAT WINGERT, MARK MILLER, MARTHA BRANT, STUART TAYLOR JR., TAMARA LIPPER, JOHN BARRY, REBECCA SINDERBRAND, SARAH CHILDRESS and JULIE SCELFO. It was written by EVAN THOMAS.

THE NEW GENDER GAP

From kindergarten to grad school, boys are becoming the second sex.

BY MICHELLE CONLIN

Lawrence High is the usual fortress of manila-brick blandness and boxy 1960s architecture. At lunch, the metalheads saunter out to the smokers' park, while the AP types get pizzas at Marinara's, where they talk about—what else?—other people. The hallways are filled with lip-glossed divas in designer clothes and packs of girls in midriff-baring track tops. The guys run the gamut, too: skate punks, rich boys in Armani, and saggy-panted crews with their Eminem swaggers. In other words, they look pretty much as you'd expect.

But when the leaders of the Class of 2003 assemble in the Long Island high school's fluorescent-lit meeting rooms, most of these boys are nowhere to be seen. The senior class president? A girl. The vice-president? Girl. Head of student government? Girl. Captain of the math team, chief of the yearbook, and editor of the newspaper? Girls.

It's not that the girls of the Class of 2003 aren't willing to give the guys a chance. Last year, the juniors elected a boy as class president. But after taking office, he swiftly instructed his all-female slate that they were his cabinet and that he was going to be calling all the shots. The girls looked around and realized they had the votes, says Tufts University-bound Casey Vaughn, an Intel finalist and one of the alpha femmes of the graduating class. "So they impeached him and took over."

The female lock on power at Lawrence is emblematic of a stunning gender reversal in American education. From kindergarten to graduate school, boys are fast becoming the second sex. "Girls are on a tear through the educational system," says Thomas G. Mortenson, a senior scholar at the Pell Institute for the Study of Opportunity in Higher Education in Washington. "In the past 30 years, nearly every inch of educational progress has gone to them."

Just a century ago, the president of Harvard University, Charles W. Eliot, refused to admit women because he feared they would waste the precious resources of his school. Today, across the country, it seems as if girls have built a kind of scholastic Roman Empire alongside boys' languishing Greece. Although Lawrence High has its share of boy superstars—like this year's valedictorian—the gender takeover at some schools is nearly complete. "Every time I turn around, if something good is happening, there's a female in charge," says Terrill O. Stammler, principal of Rising Sun High School in Rising Sun, Md. Boys are missing from nearly every leadership position, academic honors slot, and student-activity post at the school. Even Rising Sun's girls' sports teams do better than the boys'.

At one exclusive private day school in the Midwest, administrators have even gone so far as to mandate that all awards and student-government positions be divvied equally between the sexes. "It's not just that boys are falling behind girls," says William S. Pollock, author of *Real Boys: Rescuing Our Sons from the Myths of Boyhood* and a professor of psychiatry at Harvard Medical School. "It's that boys themselves are falling behind their own functioning and doing worse than they did before."

It may still be a man's world. But it is no longer, in any way, a boy's. From his first days in school, an average boy is already developmentally two years behind the girls in reading and writing. Yet he's often expected to learn the same things in the same way in the same amount of time.

While every nerve in his body tells him to run, he has to sit still and listen for almost eight hours a day. Biologically, he needs about four recesses a day, but he's lucky if he gets one, since some lawsuit-leery schools have banned them altogether. Hug a girl, and he could be labeled a "toucher" and swiftly suspended—a result of what some say is an increasingly anti-boy culture that pathologizes their behavior.

If he falls behind, he's apt to be shipped off to special ed, where he'll find that more than 70% of his classmates are also boys. Squirm, clown, or interrupt, and he is four times as likely to be diagnosed with attention deficit hyperactivity disorder. That often leads to being forced to take Ritalin or risk being expelled, sent to special ed, or having parents accused of negligence. One study of public schools in Fairfax County, Va., found that more than 20% of upper-middle-class white boys were taking Ritalin-like drugs by fifth grade.

Once a boy makes it to freshman year of high school, he's at greater risk of falling even further behind in grades, extracurricular activities, and advanced placement. Not even science and math remain his bastions. And while the girls are busy working on sweeping the honor roll at graduation, a boy is more likely to be bulking up in the weight room to enhance his steroid-fed Adonis complex, playing Grand Theft Auto: Vice City on his PlayStation2, or downloading rapper 50 Cent on his iPod. All the while, he's 30% more likely to drop out, 85% more likely to commit murder, and four to six times more likely to kill himself, with boy suicides tripling since 1970. "We get a bad rap," says Steven Covington, a sophomore at Ottumwa High School in Ottumwa, Iowa. "Society says we can't be trusted."

As for college—well, let's just say this: At least it's easier for the guys who get there to find a date. For 350 years, men outnumbered women on college campuses. Now, in every state, every income bracket, every racial and ethnic group, and most industrialized Western nations, women reign, earning an average 57% of all BAs and 58% of all master's degrees in the U.S. alone. There are 133 girls getting BAs for every 100 guys—a number that's projected to grow to 142 women per 100 men by 2010, according to the U.S. Education Dept. If current trends continue, demographers say, there will be 156 women per 100 men earning degrees by 2020.

Overall, more boys and girls are in college than a generation ago. But when adjusted for population growth, the percentage of boys entering college, master's programs, and most doctoral programs—except for PhDs in fields like engineering and computer science—has mostly stalled out, whereas for women it has continued to rise across the board. The trend is most pronounced among Hispanics, African Americans, and those from low-income families.

The female-to-male ratio is already 60–40 at the University of North Carolina, Boston University, and New York University. To keep their gender ratios 50–50, many Ivy League and other elite schools are secretly employing a kind of stealth affirmative action for boys. "Girls present better qualifications in the application process—better grades, tougher classes, and more thought in their essays," says Michael S. McPherson, president of Macalester College in St. Paul, Minn., where 57% of enrollees are women. "Boys get off to a slower start."

The trouble isn't limited to school. Once a young man is out of the house, he's more likely than his sister to boomerang back home and sponge off his mom and dad. It all adds up to the fact that before he reaches adulthood, a young man is more likely than he was 30 years ago to end up in the new and growing class of underachiever—what the British call the "sink group."

For a decade, British educators have waged successful classroom programs to ameliorate "laddism" (boys turning off to school) by focusing on teaching techniques that re-engage them. But in the U.S., boys' fall from alpha to omega status doesn't even have a name, let alone the public's attention. "No one wants to speak out on behalf of boys," says Andrew Sum, director of the Northeastern University Center for Labor Market Studies. As a social-policy or educational issue, "it's near nonexistent."

Women are rapidly closing the M.D. and PhD gap and make up almost half of law students.

On the one hand, the education grab by girls is amazing news, which could make the 21st the first female century. Already, women are rapidly closing the M.D. and PhD gap and are on the verge of making up the majority of law students, according to the American Bar Assn. MBA programs, with just 29% females, remain among the few old-boy domains.

Still, it's hardly as if the world has been equalized: Ninety percent of the world's billionaires are men. Among the super rich, only one woman, Gap Inc. cofounder Doris F. Fisher, made, rather than inherited, her wealth. Men continue to dominate in the highest-paying jobs in such leading-edge industries as engineering, investment banking, and high tech—the sectors that still power the economy and build the biggest fortunes. And women still face sizable obstacles in the pay gap, the glass ceiling, and the still-Sisyphean struggle to juggle work and child-rearing.

But attaining a decisive educational edge may finally enable females to narrow the earnings gap, punch through more of the glass ceiling, and gain an equal hand in rewriting the rules of corporations, government, and society. "Girls are better able to deliver in terms of what modern society requires of people—paying attention, abiding by rules, being verbally competent, and dealing with interpersonal relationships in offices," says James Garbarino, a professor of human development at Cornell

University and author of *Lost Boys: Why Our Sons Turn Violent and How We Can Save Them.*

Righting boys' problems needn't end up leading to reversals for girls. But some feminists say the danger in exploring what's happening to boys would be to mistakenly see any expansion of opportunities for women as inherently disadvantageous to boys. "It isn't a zero-sum game," says Susan M. Bailey, executive director of the Wellesley Centers for Women. Adds Macalester's McPherson: "It would be dangerous to even out the gender ratio by treating women worse. I don't think we've reached a point in this country where we are fully providing equal opportunities to women."

Men could become losers in a global economy that values mental powers over might.

Still, if the creeping pattern of male disengagement and economic dependency continues, more men could end up becoming losers in a global economy that values mental powers over might—not to mention the loss of their talent and potential. The growing educational and economic imbalances could also create societal upheavals, altering family finances, social policies, and work-family practices. Men are already dropping out of the labor force, walking out on fatherhood, and disconnecting from civic life in greater numbers. Since 1964, for example, the voting rate in Presidential elections among men has fallen from 72% to 53%—twice the rate of decline among women, according to Pell's Mortenson. In a turnaround from the 1960s, more women now vote than men.

Boys' slide also threatens to erode male earnings, spark labor shortages for skilled workers, and create the same kind of marriage squeeze among white women that already exists for blacks. Among African Americans, 30% of 40- to 44-year-old women have never married, owing in part to the lack of men with the same academic credentials and earning potential. Currently, the never-married rate is 9% for white women of the same age. "Women are going to pull further and further ahead of men, and at some point, when they want to form families, they are going to look around and say, 'Where are the guys?'" says Mortenson.

Corporations should worry, too. During the boom, the most acute labor shortages occurred among educated workers—a problem companies often solved by hiring immigrants. When the economy reenergizes, a skills shortage in the U.S. could undermine employers' productivity and growth.

Better-educated men are also, on average, a much happier lot. They are more likely to marry, stick by their children, and pay more in taxes. From the ages of 18 to 65, the average male college grad earns $2.5 million over his lifetime, 90% more than his high school counterpart. That's

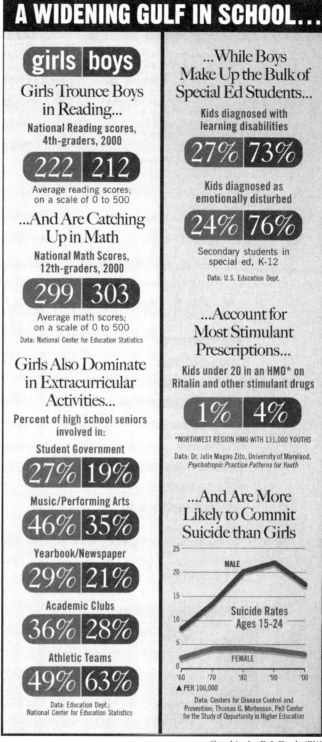

Graphics by Rob Doyle/BW

up from 40% more in 1979, the peak year for U.S. manufacturing. The average college diploma holder also contributes four times more in net taxes over his career than a high school grad, according to Northeastern's Sum. Meanwhile, the typical high school dropout will usually get $40,000 more from the government than he pays in, a net drain on society.

Certainly, many boys continue to conquer scholastic summits, especially boys from high-income families with

...LEADS MORE AND MORE TO A GIRLS' CLUB IN COLLEGE

The Gender Gap Spans Every Racial and Ethnic Group...
Bachelor's degrees awarded to students by race/ethnicity, as a percent of total

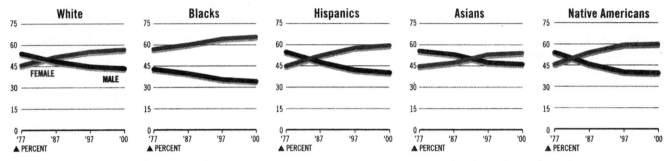

...And Most of the Industrialized World...

Ages 25 to 34, with at least a college education, plus advanced degrees

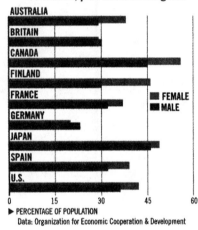

▶ PERCENTAGE OF POPULATION
Data: Organization for Economic Cooperation & Development

...And Is Projected to Get Worse...

Number of U.S. women awarded degrees per 100 men

Bachelor's Degrees

1999-2000	Est. 2009-10
133	142

Master's Degrees

1999-2000	Est. 2009-10
138	151

Data: Andrew Sum, Northeastern University Center for Labor Market Studies

...Threatening the Marriage Squeeze Among Whites That Blacks Already Face

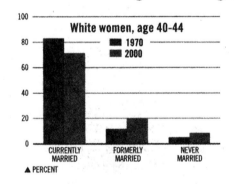

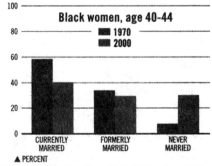

Data: *Mismatch*, by Andrew Hacker; National Center for Education Statistics; Bureau of Labor Statistics; Census Bureau

Graphics by Rob Doyle/BW

educated parents. Overall, boys continue to do better on standardized tests such as the scholastic aptitude test, though more low-income girls than low-income boys take it, thus depressing girls' scores. Many educators also believe that standardized testing's multiple-choice format favors boys because girls tend to think in broader, more complex terms. But that advantage is eroding as many colleges now weigh grades—where girls excel— more heavily than test scores.

Still, it's not as if girls don't face a slew of vexing issues, which are often harder to detect because girls are likelier to internalize low self-esteem through depression or the

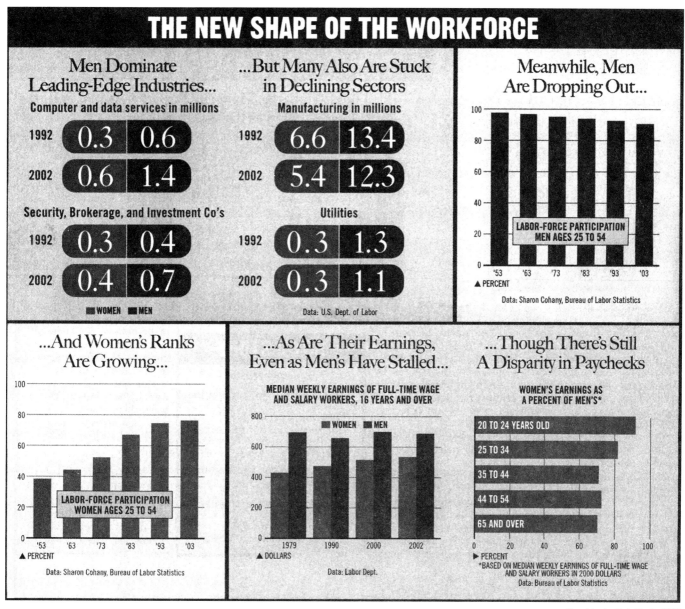

THE NEW SHAPE OF THE WORKFORCE

Men Dominate Leading-Edge Industries...

Computer and data services in millions

	WOMEN	MEN
1992	0.3	0.6
2002	0.6	1.4

Security, Brokerage, and Investment Co's

	WOMEN	MEN
1992	0.3	0.4
2002	0.4	0.7

■ WOMEN ■ MEN

...But Many Also Are Stuck in Declining Sectors

Manufacturing in millions

1992	6.6	13.4
2002	5.4	12.3

Utilities

1992	0.3	1.3
2002	0.3	1.1

Data: U.S. Dept. of Labor

Meanwhile, Men Are Dropping Out...

LABOR-FORCE PARTICIPATION MEN AGES 25 TO 54

▲ PERCENT

Data: Sharon Cohany, Bureau of Labor Statistics

...And Women's Ranks Are Growing...

LABOR-FORCE PARTICIPATION WOMEN AGES 25 TO 54

▲ PERCENT

Data: Sharon Cohany, Bureau of Labor Statistics

...As Are Their Earnings, Even as Men's Have Stalled...

MEDIAN WEEKLY EARNINGS OF FULL-TIME WAGE AND SALARY WORKERS, 16 YEARS AND OVER

■ WOMEN ■ MEN

▲ DOLLARS

Data: Labor Dept.

...Though There's Still A Disparity in Paychecks

WOMEN'S EARNINGS AS A PERCENT OF MEN'S*

20 TO 24 YEARS OLD
25 TO 34
35 TO 44
44 TO 54
65 AND OVER

▶ PERCENT
*BASED ON MEDIAN WEEKLY EARNINGS OF FULL-TIME WAGE AND SALARY WORKERS IN 2000 DOLLARS
Data: Bureau of Labor Statistics

Graphics by Rob Doyle/BW

desire to starve themselves into perfection. And while boys may act out with their fists, girls, given their superior verbal skills, often do so with their mouths in the form of vicious gossip and female bullying. "They yell and cuss," says 15-year-old Keith Gates, an Ottumwa student. "But we always get in trouble. They never do."

Before educators, corporations, and policymakers can narrow the new gender gap, they will have to understand its myriad causes. Everything from absentee parenting to the lack of male teachers to corporate takeovers of lunch rooms with sugar-and-fat-filled food, which can make kids hyperactive and distractable, plays a role. So can TV violence, which hundreds of studies—including recent ones by Stanford University and the University of Michigan—have linked to aggressive behavior in kids. Some believe boys are responding to cultural signals—downsized dads cast adrift in the New Economy, a dumb-and-

dumber dude culture that demeans academic achievement, and the glamorization of all things gangster that makes school seem so uncool. What can compare with the allure of a gun-wielding, model-dating hip hopper? Boys, who mature more slowly than girls, are also often less able to delay gratification or take a long-range view.

Schools have inadvertently played a big role, too, losing sight of boys—taking for granted that they were doing well, even though data began to show the opposite. Some educators believed it was a blip that would change or feared takebacks on girls' gains. Others were just in denial. Indeed, many administrators saw boys, rather than the way schools were treating them, as the problem.

Thirty years ago, educational experts launched what's known as the "Girl Project." The movement's noble objective was to help girls wipe out their weaknesses in math and science, build self-esteem, and give them the undisputed message: The opportunities are yours; take them. Schools focused on making the classroom more girl-friendly by including teaching styles that catered to them. Girls were also powerfully influenced by the women's movement, as well as by Title IX and the Gender & Equity Act, all of which created a legal environment in which discrimination against girls—from classrooms to the sports field—carried heavy penalties. Once the chains were off, girls soared.

For 30 years, the focus at schools has been to empower girls, in and out of the classroom.

Yet even as boys' educational development was flat-lining in the 1990s—with boys dropping out in greater numbers and failing to bridge the gap in reading and writing—the spotlight remained firmly fixed on girls. Part of the reason was that the issue had become politically charged and girls had powerful advocates. The American Association of University Women, for example, published research cementing into pedagogy the idea that girls had deep problems with self-esteem in school as a result of teachers' patterns, which included calling on girls less and lavishing attention on boys. Newspapers and TV newsmagazines lapped up the news, decrying a new confidence crisis among American girls. Universities and research centers sponsored scores of teacher symposiums centered on girls. "All the focus was on girls, all the grant monies, all the university programs—to get girls interested in science and math," says Steve Hanson, principal of Ottumwa High School in Iowa. "There wasn't a similar thing for reading and writing for boys."

Some boy champions go so far as to contend that schools have become boy-bashing laboratories. Christina Hoff Sommers, author of *The War Against Boys*, says the AAUW report, coupled with zero-tolerance sexual harassment laws, have hijacked schools by overly feminizing classrooms and attempting to engineer androgyny.

The "earliness" push, in which schools are pressured to show kids achieving the same standards by the same age or risk losing funding, is also far more damaging to boys, according to Lilian G. Katz, co-director of ERIC Clearinghouse on Elementary and Early Childhood Education. Even the nerves on boys' fingers develop later than girls', making it difficult to hold a pencil and push out perfect cursive. These developmental differences often unfairly sideline boys as slow or dumb, planting a distaste for school as early as the first grade.

Instead of catering to boys' learning styles, Pollock and others argue, many schools are force-fitting them into an unnatural mold. The reigning sit-still-and-listen paradigm isn't ideal for either sex. But it's one girls often tolerate better than boys. Girls have more intricate sensory capacities and biosocial aptitudes to decipher exactly what the teacher wants, whereas boys tend to be more

anti-authoritarian, competitive, and risk-taking. They often don't bother with such details as writing their names in the exact place instructed by the teacher.

Experts say educators also haven't done nearly enough to keep up with the recent findings in brain research about developmental differences. "Ninety-nine-point-nine percent of teachers are not trained in this," says Michael Gurian, author of *Boys and Girls Learn Differently*. "They were taught 20 years ago that gender is just a social function."

In fact, brain research over the past decade has revealed how differently boys' and girls' brains can function. Early on, boys are usually superior spatial thinkers and possess the ability to see things in three dimensions. They are often drawn to play that involves intense movement and an element of make-believe violence. Instead of straitjacketing boys by attempting to restructure this behavior out of them, it would be better to teach them how to harness this energy effectively and healthily, Pollock says.

As it stands, the result is that too many boys are diagnosed with attention-deficit disorder or its companion, attention-deficit hyperactivity disorder. The U.S.—mostly its boys—now consumes 80% of the world's supply of methylphenidate (the generic name for Ritalin). That use has increased 500% over the past decade, leading some to call it the new K–12 management tool. There are school districts where 20% to 25% of the boys are on the drug, says Paul R. Wolpe, a psychiatry professor at the University of Pennsylvania and the senior fellow at the school's Center for Bioethics: "Ritalin is a response to an artificial social context that we've created for children."

Instead of recommending medication—something four states have recently banned school administrators from doing—experts say educators should focus on helping boys feel less like misfits. Experts are designing new developmentally appropriate, child-initiated learning that concentrates on problem-solving, not just test-taking. This approach benefits both sexes but especially boys, given that they tend to learn best through action, not just talk. Activities are geared toward the child's interest level and temperament. Boys, for example, can learn math through counting pinecones, biology through mucking around in a pond. They can read *Harry Potter* instead of *Little House on the Prairie*, and write about aliens attacking a hospital rather than about how to care for people in the hospital. If they get antsy, they can leave a teacher's lecture and go to an activity center replete with computers and manipulable objects that support the lesson plan.

Paying attention to boys' emotional lives also delivers dividends. Over the course of her longitudinal research project in Washington (D.C.) schools, University of Northern Florida researcher Rebecca Marcon found that boys who attend kindergartens that focus on social and emotional skills—as opposed to only academic learning—perform better, across the board, by the time they reach junior high.

Indeed, brain research shows that boys are actually more empathic, expressive, and emotive at birth than girls. But Pollock says the boy code, which bathes them in a culture of stoicism and reticence, often socializes those aptitudes out of them by the second grade. "We now have executives paying $10,000 a week to learn emotional intelligence," says Pollock. "These are actually the skills boys are born with."

The gender gap also has roots in the expectation gap. In the 1970s, boys were far more likely to anticipate getting a college degree—with girls firmly entrenched in the cheerleader role. Today, girls' expectations are ballooning, while boys' are plummeting. There's even a sense, including among the most privileged families, that today's boys are a sort of payback generation—the one that has to compensate for the advantages given to males in the past. In fact, the new equality is often perceived as a loss by many boys who expected to be on top. "My friends in high school, they just didn't see the value of college, they just didn't care enough," says New York University sophomore Joe Clabby. Only half his friends from his high school group in New Jersey went on to college.

They will face a far different world than their dads did. Without college diplomas, it will be harder for them to find good-paying jobs. And more and more, the positions available to them will be in industries long thought of as female. The services sector, where women make up 60% of employees, has ballooned by 260% since the 1970s. During the same period, manufacturing, where men hold 70% of jobs, has shrunk by 14%.

These men will also be more likely to marry women who outearn them. Even in this jobless recovery, women's wages have continued to grow, with the pay gap the smallest on record, while men's earnings haven't managed to keep up with the low rate of inflation. Given that the recession hit male-centric industries such as technology and manufacturing the hardest, native-born men experienced more than twice as much job loss as native-born women between 2000 and 2002.

Some feminists who fought hard for girl equality in schools in the early 1980s and '90s say this: So what if girls have gotten 10, 20 years of attention—does that make up for centuries of subjugation? Moreover, what's wrong with women gliding into first place, especially if they deserve it? "Just because girls aren't shooting 7-Eleven clerks doesn't mean they should be ignored," says Cornell's Garbarino. "Once you stop oppressing girls, it stands to reason they will thrive up to their potential."

Moreover, girls say much of their drive stems from parents and teachers pushing them to get a college degree because they have to be better to be equal—to make the same money and get the same respect as a guy. "Girls are more willing to take the initiative… they're not afraid to do the work," says Tara Prout, the Georgetown-bound senior class president at Lawrence High. "A lot of boys in my school are looking for credit to get into college to look good, but they don't really want to do the grunt work."

A new world has opened up for girls, but unless a symmetrical effort is made to help boys find their footing, it may turn out that it's a lonely place to be. After all, it takes more than one gender to have a gender revolution.

BOYS' STORY

For further reading:

- *Lost Boys* by James Garbarino
- *Boys and Girls Learn Differently* by Michael Gurian
- *Mismatch* by Andrew Hacker
- *Raising Cain* by Dan Kindlon and Michael Thompson
- *Real Boys* by William Pollack
- *The War Against Boys* by Christina Hoff Sommers

When Baby Boomers Grow Old

How will the United States meet the housing and elder-care needs
of its growing population of seniors?

BY ELIZABETH BENEDICT

Last year, without warning, a close friend and gifted writer committed suicide. She was 75 and affluent, facing major surgery, a wheelchair, permanent incapacity; she declined that new life as unambiguously as she could. Several nights later, still raw from the news, I received a letter from the hotel-turned-assisted-living-facility—let us call it Shangri-la—where my 76-year-old divorced mother and her 88-year-old widowed sister live. They share a single room in a modest suburb of New York City. "Your aunt and mother's lease is due to expire on August 31, 2000" the director of admissions wrote. "We are pleased to offer them a renewal of their lease. Please note, there is a 5% increase over last year's rent. The new rent will be $3,780 per month."

Please note, my mother and aunt have no idea how much Shangri-la costs. The times I have mentioned it, they have been flabbergasted. But a minute later, they cannot remember the number. They are sociable, spry, eager participants in the cruise-like flurry of events and entertainments that fill their days, but there are craters in their memories and their cognitive abilities.

Their Social Security paid for a little less than half of their expenses in 2000; their lifetime savings paid the rest. I am their money manager. When they run through their funds in several years, they may have to go to a nursing home as Medicaid patients, if they can get into one. Then the government will pay about $300 a day for each of them. If they stay at Shangri-la, the government will pay nothing, even though it's cheaper than a nursing home. I would like to move them to one of the few subsidized assisted-living communities for people with low and middle incomes, but because of the demand and rigid eligibility requirements, I am not sanguine about the possibility. My sister and I have neither room for them in our small apartments nor the money to keep them indefinitely at Shangri-la. My mother can no longer understand directions on a bottle of pills. Yet when she asks if I am going to have children, and I remind her that I am 45, divorced, and not interested, her answer leaves me speechless: "But who will take care of you when you're old the way you take care of us?"

> With the increase in prosperous seniors during the past 10 years, assisted living has become a popular, though costly, alternative to living alone or to nursing homes for those who can no longer manage a household.

I mumble something about my boyfriend's young daughter, and she is comforted for as long as she can remember. But the truth is, I have no idea. Like most of my fellow 77 million baby boomers, I would rather not dream so far into the future, though questions have begun to gnaw at me. Where might we live when we need bathtub grip bars and someone to tell us when to take our Prozac, when it is problematic to live alone but before we become severely incapacitated? Will the country be strewn with Shangri-las and their stylish, Dean-and-DeLucafied offspring, tailor-made for the "bo-urgeois bo-hemians"

David Brooks mocks in *Bobos in Paradise*? Will the Hyatts and Marriots of today, which have captured a chunk of the luxury assisted-living market, have put all their competition out of business in time for our twilight years? And where in the world will everyone else live—those who can't afford the top of the line or much of anything else? Might Motel 6, like its posh counterparts, move into housing seniors?

With the increase in prosperous seniors during the past 10 years, assisted living has become a popular, though costly, alternative to living alone or to nursing homes for those who can no longer manage a household. Without federal regulations or uniform definitions, numbers are imprecise, though the funding sources are not: It's every senior for him- or herself, with almost no help from Medicaid. *Consumer Reports* claims that "500,000 Americans live in places loosely called assisted-living facilities"; the Assisted Living Federation of America believes that a million dwell in some 30,000 facilities. (The more reliable figures for nursing homes put about 1.5 million frail seniors living in some 17,000 nursing homes, with Medicaid picking up the tab for 68 percent of these residents.) All agree that there is a great need for more affordable assisted living; seniors with incomes below $30,000 a year outnumber others by two to one. The 6.5 million low-income seniors who need day-to-day assistance—most of them women—have a higher prevalence of frailty than the more affluent.

UPBEAT AGING

As we boomers consider where we'll grow old, we'll need first to look at the larger question of *how*. If the prevailing American dream for our parents was to retire to the Sun-belt and play golf, today that aspiration is just one of many possibilities. Gerontologist, psychologist, and elder-care consultant Lenise Dolen has observed that some people now retire and relax for a few years in the old-fashioned way before training for a second or third career. She predicts that senior centers of the future will be places for educational and vocational retraining. By the time we reach old age, it will be a different country than it was when my robust grandfather was forced to retire from his traveling-salesman career at 65 and then went on to work for the family business until he was 89.

In 1958, when youthful Muriel Spark published *Memento Mori*, a classic of geriatric literature, old age meant isolation and shame. These days, with climbing longevity rates, the golden years are, for some, high time to start a new family, as John Updike's Jewish alter-ego does in *Bech at Bay* and as octogenarian Saul Bellow recently did in real life. But even seniors who are not literally spreading their seed are being fruitful and finding inspiration in the lives of John Glenn, Jimmy and Rosalynn Carter, Gloria Steinem (who married for the first time at age 66), and the artists, composers, and more ordinary elders de-

scribed in psychiatrist-gerontologist Gene Cohen's recent work *The Creative Age: Awakening Human Potential in the Second Half of Life* and in Marc Freedman's *Prime Time: How Baby Boomers Will Revolutionize Retirement and Transform America*. Freedman promotes the idea of "transformed retirement" in the examples of men and women who devote "the next third of life" to community and volunteer work and to new pursuits in which the experience itself—being a physician's assistant, for example—is more important than the prestige or the paycheck.

> Where might boomers live when they need bathtub grip bars and someone to tell them when to take their Prozac—when it is problematic to live alone, but before they become severely incapacitated?

At a recent conference hosted by New York's International Longevity Center (ILC), the center's president and CEO, Dr. Robert Butler—an ardent, soft-spoken, 73-year-old dynamo—pointed out that America is becoming a "gerontocracy": that in 30 years we will have the same proportion of population 65 and older—one in five—as Florida does today. One bit of evidence that we're heading in this direction is the extraordinarily high membership of AARP. With its 32 million members (median age: 64), AARP publishes the country's highest-circulation magazine, *Modern Maturity* (which has 20 million readers and commands up to $270,000 per advertising page), and has just launched a boomer-friendly version, *My Generation*, for AARPies closer to 50.

But according to Robert Blancato, an activist and lobbyist who's been involved in national aging policy for 20 years, boomers may not join AARP, or any other group, the way their parents did, if his experience is any indication. In 1998 he founded Boomer Agenda, which he just disbanded for prospective members' lack of interest. "We surveyed a few thousand boomers on long-term-care insurance, age discrimination, privacy," he said. "They cared about the issues but didn't want to join an organization." With baby boomers at the helm, with cultural icons like Steinem, Ram Dass, and Hillary Clinton—people who understand that the personal is political, that private life easily becomes public, and that we have the capacity and longevity to reinvent ourselves any number of times—old age seems poised to become a period associated with liberation, innovation, the next cool thing: a sort of Woodstock Nation redux.

Except, of course, we won't want to thrash around half-naked in the mud anymore. We will need somewhere to live or some kind of help when we can't do it all ourselves; and in this area, too, we will be doing our best to rewrite the rules. Not only are we more highly educated than any previous generation, but we are more exacting consumers. By the time we need help getting around, most of us will have been exposed, in taking care of our parents, to the wretched current system—or non-system—of long-term care, "which means impoverishing and institutionalizing our elders if they are to receive any kind of public support," as author Trudy Lieberman (with the editors of *Consumer Reports*) explains in the *Complete Guide to Health Services for Seniors*.

The best-case scenario is that numbers and savvy will translate into political power that can bring about major change. The worst-case scenario is reduced access to Social Security, Medicare, and Medicaid.

The best-case scenario is that our numbers, our savvy, and our needs will translate into political power that can bring about major change. Given the predictions about the coming insolvency of Social Security, Medicare, and Medicaid, major change may consist of simply finding a way to fund these programs at levels that will support elderly baby boomers. Radical change could include fixing them so that the system provides what's known as "a seamless continuum of care," instead of what Lieberman calls the current "fragmented, inhumane system of care that is a nightmare to navigate."

It's daydreaming to envision universal medical coverage or even a comprehensive social-insurance or pension policy for the elderly in the United States. Although several developed countries, including the United Kingdom, Germany, and Japan, have impressive home- and community-based services for long-term care, the United States has made no real effort to emulate their programs. Not surprisingly, in our era of bottom-line legislating, a country that lacks the political will to protect 44 million of its inhabitants without medical coverage has taken no bold steps in this direction. The distance we have yet to travel in even thinking about long-term care is encapsulated in a statistic Dr. Butler of the ILC often quotes: In our 126 accredited medical schools, we have three departments of geriatrics, while every medical school in England has its own. Why do we give the elderly such short shrift? Time, money, and prestige. They are labor-intensive to treat, Medicare reimbursements are slender, and

no one is going to discover a cure for old age. In the face of such systemic obstacles, elderly baby boomers may continue to do what's currently being done: tinker with federal programs and make piecemeal improvements.

LONG-TERM PROSPECTS

Echoing UN High Commissioner for Human Rights Mary Robinson's assertion that old age is a human rights issue, Dr. Butler warns of the potential for displacement, suffering, and widespread poverty among elderly baby boomers ill prepared for their old age. One recent trend touted as a positive development for seniors who own property and have assets to protect is long-term-care insurance. It is endorsed in certain circumstances by a wide array of organizations—including AARP, which sells policies, the National Alliance for Caregiving and United Seniors Health Cooperative, which do not, and *Consumer Reports*. Age guru and best-selling writer Ken Dychtwald believes it should be part of a family's long-term financial planning. As president, Bill Clinton recently made it available to be purchased by federal employees.

Still, long-term-care insurance remains controversial, both as an insurance product and as an investment. It is expensive and asks you to pay for a benefit you may not need for 30 years—a nursing home, a home health aide, assisted living. And in 30 years, when you need that benefit, it may be called something else and your policy may not cover the service under its new name. While you can purchase a policy that has inflation protection, you will pay a higher premium. I have heard stories of brokers so eager to make a sale that they sell someone a policy without inflation protection; when the benefit is needed—20 or 30 years later—it may be worth a fraction of what is necessary.

"It's not a scam," said Ron Pollack, executive director of Families USA. "It's just not a good buy." When I asked him why so many senior organizations and advocates encourage it, his heartbreaking answer spoke to the paucity of choices before us: "What else can they say?"

The issue of long-term care is so deeply enmeshed in almost every aspect of life—from our spending, savings, and eating habits to our day-to-day dealings with our aging parents—that imagining how and where we might live 30 years from now is a dizzying prospect. But as we begin, tentatively, to envision these brave new worlds, there are four general housing and social trends to bear in mind.

1. People want to stay home rather than move to an institution. In a May 2000 AARP study of people 45 and older, the vast majority—82 percent—said they would rather not move from their current home if they were to need help caring for themselves. Only 9 percent would prefer "moving to a facility where care is provided," and only 4 percent to a relative's home. It's a good thing that most would choose to stay put: If worst-case scenarios come true, baby boomers will have reduced access to Social Security, Medicare, and Medicaid, and the least affluent may have to find ways to stay safely at home. In senior-housing jargon, staying home in all of its forms is known as "aging in place." Either people fix up their houses to make them infirmity-friendly or, if they are well-to-do and don't mind planned communities, they relocate before they become frail and move to one of a growing number of continuing-care retirement communities. Residents pay a hefty entrance fee in addition to monthly maintenance ($1,500 to $5,000) for housing that accommodates their needs at every stage. They begin in an apartment and move when necessary to the assisted-living wing, then to the nursing wing. It's expensive and becomes even more so when an elderly couple's needs diverge and they are paying for both an apartment and a bed in the nursing wing.

A house retrofitted to infirmities is known as a "smart house." Many observers, including consultant Lenise Dolen, believe that smart houses as well as food-delivery services and chore helpers will change baby boomers' frail old age to a stay-at-home proposition. The huge demand for these services will make them affordable. We might also see an increase in community-based "adult day care" services or community-based home help.

In creating smart houses, innovation is coming from both sides of the Atlantic, with the English excelling in charm and the Americans in efficiency. "A Smart House for People with Dementia," a project of the University of Bath, is a real model house in Gloucester, England, outfitted with computer-driven household systems that issue warnings ("Don't forget, you've left the bath running, Mum"), locate lost objects (pressing an image on the computer pad will make the object warble until you find it), and turn on lights when you get out of bed at night. In a suburb of Portland, Oregon, a new assisted-living facility—Oatfield Estates, run by Elite Care—has incorporated institutional versions of these concepts to help rather than replace human staff members; some residents are even hooked up to electronic locating badges. The pioneering owner, Bill Reed, who was influenced by seeing how his mother had taken care of her mother in her later years, seems to understand that his community is something of a work in progress and that there are complicated challenges in meshing the wonders of technology with human needs for care and attention.

Alan Solomont, a prominent Democratic Party donor who for decades was a leader in building nursing homes and assisted-living communities in Massachusetts, now finances HouseWorks, a smart-house company in Newton, Massachusetts. "We're used to taking people to services they need, but now that the era of big government has begun to wane, we're trying to reverse that and take the services to the people," he said. "I don't know a family that isn't struggling with this issue. The most important thing our country can do now is to recognize that long-

term care is an issue and that there is not a big safety net to jump into."

2. Medicaid supports alternatives to nursing homes for poor people, but at pitifully inadequate levels. Since 1981, Medicaid, the federally funded and state administered health agency for the indigent of all ages, has allowed states to apply to the Health Care Financing Administration (HCFA) for what are called "Medicaid waivers," targeted, small-scale exemptions to the rule that Medicaid will pay for indigent care only if the beneficiaries are in nursing homes. Individual states, which must get approval from their legislatures, petition HCFA to provide certain services (such as home health aides, adult day care, transportation, and minor home modification) to a specified number of people, hundreds or several thousand, in a specific population—elderly, disabled, or mentally ill. (To be eligible to participate in a Medicaid waiver program, individuals must meet the same criteria they would for Medicaid to pick up a tab in a nursing home: They must be frail and have no more in total assets than $2,000 to $3,000, depending on the state, not including Social Security payments.) If approved, the states administer these programs for three- to five-year periods. All states currently have Medicaid waiver programs; 37 states have waivers that offer aid to the elderly poor for assisted living. Sadly, Medicaid waivers nationwide are helping only about 60,000 poor seniors to live somewhere other than a nursing home, while every year Medicaid pays the nursing home bill for 68 percent of residents: an average of $56,000, for about 1.02 million people.

The Medicaid waiver program is so modest for two reasons. First, the nursing-home industry depends on Medicaid reimbursements for most of its income and is threatened by anything that directs money elsewhere. (Some traditional nursing homes have minimized the blow from the surge in assisted living by converting properties and getting into the business themselves, though the absence of regulation makes it impossible to monitor the extent and quality of these efforts.) Second, state administrators, whose Medicaid waiver programs must be "budget neutral," keep programs small for fear of the potential "woodwork effect": Poor people who would otherwise not choose a nursing home might swarm out of the woodwork if they knew they could get Medicaid funds to help them stay safely at home—and budgets would soar.

Yet in states where waivers exist, some have saved the state money and kept people where they want to be: at home. According to the 7,000-member Assisted Living Federation of America, Oregon's waivers saved the state an estimated $227 million between 1981 and 1991, from a projected expenditure of $1.35 billion. Maine reduced total long-term-care spending from $228 million in 1995 to $185 million in 1998 and served 3,700 more people.

Again, the question for baby boomers will be whether we reinvent the hydra-headed monster that Medicaid has become or continue to allow our poorest citizens—and their caregiving families—to be subjected to the systemic indignities, inequities, and corruption of these programs.

3. Other government programs are being adjusted to meet the housing needs of the poor and low-income elderly. Again, the United States is taking baby steps toward addressing an overwhelming nationwide need for affordable assisted living. In December 2000, Andrew Cuomo's Department of Housing and Urban Development (HUD) announced a new, $50-million effort—the Assisted Living Conversion Program—to convert subsidized housing for poor seniors into affordable assisted-living space. One wants to applaud any efforts in this direction, but $50 million is hardly a resounding display of federal commitment. Since its founding in 1959, Section 202—the only federally funded housing program specifically designed for seniors—has supported the construction of more than 300,000 individual units in 5,000 housing complexes. But new building has tapered off over the past 20 years, falling from around 15,000 new units annually in 1981, when Ronald Reagan took office, to a projected 6,500 this year. (Poor seniors are also eligible for Section 8 housing, a voucher program administered by HUD, but such assistance can only help defray costs and does not address the needs that may go along with aging.)

Bush administration policies don't inspire hope that the Assisted Living Conversion Program will flourish. Even a partial list of the facilities lucky enough to get grants last year suggests the depth of our nation's collective denial about this problem. One subsidized housing project in New Haven, Connecticut, was awarded $4.2 million to convert or modify 33 apartments; another in Jacksonville, Florida, received $2.7 million to transform 36 apartments into assisted-living units.

Positive news is largely restricted to the local level—and measured in two- and three-digit numbers. A builder of relatively upscale senior residences in Michigan has been an innovator at using federal and state programs in tandem to keep diminishing funds from forcing some of his state's seniors out of assisted-living facilities and into nursing homes. J. Robert Gillette, the president of American House Senior Living Residences, has built 27 senior-housing facilities in metropolitan Detroit; costs for building six of them were subsidized by federal and state tax credits that require a certain percentage of units be rented to low-income tenants at below-market rates.

In addition to the tax subsidies—through the federal Low-Income Housing Tax Credit program and the Michigan State Housing Development Authority—Gillette has incorporated Medicaid waiver programs that help 160 poorer residents pay for housework, meals, dressing, and medication reminders. Because of the size of his operation, Gillette is in a position to have some of his residences subsidize others whose profits are not as high; but he is also willing to reach out creatively to people who need help.

Though the federal government's overall approach to long-term care hasn't changed much since 1965, Gillette and others have taken advantage of the several highly technical tax-credit and financing programs geared toward developers and local governments, rather than consumers, to help bring more affordable senior housing to the market. Such federal initiatives include the Low-Income Housing Tax Credit program, the HUD-FHA 232 Mortgage Insurance program, the Federal Home Loan Bank program, the HOME program, and the HUD Community Development Block Grants. But again, the challenges of coordinating these limited and disparate programs with other public and private funds militate against large-scale changes.

4. Baby boomers are beginning to create their own unique assisted-living communities. Writer Vivian Gornick has spearheaded an ambitious project, still being developed, that would allow women in the arts to age in place once they have moved to a desirable place in which to do it. Gornick's nonprofit organization, the House of Elder Artists, aims to build a 100-apartment building in New York City, a project she described in an interview as a "senior residence for women in the arts in which we can go on living and working until the end of life." She envisions a set of public rooms—dining and living rooms—where residents will give lectures, hold readings, and show artwork. "The most important thing," she emphasized, "is to keep a working mind alive, not to play golf or bingo."

If Gornick's project exemplifies the philosophy of "productive aging" (continuing to achieve and extending work life), another innovative senior-housing project in Santa Fe, New Mexico—primarily for those with low and limited incomes—very openly follows the "conscious aging" movement (seeking spiritual growth and talking openly about aging and death). Artist Geoffrey Landis and psychologist and educator Stefan Dobuszynski, both community activists, are working toward building Jubilados. (Spanish for "those who have joy," *jubilados* is a term used in Central and South America for "retired people.") The project is based on Buddhist principles of interconnectedness and respect for the earth. Landis and Dobuszynski plan for the 128 units, on 13 acres of arable land just outside Santa Fe, to include a meditation hall, health care unit, and hospice, to house up to 160 people, and to be open for business in 2003. Expecting to attract residents who have devoted their lives to social activism and spiritual development rather than to amassing money, they also anticipate that 30 percent of the residents will be nonelderly individuals. As a nonprofit corporation, they are seeking funding from foundations and government financing programs, including some of those mentioned above.

It's hokey to talk about revolution anymore, but as baby boomers grow old in new ways, we might initiate another one to add to the sexual revolution, the women's movement, and our explorations in cyberspace. We'll have longer and healthier life expectancy than any previous population, and we're slated to add seven or eight years to it by 2030. Though we won't have as many children or spouses to take care of us as our predecessors did, we'll have had a lifetime of practice taking care of ourselves. And we won't all be heading for Florida or Arizona.

But what must be done to spare ourselves the same future that makes so many of our parents' later years a nightmarish tangle with dysfunctional bureaucracies? With only one in three or four seniors able to afford appropriate care now, and with a widespread perception that the elderly are reaping more than their share of the social-welfare bounty, we are getting a taste of the conflicts that will come on a much larger scale. To minimize the pervasive poverty and hardship that Dr. Butler and others predict, Medicare, Medicaid, and Social Security must be reinvented for the twenty-first century. President Bush and Congress ought not rush to "return the people's money to the people." The rest of us, individually, should start stockpiling savings. Collectively, we'd do well to take the standard advice given to addicts: Admit that we have a problem and ask for help.

One of the cruel tricks of life is how fast it seems to go by; how young we often feel and how old we look in the mirror. I joke with a friend that when we move to Shangri-la ourselves, her room will be bigger than mine. Her answer makes me laugh and cry: "And we'll be there in two minutes." I will blink a dozen times and be 60, but what a long, long way our country has to go to begin to address the crushing, hugely complicated problem of how and where the elderly should live. "The biggest surprise that comes to a man is old age," said Leon Trotsky, whose views are out of favor these days. But the biggest surprise coming to millions of baby boomers is how complicated and costly it is to be old in America—and how soon that is going to start to matter to so many of us.

ELIZABETH BENEDICT'S fourth novel, *Almost*, was published in August 2001 by Houghton Mifflin.

UNIT 4
Institutional Problems

Unit Selections

Key Points to Consider

- What changes in the family do you think are good and what changes do you think are bad? What can be done about the bad changes?

- Discuss the good and bad aspects of divorce. What are the forces behind the high divorce rates? Will these forces decline or increase? Defend your answer.

- What is wrong with America's education system and how can it be improved?

- What is your assessment of the health care system in America? What are its major faults? How should it be fixed?

 **Links: www.dushkin.com/online/**
These sites are annotated in the World Wide Web pages.

The Center for Education Reform
http://edreform.com/school_choice/

Go Ask Alice!
http://www.goaskalice.columbia.edu

The National Academy for Child Development (NACD)
http://www.nacd.org

National Council on Family Relations (NCFR)
http://www.ncfr.com

National Institute on Aging (NIA)
http://www.nih.gov/nia/

National Institute on Drug Abuse (NIDA)
http://165.112.78.61

National Institutes of Health (NIH)
http://www.nih.gov

Parenting and Families
http://www.cyfc.umn.edu/features/index.html

A Sociological Tour Through Cyberspace
http://www.trinity.edu/~mkearl/index.html

World Health Organization (WHO)
http://www.who.int/home-page/

This unit looks at the problems in three institutional areas: the family, education, and health care. The first subsection deals with the problems of the family. The family is important. Politicians and preachers are earnestly preaching this message today as though most people need to be converted. Of course, since everyone already agrees, the preaching is mostly ritual. Nevertheless, families are having real problems. The causes of the problems are not due to a lack of commitment as much as to numerous changes in society that have had an impact on the family. For example, women have to work because many men do not make enough income to support a family adequately. Women are working not only to enjoy a career but also out of necessity. With women working, they are less dependent on their husbands. As a result, divorce becomes more of an option and psychologically more likely. Since there are many other forces that make divorce more likely, the issue of strong families is complex and the articles in this section shed some helpful light on the problems. In the first article, Stephanie Coontz corrects many common misunderstandings about the family. She takes issue with the data presented for the decline of marriage and the family thesis and offers evidence that marriage is strong today even though divorce is common. In fact, she argues that today's families are better than families a century ago in many ways. According to Coontz "the biggest problem facing most families… is not that our families have changed too much but that our institutions have changed too little." In the second article Kathleen Deveny discusses the problem of modern couples often overworking or having so many activities that they do not have enough energy for much of a sex life. Many couples, however, make special efforts to overcome this problem.

The next two articles look at divorce. The first, by James Q. Wilson, analyzes why the "illegitimacy ratio" has risen to 33 percent. Using history and statistics, Wilson searches for the major causes. He argues that welfare is a cause, although a small one. The big cause is cultural changes that have removed the stigma of both welfare and unmarried motherhood. Cultural changes have also weakened the moral underpinnings of marriage. Since Wilson believes in the power of culture, he also believes that it is very hard to change the situation. The next article, by Walter Kirn presents a fairly complete examination of the consequences of divorce on the children. He reviews the debate over whether a bad marriage or a divorce is more harmful for the children. The evidence shows that both are bad.

The second subsection deals with education, a perennial problem area. John Taylor Gatto attacks the American school system for slowing the maturation of students and being boring.

He suspects that this result is exactly what those who control the school system want schools to do. In arguing his radical thesis he presents a very provocative history of the evolution of the American school system.

The last subsection deals with health issues. The first article, by Daniel Eisenberg and Maggie Sieger Joliet discuss the problem of the soaring costs of malpractice insurance which are driving many doctors out of business. Health care suffers as a result so the legal structure of health care needs reform. The next article reports pain and death involved in the worldwide epidemic of AIDS, with its focus on sub-Saharan Africa where 70 percent of those infected with HIV/AIDS reside. Of course, we would expect the various governments to do everything in their power to stop the epidemic and help the victims, and for the friends and relatives of the victims to have compassion on them. Unfortunately the true story is quite ugly. The shocking failure of many societies in the AIDS crisis reveals the fragility of these societies. The unbelievable brutality of the treatment of AIDS victims by relatives and others reveals the depths of the evil that many people are capable of when they are afraid.

THE AMERICAN FAMILY

New research about an old institution challenges the conventional wisdom that the family today is worse off than in the past. Essay by Stephanie Coontz

As the century comes to an end, many observers fear for the future of America's families. Our divorce rate is the highest in the world, and the percentage of unmarried women is significantly higher than in 1960. Educated women are having fewer babies, while immigrant children flood the schools, demanding to be taught in their native language. Harvard University reports that only 4 percent of its applicants can write a proper sentence.

Things were worse at the turn of the last century than they are today. Most workers labored 10 hours a day, six days a week, leaving little time for family life.

There's an epidemic of sexually transmitted diseases among men. Many streets in urban neighborhoods are littered with cocaine vials. Youths call heroin "happy dust." Even in small towns, people have easy access to addictive drugs, and drug abuse by middle-class wives is skyrocketing. Police see 16-year-old killers, 12-year-old prostitutes, and gang members as young as 11.

America at the end of the 1990s? No, America at the end of the 1890s.

The litany of complaints may sound familiar, but the truth is that many things were worse at the start of this century than they are today. Then, thousands of children worked full-time in mines, mills and sweatshops. Most

workers labored 10 hours a day, often six days a week, which left them little time or energy for family life. Race riots were more frequent and more deadly than those experienced by recent generations. Women couldn't vote, and their wages were so low that many turned to prostitution.

DAHLSTROM COLLECTION/TIME INC.

c. **1890** A couple and their six children sit for a family portrait. With smaller families today, mothers spend twice as much time with each kid.

In 1900 a white child had one chance in three of losing a brother or sister before age 15, and a black child had a fifty-fifty chance of seeing a sibling die. Children's-aid groups reported widespread abuse and neglect by parents. Men who deserted or divorced their wives rarely paid child support. And only 6 percent of the children graduated from high school, compared with 88 percent today.

LEWIS HINE/CULVER PICTURES

1915 An Italian immigrant family gathers around the dinner table in an apartment on the East Side of New York City. Today, most families still eat together—but often out.

Why do so many people think American families are facing worse problems now than in the past? Partly it's because we compare the complex and diverse families of the 1990s with the seemingly more standard-issue ones of the 1950s, a unique decade when every long-term trend of the 20th century was temporarily reversed. In the 1950s, for the first time in 100 years, the divorce rate fell while marriage and fertility rates soared, crating a boom in nuclear-family living. The percentage of foreign-born individuals in the country decreased. And the debates over social and cultural issues that had divided Americans for 150 years were silenced, suggesting a national consensus on family values and norms.

Some nostalgia for the 1950s is understandable: Life looked pretty good in comparison with the hardship of the Great Depression and World War II. The GI Bill gave a generation of young fathers a college education and a subsidized mortgage on a new house. For the first time, a majority of men could support a family and buy a home without pooling their earnings with those of other family members. Many Americans built a stable family life on these foundations.

But much nostalgia for the 1950s is a result of selective amnesia—the same process that makes childhood memories of summer vacations grow sunnier with each passing year. The superficial sameness of 1950s family life was achieved through censorship, coercion and discrimination. People with unconventional beliefs faced governmental investigation and arbitrary firings. African Americans and Mexican Americans were prevented from voting in some states by literacy tests that were not administered to whites. Individuals who didn't follow the rigid gender and sexual rules of the day were ostracized.

Leave It to Beaver did not reflect the real-life experience of most American families. While many moved into the middle class during the 1950s, poverty remained more widespread than in the worst of our last three recessions. More children went hungry, and poverty rates for the elderly were more than twice as high as today's.

Even in the white middle class, not every woman was as serenely happy with her lot as June Cleaver was on TV. Housewives of the 1950s may have been less rushed than today's working mothers, but they were more likely to suffer anxiety and depression. In many states, women couldn't serve on juries or get loans or credit cards in their own names.

And not every kid was as wholesome as Beaver Cleaver, whose mischievous antics could be handled by Dad at the dinner table. In 1955 alone, Congress discussed 200 bills aimed at curbing juvenile delinquency. Three years later, LIFE reported that urban teachers were being terrorized by their students. The drugs that were so freely available in 1900 had been outlawed, but many children grew up in families ravaged by alcohol and barbiturate abuse.

Rates of unwed childbearing tripled between 1940 and 1958, but most Americans didn't notice because unwed mothers generally left town, gave their babies up for adoption and returned home as if nothing had happened. Troubled youths were encouraged to drop out of high school. Mentally handicapped children were warehoused in institutions like the Home for Idiotic and Imbecilic Children in Kansas, where a woman whose sister had lived there for most of the 1950s once took me. Wives routinely told pollsters that being disparaged or ignored by their husbands was a normal part of a happier than-average marriage.

Many of our worries today reflect how much better we want to be, not how much better we used to be.

Denial extended to other areas of life as well. In the early 1900s, doctors refused to believe that the cases of gonorrhea and syphilis they saw in young girls could have been caused by sexual abuse. Instead, they reasoned, girls could get these diseases from toilet seats, a myth that terrified generations of mothers and daughters. In the 1950s, psychiatrists dismissed incest reports as Oedipal fantasies on the part of children.

Spousal rape was legal throughout the period and wife beating was not taken seriously by authorities. Much of what we now label child abuse was accepted as a normal part of parental discipline. Physicians saw no reason to question parents who claimed that their child's broken bones had been caused by a fall from a tree.

MARGARET BOURKE-WHITE

1937: The Hahn family sits in the living room of a working-class Muncie home, which rents for $10 a month. Class distinctions have eroded over 60 years.

American Mirror

Muncie, Ind. (pop. 67,476), calls itself America's Hometown. But to generations of sociologists it is better known as America's Middletown—the most studied place in the 20th century American landscape. "Muncie has nothing extraordinary about it," says University of Virginia professor Theodore Caplow, which is why, for the past 75 years, researchers have gone there to observe the typical American family. Muncie's averageness first drew sociologists Robert and Helen Lynd in 1924. They returned in 1935 (their follow-up study was featured in a LIFE photo essay by Margaret Bourke-White). And in 1976, armed with the Lynds' original questionnaires, Caplow launched yet another survey of the town's citizens.

Caplow discovered that family life in Muncie was much healthier in the 1970s than in the 1920s. No only were husbands and wives communicating more, but unlike married couples in the 1920s, they were also shopping, eating out, exercising and going to movies and concerts together. More than 90 percent of Muncie's couples characterized their marriages as "happy" or "very happy." In 1929 the Lynds had described partnerships of a drearier kind, "marked by sober accommodation of each partner to his share in the joint undertaking of children, paying off the mortgage and generally 'getting on.'"

Caplow's five-year study, which inspired a six-part PBS series, found that even though more moms were working outside the home, two thirds of them spent at least two hours a day with their children; in 1924 fewer than half did. In 1924 most children expected their mothers to be good cooks and housekeepers, and wanted their fathers to spend time with them and respect their opinions. Fifty years later, expectations of fathers were unchanged, but children wanted the same—time and respect—from their mothers.

This year, Caplow went back to survey the town again. The results (and another TV documentary) won't be released until December 2000.

—*Sora Song*

There are plenty of stresses in modern family life, but one reason they seem worse is that we no longer sweep them under the rug. Another is that we have higher expectations of parenting and marriage. That's a good thing. We're right to be concerned about inattentive parents, conflicted marriages, antisocial values, teen violence and child abuse. But we need to realize that many of our worries reflect how much better we *want* to be, not how much better we *used* to be.

Fathers in intact families are spending more time with their children than at any other point in the past 100 years. Although the number of hours the average woman spends at home with her children has declined since the early 1900s, there has been a decrease in the number of children per family and an increase in individual attention to each child. As a result, mothers today, including working moms, spend almost twice as much time with each child as mothers did in the 1920s. People who raised children in the 1940s and 1950s typically report that their own adult children and grandchildren communicate far better with their kids and spend more time helping with homework than they did—even as they complain that other parents today are doing a worse job than in the past.

Despite the rise in youth violence from the 1960s to the early 1990s, America's children are also safer now than they've ever been. An infant was four times more likely to die in the 1950s than today. A parent then was three times more likely than a modern one to preside at the funeral of a child under the age of 15, and 27 percent more likely to lose an older teen to death.

If we look back over the last millennium, we can see that families have always been diverse and in flux. In each period, families have solved one set of problems only to face a new array of challenges. What works for a family in one economic and cultural setting doesn't work for a family in another. What's helpful at one stage of a family's life may be destructive at the next stage. If there is one lesson to be drawn from the last millennium of family history, it's that families are always having to play catch-up with a changing world.

Take the issue of working mothers. Families in which mothers spend as much time earning a living as they do raising children are nothing new. They were the norm throughout most of the last two millennia. In the 19th century, married women in the United States began a withdrawal from the workforce, but for most families this was made possible only by sending their children out to work instead. When child labor was abolished, married women began reentering the workforce in ever large numbers.

For a few decades, the decline in child labor was greater than the growth of women's employment. The result was an aberration: the male-breadwinner family. In the 1920s, for the first time, a bare majority of American children grew up in families where the husband provided all the income, the wife stayed home full-time, and they and their siblings went to school instead of work. During the 1950s, almost two thirds of children grew up in such

MARK KAUFFMAN

1955 A family poses in Seattle. Husbands today are doing more housework.

families, an all-time high. Yet that same decade saw an acceleration of workforce participation by wives and mothers that soon made the dual-earner family the norm, a trend not likely to be reversed in the next century.

What's new is not that women make half their families' living, but that for the first time they have substantial control over their own income, along with the social freedom to remain single or to leave an unsatisfactory marriage. Also new is the declining proportion of their lives that people devote to rearing children, both because they have fewer kids and because they are living longer. Until about 1940, the typical marriage was broken by the death of one partner within a few years after the last child left home. Today, couples can look forward to spending more than two decades together after the children leave.

The growing length of time partners spend with only each other for company has made many individuals less willing to put up with an unhappy marriage, while women's economic independence makes it less essential for them to do so. It is no wonder that divorce has risen steadily since 1900. Disregarding a spurt in 1946, a dip in the 1950s and another peak around 1980, the divorce rate is just where you'd expect to find it, based on the rate of

increase from 1900 to 1950. Today, 40 percent of all marriages will end in divorce before a couple's 40th anniversary. Yet despite this high divorce rate, expanded life expectancies mean that more couples are reaching that anniversary than ever before.

Families and individuals in contemporary America have more life choices than in the past. That makes it easier for some to consider dangerous or unpopular options. But it also makes success easier for many families that never would have had a chance before—interracial, gay or lesbian, and single-mother families, for example. And it expands horizons for most families.

Women's new options are good not just for themselves but for their children. While some people say that women who choose to work are selfish, it turns out that maternal self-sacrifice is not good for children. Kids do better when their mothers are happy with their lives, whether their satisfaction comes from being a full-time homemaker or from having a job.

Largely because of women's new roles at work, men are doing more at home. Although most men still do less housework than their wives, the gap has been halved since the 1960s. Today, 49 percent of couples say they share childcare equally, compared with 25 percent of 1985.

Men's greater involvement at home is good for their relationships with their parents, and also good for their children. Hands-on fathers make better parents than men who let their wives do all the nurturing and childcare: They raise sons who are more expressive and daughters who are more likely to do well in school, especially in math and science.

The biggest problem is not that our families have changed too much but that our institutions have changed too little.

In 1900, life expectancy was 47 years, and only 4 percent of the population was 65 or older. Today, life expectancy is 76 years, and by 2025, about 20 percent of Americans will be 65 or older. For the first time, a generation of adults must plan for the needs of both their parents and their children. Most Americans are responding with remarkable grace. One in four households gives the equivalent of a full day a week or more in unpaid care to an aging relative, and more than half say they expect to do so in the next 10 years. Older people are less likely to be impoverished or incapacitated by illness than in the past, and they have more opportunity to develop a relationship with their grandchildren.

Even some of the choices that worry us the most are turning out to be manageable. Divorce rates are likely to remain high, but more non-custodial parents are staying in touch with their children. Child-support receipts are up. And a lower proportion of kids from divorced families are exhibiting problems than in earlier decades. Stepfamilies are learning to maximize children's access to supportive adults rather than cutting them off from one side of the family.

Out-of-wedlock births are also high, however, and this will probably continue because the age of first marriage for women has risen to an all-time high of 25, almost five years above what it was in the 1950s. Women who marry at an older age are less likely to divorce, but they have more years when they are at risk—or at choice—for a nonmarital birth.

Nevertheless, births to teenagers have fallen from 50 percent of all nonmarital births in the late 1970s to just 30 percent today. A growing proportion of women who have a nonmarital birth are in their twenties and thirties and usually have more economic and educational resources than unwed mothers of the past. While two involved parents are generally better than one, a mother's personal maturity, along with her educational and economic status, is a better predictor of how well her child will turn out than her marital status. We should no longer assume that children raised by single parents face debilitating disadvantages.

As we begin to understand the range of sizes, shapes and colors that today's families come in, we find that the differences *within* family types are more important than the differences *between* them. No particular family form guarantees success, and no particular form is doomed to fail. How a family functions on the inside is more important than how it looks from the outside.

The biggest problem facing most families as this century draws to a close is not that our families have changed too much but that our institutions have changed too little. America's work policies are 50 years out of date, designed for a time when most moms weren't in the workforce and most dads didn't understand the joys of being involved in childcare. Our school schedules are 150 years out of date, designed for a time when kids needed to be home to help with the milking and haying. And many political leaders feel they have to decide whether to help parents stay home longer with their kids or invest in better childcare, preschool and afterschool programs, when most industrialized nations have long since learned it's possible to do both.

So America's social institutions have some Y2K bugs to iron out. But for the most part, our families are ready for the next millennium.

WE'RE NOT IN THE MOOD

For married couples with kids and busy jobs, sex just isn't what it used to be. How stress causes strife in the bedroom—and beyond.

BY KATHLEEN DEVENY

FOR MADDIE WEINREICH, SEX HAD ALWAYS BEEN A JOY. IT helped her recharge her batteries and reconnect with her husband, Roger. But teaching yoga, raising two kids and starting up a business—not to mention cooking, cleaning and renovating the house—left her exhausted. She often went to bed before her husband, and was asleep by the time he joined her. Their once steamy love life slowly cooled. When Roger wanted to have sex, she would say she was too beat. He tried to be romantic; to set the mood he'd light a candle in their bedroom. "I would see it and say, 'Oh, God, not that candle'," Maddie recalls. "It was just the feeling that I had to give something I didn't have."

Lately, it seems, we're just not in the mood. We're overworked, anxious about the economy—and we have to drive our kids to way too many T-Ball games. Or maybe it's all those libido-dimming antidepressants we're taking. We resent spouses who never pick up the groceries or their dirty socks. And if we actually find we have 20 minutes at the end of the day—after bath time and story time and juice-box time and e-mail time—who wouldn't rather zone out to Leno than have sex? Sure, passion ebbs and flows in even the healthiest of relationships, but judging from the conversation of the young moms at the next table at Starbucks, it sounds like we're in the midst of a long dry spell.

It's difficult to say exactly how many of the 113 million married Americans are too exhausted or too grumpy to get it on, but some psychologists estimate that 15 to 20

percent of couples have sex no more than 10 times a year, which is how the experts define sexless marriage. And even couples who don't meet that definition still feel like they're not having sex as often as they used to. Despite the stereotype that women are more likely to dodge sex, it's often the men who decline. The number of sexless marriages is "a grossly underreported statistic," says therapist Michele Weiner Davis, author of "The Sex-Starved Marriage."

IF SO, THE PROBLEM MUST BE HUGE, GIVEN HOW MUCH WE already hear about it. Books like "The Sex-Starved Marriage," "Rekindling Desire: A Step-by-Step Program to Help Low-Sex and No-Sex Marriages" and "Resurrecting Sex" have become talk-show fodder. Dr. Phil has weighed in on the crisis; his Web site proclaims "the epidemic is undeniable." Avlimil, an herbal concoction that promises to help women put sex back into sexless marriage, had sales of 200,000 packages in January, its first month on the market. The company says it's swamped with as many as 3,000 calls a day from women who are desperately seeking desire. Not that the problem is confined to New Agers: former U.S. Labor secretary Robert Reich jokes about the pressure couples are under in speeches he gives on overworked Americans. Have you heard of DINS? he asks his audience. It stands for dual income, no sex.

Sex and the Century: A History

Over the past 100 years, our understanding of sexual behavior has changed dramatically—
and it's still evolving. From Sigmund to Sarah Jessica and Lucy to Lorena,
here are some of the highlights:

1905 Sigmund Freud's 'Three Essays on Sexuality' misinform generations about the nature of the female orgasm.

1934 Henry Miller's 'Tropic of Cancer,' a semifictional memoir, debuts in Paris. But the expatiriate's libidinous adventures get banned in the United States.

1952 Lucille Ball is the first pregnant woman to play a mother-to-be in a sitcom—but she isn't allowed to say the word 'pregnancy' on TV.

1953 Alred Kinsey publishes 'Sexual Behavior in the Human Female,' the first major U.S. survey on women's sexual habits. He finds that Americans' attitudes don't match their behavior—50 percent have had premarital sex.

December 1953 Marilyn Monroe takes it all off in the first issue of Playboy. Hugh Hefner's open love letter to bachelorhood.

1960 The Food and Drug Administration OKs the birth-control pill, fueling the sexual revolution.

1962 Helen Gurley Brown publishes her best-selling book 'Sex and the Single Girl.'

1965 In *Griswold v. Connecticut*, the Supreme Court rules that the government cannot regulate a married couple's use of birth control.

1966 William Masters and Virginia Johnson's 'Human Sexual Response' finds that half of all U.S. Marriages are plagued by some kind of sexual inadequacy.

1970 Female college students nationwide adopt 'Our Bodies, Ourselves' as their bible on health and sexuality.

1973 In *Roe v. Wade*, the Supreme Court decides that a woman's right to privacy encompasses her decision to terminate a pregnancy.

1981 State Supreme Court cases in Massachusetts and New Jersey rule that husbands can be prosecuted for raping their wives—overturning the centuries-old marital-rape exception.

1984 Researchers isolate the virus responsible for causing AIDS.

1987 In 'Fatal Attraction,' Michael Douglas and Glenn Close share a one-night stand that turns mighty ugly. Mmm, rabbit.

1993 Lorena Bobbit cuts off her husband's penis with a kitchen knife. Men nationwide cross their legs a little tighter.

June 2003 HBO's 'Sex and the City,' which candidly chronicles the love lives of four professional, single women in New York City, kicks off its final season.

—MELISSA BREWSTER

LOOKING FOR LOVE: New Yorkers Rosemary Breslin and her husband, Tony Dunne, joke that they've shelved sex till 2004.

Marriage counselors can't tell you how much sex you should be having, but most agree that you should be having *some*. Sex is only a small part of a good union, but happy marriages usually include it. Frequency of sex may be a measure of a marriage's long-term health; if it suddenly starts to decline, it can be a leading indicator of deeper problems, just like "those delicate green frogs that let us know when we're destroying the environment," says psychologist John Gottman, who runs the Family Research Lab (dubbed the Love Lab) at the University of Washington. Marriage pros say intimacy is often the glue that holds a couple together over time. If either member of a couple is miserable with the amount of sex in a marriage, it can cause devastating problems—and, in some cases, divorce. It can affect moods and spill over into all aspects of life—relationships with other family members, even performance in the office.

Best-selling novels and prime-time sit-coms only reinforce the idea that we're not having sex. In the opening pages of Allison Pearson's portrait of a frazzled working mom, "I Don't Know How She Does It," the novel's heroine, Kate Reddy, carefully brushes each of her molars 20 times. She's not fighting cavities. She's stalling in the hopes that her husband will fall asleep and won't try to have sex with her. (That way, she can skip a shower the next morning.) And what would Ray Romano joke about on his hit series "Everybody Loves Raymond" if he didn't have to wheedle sex out of his TV wife? Romano, who has four kids, including 10-year-old twins, says his comedy is inspired by real life. "After kids, everything changes," he told NEWSWEEK. "We're having sex about every three months. If I have sex, I know my quarterly estimated taxes must be due. And if it's oral sex, I know it's time to renew my driver's license."

"It wasn't that I didn't love him. It had nothing to do with him. What it boiled down to was being exhausted."

—TARA PATERSON

Yet some couples seem to accept that sexless marriage is as much a part of modern life as traffic and e-mail. It's a given for Ann, a 39-year-old lawyer with two kids who lives in Brooklyn. When she and her husband were first married, they had sex almost every day. Now their 5-year-old daughter comes into their bedroom every night. Pretty soon, the dog starts whining to get on the bed, too. "At 3 or 4 a.m., I kick my husband out for snoring and he ends up sleeping in my daughter's princess twin bed with the Tinkerbell night light blinking in his face," she says. "So how are we supposed to have sex?"

The statistical evidence would seem to show everything is fine. Married couples say they have sex 68.5 times a year, or slightly more than once a week, according to a 2002 study by the highly respected National Opinion Research Center at the University of Chicago, and the NORC numbers haven't changed much over the past 10 years. At least according to what people tell researchers, DINS are most likely an urban myth: working women appear to have sex just as often as their stay-at-home counterparts. And for what it's worth, married people have 6.9 more sexual encounters a year than people who have never been married. After all, you can't underestimate the value of having an (occasionally) willing partner conveniently located in bed next to you.

But any efforts to quantify our love lives must be taken with a shaker of salt. The problem, not surprisingly, is that people aren't very candid about how often they have sex. Who wants to sound like a loser when he's trying to make a contribution to social science? When pressed, nearly everyone defaults to a respectable "once or twice a week," a benchmark that probably seeped into our collective consciousness with the 1953 Kinsey Report, a study that's considered flawed because of its unrepresentative, volunteer sample.

"As a result, we have no idea what's 'normal'," says Pepper Schwartz, a sociologist and author of "Everything You Know About Love and Sex Is Wrong." Her best guess: three times a week during the first year of marriage, much less over time. When people believe they have permission to complain, she says, they often admit to having sex less than once a month: "And these are couples who like each other!"

In fact, the problem may be just as much perception as reality. Because we have the 100-times-a-year myth in our minds, and because there are so many movies and TV shows out there with characters who frequently have better-than-you-get sex, it's easy to think that everybody else is having more fun. Forget the four hotties on HBO's "Sex and the City." Even Ruth Fisher, the frumpy, middle-aged widow on the network's "Six Feet Under," gets lucky week after week. Armed with birth-control pills and dog-eared copies of "The Sensuous Woman," boomers were the front line of the sexual revolution. They practically invented guilt-free, premarital sex, and they know what they're missing better than any previous generation in history. "Boomers are the first generation to imagine that they can have exciting monogamous sex through old age," says Marty Klein, a marriage and sex therapist in Palo Alto, Calif. "The collision between that expectation and reality is pretty upsetting for most people."

And sexlessness has a long and rich tradition. In Aristophanes' bawdy play "Lysistrata," written in 411 B.C., Spartan and Athenian women agree to withhold sex from their husbands until the two warring city-states make peace. Virginia Woolf's Mrs. Dalloway was in a sexless marriage; it's likely Dorothea Brooke and Edward Casaubon, characters in George Eliot's "Middlemarch," were, too. And what about the "frigid" housewives of the 1950s?

Marriage experts say there's no single reason we're suddenly so unhappy with our sex lives. Many of us are depressed; last year Americans filled more than 200 million prescriptions for antidepressants. The sexual landscape may have been transformed in the last 40 years by birth control, legalized abortion and a better understanding of women's sexuality. But women have changed, too. Since they surged into the workplace in the 1970s, their economic power has grown steadily. Women now make up 47 percent of the work force; they're awarded 57 percent of all bachelor's degrees. About 30 percent of working women now earn more than their husbands.

Like never before, women have the financial clout to leave their husbands if they choose. In his new book, "Mismatch: The Growing Gulf Between Women and Men," sociologist Andrew Hacker says women are less and less inclined to stay married when they're not emotionally satisfied. Wives say they were the driving force in 56.2 percent of divorces, according to Hacker, while men say they were the ones who wanted out only 23.3 percent of the time. When women have those kinds of choices, marital "duties" become options and the debate over how much, or how little, sex to have is fundamentally altered.

MEANWHILE, FAMILIES HAVE CHANGED. THE YEAR AFTER the first child is born has always been a hazardous time for marriages—more divorces happen during those sleepless months than at any other time in a marriage, except for the very first year. But some researchers say parents are now obsessed with their children in a way that can be unhealthy. Kids used to go to dance class or take piano lessons once a week; now parents organize an array of activities—French classes, cello lessons and three different sports—that would make an air-traffic controller dizzy. And do you remember being a child at a restaurant with your parents and having every adult at the table focus on your happiness? No? That's probably because you weren't taken along.

Working parents who wish they could spend more time with their kids often compensate by dragging their brood everywhere with them. That means couples are sacrificing sleep and companionship. Parents of infants sometimes stop thinking of themselves as sexual beings altogether. Gottman recalls treating a couple with a 4-month-old; the wife was nursing. One morning the husband reached over and caressed his wife's breast. The woman sat bolt upright in bed and said, "Those are for *Jonathan*." "They laugh about it now," Gottman says. "But you can understand why a guy might withdraw in that kind of situation."

"We say, 'Meet me in the bedroom at noon.' We put on music and light candles and take some time to enjoy each other."

REGENA THOMASHAUER

There's another theme winding through popular culture and private conversations. Because let's face it: no one is *really* too tired to have sex. Arguing over whether you should have sex can easily take longer than the act itself. For many couples, consciously or not, sex has become a weapon. A lot of women out there are mad. Working mothers, stay-at-home moms, even women without kids. They're mad that their husband couldn't find the babysitter's home number if his life depended on it. Mad that he would never think to pick up diapers or milk on his way home. Mad that he doesn't have to sing all the verses of "The Wheels on the Bus" while trying to blow-dry his hair. Those of us who were weaned on "Fear of Flying" or "Our Bodies, Ourselves" understand that we're responsible for our own orgasms. But then couldn't somebody else take responsibility for the laundry once in a while?

Researchers say women have some legitimate gripes. Most two-income couples without children divide up the household chores pretty evenly. After the kids come, however, men may be happy to play with Junior, but they actually do *less* around the house. Men's contributions to household chores increased dramatically in the '70s and '80s, but haven't changed much since then, according to Andrew Cherlin, a sociologist at Johns Hopkins. And it isn't just that Dad isn't doing the dishes. Researchers say many new fathers—55 percent—actually start spending *more time* at work after a child is born. Experts can only

speculate on why: fathers may suddenly take their role as breadwinner more seriously. Others may feel slighted by how much attention their wives lavish on the new baby.

But men are mad, too. "The big loser between job, kids and the dogs is me," says Alex, a 35-year-old financial executive from Manhattan. "I need more sex, but that's not the whole story. I want more time alone with my wife and I want more attention." They may not be perfect, but most husbands today do far more around the house than their fathers would have ever dreamed of doing. They're also more involved than ever in their children's lives. And they want points for it, points they're not getting.

Experts say very few women openly withhold sex. More often, lingering resentments slowly drive a wedge between partners. After two kids and 10 years of marriage, Bill, an actor in his 50s, loves his wife, Laurie (not their real names), though he'd like to have sex more often than the once or twice a month they average now. Laurie, a graphic designer in her 40s, agreed to hire a babysitter and make a standing Saturday-night date. But when Saturday rolled around, she was too tired to go out. They missed the next week's appointment, too. She's tired, she says, but resentful, too. "I get angry because he doesn't help around the house enough or with the kids. He sees the groceries sitting on the counter. Why doesn't he take them out of the bag and put them away? How can I get sexy when I'm ticked off all the time?"

Advice on how to stay connected, however, varies widely. Traditionally, marriage counselors have focused on bridging emotional gaps between husbands and wives, with the idea that better sex flows out of better communication. More important than a fancy meal at a restaurant (where you can still have a rip-roaring fight, of course) is to just make time to sit down and talk. The Weinreichs managed to rekindle romance after their sons, now 18 and 21, got a little older. All it really took, Maddie says, was being more committed to intimacy.

But a new breed of marriage therapists take a more action-oriented approach. Regena Thomashauer, a relationship counselor and author of "Mama Gena's Owner's and Operator's Guide to Men," agrees that scheduling time together is essential. Use the time to have sex, she urges. Michele and Marcelo Sandoval, 40 and 42, respectively, sought help from Thomashauer when they were expecting their first child; now they make two "dates" a week. "We call them dates," says Marcelo, "but we know it means sex, and we make it a priority."

Author Weiner Davis has a similar strategy: just do it. Don't wait until you're in the mood. And view thoughtful gestures, such as letting your spouse sleep in, as foreplay. Chris Paterson, 31, and his wife, Tara, 29, say Weiner Davis has helped them. Early in their marriage, they had sex nearly every night. But after she gave birth to their first child, Tara lost interest. Their nightly sessions became infrequent events. In addition to raising the kids, now 6 and 2, both Tara and Chris run their own businesses—she has a Web site called justformom.com and he's a general contractor. Tara says she's just exhausted. Chris also shoulders part of the blame. "I haven't always been the most romantic, getting-her-in-the-mood kind of individual," he says. Since talking to Weiner Davis and reading her book, Chris and Tara say they now have sex almost once a week, when they "try really hard."

"When you have young children and you're working, your husband goes from the top of the food chain to the bottom."

MADDIE WEINREICH

Most therapists do agree on one thing. You can't force a sexy situation. There's nothing wrong with dressing up like a cowgirl or answering the front door in "black mesh stockings, and an apron—that's all," a la Marabel Morgan's 1973 classic, "Total Woman." But if it feels silly, it won't work. Rosemary Breslin, 45, a writer and filmmaker in New York, says she still has a great relationship with her husband, Tony Dunne. "But one of the things I ask him is, 'Are we going to have sex in 2003 or are we shelving it to 2004?' I asked him what he would do if I put on a black negligee, and he said he would laugh." Maybe she should persuade him to help out a little more around the house. After all, we know there's nothing sexier these days than a man who takes out the trash without being asked.

With HOLLY PETERSON, PAT WINGERT, KAREN SPRINGEN, JULIE SCELFO, MELISSA BREWSTER, TARA WEINGARTEN and JOAN RAYMOND

DIVORCE AND COHABITATION

Why We Don't Marry

JAMES Q. WILSON

Everyone knows that the rising proportion of women who bear and raise children out of wedlock has greatly weakened the American family system. This phenomenon, once thought limited to African Americans, now affects whites as well, so much so that the rate at which white children are born to an unmarried mother is now as high as the rate for black children in the mid-1960s, when Daniel Patrick Moynihan issued his famous report on the Negro family. For whites the rate is one-fifth; for blacks it is over one-half.

Almost everyone—a few retrograde scholars excepted—agrees that children in mother-only homes suffer harmful consequences: the best studies show that these youngsters are more likely than those in two-parent families to be suspended from school, have emotional problems, become delinquent, suffer from abuse, and take drugs. Some of these problems may arise from the economic circumstances of these one-parent families, but the best studies, such as those by Sara McLanahan and Gary Sandefur, show that low income can explain, at most, about half of the differences between single-parent and two-parent families. The rest of the difference is explained by a mother living without a husband.

And even the income explanation is a bit misleading, because single moms, by virtue of being single, are more likely to be poor than are married moms. Now that our social security and pension systems have dramatically reduced poverty among the elderly, growing up with only one parent has dramatically increased poverty among children. In this country we have managed to shift poverty from old folks to young folks. Former Clinton advisor William Galston sums up the matter this way: you need only do three things in this country to avoid poverty—finish high school, marry before having a child, and marry after the age of 20. Only 8 percent of the families who do this are poor; 79 percent of those who fail to do this are poor.

This pattern of children being raised by single parents is now a leading feature of the social life of almost all English-speaking countries and some European ones. The illegitimacy ratio in the late 1990s was 33 percent for the United States, 31 percent for Canada, and 38 percent for the United Kingdom.

Now, not all children born out of wedlock are raised by a single mother. Some, especially in Sweden, are raised by a man and woman who, though living together, are not married; others are raised by a mother who gets married shortly after the birth. Nevertheless, there has been a sharp increase in children who are not only born out of wedlock but are raised without a father. In the United States, the percentage of children living with an unmarried mother has tripled since 1960 and more than doubled since 1970. In England, 22 percent of all children under the age of 16 are living with only one parent, a rate three times higher than in 1971.

Why has this happened? There are two possible explanations to consider: money and culture.

Money readily comes to mind. If a welfare system pays unmarried mothers enough to have their own apartment, some women will prefer babies to husbands. When government subsidizes something, we get more of it. But for many years, American scholars discounted this possibility. Since the amount of welfare paid per mother had declined in inflation-adjusted terms, and since the amount paid in each state showed no correlation with each state's illegitimacy rate, surely money could not have caused the increase in out-of-wedlock births.

This view dominated scholarly discussions until the 1990s. But there are three arguments against it. First, the inflation-adjusted value of welfare benefits was not the key factor. What counted was the inflation-adjusted value of all the benefits an unmarried mother might receive—not only welfare, but also food stamps, public housing, and Medicaid. By adding these in, welfare kept up with inflation.

Second, what counted was not how much money each state paid out, but how much it paid compared with the cost of living in that state. As Charles Murray pointed out, the benefits for a woman in New Orleans ($654 a month) and those for one in San Francisco ($867 a month) made nearly identical contributions to the cost of living, because in New Orleans it cost about two-thirds as much to live as it did in San Francisco.

Third, comparing single-parent families and average spending levels neglects the real issue: how attractive is welfare to a low-income unmarried woman in a given locality? When economist Mark Rosenzweig asked this question of women who are part of the National Longitudinal Survey of Youth—a panel study of people that has been going on since 1979—he found that a 10 percent increase in welfare benefits made the chances that a poor young woman would have a baby out of wedlock before the age of 22 go up by 12 percent. And this was true for whites as well as blacks. Soon other scholars were confirming Rosenzweigs findings. Welfare made a difference.

WELFARE CHILDREN

But how big a difference? AFDC began in 1935, but by 1960 only 4 percent of the children getting welfare had a mother who had never been married; the rest had mothers who were widows or had been separated from their husbands. By 1996 that had changed dramatically: now approximately two-thirds of welfare children had an unmarried mom, and hardly any were the offspring of widows.

Why this change? At least for blacks, one well-known explanation has been offered: men did not marry because there were no jobs for them in the big cities. As manufacturing employment sharply declined in the central cities, William Julius Wilson has argued, blacks were unable to move to the suburbs as fast as the jobs. The unemployed males left behind are not very attractive as prospective husbands to the women they know, and so more and more black women do without marriage.

The argument has not withstood scholarly criticism. First, Mexican Americans, especially illegal immigrants, live in the central city also, but the absence of good jobs has not mattered, even though many Mexicans are poorer than blacks, speak English badly, and if undocumented cannot get good jobs. Nevertheless, the rate of out-of-wedlock births is much lower among these immigrants than it is among African Americans, as W. J. Wilson acknowledges.

Second, Christopher Jencks has shown that there has been as sharp a decline in marriage among employed black men as among unemployed ones, and that the supply of employed blacks is large enough to provide husbands for almost all unmarried black mothers. For these people, as Jencks concludes, "marriage must… have been losing its charms for non-economic reasons."

Moreover, the argument that single-parent families have increased because black men have not been able to move to wherever factory jobs can be found does not explain why such families have grown so rapidly among whites, for whom moving around a city should be no problem. For these whites—and I suspect for many blacks as well—there must be another explanation.

To explain the staggering increase in unmarried mothers, we must turn to culture. In this context, what I mean by culture is simply that being an unmarried mother and living on welfare has lost its stigma. At one time living on the dole was shameful; now it is much less so. As this may not be obvious to some people, let me add some facts that will support it.

STIGMA

Women in rural communities who go on welfare leave it much sooner than the same kind of women who take welfare in big cities, and this is true for both whites and blacks and regardless of the size of their families. The studies that show this outcome offer a simple explanation for it. In a small town, everyone knows who is on welfare, and welfare recipients do not have many friends in the same situation with whom they can associate. But in a big city, welfare recipients are not known to everyone, and each one can easily associate with other women living the same way. In the small town, welfare recipients tell interviewers the same story: "I always felt like I was being watched"; "they treat us like welfare cattle"; people make "nasty comments." But in a big city, recipients had a different story: Everyone "is in the same boat I am"; people "dont look down on you."

American courts have made clear that welfare laws cannot be used to enforce stigma. When Alabama tried in 1960 to deny welfare to an unmarried woman who was living with a man who was not her husband, the U.S. Supreme Court objected. Immorality, it implied, was an outdated notion. The states have no right to limit welfare to a "worthy person," and welfare belongs to the child, not the mother. If the state is concerned about immorality, it will have to rehabilitate the women by other means.

How did stigma get weakened by practice and undercut by law, when Americans—no less than Brits, Canadians, and Australians—favor marriage and are skeptical of welfare?

Let me suggest that beneath the popular support for marriage there has slowly developed, almost unnoticed, a subversion of it, which can be summarized this way: whereas marriage was once thought to be about a social union, it is now about personal preferences. Formerly, law and opinion enforced the desirability of marriage without asking what went on in that union; today, law and opinion enforce the desirability of personal happiness without worrying much about maintaining a formal relationship. Marriage was once a sacrament, then it became a contract, and now it is an arrangement. Once religion provided the sacrament, then the law enforced the contract, and now personal preferences define the arrangement.

The cultural change that made this happen was the same one that gave us science, technology, freedom, and capitalism: the Enlightenment. The Enlightenment—that extraordinary intellectual development that began in eighteenth-century England, Scotland, Holland, and Germany—made human reason the measure of all things, throwing off ancient rules if they fell short. What the king once ordered, what bishops once enforced, what tradition once required was to be set aside in the name of scientific knowledge and personal self-discovery. The Enlightenment's great spokesmen were David Hume, Adam Smith, and Immanuel Kant; its greatest accomplishment was the creation of the United States of America.

I am a great admirer of the Enlightenment. But it entailed costs. I take great pride in the vast expansion in human freedom that the Enlightenment conferred on so many people, but I also know that the Enlightenment spent little time worrying about those cultural habits that make freedom meaningful and constructive. The family was one of these.

THE ENLIGHTENMENT

It was in the world most affected by the Enlightenment that we find both its good and bad legacies. There we encounter both remarkable science and personal self-indulgence. There we find human freedom and high rates of crime. There we find democratic governments and frequent divorces. There we find regimes concerned about the poor and a proliferation of single-parent families.

Single-parent families are most common in those nations—England, America, Canada, Australia, France, the Netherlands—where the Enlightenment had its greatest effect. Such families are far less common in Italy, Spain, Eastern Europe, Russia, the Middle East, China, and Japan. It was in the enlightened nations that nuclear rather than extended families became common, that individual consent and not clan control was the basis of a marriage contract, and that divorce first became legal.

But why did the Enlightenment have its greatest effect on the English-speaking world and on northwestern Europe? I think it was because life in those countries had for so long been arranged in ways that provided fertile ground in which human reason and personal freedom could take root and prosper. Alan Macfarlane, the great English anthropologist, has shown that land in England was individually owned as far back as the thirteenth century and possibly even earlier. There, and in similar countries in northwestern Europe, land ownership had established the basis for a slow assertion of human rights and legal defenses. If you own the land, you have a right to keep, sell, or bequeath it, and you have access to courts that will defend those rights and, in defending them, will slowly add more rights.

LAND OWNERSHIP

Marriage depended on land. Until a young man inherited or bought a piece of property, he was in no position to take a wife. The rule was: no land, no marriage. As a result, English men and women married at a much older age than was true elsewhere. But with the rise of cities and the growth of industrialism, that began to change. Now a man and a woman, already defined by rights that were centuries old, could marry on an income, not on a farm, and so they married at a younger age.

English couples could get married on the basis of their individual consent, without obtaining the formal approval of their parents, though parents still might try to influence these decisions, and among the landed aristocracy such influence was often decisive. But for most people, the old rule of the Roman Catholic church was in force: no marriage was legitimate unless the man and woman freely consented. That rule found its widest observance in countries like England, where individual land ownership and personal rights reinforced it.

In Eastern Europe, to say nothing of the Middle and Far East, a different culture had been created out of a different system for owning land. In many parts of these regions, land lay in the control of families and clans. No individual owned it, and no individual could sell or bequeath it. One man might run the farm, but he did so not on the basis of ownership, but because of his seniority or skill, with the land itself remaining the property of an extended family.

In these places—where courts, unimportant in matters of real estate, tended to be unimportant in other respects as well—human rights were less likely to develop. In clan-based regimes, families often decided what man a woman might marry, and, since family labor worked family-owned land, men and women married at a young age, in hopes of adding many children to the common labor force.

The Enlightenment did not change the family immediately, because everyone took family life for granted. The most important Enlightenment thinkers assumed marriage and denounced divorce. That assumption—and in time that denunciation—slowly lost force, as people gradually experienced the widening of human freedom.

The laws, until well into the twentieth century, made it crystal clear that, though a child might be conceived by an unmarried couple, once born it had to have two parents. There was no provision for the state to pay for a single-parent child, and public opinion strongly and unanimously endorsed that policy.

But by the end of the nineteenth century and the early years of the twentieth, policies changed, and then, slowly, opinion changed. Two things precipitated the change: first, a compassionate desire to help needy children; and second, a determination to end the legal burdens under which women suffered. The first was a powerful force, especially since the aid to needy children was designed to help those who had lost their fathers owing to wars or accidents, as so many did as a consequence of the First World War and of industrial or mining accidents. Slowly, however, a needy child was redefined to include those of any mother without a husband, and not just any who had become a widow.

EMANCIPATION OF WOMEN

The emancipation of women was also a desirable process. In America and England, nineteenth-century women already had more rights than those in most of Europe, but when married they still could not easily own property, file for a divorce, or conduct their own affairs. By the 1920s most of these restrictions had ended, and once women got the vote, there was no chance of these limitations ever being reinstated.

We should therefore not be surprised that the twenties were an enthusiastic display of unchaperoned dating, provocative dress, and exhibitionist behavior. Had it not been for a time-out imposed by the Great Depression and the Second World War, we would no longer be referring to the sixties as an era of self-indulgence; we would be talking about the legacy of the twenties.

The sixties reinstated trends begun half a century earlier, but now without effective opposition. No-fault divorce laws were passed throughout most of the West, the pill and liberalized abortion laws dramatically reduced the chances of unwanted pregnancies, and popular entertainment focused on pleasing the young. As a result, family law, in Carl Schneider's term, lost its moral basis. It was easier to get out of a marriage than a mortgage. This change in culture was made crystal clear by court decisions. At the end of the nineteenth century, the Supreme Court referred to marriage as a "holy estate" and a "sacred obligation." By 1965 the same court described marriage as "an association of two individuals."

People still value marriage; but it is only that value—and very little social pressure or legal obligation—that sustains it.

But there is another part of the cultural argument, and it goes to the question of why African Americans have such high rates of mother-only families. When black scholars addressed this question, as did W. E. B. DuBois in 1908 and E. Franklin Frazier in 1939, they argued that slavery had weakened the black family. When Daniel Patrick Moynihan repeated this argument in 1965, he was denounced for "blaming the victim."

An intense scholarly effort to show that slavery did little harm to African-American families followed that denunciation; instead, what really hurt them was migrating to big cities where they encountered racism and oppression.

SLAVERY

It was an astonishing argument. Slavery, a vast and cruel system of organized repression that, for over two centuries, denied to blacks the right to marry, vote, sue, own property, or take an oath; that withheld from them the proceeds of their own labor; that sold them and their children on the auction block; that exposed them to brutal and unjust punishment: all this misery had little or no effect on family life, but moving as free people to a big city did. To state the argument is to refute it.

But since some people take academic nonsense seriously, let me add that we now know, thanks to such scholars as Orlando Patterson, Steven Ruggles, and Brenda E. Stevenson, that this argument was empirically wrong. The scholars who made it committed some errors. In calculating what percentage of black mothers had husbands, they accepted many women's claims that they were widows, when we now know that such claims were often lies, designed to conceal that the respondents had never been married. In figuring out what proportion of slaves were married, these scholars focused on large plantations, where the chance of having a spouse was high, instead of on small ones, where most slaves lived, and where the chance of having a spouse was low. On these small farms, only about one-fifth of the slaves lived in a nuclear household.

After slavery ended, sharecropping took its place. For the family, this was often no great improvement. It meant that it was very difficult for a black man to own property and thus hard for him to provide for the progress of his children or bequeath to them a financial start in life. Being a tenant farmer also meant that he needed help on the land, and so he often had many children, despite the fact that, without owning the land, he could not provide for their future.

The legacy of this sad history is twofold. First, generations of slaves grew up without having a family, or without having one that had any social and cultural meaning. Second, black boys grew up aware that their fathers were often absent or were sexually active with other women, giving the boys poor role models for marriage. Today, studies show that the African-American boys most likely to find jobs are those who reject, rather than emulate, their fathers; whereas for white boys, those most likely to find work are those who admire their fathers.

What is astonishing today is that so many African Americans are married and lead happy and productive lives. This is an extraordinary accomplishment, of which everyone should be proud. But it is an accomplishment limited to only about half of all black families, and white families seem to be working hard to catch up.

But there remains at least one more puzzle to solve. Culture has shaped how we produce and raise children, but that culture surely had its greatest impact on how educated people think. Yet the problem of weak, single-parent families is greatest among the least educated people. Why should a culture that is so powerfully shaped by upper-middle-class beliefs have so profound an effect on poor people? If some intellectuals have devalued marriage, why should ordinary people do so? If white culture has weakened marriage, why should black culture follow suit?

I suspect that the answer may be found in Myron Magnet's book *The Dream and the Nightmare*. When the haves remake a culture, the people who pay the price are the have-nots. Let me restate his argument with my own metaphor. Imagine a game of crack-the-whip, in which a line of children, holding hands, starts running in a circle. The first few children have no problem keeping up, but near the end of the line the last few must run so fast that many fall down. Those children who did not begin the turning suffer most from the turn.

There are countless examples of our cultural crack-the-whip. Heroin and cocaine use started among elites and then spread down the social scale. When the elites wanted to stop, they could hire doctors and therapists; when the poor wanted to stop, they could not hire anybody. The elites endorsed community-based centers to treat mental illness, and so mental hospitals were closed down. The elites hired psychiatrists; the poor slept on the streets. People who practiced contraception endorsed loose sexuality in writing and movies; the poor practiced loose sexuality without contraception. Divorce is more common among the affluent than the poor. The latter, who can't afford divorce, deal with unhappy marriages by not getting married in the first place. My only trivial quarrel with Magnet is that I believe these changes began a century ago and even then built on more profound changes that date back centuries.

Now you probably expect me to tell you what we can do about this, but if you believe, as I do, in the power of culture, you will realize that there is very little one can do. As a University of Chicago professor once put it, if you succeed in explaining why something is so, you have probably succeeded in explaining why it must be so. He implied what is in fact often the case: change is very hard.

The remarkable fact is that today so many Americans value marriage, get married, and want their children to marry. Many often cohabit, but when a child arrives most get married. The ones who don't make their children suffer. But to many people the future means more cohabitation—more "relationships"—and fewer marriages. Their goal is Sweden, where marriage is slowly going out of style.

The difficulty with cohabitation as opposed to marriage has been brilliantly laid out by Linda Waite and Maggie Gallagher in their book *The Case for Marriage*. In it they show that married people, especially men, benefit greatly from marriage: they are healthier, live longer, and are less depressed. But many young men today have not absorbed that lesson. They act as if sex is more important than marriage, worry more about scoring than dating, and are rewarded by their buddies when they can make it with a lot of young women. To them, marriage is at best a long-term benefit, while sex is an immediate preoccupation. This fact supplies us with a sober lesson: the sexual revolution—one that began nearly a century ago but was greatly hastened by the 1960s—was supposed to help make men and women equal. Instead it has helped men, while leaving many women unmarried spectators watching *Sex and the City* on HBO.

One could imagine an effort to change our culture, but one must recognize that there are many aspects of it that no one, least of all I, wants to change. We do not want fewer freedoms or less democracy. Most of us, myself included, do not want to change any of the gains women have made in establishing their moral and legal standing as independent actors with all the rights that men once enjoyed alone. We can talk about tighter divorce laws, but it is not easy to design one that both protects people from ending a marriage too quickly with an easy divorce and at the same time makes divorce for a good cause readily available.

The right and best way for a culture to restore itself is for it to be rebuilt, not from the top down by government policies, but from the bottom up by personal decisions. On the side of that effort, we can find churches—or at least many of them—and the common experience of adults that the essence of marriage is not sex, or money, or even children: it is commitment.

Mr. Wilson teaches at Pepperdine University. From "Why We Don't Marry," by James Q. Wilson, City Journal, Winter 2002, pages 46–55.

SHOULD YOU STAY TOGETHER FOR THE KIDS?

A controversial book argues that the damage from divorce is serious and lasting, but many argue that the remedy of parents staying hitched is worse than the ailment.

By WALTER KIRN

ONE AFTERNOON WHEN JOANNE WAS nine years old she came home from school and noticed something missing. Her father's jewelry box had disappeared from its usual spot on her parents' bureau. Worse, her mother was still in bed. "Daddy's moved out," her mother told her. Joanne panicked. She began to sob. And even though Joanne is 40 now, a married Los Angeles homemaker with children of her own, she clearly remembers what she did next that day. Her vision blurred by tears, she searched through the house that was suddenly not a home for the jewelry box that wasn't there.

Time heals all wounds, they say. For children of divorce like Joanne, though, time has a way of baring old wounds too. For Joanne, the fears that her parents' split unleashed—of abandonment, of loss, of coming home one day and noticing something missing from the bedroom—deepened as the years went by. Bursts of bitterness, jealousy and doubt sent her into psychotherapy. "Before I met my husband," she remembers, "I sabotaged all my other relationships with men because I as-

sumed they would fail. There was always something in the back of my head. The only way I can describe it is a void, unfinished business that I couldn't get to."

For America's children of divorce—a million new ones every year—unfinished business is a way of life. For adults, divorce is a conclusion, but for children it's the beginning of uncertainty. Where will I live? Will I see my friends again? Will my mom's new boyfriend leave her too? Going back to the early '70s—the years that demographers mark as the beginning of a divorce boom that has receded only slightly despite three decades of hand wringing and worry—society has debated these children's predicament in much the same way that angry parents do: by arguing over the little ones' heads or quarreling out of earshot, behind closed doors. Whenever concerned adults talk seriously about what's best for the children of divorce, they seem to hold the discussion in a setting—a courtroom or legislature or university—where young folks aren't allowed.

That's changing. The children are grown now, and a number are speaking up,

telling stories of pain that didn't go away the moment they turned 18 or even 40. A cluster of new books is fueling a backlash, not against divorce itself but against the notion that kids somehow coast through it. Stephanie Staal's *The Love They Lost* (Delacorte Press), written by a child of divorce, is part memoir and part generational survey, a melancholy volume about the search for love by kids who remember the loss of love too vividly. *The Case for Marriage* by Linda Waite and Maggie Gallagher (Doubleday) emphasizes the positive, arguing that even rocky marriages nourish children emotionally and practically.

The most controversial book, comes from Judith Wallerstein, 78, a therapist and retired lecturer at the University of California, Berkeley. In *The Unexpected Legacy of Divorce* (Hyperion) she argues that the harm caused by divorce is graver and longer lasting than we suspected. Her work raises a question that some folks felt was settled back in the days of *Love, American Style*: Should parents stay together for the kids?

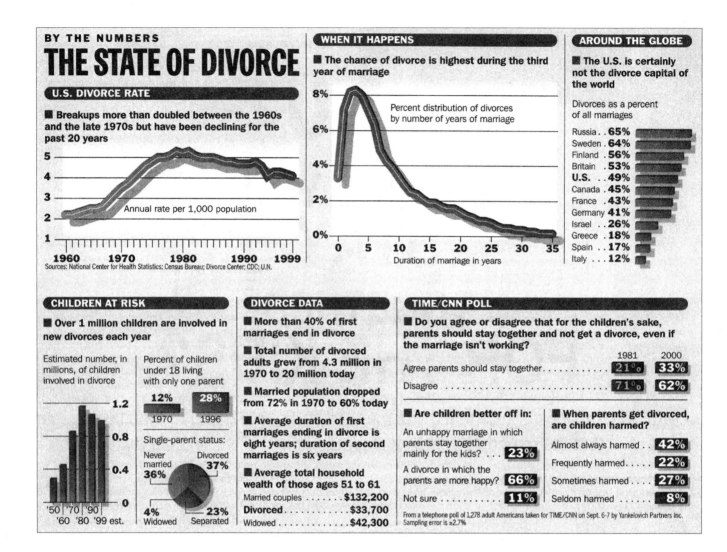

BY THE NUMBERS
THE STATE OF DIVORCE

U.S. DIVORCE RATE

■ Breakups more than doubled between the 1960s and the late 1970s but have been declining for the past 20 years

Annual rate per 1,000 population

1960   1970   1980   1990   1999

Sources: National Center for Health Statistics; Census Bureau; Divorce Center; CDC; U.N.

WHEN IT HAPPENS

■ The chance of divorce is highest during the third year of marriage

Percent distribution of divorces by number of years of marriage

Duration of marriage in years

AROUND THE GLOBE

■ The U.S. is certainly not the divorce capital of the world

Divorces as a percent of all marriages

Russia . . **65%**
Sweden . **64%**
Finland . **56%**
Britain . **53%**
U.S. . . **49%**
Canada . **45%**
France . **43%**
Germany **41%**
Israel . . **26%**
Greece . **18%**
Spain . . **17%**
Italy . . . **12%**

CHILDREN AT RISK

■ Over 1 million children are involved in new divorces each year

Estimated number, in millions, of children involved in divorce

'50 '70 '90
  '60 '80 '99 est.

Percent of children under 18 living with only one parent

12% 1970   **28%** 1996

Single-parent status:

Never married **36%**   Divorced **37%**   **4%** Widowed   **23%** Separated

DIVORCE DATA

■ More than 40% of first marriages end in divorce

■ Total number of divorced adults grew from 4.3 million in 1970 to 20 million today

■ Married population dropped from 72% in 1970 to 60% today

■ Average duration of first marriages ending in divorce is eight years; duration of second marriages is six years

■ Average total household wealth of those ages 51 to 61

Married couples **$132,200**
Divorced **$33,700**
Widowed **$42,300**

TIME/CNN POLL

■ Do you agree or disagree that for the children's sake, parents should stay together and not get a divorce, even if the marriage isn't working?

	1981	2000
Agree parents should stay together	21%	33%
Disagree	71%	62%

■ Are children better off in:

An unhappy marriage in which parents stay together mainly for the kids? . . . **23%**

A divorce in which the parents are more happy? **66%**

Not sure **11%**

■ When parents get divorced, are children harmed?

Almost always harmed . . **42%**
Frequently harmed. **22%**
Sometimes harmed **27%**
Seldom harmed **8%**

From a telephone poll of 1,278 adult Americans taken for TIME/CNN on Sept. 6-7 by Yankelovich Partners Inc. Sampling error is ±2.7%

Listening to children from broken families is Wallerstein's lifework. For nearly three decades, in her current book and two previous ones, she has compiled and reflected on the stories of 131 children of divorce. Based on lengthy, in-depth interviews, the stories are seldom happy. Some are tragic. Almost all of them are as moving as good fiction. There's the story of Paula, who as a girl told Wallerstein, "I'm going to find a new mommy," and as a young woman—too young, it turned out—impulsively married a man she hardly knew. There's Billy, born with a heart defect, whose parents parted coolly and amicably but failed to provide for his pressing medical needs.

It's the rare academic who can make a reader cry. Maybe that's why, with each new installment, Wallerstein's study has created shock waves, shaping public opinion and even the law. Her attention-getting style has proved divisive. For experts in the field of family studies (who tend to quarrel at least as bitterly as the dysfunc-

tional clans they analyze), she's a polarizing figure. To her admirers, this mother of three and grandmother of five, who has been married to the same man for 53 years, is a brave, compassionate voice in the wilderness. To her detractors, she's a melodramatic doomsayer, a crank.

What drew someone from such a stable background to the study of marital distress? At the end of the 1960s, Wallerstein, whose Ph.D. is in clinical psychology, moved from Topeka, Kans., in the ho-hum heartland, to swinging California. "Divorce was almost unheard of in the Midwest," she recalls. Not so on the Gold Coast, the state had just passed its pioneering no-fault divorce law. Wallerstein took a job consulting at a large community mental-health center in Marin County just as the social dam began to crack. "We started to get complaints," she says," from nursery school teachers and parents: 'Our children are having a very hard time. What should we do?'"

The prevailing view at the time, she says, was that divorce was no big deal for

kids. So much for the power of positive thinking. "We began to get all these questions," Wallerstein remembers. "The children were sleepless. The children in the nursery school were aggressive. They were out of control." When Wallerstein hit the library for answers, she discovered there were none. The research hardly existed, so she decided to do her own. She had a hunch about what she would learn. "I saw a lot of children very upset," she says, "but I fully expected that it would be fleeting."

Her hunch was wrong. Paradise for kids from ruptured families wasn't easily regained. Once cast out of the domestic garden, kids dreamed of getting back in. The result more often than not was frustration and anxiety. Children of divorce suffer depression, learning difficulties and other psychological problems more frequently than those of intact families. Some of Wallerstein's colleagues, not to mention countless divorced parents, felt they were being guilt-tripped by a square. They didn't want to hear this somber news.

DIVORCE/THE DEBATE

"We have to pay attention to what Judy Wallerstein says... It's another reason not to be sanguine about what happens to children following divorce and not to cling to this 1970s opinion that it's no big deal, they'll bounce back, just be happy yourself."
—BARBARA DAFOE WHITEHEAD, *author of* The Divorce Culture: Rethinking Our Commitments to Marriage and Family

"I think [Wallerstein] is wonderful at seeing the trees, but sometimes she misses the forest. For the most part, kids from divorced families are resilient. They bounce back from all the stresses. Some kids are at risk, but the majority are functioning well."
—ROBERT EMERY, *director of the University of Virginia's Center for Children, Families and the Law*

"[My parents] tried to stick it out for an extra year. That year was horrible... It's really devastating when your parents divorce. But it doesn't automatically mean that I wish my parents were still together. People who haven't gone through parental divorce don't really understand that."
—STEPHANIE STAAL, *author of* The Love They Lost: Living with the Legacy of Our Parents' Divorce

"I think the kids are better off if divorce is handled intelligently—that is, if both parents talk to the kids, explain what it is. Let's say each party remarries. The children get the benefit of now four adults in their life, instead of two. If everything works well, the kids benefit."
—LARRY KING, *five-times-divorced TV talk-show host*

"Every marriage waxes and wanes... So thinking about getting divorced when things are awful is in some ways a shortsighted view. You're cutting off your foot because you have an ingrown toenail."
—LINDA WAITE, *co-author of* The Case for Marriage: Why Married People Are Happier, Healthier and Better Off Financially

"I'm not suggesting that divorce be outlawed. But people move too quickly without trying to work through their problems in the relationship."
—MARSHALL HERSKOVITZ, *co-creator of TV's* Once and Again

"What most of the large-scale scientific research shows is that although growing up in a divorced family elevates the risk for certain kinds of problems, it by no means dooms children to having a terrible life. The fact of the matter is that most kids from divorced families do manage to overcome their problems and do have good lives."
—PAUL AMATO, *professor of sociology, Penn State University*

Now, decades later, some still don't want to hear her. For parents, her book's chief finding, to be sure, is hardly upbeat or very reassuring; children take a long time to get over divorce. Indeed, its most harmful and profound effects tend to show up as the children reach maturity and struggle to form their own adult relationships. They're gun-shy. The slightest conflict sends them running. Expecting disaster, they create disaster. "They look for love in strange places," Wallerstein says. "They make terrible errors of judgment in whom they choose."

Marcie Schwalm, 26, a Bloomington, Ill., legal secretary whose parents split when she was four, illustrates Wallerstein's thesis well. As a young woman she couldn't seem to stick with the same boyfriend. "I thought guys were for dating and for breaking up with a few weeks later," she says. "I would go into a relationship wondering how it was going to end." Finally, Marcie says, a college beau told her she had a problem. She's married now, and her feelings about divorce have a hard-line, 1950s tone: "Divorce is not something I am going to go through. I would do whatever it takes to keep the marriage together."

Kristina Herrndobler, 17, isn't so sure that harmony can be willed. Now a high

school student in Benton, Ill., she too was four when her parents called it quits. She says she has no memories of the trauma, just an abiding skepticism about marriage and a resolve to settle for nothing less than the ideal man. "I don't want my kids to wind up in a single-parent situation," she says. "And I don't want to have kids with a man I don't want to be married to forever. I don't believe in the fairy tale. I hope it exists, but I really don't believe it does."

And therein lies another problem, according to Wallerstein: the belief, quite common in children of divorce, that marriage is either a fairy tale or nothing. These jittery, idealistic children tend to hold out for the perfect mate—only to find they have a very long wait. Worse, once they're convinced they've found him, they're often let down. High romantic expectations tend to give way, Wallerstein reports, to bitter disillusionments. Children from broken families tend to marry later, yet divorce more often than those from intact homes.

So divorce often screws up kids. In itself, this isn't news, though many experts feel Wallerstein overstates the case. That divorce may screw them up for a long, long time and put them at risk for everything from drug abuse to a loveless, solitary old

age is more disturbing—and even more debatable. Christy Buchanan, a professor of psychology at Wake Forest University and co-author of *Adolescents After Divorce* (Harvard), is typical of Wallerstein's detractors. "I think the main drawback of the sort of research she does is that you can't necessarily generalize it to a broad population," Buchanan says. "The other caution I would put forth is that she has a group of divorced families but no comparison group of nondivorced families. [Perhaps in response to this longstanding complaint, Wallerstein also interviewed children of intact marriages for her new book.] There's some good research suggesting that many of the problems that have been attributed to divorce in children were actually present prior to the divorce."

Not rigorous enough. Too gloomy. Those are the leading raps against Wallerstein. Paul Amato, a sociology professor at Penn state, has researched divorce and children for 20 years, casting the sort of wide statistical net that hardheaded academics favor and Wallerstein eschews as too impersonal. While Amato agrees with her about divorce's "sleeper effect" on children—the problems that crop up only after they're grown—he finds her work a bit of a bummer. "It's a dismal kind of pic-

Is Divorce Getting a Bum Rap?

KATHA POLLITT

Are Americans a nation of frivolous divorcers who selfishly pursue the bluebird of happiness, oblivious to their children's needs? Divorce opponents like Judith Wallerstein seem to think most parents see divorce as a marvelous opportunity for the whole family. How immature do they think people are? All over America, unhappy spouses lie awake at night wondering if they and their kids can afford divorce—financially, socially, emotionally. Where will they live, how will they pay the bills, will the kids fall apart, will there be a custody battle, what will their families say? The very fact that so many people leave their marriage for a future with so many pitfalls proves that divorce is anything but a whim. Most people I know who split up (not to mention my ex and me) spend years working up to it.

SPLIT DECISIONS: "America doesn't need more 'good enough' marriages"

In her new book, Wallerstein argues that children don't care if their parents are happy—they just want the stability of a two-parent household, without which they would later flail through adulthood and have a hard time forming good relationships. This conclusion, like her other gloomy generalizations ("Parenting erodes almost inevitably at the breakup and does not get restored for years, if ever"), is based on a small, nonrepresentative sample of families who were going through divorce in 1971 in affluent Marin County, Calif. Wallerstein looks for evidence that divorce harms kids, and of course she finds it—now well into their mid-30s, her interviews still blame their parents' breakup for every rock on the path to fulfillment—but the very process of participating in a famous ongoing study about the effects of divorce encourages them to see their lives through that lens. What if she had spent as much time studying children whose parents had terrible marriages but stayed together for the kids? How many 35-year-old "children" would be blaming their problems on the nights they hid in their rooms while Mom and Dad screamed at each other in the kitchen? Wallerstein points out many children of divorce feel overly responsible for their parents' happiness. But what about the burden of knowing that one or both of your parents endured years of misery—for you?

As a matter of fact, we know the answer to that question. The baby boomers, who helped divorce become mainstream, were the products of exactly the kind of marriages the anti-divorcers approve of—the child-centered unions of the 1950s, when parents, especially Mom, sacrificed themselves on the altar of family values and the suburban respectability. To today's anti-divorcers those may seem like "good enough" marriages—husband and wife rubbing along for the sake of the children. The kids who lived with the silence and contempt said no thank you.

America doesn't need more "good enough" marriages full of depressed and bitter people. Nor does it need more pundits blaming women for destroying "the family" with what are, after all, reasonable demands for equality and self-development. We need to acknowledge that there are lots of different ways to raise competent and well-adjusted children, which—as according to virtually every family researcher who has worked with larger and more representative samples than Wallerstein's tiny handful—the vast majority of kids of divorce turn out to be. We've learned a lot about how to divorce since 1971. When Mom has enough money and Dad stays connected, when parents stay civil and don't bad-mouth each other, kids do all right. The "good enough" divorce—why isn't *that* ever the cover story?

Katha Pollitt is an author and a columnist for The Nation.

ture that she paints," he says. "What most of the large-scale, more scientific research shows is that although growing up in a divorced family elevates the risk for certain kinds of problems, it by no means dooms children to having a terrible life."

And what about children raised from the start by single moms? Last month, TIME ran a story about the challenges faced by single women having children of their own. But in all the coverage about how those women are coping, the impact on the kids is sometimes underplayed—and their issues are not that different from those of kids from divorced households. "Some studies have directly compared children who were raised by mothers who are continuously single with mothers who went through a divorce," says Amato. "In general, the outcomes for children seem to be pretty similar. It appears to increase the risk for some types of problems: in con-

duct, in school, in social relations. Neither one appears to be optimal for children."

Besides her conclusions on children's long-term prospects following divorce, Wallerstein makes another major point in her book—one that may result in talk-show fistfights. Here it is: children don't need their parents to like each other. They don't even need them to be especially civil. They need them to stay together, for better or worse. (Paging Dr. Laura!) This imperative comes with asterisks, of course, but fewer than one might think. Physical abuse, substance addiction and other severe pathologies cannot be tolerated in any home. Absent these, however, Wallerstein stands firm: a lousy marriage, at least where the children's welfare is concerned, beats a great divorce.

Them's fighting words.

The shouting has already started. Family historian Stephanie Coontz, author of

The Way We Never Were: American Families and the Nostalgia Trap (Basic), questions the value of papering over conflicts for the kids' sake. Sure, some parents can pull it off, but how many and for how long? "For many couples," Coontz says, "things only get worse and fester, and eventually, five years down the road, they end up getting divorced anyway, after years of contempt for each other and outside affairs."

Coontz doesn't believe in social time travel. She doesn't think we can go back to *Leave It to Beaver* after we've seen *Once and Again.* Unlike Wallerstein, whose investigation is deep but rather narrow (the families in her original study were all white, affluent residents of the same Northern California county, including non-working wives for whom divorce meant a huge upheaval), Coontz takes a lofty, long view of divorce. "In the 1940s

BOOK EXCERPT

Fear of Falling

A sense that love is doomed often haunts the offspring of divorce as they grow up and try to build relationships of their own, says a controversial new book based on a 25-year study of 131 children. Here we follow a young woman's painful search for love that can last

BY JUDITH WALLERSTEIN, JULIA LEWIS AND SANDRA BLAKESLEE

WHEN MOST PEOPLE HEAR THE WORD DIVORCE, THEY THINK IT means one failed marriage. The child of divorce is thought to experience one huge loss of the intact family, after which stability and a second, happier marriage comes along. But this is not what happens to most children of divorce. They experience not one, not two, but many more losses as their parents go in search of new lovers or partners. Each of these throws the child's life into turmoil and brings back painful reminders of the first loss.

Children observe their parents' courtships with a mixture of excitement and anxiety. For adolescents, the erotic stimulation of seeing their parents with changing partners can be difficult to contain. Several young teenage girls in the study began their own sexual activity when they observed a parent's involvement in a passionate affair. Children watch their parents' lovers with everything from love to resentment, hoping for some clue about the future. They participate actively as helper, critic and audience. They are not afraid to intervene. One mother returning home from a date found her school-age children asleep in her bed. Since they'd told her earlier that they didn't like her boyfriend, she took the hint. Many new lovers are attentive to the children, regularly bringing little gifts. But even the most charming lovers can disappear overnight. Second marriages with children are much more likely to end in divorce than first marriages.

The experience of Karen, whose identity I have concealed here, is typical of many I have seen. Her father's second wife, who was nice to the children, left without warning three years into the marriage. After she was gone, her father had four more girlfriends who caused him a great deal of suffering when they also left. Karen's mother had three unhappy love affairs prior to her remarriage, which ended after five years. The childhood of Karen and her siblings were filled with a history of new attachments followed by losses and consequent distress for both parents. Karen's brother, at age 30, told me: "What is marriage? Only a piece of paper and a piece of metal. If you love someone, it breaks your heart." In this study, only 7 of the 131 children experienced stable second marriages in which they had good relationships on both sides of the divorced family. Can we be surprised that so many children of divorce conclude that love is fleeting?

When I turn to the notes of my interview with Karen 15 years after her parents' divorce, the image of a young woman crying inconsolably enters my mind. Karen was sitting on the sofa in my old office, with her chin in her hands and elbows on her knees, telling me about her live-in relationship with her boyfriend Nick. "I've made a terrible mistake," she said, twisting a damp tissue into the shape of a rope. "I can't believe I've gotten myself into this. It's what I grew up dreading most and look what happened."

Karen gripped her fingers tightly until her knuckles shone like moons. "What's wrong?" I asked, as gently as I could. "Everything," she moaned. "He drinks beer. He has no ambition, no life goals, no education, no regular job. When I come home after work,

he's just sitting there in front of the TV and that's where he's been all day." Then Karen's voice dropped. "But he loves me," she said in anguish. "He would be devastated if I ever left him." Even in her great distress and anger she was intensely cognizant of her boyfriend's suffering. I thought to myself, this epitomizes Karen—she's always aware of other people's hurts and suffering.

"But then why did you move in with him?"

"I'm not sure. I knew I didn't love him. But I was scared of marriage. I was scared of divorce, and I'm terrified of being alone. When Nick asked me to live with him, I was afraid that I'd get older and that I wouldn't have another chance. I kept thinking that I'd end up lonely like my dad. And Mom."

I looked at this beautiful young woman and shook my head in disbelief. Could she really think that this was all she could hope for? Karen must have read my mind because she quickly said, "I know. People have been telling me how pretty I am since I was a child. But I don't believe it. And I don't care."

"How did you meet Nick?"

She sighed as she answered, "Well, we hardly knew each other in high school. I think that he had a crush on me from afar. Then in my junior year I broke my ankle and during the six weeks that I was hobbling around, he was very kind to me, carrying my stuff and visiting me. He was the only one who took any care of me. He also comes from a divorced family with lots of troubles. When he dropped out of school, I felt very sorry for him."

"Then how did he come back into your life?"

"I was having a real bad time. My brother was getting into serious trouble with the law and my dad wouldn't do anything to help. I was frantic and beginning to realize that all my efforts to hold my family together were wasted. So when Nick asked me to move in with him, I said yes. Anything to get away, even though I knew from the outset he had no plans for the future. After the first day, I said to myself, 'Oh, my God, what did I do?' But at least I knew he won't betray me. At least I'm safe from that."

"Karen, this fear of betrayal is pretty central to you. You keep mentioning it."

"It's been central to my life," she agreed. "Both my parents played around. I saw it all around me. They felt that if you are not getting what you want, you just look elsewhere." (I've never heard anyone put the alternative morality of our divorce culture so succinctly.)

Like a good caregiver child, Karen reinstalled her troubled relationships with her mother and father into her early relationships with men. As rescuers, most young women like Karen are used to giving priority to the needs of others. Karen confessed that she had never in her life thought about what would make her happy. "That would be like asking for the moon," she said. "I was always too worried about my family to ask for me."

(continued)

Fear of Falling *(continued)*

What prompts so many children of divorce to rush into a cohabitation or early marriage with as much forethought as buying a new pair of shoes? Answers lie in the ghosts that rise to haunt them as they enter young adulthood. They live in fear that they will repeat their parents' history, hardly daring to hope that they can do better. Dating and courtship raise their hopes of being loved sky-high—but also their fears of being hurt and rejected. This amalgam of fear and loneliness can lead to multiple affairs, hasty marriages, early divorce, and—if no take-home lessons are gleaned from it all—a second and third round of the same.

Here's how it works: at the threshold of young adulthood, relationships move center stage. But for many that stage is barren of good memories of how an adult man and woman can life together in a loving relationship. The psychological scaffolding they need to construct a happy marriage has been badly damaged by the two people they depended on while growing up. Children learn all kinds of lessons at their parents' knees from the time they are born to the time they leave home. There is no more exciting image to the child than the frame that includes Mom and Dad kissing, fighting, conferring, frowning, crying, yelling or hugging. These thousand-and-one images are internalized, and they form the template for the child's view of how men and women treat each other, how parents and children communicate, how brothers and sisters get along.

Unlike children from intact families, children of divorce in our study spoke very little about their parents' interaction. Parents who divorce may think of their decision to end the marriage as wise, courageous and the best remedy for their unhappiness—indeed, it may be so—but for the child the divorce carries one meaning: the parents have failed at one of the central tasks of adulthood. Together and separately, they failed to maintain the marriage. This failure shapes the child's inner template of self and family. If they failed, I can fail too. And if, as happens so frequently, the child observes more failed relationships in the years after divorce, the conclusion is simple. *I have never seen a man and a woman together on the same beam. Failure is inevitable.*

When I talked with Karen again nine years later, at age 34, she told me on the phone that "I'm in a whole other place than our last meeting. It's all new." As she came through my front door, she looked radiant. I was suddenly aware that in all the years we've known each other, I had rarely seen her happy. She was dressed very simply in black wool slacks, white pullover and herringbone suit jacket. Her stunning blue eyes had a new twinkle that flashed as we greeted each other warmly.

I told her how lovely she looked and congratulated her on her forthcoming marriage. "Who's the lucky man?"

"We're both lucky," she said, settling on the sofa. "Gavin and I did everything differently compared to how I lived my life before." And she launched into her story. Within months of our last meeting, she had moved out of the apartment she shared with Nick and said goodbye. As she had anticipated, he was devastated, begged her to come back, and made her feel guiltier than ever.

"How were you able to leave?" I asked.

She answered slowly, her face pale. "I felt like I was dying. It has to be the hardest thing I've ever done and it took all my courage." She described how she would come home after work and find her partner lying on the couch, waiting for her to take charge. It was just like taking care of her mom. At that point, she realized she had to get out. Her escape took her to the East Coast, graduate school, and ultimately into a dream job—directing a regional public health program for handicapped children.

It was there that Karen met her fiancé, Gavin, an assistant professor of economics. As she told me about him, I smiled and said, "I remember when you thought you didn't have choices. It looks like you've made quite a few recently."

"I decided to take a chance, and I discovered what I want. And I finally figured out what I don't want. I don't want another edition of my relationships with my mom or dad. I don't want a man who is dependent on me."

"And you do want?"

"I want a lover and a husband. I'm no longer frantic to find just anybody because if I have to, I can live alone. I can stand on my own two feet. I'm no longer afraid." And then the sadness around her eyes returned. "But it's not really all behind me. Like I told you, part of me is always waiting for disaster to strike. It never really goes away, never."

In hearing story after story like Karen's, I realized that compared with children from intact families, children of divorce follow a different trajectory for growing up. *It takes them longer.* Their adolescence is protracted and their entry into adulthood is delayed. Children of divorce need more time to grow up because they have to accomplish more: they must simultaneously let go of the past and create mental models for where they are headed, carving their own way. Those who succeed deserve gold medals for integrity and perseverance. Having rejected their parents as role models, they have to invent who they want to be and what they want to achieve in adult life. This is far beyond what most adolescents are expected to achieve.

Children of divorce are held back from adulthood because the vision of it is so frightening. The fact that Karen and others were able to turn their lives around is very good news for all of us who have been worried about the long-term effects of divorce on children. It sometimes took many years and several failed relationships, but close to half of the women and over a third of the men in our study were finally able to create a new template with themselves in starring roles. They did it the hard way—by learning from their own experience. They got hurt, kept going, and tried again. Some had relatives, especially grandparents, who loved them and provided close-up role models. Some had childhood memories from before the divorce that gave them hope and self-confidence. Only a few had mentors, but when they came along they were greatly appreciated. One young man told me, "My boss has been like a father to me, the father that I always wanted and never had." Men and women alike were especially grateful to lovers who stood by them and insisted that they stick around for the long haul. Finally, a third of the men and women in our study sought professional help from therapists and found that they could establish a trusting relationship with another person and use it to get at the roots of their difficulties.

We now come to a final, critical question. What values does this generation hold regarding marriage and divorce? Their vote is clear. Despite their firsthand experience of seeing how marriages can fail, they sincerely want lasting, faithful relationships. No single adult in this study accepts the notion that marriage is going to wither away. They want stability and a different life for their children. They want to do things better than their parents.

THE OTHER PATH

What If They Tough It Out?

People tend to believe that if a husband and wife are unhappy with each other, their children will also be unhappy. What's left out of the equation are the many families like Gary's, where the parents stay together and try to keep the peace. Gary (whose identity I've concealed) described with gusto his happy memories of childhood play, but had not revealed what he meant by the "indoor version" of his family. "What was that all about?" I asked.

"There was this feeling of tension that you could cut with a knife," Gary replied. "As things got worse between them, there were fewer words and more and more tension. My brother and sister and I spent as much time out of the house as we could."

"Things got pretty bad when I was in junior high school," he said. "One morning, after I knew Dad hadn't been home the night before, I was feeling really low. I guess I was seriously worried that he wouldn't come back. Mom had been all teary-eyed and silent during breakfast. I got on my bike to ride to school but I just couldn't face going. So I rode down to Dad's store. I thought I'd just peek in to see if he was there. He saw me looking and must've sensed something was wrong because he just left off helping a customer and came straight out to me. I remember he looked tired but he also looked kind of alarmed. He asked if anything was wrong at home and looked relieved when I told him there wasn't.

"So we went back into his office and we talked. He said he didn't know why Mom was so angry and suspicious but that sometimes he had to leave because it got to him and made him angry. He pointed to the old leather couch in the office and told me that when he did leave, this was where he slept.

"That was when I asked him if they might divorce. I'll always remember this part. His face went all saggy like he was going to cry, and he reached out and hugged me hard. 'Let me tell you something, Sport. Marriage is like a roller coaster. It has real highs and real lows. The lows have been worse than I thought, and the highs have been better than I thought. The big picture is that I love your mother, and you kids are the high point of our marriage. The picture right now is your mother and I are in a slump, but we'll work our way out of it. I know we will because we love you kids so much. Our marriage has been challenging, but it's been a good ride, and I'm hanging on till the end.'"

Gary was choking up as he recalled his father's words and blinking back tears. Finally, he said, "That was one of the most important conversations of my whole life."

"For me it was definitely better that they stayed together," he said. "But that's because they were great parents. My brother, sister and I never doubted that they loved us. My mom was lonely and, as I look back, probably depressed, but she continued to be very interested in us and our schoolwork and our activities. In other words, our world was protected. But if they *had* split up, I'd lay you bets that my father would have been remarried in a flash. And maybe had a couple more kids. We would have definitely lost out."

"How?"

"He wouldn't have been around for me. I doubt that my mom would have remarried, although who knows? It was better for me and my brother and sister, even if our folks missed out on some goodies of life. I know that's selfish of me."

"Why do you say that?"

"Because I have no idea how unhappy my parents were. After all, there are a lot of other things in life besides kids. Now that I'm an adult, I feel terribly sorry for both of them."

---

the average marriage ended with the death of the spouse," Coontz says. "But life expectancy is greater today, and there is more potential for trouble in a marriage. We have to become comfortable with the complexity and ambiguity of every family situation and its own unique needs."

That's just a lot of fancy, high-flown talk to Wallerstein and her followers. Ambiguity doesn't put dinner on the table or drive the kids to soccer practice or save for their college education. Parents do. And parents tend to have trouble doing these things after they get divorced. In observing what goes wrong for kids when their folks decide to split, Wallerstein is nothing if not practical. It's not just the absence of positive role models that bothers her, it's the depleted bank accounts, the disrupted play-group schedules, the frozen dinners. Parents simply parent better, she's found, when there are two of them. Do kids want peace and harmony at home? Of course. Still, they'll settle for hot meals.

Wallerstein didn't always feel this way. Once upon a time, she too believed that a good divorce trumped a bad marriage where children were concerned. "The central paradigm now that is subscribed to throughout the country," says Wallerstein, "is if at the time of the breakup people will be civil with each other, if they can settle financial things fairly, and if the child is able to maintain contact with both parents, then the child is home free." Wallerstein helped build this mode, she says, but now she's out to tear it down. "I'm changing my opinion," she says flatly.

The family-values crowd is pleased as punch with Wallerstein's change of heart. Take David Blankenhorn, president of the Institute for American Values. "There was a sense in the '70s especially, and even into the '80s, that the impact of divorce on children was like catching a cold: they would suffer for a while and then bounce back," he says. "More than anyone else in the country, Judith Wallerstein has shown that

that's not what happens." Fine, but does this oblige couples to muddle through misery so that Johnny won't fire up a joint someday or dump his girlfriend out of insecurity? Blankenhorn answers with the sort of certainty one expects from a man with his imposing title. "If the question is, If unhappily married parents stay together for the sake of their kids, will that decision benefit their children?, the answer is yes."

We can guess how the moral stalwarts will answer such questions. What about ordinary earthlings? Virginia Gafford, 56, a pet-product saleswoman in Pawleys Island, S.C., first married when she was 19. The marriage lasted three years. She married again, had a second child, Denyse, and divorced again. Denyse was 14. She developed the classic symptoms. Boyfriends jilted her for being too needy. She longed for the perfect man, who was nowhere to be found. "I had really high expectations," says Denyse. "I wanted Superman, so they wouldn't do what Dad had done." Denyse is in college now and getting fine grades, but her mother still has certain regrets. "If I could go back and find any way to save that marriage, I'd do it," she says. "And I'd tell anyone else to do the same."

For Wallerstein and her supporters, personal growth is a poor excuse for dragging the little ones through a custody battle that just might divide their vulnerable souls into two neat, separate halves doomed to spend decades trying to reunite. Anne Watson is a family-law attorney in Bozeman, Mont., and has served as an administrative judge in divorce cases. She opposes tightening divorce laws out of fear that the truly miserable—battered wives, the spouses of alcoholics—will lose a crucial escape route. But restless couples who merely need their space, in her opinion, had better think twice and think hard. "If people are divorcing just because of choices they want to make, I think it's pretty tough on the kids," Watson says. "Just because you're going to feel better, will they?"

That, of course, is the million-dollar question. Wallerstein's answer is no, they'll feel worse. They'll feel worse for quite a while, in fact, and may not know why until they find themselves in court, deciding where their own kids will spend Christmas. It's no wonder Wallerstein's critics find her depressing.

Does Wallerstein's work offer any hope or guidance to parents who are already divorced? Quite a bit, actually. For such parents, Wallerstein offers the following advice; First, stay strong. The child should be assured that she is not suddenly responsible for her parents' emotional well-being. Two, provide continuity for the child, maintaining her usual schedule of activities. Try to keep her in the same playgroup, the same milieu, among familiar faces and accustomed scenes. Lastly, don't let your own search for new love preoccupy you at the child's expense.

Her chief message to married parents is clear: Suck it up if you possibly can, and stick it out. But even if you agree with Wallerstein, how realistic is such spartan advice? The experts disagree. Then again, her advice is not for experts. It's directed at people bickering in their kitchen and staring up at the ceiling of their bedroom. It's directed at parents who have already divorced and are sitting alone in front of the TV, contemplating a second try.

The truth and usefulness of Wallerstein's findings will be tested in houses and apartments, in parks and playgrounds, not in sterile think tanks. Someday, assuming we're in a mood to listen, millions of children will give us the results.

—Reported by Jeanne McDowell/
Los Angeles, Timothy Padgett/Miami,
Andrea Sachs/New York and
David E. Thigpen/Chicago

AGAINST SCHOOL

How public education cripples our kids, and why

By Jon Taylor Gatto

I taught for thirty years in some of the worst schools in Manhattan, and in some of the best, and during that time I became an expert in boredom. Boredom was everywhere in my world, and if you asked the kids, as I often did, *why* they felt so bored, they always gave the same answers: They said the work was stupid, that it made no sense, that they already knew it. They said they wanted to be doing something real, not just sitting around. They said teachers didn't seem to know much about their subjects and clearly weren't interested in learning more. And the kids were right: their teachers were every bit as bored as they were.

Boredom is the common condition of schoolteachers, and anyone who has spent time in a teachers' lounge can vouch for the low energy, the whining, the dispirited attitudes, to be found there. When asked why *they* feel bored, the teachers tend to blame the kids, as you might expect. Who wouldn't get bored teaching students who are rude and interested only in grades? If even that. Of course, teachers are themselves products of the same twelve-year compulsory school programs that so thoroughly bore their students, and as school personnel they are trapped inside structures even more rigid than those imposed upon the children. Who, then, is to blame?

We all are. My grandfather taught me that. One afternoon when I was seven I complained to him of boredom, and he batted me hard on the head. He told me that I was never to use that term in his presence again, that if I was bored it was my fault and no one else's. The obligation to amuse and instruct myself was entirely my own, and peo-

ple who didn't know that were childish people, to be avoided if possible. Certainly not to be trusted. That episode cured me of boredom forever, and here and there over the years I was able to pass on the lesson to some remarkable student. For the most part, however, I found it futile to challenge the official notion that boredom and childishness were the natural state of affairs in the classroom. Often I had to defy custom, and even bend the law, to help kids break out of this trap.

DO WE REALLY NEED SCHOOL? SIX CLASSES A DAY, FIVE DAYS A WEEK, NINE MONTHS A YEAR, FOR TWELVE YEARS? IS THIS DEADLY ROUTINE REALLY NECESSARY?

The empire struck back, of course; childish adults regularly conflate opposition with disloyalty. I once returned from a medical leave to discover that all evidence of my having been granted the leave had been purposely destroyed, that my job had been terminated, and that I no longer possessed even a teaching license. After nine months of tormented effort I was able to retrieve the license when a school secretary testified to witnessing the plot unfold. In the meantime my family suffered more than I care to remember. By the time I finally retired in 1991, I had more than enough reason to think of our schools—with their long-term, cell-block-style, forced confinement of both students and teachers—as virtual factories of childishness. Yet I honestly could not see *why* they had to be that way. My own experience had revealed to me what many other teachers must learn along the way, too, yet keep to themselves for fear of reprisal: if we wanted to we could easily and inexpensively jettison the old, stupid structures and help kids *take* an education rather than merely *receive* a schooling. We could encourage the best qualities of youthfulness—curiosity, adventure, resilience, the capacity for surprising insight—simply by being more flexible about time, texts, and tests, by introducing kids to truly competent adults, and by giving each student what autonomy he or she needs in order to take a risk every now and then.

But we don't do that. And the more I asked why not, and persisted in thinking about the "problem" of schooling as an engineer might, the more I missed the point: What if there is no "problem" with our schools? What if they are the way they are, so expensively flying in the face of common sense and long experience in how children learn things, not because they are doing something wrong but because they are doing something right? Is it possible that George W. Bush accidentally spoke the truth when he said we would "leave no child behind"? Could it be that our schools are designed to make sure not one of them ever really grows up?

Do we really need school? I don't mean education, just forced schooling: six classes a day, five days a week, nine months a year, for twelve years. Is this deadly routine really necessary? And if so, for what? Don't hide behind reading, writing, and arithmetic as a rationale, because 2 million happy homeschoolers have surely put that banal justification to rest. Even if they hadn't, a considerable number of well-known Americans never went through the twelve-year wringer our kids currently go through, and they turned out all right. George Washington, Benjamin Franklin, Thomas Jefferson, Abraham Lincoln? Someone taught them, to be sure, but they were not products of a school *system*, and not one of them was ever "graduated" from a secondary school. Throughout most of American history, kids generally didn't go to high school, yet the unschooled rose to be admirals, like Farragut; inventors, like Edison; captains of industry like Carnegie and Rockefeller; writers, like Melville and Twain and Conrad; and even scholars, like Margaret Mead. In fact, until pretty recently people who reached the age of thirteen weren't looked upon as children at all. Ariel Durant, who co-wrote an enormous, and very good, multivolume history of the world with her husband, Will, was happily married at fifteen, and who could reasonably claim that Ariel Durant was an uneducated person? Unschooled, perhaps, but not uneducated.

We have been taught (that is, schooled) in this country to think of "success" as synonymous with, or at least dependent upon, "schooling," but historically that isn't true in either an intellectual or a financial sense. And plenty of people throughout the world today find a way to educate themselves without resorting to a system of compulsory secondary schools that all too often resemble prisons. Why, then, do Americans confuse education with just such a system? What exactly is the purpose of our public schools?

IN 1843, HORACE MANN WROTE A PAEAN TO THE LAND OF FREDERICK THE GREAT AND CALLED FOR ITS SCHOOLING TO BE BROUGHT HERE.

Mass schooling of a compulsory nature really got its teeth into the United States between 1905 and 1915, though it was conceived of much earlier and pushed for throughout most of the nineteenth century. The reason given for this enormous upheaval of family life and cultural traditions was, roughly speaking, threefold:

1) To make good people.
2) To make good citizens.
3) To make each person his or her personal best.

These goals are still trotted out today on a regular basis, and most of us accept them in one form or another as a decent definition of public education's mission, however short schools actually fall in achieving them. But we are dead wrong. Compounding our error is the fact that the national literature holds numerous and surprisingly consistent statements of compulsory schooling's true purpose. We have, for example, the great H. L. Mencken, who wrote in *The American Mercury* for April 1924 that the aim of public education is not

> to fill the young of the species with knowledge and awaken their intelligence.… Nothing could be further from the truth. The aim… is simply to reduce as many individuals as possible to the same safe level, to breed and train a standardized citizenry, to put down dissent and originality. That is its aim in the United States… and that is its aim everywhere else.

Because of Mencken's reputation as a satirist, we might be tempted to dismiss this passage as a bit of hyperbolic sarcasm. His article, however, goes on to trace the template for our own educational system back to the now vanished, though never to be forgotten, military state of Prussia. And although he was certainly aware of the irony that we had recently been at war with Germany, the heir to Prussian thought and culture, Mencken was being perfectly serious here. Our educational system really is Prussian in origin, and that really is cause for concern.

The odd fact of a Prussian provenance for our schools pops up again and again once you know to look for it. William James alluded to it many times at the turn of the century. Orestes Brownson, the hero of Christopher Lasch's 1991 book, *The True and Only Heaven*, was publicly denouncing the Prussianization of American schools back in the 1840s. Horace Mann's "Seventh Annual Report" to the Massachusetts State Board of Education in 1843 is essentially a paean to the land of Frederick the Great and a call for its schooling to be brought here. That Prussian culture loomed large in America is hardly surprising, given our early association with that utopian state. A Prussian served as Washington's aide during the Revolutionary War, and so many German-speaking people had settled here by 1795 that Congress considered publishing a German-language edition of the federal laws. But what shocks is that we should so eagerly have adopted one of the very worst aspects of Prussian culture: an educational system deliberately designed to produce mediocre intellects, to hamstring the inner life, to deny students appreciable leadership skills, and to ensure docile and incomplete citizens—in order to render the populace "manageable."

MODERN, INDUSTRIALIZED, COMPULSORY SCHOOLING WAS TO MAKE A SURGICAL INCISION INTO THE PROSPECTIVE UNITY OF THE UNDERCLASSES.

It was from James Bryant Conant—president of Harvard for twenty years, WWI poison-gas specialist, WWII executive on the atomic-bomb project, high commissioner of the American zone in Germany after WWII, and truly one of the most influential figures of the twentieth century—that I first got wind of the real purposes of American schooling. Without Conant, we would probably not have the same style and degree of standardized testing that we enjoy today, nor would we be blessed with gargantuan high schools that warehouse 2,000 to 4,000 students at a time, like the famous Columbine High in Littleton, Colorado. Shortly after I retired from teaching I picked up Conant's 1959 book-length essay, *The Child the Parent and the State*, and was more than a little intrigued to see him mention in passing that the modern schools we attend were the result of a "revolution" engineered between 1905 and 1930. A revolution? He declines to elaborate, but he does direct the curious and the uninformed to Alexander Inglis's 1918 book, *Principles of Secondary Education*, in which "one saw this revolution through the eyes of a revolutionary."

Inglis, for whom a lecture in education at Harvard is named, makes it perfectly clear that compulsory schooling on this continent was intended to be just what it had been for Prussia in the 1820s: a fifth column into the burgeoning democratic movement that threatened to give the peasants and the proletarians a voice at the bargaining table. Modern, industrialized, compulsory schooling was to make a sort of surgical incision into the prospective unity of these underclasses. Divide children by subject, by age-grading, by constant rankings on tests, and by

many other more subtle means, and it was unlikely that the ignorant mass of mankind, separated in childhood, would ever re-integrate into a dangerous whole.

Inglis breaks down the purpose—the *actual* purpose—of modern schooling into six basic functions, any one of which is enough to curl the hair of those innocent enough to believe the three traditional goals listed earlier:

1) The *adjustive* or *adaptive* function. Schools are to establish fixed habits of reaction to authority. This, of course, precludes critical judgment completely. It also pretty much destroys the idea that useful or interesting material should be taught, because you can't test for *reflexive* obedience until you know whether you can make kids learn, and do, foolish and boring things.

2) The *integrating* function. This might well be called "the conformity function," because its intention is to make children as alike as possible. People who conform are predictable, and this is of great use to those who wish to harness and manipulate a large labor force.

3) The *diagnostic* and *directive* function. School is meant to determine each student's proper social role. This is done by logging evidence mathematically and anecdotally on cumulative records. As in "your permanent record." Yes, you do have one.

4) The *differentiating* function. Once their social role has been "diagnosed," children are to be sorted by role and trained only so far as their destination in the social machine merits—and not one step further. So much for making kids their personal best.

SCHOOL DIDN'T HAVE TO TRAIN KIDS TO THINK THEY SHOULD CONSUME NONSTOP; IT SIMPLY TAUGHT THEM NOT TO THINK AT ALL.

5) The *selective* function. This refers not to human choice at all but to Darwin's theory of natural selection as applied to what he called "the favored races." In short, the idea is to help things along by consciously attempting to improve the breeding stock. Schools are meant to tag the unfit—with poor grades, remedial placement, and other punishments—clearly enough that their peers will accept them as inferior and effectively bar them from the reproductive sweepstakes. That's what all those little humiliations from first grade onward were intended to do: wash the dirt down the drain.

6) The *propaedeutic* function. The societal system implied by these rules will require an elite group of caretakers. To that end, a small fraction of the kids will quietly be taught how to manage this continuing project, how to watch over and control a population deliberately dumbed down and declawed in order that government might proceed unchallenged and corporations might never want for obedient labor.

That, unfortunately, is the purpose of mandatory public education in this country. And lest you take Inglis for an isolated crank with a rather too cynical take on the educational enterprise, you should know that he was hardly alone in championing these ideas. Conant himself, building on the ideas of Horace Mann and others, campaigned tirelessly for an American school system designed along the same lines. Men like George Peabody, who funded the cause of mandatory schooling throughout the South, surely understood that the Prussian system was useful in creating not only a harmless electorate and a servile labor force but also a virtual herd of mindless consumers. In time a great number of industrial titans came to recognize the enormous profits to be had by cultivating and tending just such a herd via public education, among them Andrew Carnegie and John D. Rockefeller.

There you have it. Now you know. We don't need Karl Marx's conception of a grand warfare between the classes to see that it is in the interest of complex management, economic or political, to dumb people down, to demoralize them, to divide them from one another, and to discard them if they don't conform. Class may frame the proposition, as when Woodrow Wilson, then president of Princeton University, said the following to the New York City School Teachers Association in 1909: " We want one class of persons to have a liberal education, and we want another class of persons, a very much larger class, of necessity, in every society, to forgo the privileges of a liberal education and fit themselves to perform specific difficult manual tasks." But the motives behind the disgusting decisions that bring about these ends need not be class-based at all. They can stem purely from fear, or from the by now familiar belief that "efficiency" is the paramount virtue, rather than love, liberty, laughter, or hope. Above all, they can stem from simple greed.

There were vast fortunes to be made, after all, in an economy based on mass production and organized to favor the large corporation rather than the small business or the family farm. But mass production required mass consumption, and at the turn of the twentieth century most Americans considered it both unnatural and unwise to buy things they didn't actually need. Mandatory schooling was a godsend on that count. School didn't have to train kids in any direct sense to think they should consume nonstop, because it did something even better: it encouraged them not to think at all. And that left them sitting ducks for another great invention of the modern era—marketing.

Now, you needn't have studied marketing to know that there are two groups of people who can always be convinced to consume more than they need to: addicts and children. School has done a pretty good job of turning our children into addicts, but it has done a spectacular job of turning our children into children. Again, this is no accident. Theorists from Plato to Rousseau to our own Dr. Inglis knew that if children could be cloistered with other children, stripped of responsibility and independence, encouraged to develop only the trivializing emotions of greed, envy, jealousy, and fear, they would grow older but never truly grow up. In the 1934 edition of his once well-known book *Public Education in the United States*, Ellwood P. Cubberley detailed and praised the way the strategy of successive school enlargements had extended childhood by two to six years, and forced schooling was at that point still quite new. This same Cubberley—who was dean of Stanford's School of Education, a textbook editor at Houghton Mifflin, and Conant's friend and correspondent at Harvard—had written the following in the 1922 edition of his book *Public School Administration*: "Our schools are… factories in which the raw products (children) are to be shaped and fashioned…. And it is the business of the school to build its pupils according to the specifications laid down."

MANDATORY SCHOOLING'S PURPOSE IS TO TURN KIDS INTO SERVANTS. DON'T LET YOUR OWN HAVE THEIR CHILDHOODS EXTENDED, NOT EVEN FOR A DAY.

It's perfectly obvious from our society today what those specifications were. Maturity has by now been banished from nearly every aspect of our lives. Easy divorce laws have removed the need to work at relationships; easy credit has removed the need for fiscal self-control; easy entertainment has removed the need to learn to entertain oneself; easy answers have removed the need to ask questions. We have become a nation of children, happy to surrender our judgments and our wills to political exhortations and commercial blandishments that would insult actual adults. We buy televisions, and then we buy the things we see on the television. We buy computers, and then we buy the things we see on the computer. We buy $150 sneakers whether we need them or not, and when they fall apart too soon we buy another pair. We drive SUVs and believe the lie that they constitute a kind of life insurance, even when we're upside-down in them. And, worst of all, we don't bat an eye when Ari Fleischer tells us to "be careful what you say," even if we remember having been told somewhere back in school that America is the land of the free. We simply buy that one too. Our schooling, as intended, has seen to it.

Now for the good news. Once you understand the logic behind modern schooling, its tricks and traps are fairly easy to avoid. School trains children to be employees and consumers; teach your own to be leaders and adventurers. School trains children to obey reflexively; teach your own to think critically and independently. Well-schooled kids have a low threshold for boredom; help your own to develop an inner life so that they'll never be bored. Urge them to take on the serious material, the *grown-up* material, in history, literature, philosophy, music, art, economics, theology—all the stuff schoolteachers know well enough to avoid. Challenge your kids with plenty of solitude so that they can learn to enjoy their own company, to conduct inner dialogues. Well-schooled people are conditioned to dread being alone, and they seek constant companionship through the TV, the computer, the cell phone, and through shallow friendships quickly acquired and quickly abandoned. Your children should have a more meaningful life, and they can.

First, though, we must wake up to what our schools really are: laboratories of experimentation on young minds, drill centers for the habits and attitudes that corporate society demands. Mandatory education serves children only incidentally; its real purpose is to turn them into servants. Don't let your own have their childhoods extended, not even for a day. If David Farragut could take command of a captured British warship as a pre-teen, if Thomas Edison could publish a broadsheet at the age of twelve, if Ben Franklin could apprentice himself to a printer at the same age (then put himself through a course of study that would choke a Yale senior today), there's no telling what your own kids could do. After a long life, and thirty years in the public school trenches, I've concluded that genius is as common as dirt. We suppress our genius only because we haven't yet figured out how to manage a population of educated men and women. The solution, I think, is simple and glorious. Let them manage themselves.

John Taylor Gatto is a former New York State and New York City Teacher of the Year and the author, most recently, of The Underground History of American Education. *He was a participant in the* Harper's Magazine *forum "School on a Hill," which appeared in the September 2001 issue.*

THE DOCTOR WON'T SEE YOU NOW

THE SOARING COST OF MALPRACTICE insurance may seem a problem just for errant physicians. But it's becoming a worry for everyone, especially patients who see their doctors move away, change specialties—or quit medicine altogether

By DANIEL EISENBERG AND MAGGIE SIEGER JOLIET

DR. ALEXANDER SOSENKO IS PROUD OF HIS SKILLS, BUT these days they don't seem to be the ones he needs to keep his medical practice going. A pulmonologist for 19 years, he knows just about everything there is to know about the lungs and is cherished by patients for his concerned, direct manner. But by his own admission, he's not great at lobbying. And, unfortunately, that's how Sosenko, 49, has lately been spending much of his time—circulating petitions at the local hospital, pleading with politicians for help. He has spent sleepless nights worrying that he may have to uproot his wife and three children from their home in Joliet, Ill., or else give up the profession he loves—all because he can't find affordable malpractice insurance.

An Abandoned Patient
Taking the Highway to Have a Baby

It wasn't morning sickness that made Vanessa Valdez's first trimester of pregnancy so hard—it was homesickness. So when the check-cashing company she worked for in Tucson, Ariz., offered her a transfer to her hometown of Douglas, she jumped at the chance. Four months pregnant at the time, Valdez, 24, was delighted to come home to her boyfriend, her parents and the 2-year-old son she left in their care when her job took her out of town. But now, as she prepares to give birth to a baby girl, she is dealing with a major drawback: there is no obstetrician within an hour's drive to deliver her child.

Valdez gave birth to her first child at Copper Queen Community Hospital in Bisbee, an old mining town just 26 miles northwest of Douglas. But when six family practitioners decided they couldn't afford the soaring malpractice premiums required for them to keep delivering babies, the hospital was forced to close its delivery room. Suddenly rural Cochise County, a 6,000-sq.-mi. expanse of mountains and desert along the Mexican border, had but one delivery room left for its 118,000 residents. It is in Sierra Vista, 50 miles northwest of Valdez's home. Which means that a week before her Aug. 4 due date, Valdez will pack her bags and camp out at a home of family friends near the hospital. "It sucks. It's not the same as being in your house, with your friends and your family," says Valdez, a petite woman who is otherwise quick to laugh.

As rising malpractice-insurance costs force a growing number of physicians to change states, drop certain procedures and even quit medicine, many patients like Valdez are finding themselves abandoned. In Las Vegas, where a number of obstetricians have stopped accepting patients, forcing some women to drive to Utah for prenatal care, a pregnant radio host took to the airwaves and begged her listeners to help her find an ob-gyn. (Her unorthodox method worked.)

In Pennsylvania, a particularly unlucky senior has lost his neurosurgeon and orthopedic surgeon to other states, and now his rheumatologist and urologist are threatening to move as well.

Valdez doesn't have it quite so bad—but don't try to tell her that. While she is busy looking for a new doctor in Sierra Vista for the big day in August, she is still commuting two hours to keep appointments with her current doctor in Tucson. The road to Sierra Vista winds through mountains and creosote flats. "It's going to be summer now, and it's getting hotter here," she says. "I'm afraid of the car breaking down again"—as it did recently while Valdez was driving alone on her way home from Tucson.

Some expectant couples rent motel rooms in Sierra Vista for when their babies are due. But some who can't afford a room or whose timing is off end up with the baby arriving in the middle of the night while they're racing along the highway, according to Copper Queen Hospital CEO James Dickson. The intersection of Highways 80 and 90 is listed as the place of birth on the certificate of a baby girl born in the front passenger seat of a car where those highways cross. Women lacking transportation, a common problem in this working-poor area, have given birth in ambulances. Others may be giving birth across the border in Mexico or at home, says Dr. Jennifer Ryan, CEO of the Elfrida-based Chiricahua Community Health Centers.

Health-care administrators in Cochise County plan to open a birthing center in Bisbee, which would be run by the federally qualified Chiricahua clinic and would be able to shelter doctors from high malpractice-insurance premiums. If all goes well, the center will be open next spring. But for Valdez and many other new mothers, that will be too late. Valdez doesn't know whom to blame—doctors, lawyers or insurance companies. She just knows that come late July, she will have to spend the final, awkward week of her pregnancy waddling around as a houseguest. That's enough to make anyone feel homesick.

—By Leslie Berestein

A Malpractice Victim
How the System Failed One Sufferer

Jim McDonough went into the hospital in 1997 to have a calcified growth, which the doctor said could be cancerous, removed from his neck. Two days later he awoke to find himself paralyzed from the chest down. Still in the intensive-care unit, he felt strangled by a noose of pain and needed three excruciating gasps of air to cry for help. "I was crushed," says McDonough, 69, a former weapons-plant inspector from Littleton, Colo. He once loved to fish and dreamed of restoring his ideal car: a 1965 Chrysler. But he soon realized that he could do neither and came to believe that his surgery had been unnecessary. A jury agreed. It found his neurosurgeon guilty of malpractice and in 2001 awarded McDonough $5.8 million. He has yet to see a dollar.

Jim McDonough feels he was mistreated by his doctor and by caps on his malpractice award

McDonough is a victim again, this time of the move to cap jury awards. Colorado is one of the few states that limit jury awards of both economic damages (say, for lost income) and noneconomic ones (for pain and suffering). Judge Warren Martin, now retired, cut McDonough's award to $1.33 million, concluding that although his injuries merited an exception to the $1 million cap, the jury had gone too far. (Colorado's caps limit economic damages to $750,000 and pain-and-suffering awards to $250,000. The former can be increased if a plaintiff shows future economic loss that exceeds that level.) McDonough appealed to the Colorado Supreme Court but was denied. He later tried to settle, but the defense argued that he had waited too long, and another judge ordered a new trial to determine damages. It will begin in August—a fresh chapter in McDonough's nightmare.

Proponents of damage caps say they simplify malpractice cases and weed out frivolous claims. But they can also entangle victims of heartbreaking tragedy like McDonough. No longer able to work, he spends his days doing crossword puzzles and preparing again for court. That was not the intention of the first jury, whose award was based not on mere sympathy but on calculations of McDonough's direct financial burden. According to foreman Joanne Kramer, in arriving at the $5.8 million in damages, the jury considered everything from home health-care aides to a van, a wheelchair, the loss of his home and the loss of income for his wife, who spends hours every day caring for him. Jurors also discussed whether McDonough's award would add to rising malpractice premiums but decided he should not be penalized for that. "We still had a responsibility to Mr. McDonough, who was a victim," says Kramer. "What's the point of having a jury if the judge can basically do what he wants?"

McDonough isn't giving up the fight. In February he wheeled himself into a state legislative hearing on damage caps. The Colorado Supreme Court ruled that "physical impairment and disfigurement" are exempt from limits on jury awards, but this spring the state's lawmakers limited the effect of the court's decision. "The doctor who performed this unnecessary operation has left the state and is continuing with his life elsewhere," McDonough testified. That neurosurgeon, Richard Branan, 59, declined to comment about McDonough. Branan practices in Los Angeles and faces two other trials this year in Colorado. His attorney in one case, in which the patient died, says, "We have a very defensible case." His attorney in the other trial, also a spinal-surgery case, says Branan "did not cause any injuries to the patient."

Despite Colorado's unusually strict damage cap, the state's largest insurer raised premiums 14% this year, the biggest jump in 15 years. So far at least, the cap law is failing to deliver the relief that it promised to doctors even as it blocks relief to acknowledged victims like Jim McDonough.

—By Rita Healy/Denver

An Uninsured Doctor
Alexander Sosenko, a pulmonologist in Joliet, Ill., can't find affordable malpractice coverage.

A few months ago, Sosenko and the five other doctors at the practice he founded, Midwest Pulmonary Consultants, learned that their malpractice insurer, American Physicians Capital, would not be renewing their policy when it expired at the end of March. They weren't exactly shocked. Over the past two years, insurers of doctors in Illinois, worried by a rise in malpractice awards by juries in the state, have dwindled in number from more than two dozen to six. But then it got personal. Sosenko and his partners discovered that their insurer was not leaving Illinois entirely but was limiting its exposure. Although Sosenko and his colleagues had not lost or settled a single lawsuit over the years—an impressive record in this litigious age—they are named in a couple of cases that have been grinding through the courts since the late 1990s. Sosenko and his colleagues have denied all the allegations and refuse to settle.

When the doctors started looking for an insurer to replace APC, none of the mainstream malpractice insurers offered coverage. One smaller firm came up with a package for nearly $100,000 a doctor (up from about $14,000 only two years earlier), plus $500,000 a year for "tail" coverage, to insure the practice for any suits that might arise from care provided before the new policy took effect. The doctors couldn't afford it. So after one of them left the practice to try to go it alone, the rest enlisted their state senator, who persuaded their original carrier to give them an extension—which expired at the end of last week. What next? Will they change specialties? Will they change addresses to a less litigious state? And what of their 6,000 patients, who would have to drive an hour to

A Chastened Insurer
He Sets Your Doctor's Bill

You don't have to feel sorry for the insurance industry to appreciate Donald Zuk's predicament. The CEO of SCPIE Holdings, California's second largest malpractice insurer, Zuk launched an ambitious plan in 1996 to expand into new states like Texas and Georgia and into new lines of business, such as insuring dentists and higher-risk doctors. It was a disaster.

Zuk, 66, a burly former football player, found himself fighting a multistate price war, cutting premiums to grab market share and badly underestimating how much his firm would pay out for claims against doctors. "The loss ratios were going through the roof," Zuk says. SCPIE raised premiums for policies outside California about 40% in 2001 and 30% in 2002. Yes, Zuk is one of the people responsible for the malpractice-insurance crisis that is disrupting the lives of so many doctors and patients. But he's not exactly profiteering. His firm has posted $96 million in losses over the past two years.

The Los Angeles-based company has retreated to California, pulling out of the malpractice business in other states. Says Zuk: "We knew that there was a risk when you go into a state without tort reform"—limits placed on personal-injury lawsuits and damages. "We thought the rates were sufficient, so we went with it. Today I know what's going on around the country. I won't go into Texas, Florida or any of the states I pulled back from until there's some semblance of tort reform."

As long as investment income held up, insurers could ignore rising claims.

Zuk has plenty of company in his malpractice losses and in his zeal for reform. In 2001 medical-malpractice insurers paid out $1.53 in claims and expenses for each $1 in premiums they collected. The industry has lost a combined $8 billion since 1995, and its reserves for estimated future claims are underfunded by about $4.6 billion. So if insurers aren't profiting from higher premiums, who is? Zuk and his peers point to trial lawyers and frivolous claimants. Insurers are lobbying alongside doctors for caps on noneconomic damages (for pain and suffering), like the ones in California and 18 other states. Rising awards, Zuk says, are bleeding money out of the system and forcing insurers to raise premiums. Cap the damages, and premiums will fall in line, he says.

Not everyone accepts that link. "In theory, tort reform would have an impact on premiums. In reality, that has not been the case," says Martin Weiss, chairman of Weiss Ratings, an independent insurance-rating agency in Palm Beach Gardens, Fla. In a study published this week, Weiss Ratings found that in states without caps on noneconomic damages, median annual premiums for standard medical-malpractice coverage rose 36% between 1991 and 2002. But in states with caps, premiums rose even more—48%. In the two groups of states, median 2002 premiums were about the same. Weiss found nine states with flat or declining premiums; two of them had caps, seven didn't. Weiss speculates that regulation of premium increases made the difference. In California, consumer groups argue that the state's tough oversight of the insurance industry, not its caps on damages, explains why rates have grown more slowly.

Caps on noneconomic damages may not hold down doctors' insurance costs, but they have boosted insurers' profits. In states with caps, the Weiss study found, claims payments grew only 38%, compared with 71% in states without them. By raising premiums, insurers have improved their ratio of claims to premiums, a key measure of profitability, from 110% in 2000 to 89% in 2002. "The caps are great for insurers," Weiss says. "Their payouts will be lower. In a perfect world, they would pass that savings on." But the industry's losses have been so large that lower claims will not reverse them; insurers are likely to keep raising premiums.

Raising rates is exactly what malpractice insurers failed to do in the 1990s, even as claims were rising. Zuk concedes that the industry has to accept some blame. "No one wanted to be the first guy to say, 'We've got to start charging the right premium,'" he says. The insurers feared losing market share, and as long as investment income held up, they could ignore rising claims.

The malpractice-insurance industry went through similar cycles of low rates, squeezed profits and price hikes in the mid-1970s and again in the mid-'80s. Zuk, who enrolled in law school in the '70s just to learn torts, says ballooning malpractice claims make the current crisis worse than previous ones. From 1997 to 2001, the median malpractice jury award doubled, to $1 million, but that counts results only in the 1% of lawsuits that are won by plaintiffs. The number of malpractice suits has remained stable, and although some states have seen sharp jumps, the average claim payment has grown about 8% a year, close to the rate of medical inflation.

Industry analysts say insurers' investment losses, not just jury awards, are behind the crisis. In bull markets, insurers count on investment income to offset underwriting losses; that ended when the 1990s' stock bubble burst. Although malpractice insurers make only about 20% of their investment income from stocks, the losses were steep and came in tandem with low bond yields.

Insurance firms, Zuk says, must stabilize the disruptive cycle of cutting rates and then raising them when losses grow too big. Regulators could stop an insurer from underpricing premiums and "protect it from its own stupidity," as Zuk puts it. "The industry has to say, 'Forget investment income. Let's just write to an underwriting profit.'"

Some industry experts suggest national standards for acceptable outcomes in medical procedures. Zuk says a separate malpractice torts system would be a better solution. New standards, he argues, would only put doctors on the defensive. He recalls his own knee replacement in 2001. His doctors, he says, focused on treating him, not providing disclaimers or ordering tests. Zuk is convinced he knows why: "They don't have to worry about me suing them."

—By Jyoti Thottam

the nearest lung specialist, in Chicago? "We doctors can move on," says Sosenko, tilting back in his office chair. "But our patients can't."

LIKE SOSENKO'S PATIENTS, MILLIONS across America might turn up for an appointment one day soon and find the doctor is out—for good. Thousands have already lost their doctors to a malpractice crisis that, while concentrated for now in certain states and specialties, is spreading. Doctors are being handed malpractice-insurance bills that are double those of a couple of years ago, forcing many of them to move from high-premium states—like Florida, Nevada and Pennsylvania—to more affordable venues like California and Indiana. The crisis is compelling some doctors and medical students to switch from lawsuit-magnet specialties like obstetrics, neurology and pulmonology to "safer" ones like dermatology and ophthalmology, or to refuse to perform high-risk procedures like delivering babies and operating on spines.

How They're Coping
DOCTORS DRIVEN AWAY

Smacked by big insurance bills, many physicians are moving, scaling back or quitting. Three M.D.s describe their tough choices.

I Had to Quit Medicine—
And Became a Lawyer

While most doctors and lawyers blame each other, Dr. Stephanie Rifkinson-Mann, 51, sees malpractice from both sides. Two years ago, after reimbursements fell as insurance premiums rose, the veteran pediatric neurosurgeon from Mount Kisco, N.Y., became a product-liability lawyer. She still does medical consultations one day a week. She quips, "Now that I'm a lawyer, I can afford to see patients."

I Had to Stop Delivering Babies

Dr. Mary-Emma Beres, a family practitioner in Sparta, N.C., has always loved delivering babies. But last year Beres, 35, concluded that she couldn't afford a tripling of her $17,000 malpractice premium and had to stop. With just one obstetrician left in town for high-risk cases, some women who need C-sections now must take a 40-minute ambulance ride.

I Had to Move My Practice

"I was happy taking care of my high school friends and their families," says neurosurgeon Brian Holmes, 42, who left his hometown of Scranton, Pa., last fall. Facing an estimated $200,000 annual malpractice premium, Holmes moved his wife and three children 190 miles southeast to Hagerstown, Md., where a policy cost just $30,000. "The move continues to be difficult."

WHILE THERE IS NO EVIDENCE that the total number of physicians in the U.S. has declined, some veteran practitioners in states with sky-high malpractice premiums are quitting medicine. Even in states where malpractice insurance remains relatively affordable, doctors are increasingly practicing more "defensive medicine," trying to gird themselves against possible lawsuits by ordering unnecessary tests and thereby driving up health-care costs.

In one 6,000-sq.-mi. expanse of Arizona, high malpractice premiums have prompted six obstetricians to stop delivering babies. Many women now have to drive an hour or more to reach a hospital with a delivery room, forcing several, like Melinda Sallard, 22, to give birth in the car en route to the hospital. Seniors in parts of Pennsylvania travel an hour or two to see a neurosurgeon, and one orthopedic surgeon from Philadelphia commutes every week to see patients in the Midwest, where malpractice-insurance costs are lower. Emergency rooms from Orlando, Fla., to Belleville, Mo., report that rising insurance premiums are making it difficult for them to employ the trauma specialists needed to treat car-accident victims. In protest, doctors from New Jersey to Washington State are taking to the streets and engaging in work slowdowns and strikes. Nearly 100 physicians in and around Jacksonville, Fla., have stopped performing elective surgery, making the county activate an emergency response system that it typically uses to deal with natural disasters like hurricanes.

The system is clearly broken, and there is no quick fix in sight. To doctors like Sosenko, the main problems are frivolous lawsuits and multimillion-dollar judgments awarded for tragic but sometimes unavoidable outcomes. (A banner at a rally read SICK? CALL A LAWYER.) The waiting room at Sosenko's Midwest Pulmonary these days looks almost like a campaign headquarters. Banners declaring WE HAVE A CRISIS! hang alongside lists of politicians' names and phone numbers. Sosenko's patients have signed petitions calling on politicians to make malpractice reform a top priority.

It's easy to see why they want to help. Sosenko is a native and a favorite son of Joliet, a middle-class town about 45 miles southwest of Chicago. The child of Ukrainian immigrants who fled a displaced-persons camp in Germany after World War II, Sosenko grew up in Joliet watching his father, Roman, serve the town as a family doctor. He wanted to do the same for his friends and neighbors, treating people suffering from diseases such as asthma, bronchitis, emphysema and lung cancer.

Over the years, Sosenko and his colleagues at MPC have earned a reputation as not only capable but also unusually attentive. Phone calls are promptly returned, day or night, and doctors make house calls when necessary. "It's such a relief, just knowing he's here," says Pat Falkenberg, 48, a patient of Sosenko's who is battling pulmonary fibrosis and awaiting a lung transplant. During a stay in the hospital, Falkenberg says, Sosenko stopped by her room so many times that she "often wondered if he ever went home."

A math whiz with almost total recall, Sosenko is legendary around the office for remembering practically every one of the several thousand patients he has seen—and details of their conditions—even if it's been 15 years between visits. He personally coordinates most of his patients' care, calling other specialists for tests and appointments. "Any wheezing? How about panting?" Sosenko asks Richard Escherick, 61, during an office visit. In his blunt but friendly style, Sosenko quizzes the man about his nighttime cough. "Is it like this?" he asks, making a hacking sound. "Or like this?"—and he rattles his throat, sounding like a tom turkey. Sitting on a round

Where It's Spreading

The medical-malpractice crisis is concentrated mostly in litigious states
with generous juries and financially shaky insurers—but its contagious

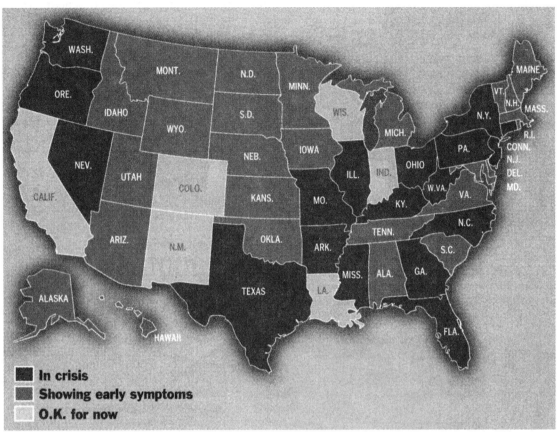

In crisis
Showing early symptoms
O.K. for now

Source: American Medical Association

WASHINGTON Nearly 1,000 doctors rallied last week to support medical-liability reforms. In May the state's largest neurosurgery group lost its insurance, leaving many hospitals without emergency-room coverage. Half of Tacoma's ob-gyns won't deliver babies

NEVADA More than 30 ob-gyns have closed their practices, and last summer the only first-rate trauma center in Las Vegas shut down for 10 days, prompting state legislators to pass a cap on noneconomic awards

ILLINOIS Thousands of physicians rallied in Chicago last month to protest skyrocketing medical-malpractice liability premiums. In Joliet last year three neurosurgeons stopped performing brain surgery. Head-trauma patients now need to be flown by helicopter to a center 45 miles away

MISSISSIPPI About 100 doctors have left or plan to leave the state. The only pediatric specialist in Rolling Fork has moved to North Dakota

PENNSYLVANIA Since 2001 some 900 doctors have closed practices, limited their services or left the state. The biggest loss: young doctors. Fewer than 5% of the state's M.D.s are younger than 35, down from 12% in 1989

NEW JERSEY Doctors have staged three rallies to urge state legislators to pass medical-liability reforms. A three-day walkout in February led to a 60% hike in the number of patients treated in emergency rooms

FLORIDA Seven hospital obstetric units have closed, and six medical centers no longer perform mammographies. Some South Florida women now must wait four months for the test

stool, with his legs crossed, and peering over the top of his reading glasses, Sosenko gives his patients as much time as they need to ask questions and voice concerns. These days, their worries often go beyond what medication to take. When Sosenko tells Richard Tea, 73, that he wants to see him again in three months, Tea's wife Mary Ellen nervously asks, "Are *you* going to be here in three months?"

Sosenko's petition drive generated more than 1,000 letters to Illinois' congressional delegation in Washington

and to state legislators in Springfield. It got the attention of state senator Larry Walsh, a Democrat from Joliet. Concerned about the availability of medical care in his hometown, Walsh persuaded Midwest Pulmonary's original carrier to give the practice a special two-month extension—albeit a pricey one, costing about $35,000. Walsh has reason to be worried. Sosenko's practice isn't the only one in Joliet that is perilously close to shutting down. The area's last remaining neurosurgeon, after learning he would have to pay $468,000 a year for insurance, up from

Who's Paying the Most

	NEUROSURGEON	OB-GYN	EMERGENCY PHYSICIAN	ORTHOPEDIC SURGEON	GENERAL SURGEON
Average annual cost of medical-liability premium	**$71,200**	**$56,546**	**$53,500**	**$38,000**	**$36,354**
Percentage increase	35.6% *from 2001 to 2002*	19.6% *from 2001 to 2002*	56.2% *from 2002 to 2003*	22.5% *from 2001 to 2002*	25% *from 2001 to 2002*
Cities with the highest premiums	$283,000 *Chicago* $267,000 *Philadelphia*	$210,576 *Miami* $152,496 *Cleveland*	$150,000 *Miami* $102,000 *Houston*	$135,000 *Philadelphia* $110,000 *Chicago*	$174,268 *Miami* $107,139 *Detroit*

SOURCES: American Academy of Orthopaedic Surgeons; American Association of Neurological Surgeons/Congress of Neurological Surgeons; American College of Emergency Physicians; American College of Obstetricians and Gynecologists; American Medical Association; Medical Liability Monitor

An Undisciplined Doctor
Why Wasn't He Stopped Sooner?

For years, Raymond Hilson thought the infection that left him disfigured was just a stroke of bad luck. Today he thinks it could have been worse. A school-bus driver from Colfax, Wis., Hilson, now 73, underwent heart-bypass surgery in 1994 at Luther Hospital in Eau Claire. At first the procedure seemed to have gone well. But Hilson contracted a severe staph infection. To treat it, doctors "kept cutting back the flesh and bone," he recalls, until his entire sternum was removed, leaving his beating heart visible just under the skin.

While there is no evidence that Hilson's surgeon was responsible for the infection, the hospital volunteered cash compensation to Hilson, which he accepted. And there are many things he knows today that he wishes he had known before his surgery. Only six months earlier, the physician operating on him, Dr. Michael McEnany, then 55, had resigned as chief of cardiovascular surgery at San Francisco Kaiser Permanente Medical Center after peers raised serious questions about his competency. He had been forbidden to operate without another surgeon assisting. Hilson had no way of knowing that background, or that the medial board of California would later accuse McEnany of incompetence and gross negligence in eight surgeries that went awry during his time at Kaiser, or that McEnany would experience other complications, including sternal wound infections, among his surgical patients in Wisconsin.

A small group of doctors causes the lion's share of malpractice payouts

You might think that McEnany would have had a hard time landing the Wisconsin job after his California experience. But as part of his resignation deal, according to California officials, Kaiser agreed to terminate McEnany's practice review and not file a report to the medical board of California, as the hospital was required to do. When officials at Luther Hospital ran a routine background check on McEnany, there were no red flags. Had a Kaiser whistle-blower not tipped off the medical board in 1996, sparking an investigation that led to McEnany's surrender of his licenses in California and Wisconsin, he could still be practicing. Instead, he is fighting off the remainder of 28 lawsuits filed against him between 1998 and 2000.

Although McEnany declined requests for interviews, one of his attorneys, Steven Sager of Fond du Lac, Wis., says, "I think that the doctor provided good care." He noted that several cases have been dismissed and McEnany has so far made no payments in Wisconsin.

For critics of doctor discipline, the McEnany case represents an extreme example of a familiar problem. While the vast majority of doctors perform with care and lose few, if any, legal judgments or settlements, a small number of negligent or incompetent doctors endanger patients and drive up malpractice-insurance costs for everyone. Since 1990, one-third of malpractice awards and settlements have resulted from just 5% of doctors making such payouts, according to the National Practitioner Data Bank (NPDB). Yet doctors and hospitals too often fail to discipline repeat offenders.

Hospitals are required to report to their state medical board and NPDB any revocation, suspension or restriction of a doctor's clinical privileges for more than 30 days. But hospitals don't always comply. By the end of 2001, 55% of all nonfederal hospitals registered with the NPDB had not reported a single disciplinary action against a doctor. (Two Kaiser administrators paid nearly $20,000 to settle with the state after failing to report McEnany, and the medical center says reporting procedures "are definitely different now.")

Hospitals face many incentives not to report a disciplined doctor—and not to discipline him at all. A hospital may want to limit its liability by not airing the problem. Or it may be afraid of a legal battle with the physician. And doctors are loath to report a colleague's bad behavior. Consumer advocates say that self-policing by doctors and hospitals is not sufficient and that patients need access to state medical board and NPDB records that are denied to them today.

That's why Raymond Hilson didn't know about the $200,000 settlement that Kaiser paid in 1992 to Richard Lord and his family for the loss of his wife Eleanor, who, according tho the California investigation, bled to death while in McEnany's care. If Hilson had known more, he says, he would have gone elsewhere. Learning the surgeon's history has made him see things in a different light. Strange as it may sound, he says, "I feel lucky to be a survivor."

—By Leslie Berestein/Los Angeles

$180,000, is considering moving to South Dakota or quitting for good. And a local group of 16 cardiologists—as well as 60 general practitioners—may lose their insurance at the end of this month.

A Medical Student
Today's Lesson: Switch Specialty

Martin Palmeri has changed his mind before. Until his fourth year of college, he was planning a career in investment banking. But one afternoon, while volunteering in a North Carolina medical clinic, Palmeri realized that he was much happier in the hospital than in economics class. Palmeri was drawn to obstetrics and gynecology, he says, for the "emotion and passion" involved in delivering babies. "It's tremendously rewarding."

Or so he thought. Last year, his third at the Brody School of Medicine at East Carolina University, Palmeri, 28, began investigating what he calls the "litigious juggernaut" of ob-gyn and decided the risks of the specialty were greater than its rewards. He's not alone. More than 10% of respondents to an informal poll on the American Medical Student Association website say they have switched their intended specialty because of the rising cost of malpractice insurance. An additional 36% are considering a change for the same reason. In the first round of the process that matches medical-school graduates to most residency programs, 30% of positions in ob-gyn and 20% in E.R. medicine went unfilled by this year's U.S. graduates. (Most spots were ultimately taken by foreign-school graduates and U.S. students who did not get their first choice.)

Palmeri did his homework before giving up on ob-gyn. He attended a workshop held by the American College of Obstetricians and Gynecologists, at which he heard alarming stories of physicians turning away high-risk patients for fear of litigation, or losing their practice because of skyrocketing insurance costs. Palmeri then observed the civil trial of a Wilson, N.C., obstetrician who was sued after the plaintiff's baby suffered neurological damage during birth. The doctor claimed that the plaintiff had refused to have a C-section despite his insistence that a vaginal birth would endanger both mother and baby. The plaintiff claimed she had received no such advice. Palmeri says he was disturbed to see that "the trial focused on the poor outcome and not on what the physician actually did." The jury was hung, and the doctor—who says he had to pay at least $30,000 in office overhead while he earned nothing sitting in court—settled the case. His insurance premiums jumped from $22,000 in 1998, the year he delivered the baby, to almost $70,000 this year. "I just couldn't imagine having to go through what he did every couple of years," Palmeri says. He's now considering radiology.

Professional groups for high-risk specialties are concerned about the loss of people like Palmeri and Peter Chien Jr., a New York University medical student who contemplated orthopedics but is opting for dermatology, a less litigious field. Perhaps even more troubling, a quarter of final-year medical students polled said they would not study medicine if they started their education over. Thankfully for his patients, that's a change of attitude Palmeri hasn't shared.

—By Amanda Bower

Soon after he got the two-month extension of his group's insurance, Sosenko thought he might have found a more permanent solution, courtesy of the local Provena Saint Joseph Hospital. Surgeons like to have a pulmonologist standing by when they perform a complicated procedure like open heart surgery. So the hospital offered to hire Sosenko and his colleagues as staff physicians and cover them under its liability insurance. However, Provena's insurance company wouldn't cover the doctors if they continued to see patients outside the hospital, even part time. "Maybe it was silly to take the two-month extension," says Dr. Gregg Cohan, 41, one of Sosenko's partners. "Maybe all we did was prolong the death."

The insurers blame rate hikes and policy cancellations on what they describe as a rising tide of lawsuits and $1 million–plus jury awards. Their solution (which many doctors, including Sosenko, support): caps of $250,000 on noneconomic damages awarded for pain and suffering. President Bush and other Republicans, whose campaigns are supported by doctors and insurance firms, endorse such legislation, and the House of Representatives has passed a bill along those lines. But plaintiffs' lawyers, who contribute heavily to the campaigns of Democrats, are lobbying their friends in the Senate, and national "tort reform" may remain more of a rallying cry than a real prospect.

The states could step in. Sosenko would love to see Illinois politicians ride to his rescue—and at the very least require a panel of qualified medical experts, rather than one hired gun, to sign off on a suit before it can go forward. But he doesn't hold out much hope. Twice in the past two decades, the state legislature has passed caps on noneconomic jury awards only to have them struck down as unconstitutional by the state supreme court. (Courts in other states, including California, have upheld similar caps.) Many state politicians are more than happy to hand the thorny issue off to Congress. State senator Walsh says some of his colleagues believe that the crisis eventually "will just work itself out." Sosenko says with disgust, "Talking to politicians is like hitting your head against a wall."

But the legal system is not the only culprit in the malpractice mess. Critics say soaring premiums are less the result of lawsuits than of insurers rushing to make up for their losses in underpriced premiums and poorly performing investments. An independent study by Weiss Ratings to be released this week shows that states with caps on malpractice damages have not enjoyed much relief in malpractice-insurance premiums but have instead seen insurers shore up profits. Sosenko's anger at the insurers moved him to join several hundred other Illinois physicians at a rally in the state capital earlier this year, calling on legislators to freeze malpractice premiums for six months and investigate the industry's pricing practices. "These companies pretty much have a free hand to do what they want," he says.

A Frustrated Lawmaker
Why Nothing Gets Fixed

The medical malpractice issue is a great one if you're a Republican looking out for the doctors and insurers who get sued. It's not so great if you're trying to find a compromise among these powerful, warring professions. But Senator Dianne Feinstein, a liberal Democrat from California, decided to give it a try, and her experience is a case study in how the politics of malpractice insurance works—or doesn't—in Washington.

Feinstein, 69, would seem well positioned to broker a deal. A member of the Senate Judiciary Committee, she has close ties with lawyers, who contributed almost $500,000 to her campaigns over the past five years, more than she received from any other group. Yet she sponsored a bill to protect high-tech firms from Y2K liability, which trial lawyers opposed. And she comes from a medical family. Her father was chairman of the department of surgery at the University of California Medical Center, and her second husband Dr. Bertram Feinstein, who died in 1978, was a neurosurgeon. He had eight malpractice suits filed against him but neurosurgeons get sued a lot because of their high-risk operations.

Late last year Senator Feinstein began meeting with California doctors in an effort to come up with a national version of her state's malpractice law. California allows unlimited amounts to be awarded for the economic damages a patient suffers as a result of a doctor's error, such as lost wages and medical bills, but caps noneconomic awards for pain and suffering at $250,000. The cap works, Feinstein believes. Nationwide, doctors' insurance premiums grew 420% from 1975 to 2001, while California's premiums, she says, are up only 168%. (Some experts credit the lower premiums to insurance reforms the state also adopted.)

After President Bush praised the California law in January, Feinstein said she would work with the White House. The next day she got a call from new Senate majority leader Bill Frist. A renowned surgeon, Frist desperately wanted the Senate to pass a bill curbing mal-practice-insurance costs. And he just as desperately needed a Democrat to co-sponsor the measure. Feinstein agreed to help.

It was complicated from the start. Doctors and lawyers spend heavily to protect their interests on Capitol Hill. The American Medical Association contributed $2.7 million to candidates in the 2002 congressional elections (60% went to Republicans), and the Association of Trial Lawyers gave out $3.7 million (89% went to Democrats). Feinstein was hit from all sides. Senate Democrats, most of whom oppose curbs on jury awards, were angry with her for breaking ranks. Lawyers' groups and consumer activists complained that the caps discriminated against low-income victims of malpractice. Some said she couldn't be objective because her late husband had faced malpractice suits.

Feinstein and Frist drafted a compromise. Since California's $250,000 cap was set 28 years ago, says Feinstein, today it would be an inflation-adjusted $780,000. So she and Frist suggested doubling the cap to $500,000. For catastrophic cases that resulted in severe disfigurement, severe physical disability or death, says Feinstein, the cap would be the greater of $2 million or $50,000 times the number of years of life expectancy. The 25 states that have laws limiting damages could keep their caps if they did not want to adopt the Federal Government's.

When Feinstein floated the draft measure, she hit two walls. Trial lawyers hated caps. And doctors said the caps were too high and wouldn't stabilize their malpractice premiums. "There's just no way to proceed at this time," Feinstein says. The House, where Republicans have firmer control, has passed the $250,000 cap Bush wants. But for now, a bill like Feinstein's won't pass in the Senate. She blames the deadlock mostly on doctors who won't compromise. "There has to be a change of heart in the medical profession," she says, "for something to proceed."

—*By Douglas Waller/Washington*

However, physicians themselves deserve at least part of the blame. "Doctors," says Dr. John Walsh, 46, one of Sosenko's partners, "haven't sold themselves as a self-policing group." The vast majority of conscientious physicians have been forced to subsidize the higher insurance costs of a few incompetents. Consider this: between September 1990 and March 2003, just 5% of the doctors who have made medical malpractice payments accounted for a third of all the money paid out, according to the Federal Government's National Practitioner Data Bank.

SOSENKO'S CRASH COURSE IN LAW and politics is taking an emotional toll on him and his family. An avid windsurfer and science-fiction buff whose favorite books are *The Hobbitt* and *The Lord of the Rings*, Sosenko hasn't been able to enjoy himself much for the past several months. He hardly has the time or energy to play video games with his son Nick, 10. For the first time in recent memory, he has missed some of his 12-year-old daughter Teresa's afterschool volleyball games, though he still manages to take the kids to their classes at the Ukrainian cultural center on Saturdays. (The family speaks Ukrainian at home.) Sosenko has always been a bit moody. His office is littered with Tasmanian-devil toys given to him by his family, an inside joke alluding to his occasional temper. But nowadays he is regularly depressed and irritable. "Alex takes everything to heart," says his wife Maria, 46, a rheumatologist (whose malpractice premiums nearly doubled this year, from $8,592 to $15,472). "He's frantically searching for help."

With Medicare, Medicaid and HMO reimbursements falling and malpractice premiums steadily rising, Sosenko's income has dropped 40% over the past five years, to about $200,000 last year. That might sound like a lot, until you consider the 13 years he studied after high school, the debts he built up, the nights and weekends he works. As his colleague Cohan says, with only a little exaggeration, "Our income is completely controlled by the government, but we have no control on our expenses." Both men are bracing for a potentially bigger pay cut. Sosenko has put off indefinitely any major expenditures, including having the house repainted. But while his colleagues and even his wife have considered moving across Illinois' eastern border to Indiana, where malpractice premiums are lower, Sosenko can't imagine cutting his ties to his hometown. Not only would he have to take his kids away from their school and friends, but he would have to relocate his wife's elderly parents, whom he and his wife recently moved to Joliet. "I don't want to leave here. I'm too old to start from scratch," Sosenko says.

Early retirement is an equally unattractive prospect for Sosenko, a driven perfectionist who avidly reads medical journals to stay current with his specialty and holds his children to his exacting standards. If necessary, Sosenko says, he would "probably work without insurance," a dangerous gamble for any doctor these days but one that some physicians, particularly in Florida, are now taking. Another option he's exploring is work as a cardiopulmonary trainer and tester for fire fighters and others who must have good respiratory fitness for their job. As for the career plans of his children, Sosenko probably won't en-

courage his oldest son Alexander, 18, to follow in Dad's or his grandfather's footsteps. "I want him to be successful," Sosenko says. "I'm not sure [anymore] that the doctor has job security."

That has been painfully clear to Sosenko in recent weeks. After the collapse of their talks with Provena Hospital, the doctors of MPC, who had pledged to stick it out together, suddenly fractured. The three who haven't been named in either of the lawsuits pending against the practice—Drs. Walsh, Visvanatha Giri and Phillip Leung—created a separate partnership and secured malpractice insurance. Sosenko is planning to take the next couple of weeks off now that his policy has run out and then try to find a new medical group to join. Even so, he says, there are no hard feelings against his former colleagues. He's too busy for that. There are too many patients to treat. And too many people to lobby.

—*With reporting by Dody Tsiantar/New York, Anne Berryman/Athens, Ga., Paul Cuadros/Sparta, N.C., and Michael Peltier/Tallahassee*

DEATH STALKS A CONTINENT

In the dry timber of African societies, AIDS was a spark. The conflagration it set off continues to kill millions. Here's why

By Johanna McGeary

IMAGINE YOUR LIFE THIS WAY. You get up in the morning and breakfast with your three kids. One is already doomed to die in infancy. Your husband works 200 miles away, comes home twice a year and sleeps around in between. You risk your life in every act of sexual intercourse. You go to work past a house where a teenager lives alone tending young siblings without any source of income. At another house, the wife was branded a whore when she asked her husband to use a condom, beaten silly and thrown into the streets. Over there lies a man desperately sick without access to a doctor or clinic or medicine or food or blankets or even a kind word. At work you eat with colleagues, and every third one is already fatally ill. You whisper about a friend who admitted she had the plague and whose neighbors stoned her to death. Your leisure is occupied by the funerals you attend every Saturday. You go to bed fearing adults your age will not live into their 40s. You and your neighbors and your political and popular leaders act as if nothing is happening.

Across the southern quadrant of Africa, this nightmare is real. The word not spoken is AIDS, and here at ground zero of humanity's deadliest cataclysm, the ultimate tragedy is that so many people don't know—or don't want to know—what is happening.

As the HIV virus sweeps mercilessly through these lands—the fiercest trial Africa has yet endured—a few try to address the terrible depredation. The rest of society looks away. Flesh and muscle melt from the bones of the sick in packed hospital wards and lonely bush kraals. Corpses stack up in morgues until those on top crush the identity from the faces underneath. Raw earth mounds scar the landscape, grave after grave without name or number. Bereft children grieve for parents lost in their prime, for siblings scattered to the winds.

The victims don't cry out. Doctors and obituaries do not give the killer its name. Families recoil in shame. Leaders shirk responsibility. The stubborn silence heralds victory for the disease: denial cannot keep the virus at bay.

The developed world is largely silent too. AIDS in Africa has never commanded the full-bore response the West has brought to other, sometimes lesser, travails. We pay sporadic attention, turning on the spotlight when an international conference occurs, then turning it off. Good-hearted donors donate; governments acknowledge that more needs to be done. But think how different the effort would be if what is happening here were happening in the West.

By now you've seen pictures of the sick, the dead, the orphans. You've heard appalling numbers: the number of new infections, the number of the dead, the number who are sick without care, the number walking around already fated to die.

But to comprehend the full horror AIDS has visited on Africa, listen to the woman we have dubbed Laetitia Hambahlane in

Durban or the boy Tsepho Phale in Francistown or the woman who calls herself Thandiwe in Bulawayo or Louis Chikoka, a long-distance trucker. You begin to understand how AIDS has struck Africa—with a biblical virulence that will claim tens of millions of lives—when you hear about shame and stigma and ignorance and poverty and sexual violence and migrant labor and promiscuity and political paralysis and the terrible silence that surrounds all this dying. It is a measure of the silence that some asked us not to print their real names to protect their privacy.

HALF A MILLION AFRICAN CHILDREN WERE INFECTED WITH HIV LAST YEAR

Theirs is a story about what happens when a disease leaps the confines of medicine to invade the body politic, infecting not just individuals but an entire society. As AIDS migrated to man in Africa, it mutated into a complex plague with confounding social, economic and political mechanics that locked together to accelerate the virus' progress. The region's social dynamics colluded to spread the disease and help block effective intervention.

We have come to three countries abutting one another at the bottom of Africa—Botswana, South Africa, Zimbabwe—the heart of the heart of the epidemic. For nearly a decade, these nations suffered a hidden invasion of infection that concealed the dimension of the coming calamity. Now the omnipresent dying reveals the shocking scale of the devastation.

AIDS in Africa bears little resemblance to the American epidemic, limited to specific high-risk groups and brought under control through intensive education, vigorous political action and expensive drug therapy. Here the disease has bred a Darwinian perversion. Society's fittest, not its frailest, are the ones who die—adults spirited away, leaving the old and the children behind. You cannot define risk groups: everyone who is sexually active is at risk. Babies too, unwittingly infected by mothers. Barely a single family remains untouched. Most do not know how or when they caught the virus, many never know they have it, many who do know don't tell anyone as they lie dying. Africa can provide no treatment for those with AIDS.

They will all die, of tuberculosis, pneumonia, meningitis, diarrhea, whatever overcomes their ruined immune systems first. And the statistics, grim as they are, may be too low. There is no broad-scale AIDS testing: infection rates are calculated mainly from the presence of HIV in pregnant women. Death certificates in these countries do not record AIDS as the cause. "Whatever stats we have are not reliable," warns Mary Crewe of the University of Pretoria's Center for the Study of AIDS. "Everybody's guessing."

THE TB PATIENT

CASE NO. 309 IN THE TUGELA FERRY HOME-CARE PROGRAM shivers violently on the wooden planks someone has knocked into a bed, a frayed blanket pulled right up to his nose. He has the flushed skin, overbright eyes and careful breathing of the tubercular. He is alone, and it is chilly within the crumbling mud walls of his hut at Msinga Top, a windswept outcrop high above the Tugela River in South Africa's KwaZulu-Natal province. The spectacular view of hills and veld would gladden a well man, but the 22-year-old we will call Fundisi Khumalo, though he does not know it, has AIDS, and his eyes seem to focus inward on his simple fear.

Before he can speak, his throat clutches in gasping spasms. Sharp pains rack his chest; his breath comes in shallow gasps. The vomiting is better today. But constipation has doubled up his knees, and he is too weak to go outside to relieve himself. He can't remember when he last ate. He can't remember how long he's been sick—"a long time, maybe since six months ago." Khumalo knows he has TB, and he believes it is just TB. "I am only thinking of that," he answers when we ask why he is so ill.

But the fear never leaves his eyes. He worked in a hair salon in Johannesburg, lived in a men's hostel in one of the cheap townships, had "a few" girlfriends. He knew other young men in the hostel who were on-and-off sick. When they fell too ill to work anymore, like him, they straggled home to rural villages like Msinga Top. But where Khumalo would not go is the hospital. "Why?" he says. "You are sick there, you die there."

"He's right, you know," says Dr. Tony Moll, who has driven us up the dirt track from the 350-bed hospital he heads in Tugela Ferry. "We have no medicines for AIDS. So many hospitals tell them, 'You've got AIDS. We can't help you. Go home and die.'" No one wants to be tested either, he adds, unless treatment is available. "If the choice is to know and get nothing," he says, "they don't want to know."

Here and in scattered homesteads all over rural Africa, the dying people say the sickness afflicting their families and neighbors is just the familiar consequence of their eternal poverty. Or it is the work of witchcraft. You have done something bad and have been bewitched. Your neighbor's jealousy has invaded you. You have not appeased the spirits of your ancestors, and they have cursed you. Some in South Africa believe the disease was introduced by the white population as a way to control black Africans after the end of apartheid.

Ignorance about AIDS remains profound. But because of the funerals, southern Africans can't help seeing that something more systematic and sinister lurks out there. Every Saturday and often Sundays too, neighbors trudge to the cemeteries for costly burial rites for the young and the middle-aged who are suddenly dying so much faster than the old. Families say it was pneumonia, TB, malaria that killed their son, their wife, their baby. "But you starting to hear the truth," says Durban home-care volunteer Busi Magwazi. "In the church, in the graveyard, they saying, 'Yes, she died of AIDS.' Oh, people talking about it even if the families don't admit it." Ignorance is the crucial reason the epidemic has run out of control. Surveys say many Africans here are becoming aware there is a sexually transmitted disease called AIDS that is incurable. But they don't think the risk applies to them. And their vague knowledge does not translate into changes in their sexual behavior. It's easy to see why so many don't yet sense the danger when few talk openly about the disease. And Africans are beset by so plentiful a roster of perils—famine, war, the violence of desperation or ethnic hatred, the regular illnesses of poverty, the dangers inside mines or on the roads—that the delayed risk of AIDS ranks low.

A CONTINENT IN PERIL

17 million Africans have died since the AIDS epidemic began in the late 1970s, more than 3.7 million of them children. An additional 12 million children have been orphaned by AIDS. An estimated 8.8% of adults in Africa are infected with HIV/AIDS, and in the following seven countries, at least 1 adult in 5 is living with HIV

1. Botswana

Though it has the highest per capita GDP, it also has the highest estimated adult infection rate—**36%**. 24,000 die each year. 66,000 children have lost their mother or both parents to the disease.

2. Swaziland

More than **25%** of adults have HIV/AIDS in this small country. 12,000 children have been orphaned, and 7,100 adults and children die each year.

3. Zimbabwe

One-quarter of the adult population is infected here. 160,000 adults and children died in 1999, and 900,000 children have been orphaned. Because of AIDS, life expectancy is 43.

4. Lesotho

24% of the adults are infected with HIV/AIDS. 35,000 children have been orphaned, and 16,000 adults and children die each year.

5. Zambia

20% of the adult population is infected, 1 in 4 adults in the cities. 650,000 children have been orphaned, and 99,000 Zambians died in 1999.

6. South Africa

This country has the largest number of people living with HIV/AIDS, about **20%** of its adult population, up from 13% in 1997. 420,000 children have been orphaned, and 250,000 people die each year from the disease.

7. Namibia

19.5% of the adult population is living with HIV. 57% of the infected are women. 67,000 children are AIDS orphans, and 18,000 adults and children die each year.

Source: UNAIDS

THE OUTCAST

TO ACKNOWLEDGE AIDS IN YOURSELF IS TO BE BRANDED AS monstrous. Laetitia Hambahlane (not her real name) is 51 and sick with AIDS. So is her brother. She admits it; he doesn't. In her mother's broken-down house in the mean streets of Umlazi township, though, Laetitia's mother hovers over her son, nursing him, protecting him, resolutely denying he has anything but TB, though his sister claims the sure symptoms of AIDS mark him. Laetitia is the outcast, first from her family, then from her society.

For years Laetitia worked as a domestic servant in Durban and dutifully sent all her wages home to her mother. She fell in love a number of times and bore four children. "I loved that last man," she recalls. "After he left, I had no one, no sex." That was 1992, but Laetitia already had HIV.

She fell sick in 1996, and her employers sent her to a private doctor who couldn't diagnose an illness. He tested her blood and found she was HIV positive. "I wish I'd died right then," she says, as tears spill down her sunken cheeks. "I asked the doctor, 'Have you got medicine?' He said no. I said, 'Can't you keep me alive?' " The doctor could do nothing and sent her away. "I couldn't face the word," she says. "I couldn't sleep at night. I sat on my bed, thinking, praying. I did not see anyone day or night. I ask God, Why?"

Laetitia's employers fired her without asking her exact diagnosis. For weeks she could not muster the courage to tell anyone. Then she told her children, and they were ashamed and frightened. Then, harder still, she told her mother. Her mother raged about the loss of money if Laetitia could not work again. She was so angry she ordered Laetitia out of the house. When her daughter wouldn't leave, the mother threatened to sell the house to get rid of her daughter. Then she walled off her daughter's room with plywood partitions, leaving the daughter a pariah, alone in a cramped, dark space without windows and only a flimsy door opening into the alley. Laetitia must earn the pennies to feed herself and her children by peddling beer, cigarettes and candy from a shopping cart in her room, when people are brave enough to stop by her door. "Sometimes they buy, sometimes not," she says. "That is how I'm surviving."

Her mother will not talk to her. "If you are not even accepted by your own family," says Magwazi, the volunteer home-care giver from Durban's Sinoziso project who visits Laetitia, "then others will not accept you." When Laetitia ventures outdoors, neighbors snub her, tough boys snatch her purse, children taunt her. Her own kids are tired of the sickness and don't like to help her anymore. "When I can't get up, they don't bring me food," she laments. One day local youths barged into her room, cursed her as a witch and a whore and beat her. When she told the police, the youths returned, threatening to burn down the house.

But it is her mother's rejection that wounds Laetitia most. "She is hiding it about my brother," she cries. "Why will she do nothing for me?" Her hands pick restlessly at the quilt covering her paper-thin frame. "I know my mother will not bury me properly. I know she will not take care of my kids when I am gone."

Jabulani Syabusi would use his real name, but he needs to protect his brother. He teaches school in a red, dusty district of KwaZulu-Natal. People here know the disease is all around them, but no one speaks of it. He eyes the scattered huts that make up his little settlement on an arid bluff. "We can count 20 who died just here as far as we can see. I personally don't remember any family that told it was AIDS," he says. "They hide it if they do know."

Syabusi's own family is no different. His younger brother is also a teacher who has just come home from Durban too sick to work anymore. He says he has tuberculosis, but after six months the tablets he is taking have done nothing to cure him. Syabusi's wife Nomsange, a nurse, is concerned that her 36-year-old brother-in-law may have something worse. Syabusi finally asked the doctor tending his brother what is wrong. The doctor said the information is confidential and will not tell him. Neither will his brother. "My brother is not brave enough to tell me," says Syabusi, as he stares sadly toward the house next door, where his only sibling lies ill. "And I am not brave enough to ask him."

Kennedy Fugewane, a cheerful, elderly volunteer counselor, sits in an empty U.S.-funded clinic that offers fast, pinprick blood tests in Francistown, Botswana, pondering how to break through the silence. This city suffers one of the world's highest infection rates, but people deny the disease because HIV is linked with sex. "We don't reveal anything," he says. "But people are so stigmatized even if they walk in the door." Africans feel they must keep private anything to do with sex. "If a man comes here, people will say he is running around," says Fugewane, though he acknowledges that men never do come. "If a woman comes, people will say she is loose. If anyone says they got HIV, they will be despised."

Pretoria University's Mary Crewe says, "It is presumed if you get AIDS, you have done something wrong." HIV labels you as living an immoral life. Embarrassment about sexuality looms more important than future health risks. "We have no language to talk candidly about sex," she says, "so we have no civil language to talk about AIDS." Volunteers like Fugewane try to reach out with flyers, workshops, youth meetings and free condoms, but they are frustrated by a culture that values its dignity over saving lives. "People here don't have the courage to come forward and say, 'Let me know my HIV status,'" he sighs, much less the courage to do something about it. "Maybe one day…"

Doctors bow to social pressure and legal strictures not to record AIDS on death certificates. "I write TB or meningitis or diarrhea but never AIDS," says South Africa's Dr. Moll. "It's a public document, and families would hate it if anyone knew." Several years ago, doctors were barred even from recording compromised immunity or HIV status on a medical file; now they can record the results of blood tests for AIDS on patient charts to protect other health workers. Doctors like Moll have long agitated to apply the same openness to death certificates.

THE TRUCK DRIVER

HERE, MEN HAVE TO MIGRATE TO WORK, INSIDE THEIR COUNTRIES or across borders. All that mobility sows HIV far and wide, as Louis Chikoka is the first to recognize. He regularly drives the highway that is Botswana's economic lifeline and its curse. The road runs for 350 miles through desolate bush that is the Texas-size country's sole strip of habitable land, home to a large majority of its 1.5 million people. It once brought prospectors to Botswana's rich diamond reefs. Now it's the link for transcontinental truckers like Chikoka who haul goods from South Africa to markets in the continent's center. And now the road brings AIDS.

Chikoka brakes his dusty, diesel-belching Kabwe Transport 18-wheeler to a stop at the dark roadside rest on the edge of Francistown, where the international trade routes converge and at least 43% of adults are HIV-positive. He is a cheerful man even after 12 hard hours behind the wheel freighting rice from Durban. He's been on the road for two weeks and will reach his destination in Congo next Thursday. At 39, he is married, the father of three and a long-haul trucker for 12 years. He's used to it.

Lighting up a cigarette, the jaunty driver is unusually loquacious about sex as he eyes the dim figures circling the rest stop. Chikoka has parked here for a quickie. See that one over there, he points with his cigarette. "Those local ones we call bitches. They always waiting here for short service." Short service? "It's according to how long it takes you to ejaculate," he explains. "We go to the 'bush bedroom' over there [waving at a clump of trees 100 yds. away] or sometimes in the truck. Short service, that costs you 20 rands [$2.84]. They know we drivers always got money."

Chikoka nods his head toward another woman sitting beside a stack of cardboard cartons. "We like better to go to them," he says. They are the "businesswomen," smugglers with gray-market cases of fruit and toilet paper and toys that they need to transport somewhere up the road. "They come to us, and we negotiate privately about carrying their goods." It's a no-cash deal, he says. "They pay their bodies to us." Chikoka shrugs at a suggestion that the practice may be unhealthy. "I been away two weeks, madam. I'm human. I'm a man. I have to have sex."

What he likes best is dry sex. In parts of sub-Saharan Africa, to please men, women sit in basins of bleach or saltwater or stuff astringent herbs, tobacco or fertilizer inside their vagina. The tissue of the lining swells up and natural lubricants dry out. The resulting dry sex is painful and dangerous for women. The drying agents suppress natural bacteria, and friction easily lacerates the tender walls of the vagina. Dry sex increases the risk of HIV infection for women, already two times as likely as men to contract the virus from a single encounter. The women, adds

Chikoka, can charge more for dry sex, 50 or 60 rands ($6.46 to $7.75), enough to pay a child's school fees or to eat for a week.

UNVANQUISHED

A Fighter in a Land of Orphans

Silence and the ignorance it promotes have fed the AIDS epidemic in Africa perhaps more than any other factors. In Malawi, where until the end of dictator Hastings Banda's rule in 1994 women were barred from wearing short skirts and men could be jailed for having long hair, public discussion of AIDS was forbidden. According to the government, AIDS didn't exist inside Malawi. Catherine Phiri, 38, knew otherwise. She tested positive in 1990, after her husband had died of the disease. Forced to quit her job as a nurse when colleagues began to gossip, she sought refuge with relatives in the capital, Lilongwe. But they shunned her and eventually forced her to move, this time to Salima on beautiful Lake Malawi. "Even here people gossiped," says Phiri, whose brave, open face is fringed by a head of closely cropped graying hair.

Determined to educate her countrymen, Phiri set up a group that offers counseling, helps place orphans and takes blood that can then be tested in the local hospital. "The community began to see the problem, but it was very difficult to communicate to the government. They didn't want to know."

They do now. According to a lawmaker, AIDS has killed dozens of members of Parliament in the past decade. And Malawi's government has begun to move. President Bakili Muluzi incorporates AIDS education into every public rally. In 1999 he launched a five-year plan to fight the disease, and last July he ordered a crackdown on prostitution (though the government is now thinking of legalizing it). At the least, his awareness campaign appears to be working: 90% of Malawians know about the dangers of AIDS. But that knowledge comes too late for the estimated 8% of HIV-positive citizens—800,000 people in 1999—or the 276,000 children under 15 orphaned by the disease.

Last October, Phiri picked up an award for her efforts from the U.N. But, she says, "I still have people who look at me like trash…" Her voice trails off. "Sometimes when I go to sleep I fear for the future of my children. But I will not run away now. Talking about it: that's what's brave."

—By Simon Robinson/Salima

Chikoka knows his predilection for commercial sex spreads AIDS; he knows his promiscuity could carry the disease home to his wife; he knows people die if they get it. "Yes, HIV is terrible, madam," he says as he crooks a finger toward the businesswoman whose favors he will enjoy that night. "But, madam, sex is natural. Sex is not like beer or smoking. You can stop them.

But unless you castrate the men, you can't stop sex—and then we all die anyway."

Millions of men share Chikoka's sexually active lifestyle, fostered by the region's dependence on migrant labor. Men desperate to earn a few dollars leave their women at hardscrabble rural homesteads to go where the work is: the mines, the cities, the road. They're housed together in isolated males-only hostels but have easy access to prostitutes or a "town wife" with whom they soon pick up a second family and an ordinary STD and HIV. Then they go home to wives and girlfriends a few times a year, carrying the virus they do not know they have. The pattern is so dominant that rates of infection in many rural areas across the southern cone match urban numbers.

IN SOME AFRICAN COUNTRIES, THE INFECTION RATE OF TEEN GIRLS IS FOUR TIMES THAT OF BOYS

If HIV zeros in disproportionately on poor migrants, it does not skip over the educated or the well paid. Soldiers, doctors, policemen, teachers, district administrators are also routinely separated from families by a civil-service system that sends them alone to remote rural posts, where they have money and women have no men. A regular paycheck procures more access to extramarital sex. Result: the vital professions are being devastated.

Schoolmaster Syabusi is afraid there will soon be no more teachers in his rural zone. He has just come home from a memorial for six colleagues who died over the past few months, though no one spoke the word AIDS at the service. "The rate here—they're so many," he says, shaking his head. "They keep on passing it at school." Teachers in southern Africa have one of the highest group infection rates, but they hide their status until the telltale symptoms find them out.

Before then, the men—teachers are mostly men here—can take their pick of sexual partners. Plenty of women in bush villages need extra cash, often to pay school fees, and female students know they can profit from a teacher's favor. So the schoolmasters buy a bit of sex with lonely wives and trade a bit of sex with willing pupils for A's. Some students consider it an honor to sleep with the teacher, a badge of superiority. The girls brag about it to their peers, preening in their ability to snag an older man. "The teachers are the worst," says Jabulani Siwela, an AIDS worker in Zimbabwe who saw frequent teacher-student sex in his Bulawayo high school. They see a girl they like; they ask her to stay after class; they have a nice time. "It's dead easy," he says. "These are men who know better, but they still do it all the time."

THE PROSTITUTE

THE WORKINGWOMAN WE MEET DIRECTS OUR CAR TO A reedy field fringing the gritty eastern townships of Bulawayo, Zimbabwe. She doesn't want neighbors to see her being interviewed. She is afraid her family will find out she is a prostitute, so we will call her Thandiwe. She looked quite prim and proper in her green calf-length dress as she waited for johns outside 109 Tongogaro Street in the center of downtown. So, for that matter, do the dozens of other women cruising the city's dim street corners: not a mini or bustier or bared navel in sight. Zimbabwe is in many ways a prim and proper society that frowns on commercial sex work and the public display of too much skin.

FINANCIAL AID

A Lending Tree

Getting ahead in Africa is tough. Banks lend money only to the middle class and the wealthy. Poor Africans—meaning most Africans—stay poor. It's even harder if you're sick. Without savings to fall back on, many HIV-positive parents pull their kids out of school. They can't afford the fees and end up selling their few possessions to feed the family. When they die, their kids are left with nothing.

Though not directly targeted at people with AIDS, microcredit schemes go some way toward fixing that problem. The schemes work like minibanks, lending small amounts—often as little as $100—to traders or farmers. Because they lack the infrastructure of banks and don't charge fees, most charge an interest rate of as much as 1% a week and repayment rates of over 99%—much better than that for banks in Africa, or in most places.

Many microcredit schemes encourage clients to set aside some of the extra income generated by the loan as savings. This can be used for medical bills or to pay school fees if the parents get sick. "Without the loans I would have had to look for another way to make money," says Florence Muriungi, 40, who sings in a Kampala jazz band and whose husband died of AIDS four years ago. Muriungi, who cares for eight children—five of her own and three her sister left when she too died of AIDS—uses the money to pay school fees in advance and fix her band's equipment. Her singing generates enough money for her to repay the loans and save a bit.

Seventeen of the 21 women at a weekly meeting of regular borrowers in Uganda care for AIDS orphans. Five are AIDS widows. "I used to buy just one or two bunches of bananas to sell. Now I buy 40, 50, 60," says Elizabeth Baluka, 47, the group's secretary. "Every week I put aside a little bit of money to help my children slowly by slowly."

—By Simon Robinson/Kampala

That doesn't stop Thandiwe from earning a better living turning tricks than she ever could doing honest work. Desperate for a job, she slipped illegally into South Africa in 1992. She cleaned floors in a Johannesburg restaurant, where she met a cook from back home who was also illegal. They had two daughters, and they got married; he was gunned down one night at work.

She brought his body home for burial and was sent to her in-laws to be "cleansed." This common practice gives a dead husband's brother the right, even the duty, to sleep with the widow. Thandiwe tested negative for HIV in 1998, but if she were positive, the ritual cleansing would have served only to pass on the disease. Then her in-laws wanted to keep her two daughters because their own children had died, and marry her off to an old uncle who lived far out in the bush. She fled.

Alone, Thandiwe grew desperate. "I couldn't let my babies starve." One day she met a friend from school. "She told me she was a sex worker. She said, 'Why you suffer? Let's go to a place where we can get quick bucks.'" Thandiwe hangs her head. "I went. I was afraid. But now I go every night."

She goes to Tongogaro Street, where the rich clients are, tucking a few condoms in her handbag every evening as the sun sets and returning home strictly by 10 so that she won't have to service a taxi-van driver to get a ride back. Thandiwe tells her family she works an evening shift, just not at what. "I get 200 zim [$5] for sex," she says, more for special services. She uses two condoms per client, sometimes three. "If they say no, I say no." But then sometimes resentful johns hit her. It's pay-and-go until she has pocketed 1,000 or 1,500 Zimbabwe dollars and can go home—with more cash than her impoverished neighbors ever see in their roughneck shantytown, flush enough to buy a TV and fleece jammies for her girls and meat for their supper.

"I am ashamed," she murmurs. She has stopped going to church. "Every day I ask myself, 'When will I stop this business?' The answer is, 'If I could get a job'…" Her voice trails off hopelessly. "At the present moment, I have no option, no other option." As trucker Chikoka bluntly puts it, "They give sex to eat. They got no man; they got no work; but they got kids, and they got to eat." Two of Thandiwe's friends in the sex trade are dying of AIDS, but what can she do? "I just hope I won't get it."

In fact, casual sex of every kind is commonplace here. Prostitutes are just the ones who admit they do it for cash. Everywhere there's premarital sex, sex as recreation. Obligatory sex and its abusive counterpart, coercive sex. Transactional sex: sex as a gift, sugar-daddy sex. Extramarital sex, second families, multiple partners. The nature of AIDS is to feast on promiscuity.

79% OF THOSE WHO DIED OF AIDS LAST YEAR WERE AFRICAN

Rare is the man who even knows his HIV status: males widely refuse testing even when they fall ill. And many men who suspect they are HIV positive embrace a flawed logic: if I'm already infected, I can sleep around because I can't get it again. But women are the ones who progress to full-blown AIDS first and die fastest, and the underlying cause is not just sex but power. Wives and girlfriends and even prostitutes in this part of the world can't easily say no to sex on a man's terms. It matters little what comes into play, whether it is culture or tradition or the pathology of violence or issues of male identity or the subservient status of women.

Beneath a translucent scalp, the plates of Gertrude Dhlamini's cranium etch a geography of pain. Her illness is obvious in the thin, stretched skin under which veins throb with the shingles that have blinded her left eye and scarred that side of her face. At 39, she looks 70. The agonizing thrush, a kind of fungus, that paralyzed her throat has ebbed enough to enable her to swallow a spoon or two of warm gruel, but most of the nourishment flows away in constant diarrhea. She struggles to keep her hand from scratching restlessly at the scaly rash flushing her other cheek. She is not ashamed to proclaim her illness to the world. "It must be told," she says.

Gertrude is thrice rejected. At 19 she bore a son to a boyfriend who soon left her, taking away the child. A second boyfriend got her pregnant in 1994 but disappeared in anger when their daughter was born sickly with HIV. A doctor told Gertrude it was her fault, so she blamed herself that little Noluthando was never well in the two years she survived. Gertrude never told the doctor the baby's father had slept with other women. "I was afraid to," she says, "though I sincerely believe he gave the sickness to me." Now, she says, "I have rent him from my heart. And I will never have another man in my life."

Gertrude begged her relatives to take her in, but when she revealed the name of her illness, they berated her. They made her the household drudge, telling her never to touch their food or their cooking pots. They gave her a bowl and a spoon strictly for her own use. After a few months, they threw her out.

Gertrude sits upright on a donated bed in a cardboard shack in a rough Durban township that is now the compass of her world. Perhaps 10 ft. square, the little windowless room contains a bed, one sheet and blanket, a change of clothes and a tiny cooking ring, but she has no money for paraffin to heat the food that a home-care worker brings. She must fetch water and use a toilet down the hill. "Everything I have," she says, "is a gift." Now the school that owns the land under her hut wants to turn it into a playground and she worries about where she will go. Gertrude rubs and rubs at her raw cheek. "I pray and pray to God," she says, "not to take my soul while I am alone in this room."

Women like Gertrude were brought up to be subservient to men. Especially in matters of sex, the man is always in charge. Women feel powerless to change sexual behavior. Even when a woman wants to protect herself, she usually can't: it is not uncommon for men to beat partners who refuse intercourse or request a condom. "Real men" don't use them, so women who want their partners to must fight deeply ingrained taboos. Talk to him about donning a rubber sheath and be prepared for accusations, abuse or abandonment.

A nurse in Durban, coming home from an AIDS training class, suggested that her mate should put on a condom, as a kind of homework exercise. He grabbed a pot and banged loudly on it with a knife, calling all the neighbors into his house. He pointed the knife at his wife and demanded: "Where was she between 4 p.m. and now? Why is she suddenly suggesting this? What has changed after 20 years that she wants a condom?"

Schoolteacher Syabusi is an educated man, fully cognizant of the AIDS threat. Yet even he bristles when asked if he uses a condom. "Humph," he says with a fine snort. "That question is nonnegotiable." So despite extensive distribution of free condoms, they often go unused. Astonishing myths have sprung up. If you don one, your erection can't grow. Free condoms must be too cheap to be safe: they have been stored too long, kept too hot, kept too cold. Condoms fill up with germs, so they spread AIDS. Condoms from overseas bring the disease with them. Foreign governments that donate condoms put holes in them so that Africans will die. Education programs find it hard to compete with the power of the grapevine.

THE CHILD IN NO. 17

IN CRIB NO. 17 OF THE SPARTAN BUT CROWDED CHILDREN'S ward at the Church of Scotland Hospital in KwaZulu-Natal, a tiny, staring child lies dying. She is three and has hardly known a day of good health. Now her skin wrinkles around her body like an oversize suit, and her twig-size bones can barely hold her vertical as nurses search for a vein to take blood. In the frail arms hooked up to transfusion tubes, her veins have collapsed. The nurses palpate a threadlike vessel on the child's forehead. She mews like a wounded animal as one tightens a rubber band around her head to raise the vein. Tears pour unnoticed from her mother's eyes as she watches the needle tap-tap at her daughter's temple. Each time the whimpering child lifts a wan hand to brush away the pain, her mother gently lowers it. Drop by drop, the nurses manage to collect 1 cc of blood in five minutes.

The child in crib No. 17 has had TB, oral thrush, chronic diarrhea, malnutrition, severe vomiting. The vial of blood reveals her real ailment, AIDS, but the disease is not listed on her chart, and her mother says she has no idea why her child is so ill. She breast-fed her for two years, but once the little girl was weaned, she could not keep solid food down. For a long time, her mother thought something was wrong with the food. Now the child is afflicted with so many symptoms that her mother had to bring her to the hospital, from which sick babies rarely return.

VIRGINITY TESTING IS BACK The practice of virginity testing used to be part of traditional Zulu rites. It is regaining popularity among anxious mothers who believe that if their daughters remain virgins, they won't get AIDS.

She hopes, she prays her child will get better, and like all the mothers who stay with their children at the hospital, she tends her lovingly, constantly changing filthy diapers, smoothing sheets, pressing a little nourishment between listless lips, trying to tease a smile from the vacant, staring face. Her husband works in Johannesburg, where he lives in a men's squatter camp. He comes home twice a year. She is 25. She has heard of

AIDS but does not know it is transmitted by sex, does not know if she or her husband has it. She is afraid this child will die soon, and she is afraid to have more babies. But she is afraid too to raise the subject with her husband. "He would not agree to that," she says shyly. "He would never agree to have no more babies."

Dr. Annick DeBaets, 32, is a volunteer from Belgium. In the two years she has spent here in Tugela Ferry, she has learned all about how hard it is to break the cycle of HIV transmission from mother to infant. The door to this 48-cot ward is literally a revolving one: sick babies come in, receive doses of rudimentary antibiotics, vitamins, food; go home for a week or a month; then come back as ill as ever. Most, she says, die in the first or second year. If she could just follow up with really intensive care, believes Dr. DeBaets, many of the wizened infants crowding three to a crib could live longer, healthier lives. "But it's very discouraging. We simply don't have the time, money or facilities for anything but minimal care."

Much has been written about what South African Judge Edwin Cameron, himself HIV positive, calls his country's "grievous ineptitude" in the face of the burgeoning epidemic. Nowhere has that been more evident than in the government's failure to provide drugs that could prevent pregnant women from passing HIV to their babies. The government has said it can't afford the 300-rand-per-dose, 28-dose regimen of AZT that neighboring nations like Botswana dole out, using funds and drugs from foreign donors. The late South African presidential spokesman Parks Mankahlana even suggested publicly that it was not cost effective to save these children when their mothers were already doomed to die: "We don't want a generation of orphans."

Yet these children—70,000 are born HIV positive in South Africa alone every year—could be protected from the disease for about $4 each with another simple, cheap drug called nevirapine. Until last month, the South African government steadfastly refused to license or finance the use of nevirapine despite the manufacturer's promise to donate the drug for five years, claiming that its "toxic" side effects are not yet known. This spring, however, the drug will finally be distributed to leading public hospitals in the country, though only on a limited basis at first.

The mother at crib No. 17 is not concerned with potential side effects. She sits on the floor cradling her daughter, crooning over and over, "Get well, my child, get well." The baby stares back without blinking. "It's sad, so sad, so sad," the mother says. The child died three days later.

The children who are left when parents die only add another complex dimension to Africa's epidemic. At 17, Tsepho Phale has been head of an indigent household of three young boys in the dusty township of Monarch, outside Francistown, for two years. He never met his father, his mother died of AIDS, and the grieving children possess only a raw concrete shell of a house. The doorways have no doors; the window frames no glass. There is not a stick of furniture. The boys sleep on piled-up blankets, their few clothes dangling from nails. In the room that passes for a kitchen, two paraffin burners sit on the dirt floor alongside the month's food: four cabbages, a bag of oranges and one of potatoes, three sacks of flour, some yeast, two jars of oil

and two cartons of milk. Next to a dirty stack of plastic pans lies the mealy meal and rice that will provide their main sustenance for the month. A couple of bars of soap and two rolls of toilet paper also have to last the month. Tsepho has just brought these rations home from the social-service center where the "orphan grants" are doled out.

Tsepho has been robbed of a childhood that was grim even before his mother fell sick. She supported the family by "buying and selling things," he says, but she never earned more than a pittance. When his middle brother was knocked down by a car and left physically and mentally disabled, Tsepho's mother used the insurance money to build this house, so she would have one thing of value to leave her children. As the walls went up, she fell sick. Tsepho had to nurse her, bathe her, attend to her bodily functions, try to feed her. Her one fear as she lay dying was that her rural relatives would try to steal the house. She wrote a letter bequeathing it to her sons and bade Tsepho hide it.

As her body lay on the concrete floor awaiting burial, the relatives argued openly about how they would divide up the profits when they sold her dwelling. Tsepho gave the district commissioner's office the letter, preventing his mother's family from grabbing the house. Fine, said his relations; if you think you're a man, you look after your brothers. They have contributed nothing to the boys' welfare since. "It's as if we don't exist anymore either," says Tsepho. Now he struggles to keep house for the others, doing the cooking, cleaning, laundry and shopping.

The boys look at the future with despair. "It is very bleak," says Tsepho, kicking aimlessly at a bare wall. He had to quit school, has no job, will probably never get one. "I've given up my dreams. I have no hope."

Orphans have traditionally been cared for the African way: relatives absorb the children of the dead into their extended families. Some still try, but communities like Tsepho's are becoming saturated with orphans, and families can't afford to take on another kid, leaving thousands alone.

Now many must fend for themselves, struggling to survive. The trauma of losing parents is compounded by the burden of becoming a breadwinner. Most orphans sink into penury, drop out of school, suffer malnutrition, ostracism, psychic distress. Their makeshift households scramble to live on pitiful handouts—from overstretched relatives, a kind neighbor, a state grant—or they beg and steal in the streets. The orphans' present desperation forecloses a brighter future. "They hardly ever succeed in having a life," says Siphelile Kaseke, 22, a counselor at an AIDS orphans' camp near Bulawayo. Without education, girls fall into prostitution, and older boys migrate illegally to South Africa, leaving the younger ones to go on the streets.

1 IN 4 SOUTH AFRICAN WOMEN AGES 20 TO 29 IS INFECTED WITH HIV

EVERY DAY SPENT IN THIS PART OF AFRICA IS ACUTELY DEPRESSING: there is so little countervailing hope to all the stories of the dead and the doomed. "More than anywhere else in the world, AIDS in Africa was met with apathy," says Suzanne LeClerc-

Madlala, a lecturer at the University of Natal. The consequences of the silence march on: infection soars, stigma hardens, denial hastens death, and the chasm between knowledge and behavior widens. The present disaster could be dwarfed by the woes that loom if Africa's epidemic rages on. The human losses could wreck the region's frail economies, break down civil societies and incite political instability.

In the face of that, every day good people are doing good things. Like Dr. Moll, who uses his after-job time and his own fund raising to run an extensive volunteer home-care program in KwaZulu-Natal. And Busi Magwazi, who, along with dozens of others, tends the sick for nothing in the Durban-based Sinoziso project. And Patricia Bakwinya, who started her Shining Stars orphan-care program in Francistown with her own zeal and no money, to help youngsters like Tsepho Phale. And countless individuals who give their time and devotion to ease southern Africa's plight.

But these efforts can help only thousands; they cannot turn the tide. The region is caught in a double bind. Without treatment, those with HIV will sicken and die; without prevention, the spread of infection cannot be checked. Southern Africa has no other means available to break the vicious cycle, except to change everyone's sexual behavior—and that isn't happening.

The essential missing ingredient is leadership. Neither the countries of the region nor those of the wealthy world have been able or willing to provide it.

South Africa, comparatively well off, comparatively well educated, has blundered tragically for years. AIDS invaded just when apartheid ended, and a government absorbed in massive transition relegated the disease to a back page. An attempt at a national education campaign wasted millions on a farcical musical. The premature release of a local wonder drug ended in scandal when the drug turned out to be made of industrial solvent. Those fiascoes left the government skittish about embracing expensive programs, inspiring a 1998 decision not to provide AZT to HIV-positive pregnant women. Zimbabwe too suffers savagely from feckless leadership. Even in Botswana, where the will to act is gathering strength, the resources to follow through have to come from foreign hands.

AIDS' grip here is so pervasive and so complex that all societies—theirs and ours—must rally round to break it. These countries are too poor to doctor themselves. The drugs that could begin to break the cycle will not be available here until global pharmaceutical companies find ways to provide them inexpensively. The health-care systems required to prescribe and monitor complicated triple-cocktail regimens won't exist unless rich countries help foot the bill. If there is ever to be a vaccine, the West will have to finance its discovery and provide it to the poor. The cure for this epidemic is not national but international.

The deep silence that makes African leaders and societies want to deny the problem, the corruption and incompetence that render them helpless is something the West cannot fix. But the fact that they are poor is not. The wealthy world must help with its zeal and its cash if southern Africa is ever to be freed of the AIDS plague.

A UGANDAN TALE

Not Afraid to Speak Out

Major Rubaramira Ruranga knows something about fighting. During Idi Amin's reign of terror in Uganda in the 1970s, Ruranga worked as a spy for rebels fighting the dictator. After Amin's ouster, the military man studied political intelligence in Cuba before returning to find a new dictator at the helm and a blood war raging. Hoping for change, Ruranga supplied his old rebel friends with more secrets, this time from within the President's office. When he was discovered, he fled to the bush to "fight the struggle with guns."

The turmoil in Uganda was fueling the spread of another enemy—AIDS. Like many rebel soldiers, Ruranga was on the move constantly to avoid detection. "You never see your wife, and so you get to a new place and meet someone else," he says. "I had sex without protection with a few women." Doctors found he was HIV positive in 1989. "They told me I would die in two to three years, so I started preparing for when I was away. I told my kids, my wife. Worked on finishing the house for them. I gave up hope." But as he learned about AIDS, his attitude changed. After talking to American and European AIDS activists—some had lived with the disease for 15 years or more—"I realized I was not going to die in a few years. I was reborn, determined to live."

He began fighting again. After announcing his HIV status at a rally on World AIDS Day in 1993—an extraordinarily brave act in Africa, where few activists, let alone army officers, ever admit to having HIV—he set up a network for those living with HIV/AIDS in Uganda, "so that people had somewhere to go to talk to friends." And while Uganda has done more to slow the spread of AIDS than any other country—in some places the rate of infection has dropped by half—"we can always do better," says Ruranga. "Why are we able to buy guns and bullets to kill people and we are not able to buy drugs to save people?" The fight continues.

—By Simon Robinson/Kampala

UNIT 5

Crime, Violence, and Law Enforcement

Unit Selections

Key Points to Consider

• What are some of the reasons why America has a high crime rate? Why has the crime rate dropped recently?

• What are some of the policy options for reducing crime?

• What policies are most heavily relied upon today? What do you think are the best policies and why?

• Do you think that the public outcry over violence in the media is a gross overreaction?

• How much of a threat is terrorism toward the United States? How can the public be protected from it?

 **Links: www.dushkin.com/online/**
These sites are annotated in the World Wide Web pages.

ACLU Criminal Justice Home Page
http://aclu.org/CriminalJustice/CriminalJusticeMain.cfm

Terrorism Research Center
http://www.terrorism.com

This unit deals with criminal behavior and its control by the law enforcement system. The first line of defense against crime is the socialization of the young to internalize norms against harmful and illegal behavior. Thus families, schools, religious institutions, and social pressure are the major crime fighters, but they do not do a perfect job. The police have to handle their failures. For the last half century, crime has increased, signaling for some commentators a decline in morality. If the power of norms to control criminal behavior declines, the role of law enforcement must increase, and that is what has happened. The societal response to crime has been threefold: hire more police, build more prisons, and toughen penalties for crimes. These policies by themselves can have only limited success. For example, putting a drug dealer in prison just creates an opportunity for another person to become a drug dealer. Another approach is to give potential criminals alternatives to crime. The key factor in this approach is a healthy economy that provides many job opportunities for unemployed young men. To some extent that has happened, and the crime rate has dropped. Programs that work with inner-city youth might also help, but budget-tight cities are not funding many programs like this. Amid the policy debates there is one thing we can agree upon: Crime has declined significantly in the past decade after rising substantially for a half century.

The first subsection deals with crime which is of major concern today because crime and violence seem to be out of control. Gene Stephens describes crime trends throughout the world but focuses on the United States. Overall crime rates in the United States were the highest in the Western world in 1980 but have fallen in the United States and increased in many other nations so that several Western countries now have higher rates. Nevertheless, the US murder rate is still the highest. Stephens presents three competing explanations for the crime decline in the United States: 1) greater success of the justice system in catching and locking up criminals, 2) the lowering of the percent of the population in the high crime ages, and 3) the prevalence and success of community based approaches.

The next subsection deals with law enforcement. In the first article, Stephen Pomper proposes seven major reforms of the criminal justice system. Pomper accepts the critical view that "the guilty are over-protected, the innocent are under-served,… too many violent and dangerous felons wind up with Get-Out-of-Jail-Free cards and too many non-violent and just-plain-innocent people wind up doing time." He proposes the following reforms: (1) reduce the extent to which evidence is excluded in court, (2) create a universal DNA database, (3) truly protect witnesses, (4) police the prosecutors as well as the police, (5) abolish the insanity defense, (6) repeal the mandatory minimum laws, and (7) improve the administration of the courts. Some of the problems that these reforms seek to correct include the many existing severe impediments to the prosecution of criminals and the extreme laws that were passed out of emotional public responses to some outrageous crimes. The front line of the law enforcement system is the police.

In the next article Hugo Adam Bedau examines a troubling aspect of the judicial system which is wrongful convictions. He presents the fruit of decades of research on miscarriages of justice which establishes its prevalence. Some of the stories are shameful and shocking and justify calls for reform. Bedau identifies several major reform efforts but few changes have been made to date. Eli Lehrer, in the next article, gives us an up-close and personal picture of police work by following a policewoman on her patrol and observing a policeman who is a Community Policing Coordinator.

The final subsection deals with violence and terrorism. Dave Grossman, in the first article in this subsection, analyzes the reasons why the incidence of violent crime is rapidly rising worldwide. The key indicator of this problem is aggravated assault, which increased over sevenfold from 1957 to the mid-1990s in the United States. His explanation is that violence in the media has trained children to kill by inadvertently following the psychological principles of basic military training. In the last article Steven Simon discusses how terrorism has changed from limited violence as a tactic in political struggles to religiously motivated indiscriminate mass killings to inflict maximum harm on a hated people. How can the U.S. protect itself from such a foe? Not being land based, it is very hard to combat militarily. Its attacks will be surprises and defense is nearly impossible with so many potential targets to protect.

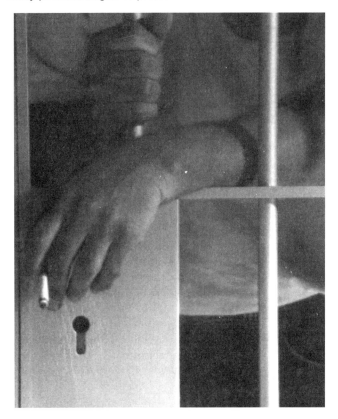

Global Trends in Crime

Crime varies greatly around the world, statistics show, but new tactics have proved effective in the United States. To keep crime in check in the twenty-first century, we'll all need to get smarter, not just tougher.

By Gene Stephens

Crime in the United States is bottoming out after a steep slide downward during the past decade. But crime in many other nations—particularly in eastern and parts of western Europe—has continued to climb. In the United States, street crime overall remains near historic lows, prompting some analysts to declare life in the United States safer than it has ever been. In fact, statistics show that, despite terrorism, the world as a whole seems to be becoming safer. This is in sharp contrast to the perceptions of Americans and others, as polls indicate they believe the world gets more dangerous every day.

Current Crime Rates Around the World

Although the United States still has more violent crime than other industrialized nations and still ranks high in overall crime, the nation has nevertheless been experiencing a decline in crime numbers. Meanwhile, a number of European countries are catching up; traditionally low-crime societies, such as Denmark and Finland, are near the top in street crime rates today. Other countries that weren't even on the crime radar—such as Japan—are also experiencing a rise in crime.

Comparing crime rates across countries is difficult (see sidebar "The Trouble with Crime Statistics"). Different definitions of crimes, among other factors, make official crime statistics notoriously unreliable. However, the periodic World Crime Survey, a UN initiative to track global crime rates, may offer the most reliable figures currently available:

• **Overall crime (homicide, rape, major assault, robbery) and property crime**. The United States in 1980 clearly led the Western world in overall crime and ranked particularly high in property crime. A decade later, statistics show a marked decline in U.S. property crime. By 2000, overall crime rates for the U.S. dropped below those of England and Wales, Denmark, and Finland, while U.S. property-crime rates also continued to decline.

• **Homicide**. The United States had consistently higher homicide rates than most Western nations from 1980 to 2000. In the 1990s, the U.S. rate was cut almost in half, but the 2000 rate of 5.5 homicides per 100,000 people was still higher than all nations except those in political and social turmoil. Colombia, for instance, had 63 homicides per 100,000 people; South Africa, 51.

• **Rape**. In 1980 and 1990, U.S. rape rates were higher than those of any Western nation, but by 2000, Canada took the lead. The lowest reported rape rates were in Asia and the Middle East.

• **Robbery** has been on a steady decline in the United States over the past two decades. As of 2000, countries with more reported robberies than the United States included England and Wales, Portugal, and Spain. Countries with fewer reported robberies include Germany, Italy, and France, as well as Middle Eastern and Asian nations.

• **Burglary**, usually considered the most serious property crime, is lower in the United States today than it was in 1980. As of 2000, the United States had lower burglary rates than Australia, Denmark, Finland, England and Wales, and Canada. It had higher reported burglary rates than Spain, Korea, and Saudi Arabia.

• **Vehicle theft** declined steadily in the United States from 1980 to 2000. The 2000 figures show that Australia, England and Wales, Denmark, Norway, Canada, France, and Italy all have higher rates of vehicle theft.

The Trouble with Crime Statistics

Accurate crime data are difficult to obtain. One reason is that most crime is not reported to police in many countries. Another reason is that police can increase or decrease the amount of crime detected and reported by their discretionary decisions at the administrative and/or street levels.

A third reason is that definitions of crime vary. Social scientists generally see crime as being what we say it is. Therefore, crime is defined by the local culture. For instance, an incident may be defined as assault by one person while being seen as "playing around" by another. Further complicating crime statistics, an officer may choose to arrest a participant in a domestic disturbance (reported as assault) or simply serve as a peacemaker and then leave (not reported).

Other obstacles to accurate crime data include intentional underreporting and manipulating of data so the statistics look good. Such conduct has been discovered in police agencies in New York, Philadelphia, Atlanta, and elsewhere.

There's also the problem that crime reported to police is not even considered to be the best measure of criminal activity. Unreported crime, termed by criminologists as "the dark figure of crime," is common: Roughly one in three crimes is actually reported to the police, according to self-reported-crime surveys by the U.S. Bureau of Justice Statistics. Asked why they didn't report crimes to police, some respondents answered, "It was too personal," "Nothing could be done," "It wasn't worth the effort," or "The offender might retaliate."

However, if you keep in mind the problems inherent in collection and reporting of crime rates, it is still worth the effort to examine the statistics. Their insight, though incomplete, can shed light on crime trends that speak to certain nations' successful crime-reduction tactics and other nations' need to do more.

—*Gene Stephens*

Overall, the United States has experienced a downward trend in crime while other Western nations, and even industrialized non-Western nations, are witnessing higher numbers. What's behind the U.S. decreases? Some analysts believe that tougher laws, enforcement, and incarceration policies have lowered crime in the United States. They point to "three-strikes" legislation, mandatory incarceration for offenses such as drug possession and domestic violence, and tougher street-level enforcement. The reason many European countries are suffering higher crime rates, analysts argue, is because of their fewer laws and more-lenient enforcement and sentencing.

Other analysts argue that socioeconomic changes—such as fewer youth in the crime-prone 15- to 25-year-old age group, a booming economy, and more community care of citizens—led to the drop in U.S. crime. They now point out that the new socioeconomic trends of growing unemployment, stagnation of wages, and the growing numbers in the adolescent male population are at work in today's terror-wary climate and may signal crime increases ahead.

Still other analysts see community-oriented policing (COP), problem-oriented policing (POP), and restorative justice (mediation, arbitration, restitution, and community service instead of criminal courts and incarceration) as the nexus of recent and future crime control successes.

Just which crime-fighting tactics have effected this U.S. crime trend is a matter of debate. Three loose coalitions offer their views:

Getting tough works. "There is, in fact, a simple explanation for America's success against crime: The American justice system now does a better job of catching criminals and locking them up," writes Eli Lehrer, senior editor of *The American Enterprise*. Lehrer says local control of policing was probably what made a critical difference between the United States and European countries where regional and national systems predominate. He holds that local control allowed police to use enforcement against loitering and other minor infractions to keep the streets clean of potential lawbreakers. He acknowledges that "positive loitering"—stickers or a pat on the back for well-behaved juveniles—was the other side of the successful effort. In addition, more people have since been imprisoned for longer periods of time, seen by "get-tough" advocates as another factor in safer streets today.

Demographics rule. Some criminologists and demographers see the crime decrease as a product of favorable socioeconomic population factors in the mid- through late-1990s. High employment rates, with jobs in some sectors going unfilled for lack of qualified candidates, kept salaries growing. Even the unemployed went back to school to gain job skills. By the end of the decade the older students filled the college classrooms, taking up the slack left by the lower numbers in the traditional student age group. In such times, both violent and property crimes have usually dropped, as economic need decreased and frustration and anger subsided.

"Get-tough" theorists hold that 200 crimes a year could be prevented for each criminal taken off the streets, but criminologist Albert Reiss counters that most offenders work in groups and are simply replaced when one leaves.

If demographic advocates are right, then the next few years could see a boom in street crime in the United States due to a combination of growing unemployment, stagnant wages, and state and local governments so strapped for funds that social programs and even education are facing major cutbacks.

Community-based approaches succeed. Whereas the "get-tough" advocates mention community policing as a factor in the crime decrease, this third group sees the service aspects (rather than strict enforcement) of COP combined with the emerging restorative-justice movement as

Crime Trends among Selected OECD Nations

Number of crimes per 100,000 population

	Total crimes		Homicides		Violent Assaults		All Thefts		Drug Offenses	
	1995	2000	1995	2000	1995	2000	1995	2000	1995	2000
Australia	4,167	7,475	3.5	3.6	560	737	3,532	6,653	n/a	n/a
Canada	9,163	8,054	5.1	4.3	165	146	4,883	4,070	208	286
Denmark	10,334	9,460	1.1	4.0	165	24	3,365	3,638	291	249
England, Wales *	7,206	9,823	2.6	2.8	17	405	6,822	6,175	42	261
Finland	7,930	8,697	0.8	0.7	38	38	2,745	2,623	177	260
France	6,317	6,446	4.4	3.7	123	182	4,137	3,990	136	177
Germany	8,179	7,625	4.9	3.4	117	142	4,797	3,703	194	297
Japan	1,486	1,985	1.0	1.1	14	24	1,253	1,683	21	22
Korea	1,181	1,635	1.5	2.0	443	69	197	379	5	8
Norway	9,167	10,087	2.2	2.7	57	77	4,541	4,677	539	984
Spain	2,313	2,213	2.4	2.9	23	22	1,789	1,768	107	252
United States	5,278	4,124	8.2	5.5	418	324	4,814	3,763	582	572

* England and Wales data for 1996 and 1998

Most of these countries in the Organization for Economic Cooperation and Development experienced an increase in total crimes from 1995 to 2000. The United States experienced a decrease in all crimes listed, yet still remains the leader in reported homicides. Its neighbor to the north, Canada, experienced a decline in all areas of crime except drug offenses.

Source: Interpol International Crime Statistics, Interpol, 200 quai Charles de Gaulle, 69006 Lyon, France. Web site www.interpol.int/Public/Statistics/ICS/.
U.S. drug offense data from FBI's annual *Crime in the United States Uniform Crime Reports*.

being the catalyst for success in crime prevention and control.

Most criminologists believe street crime is a product of socioeconomic conditions interacting on young people, primarily adolescent males. Usually their crimes occur in interaction with others in gangs or groups, especially when law-abiding alternatives (youth athletic programs, tutors, mentors, community centers, social clubs, after-school programs) are not available. Thus, any chance of success in keeping crime rates low on a long-term basis depends on constant assessment of the community and its needs to maintain a nurturing environment.

COP and POP coordinate community cohesion by identifying problems that will likely result in crime and by simply improving the quality of life in the neighborhoods. The key: partnerships among police, citizens, civic and business groups, public and private social-service agencies, and government agencies. Combined with an ongoing needs analysis in recognition of constantly changing community dynamics, the partnerships can quickly attack any problem or situation that arises.

A restorative-justice movement has grown rapidly but stayed below the radar screen in the United States. In many communities, civil and criminal incidents are more likely to be handled through mediation or arbitration, restitution, community service, and reformation/reintegration than in civil or criminal courts. The goal, besides justice for all, is the development of a symbiotic relationship and reconciliation within the community, since more than 90% of all street offenders return to the same community.

Lessons for the Future of Crime Prevention and Control

All schools of thought on why street crime is decreasing have a commonality: proactive prevention rather than reactive retribution. Even the method to achieve this goal is not really in question—only the emphasis.

Since the 1980s, progressive police agencies in the United States have adhered to the "Broken Windows" and "Weed and Seed" philosophies taken from the work of criminologists James Q. Wilson and George L. Kelling. Broken windows are a metaphor for failure to establish and maintain acceptable standards of behavior in the community. The blame, according to Wilson and Kelling, lay primarily in the change in emphasis by police from being peace officers who maintain order to law-enforcement officers who seek to capture criminals. They argue that, in healthy communities, informal but widely understood rules were maintained by citizens and police, often using extralegal ("move on") or arrest for minor infractions (vagrancy, loitering, pandering). It was, then, this citizen-police partnership that worked to stem commu-

International Law Enforcement Academies

The success of U.S. cities and states in lowering crime rates over the past decade has sparked the interest of law enforcement agencies around the globe in American police operations. At the same time, the attacks of September 11, 2001, and the resulting war on terrorism have made the United States acutely aware of its need for eyes and ears around the world, as well as for partners in the quest to make the earth safer. One of the ways to build symbiotic relationships among the world's police agencies is through International Law Enforcement Academies (ILEAs).

ILEAs "develop an extensive network of alumni, who will become the leaders and decision makers in their respective countries, to exchange information with their U.S. counterparts and assist in transnational investigations," according to the U.S. State Department. Started in 1995, ILEAs have already provided training for more than 8,000 officials from 50 countries, including Hungary, Thailand, Botswana, and Costa Rica.

One ILEA of note is the Moscow Police Command College. Coordinated by the Department of Criminology and Criminal Justice at the University of South Carolina and held in Columbia, South Carolina, MPCC has graduated five classes of command-level officers primarily from Moscow. Emphasis in this program is on the principles and implementation of community-oriented policing and victim assistance, as well as police leadership in the community. Moscow police stand to gain much from this new training, since they are dealing with crime that hardly existed under the iron fist of communism: Violence and organized crime, not just economic opportunity, are a product of Russia's free market.

—*Gene Stephens*

The Weed and Seed programs in the United States imparted the following lessons:

• Proactive prevention must be at the core of any successful crime-control strategy.

• Each community must have an ongoing needs assessment carried out by a police-citizen partnership.

• A multitude of factors—from laws and neighborhood standards to demographics and socioeconomic needs—must be considered in the assessment process.

• Weed and seed must be balanced according to specific needs—somewhat differently in each community.

• When crime does occur, community-based restorative justice should be used to provide restitution to victims and community while reforming and then reintegrating the offender as a law-abiding citizen of the community.

New Approaches for the Emerging Crime Landscape

Twenty-first-century crime is going to require new approaches to prevention and control. Street crime dominated the attention of the justice system in the twentieth century, but recent excesses of corporations, costing stockholders and retirees literally billions of dollars, do not fit into the street-crime paradigm. Nor do political or religious-motivated terrorism, Internet fraud, deception, theft, harassment, pedophilia, and terrorism on an information highway without borders, without ownership, and without jurisdiction. New attention must—and will—be paid to white-collar crimes, infotech and biotech crimes, and terrorism.

Surveys find that a large majority of corporations have been victims of computer-assisted crimes. Polls of citizens find high rates of victimization by Internet offenses ranging from identity theft to fraud, hacking to harassment. U.S. officials have maintained since the late 1990s that it is just a matter of time until there is a "Pearl Harbor" on the Internet (such as shutting down medical services networks, power grids, or financial services nationwide or even worldwide).

Following the attacks by terrorists on September 11, 2001, and later strikes abroad, doomsday scenarios have abounded, with release of radioactive or biological toxins being the most frightening. Attempts to shoot down an Israeli commercial airliner with a shoulder-held missile launcher further increased anxiety.

Clearly these crimes against victims generally unknown to the attacker and often chosen randomly cannot be stopped by community policing alone, although vigilant community partners often can spot suspicious activity and expose possible criminals and terrorists. Early response to this dilemma was to pass more laws, catch more offenders, and thus deter future incidents. This is the same response traditionally taken to street crime—the one being abandoned in preference to proactive prevention methods (COP and restorative justice). Clearly, pre-

nity deterioration and disorder, which, unattended, would lead to crime.

"Weeding" involved using street-sweeping ordinances to clean the streets of the immediate problems (drunks, drug addicts, petty thieves, panhandlers). "Seeding" involved taking a breather while these offenders were in jail and establishing "opportunity" programs designed to make the community viable and capable of self-regulating its behavioral controls (job training, new employers, day care, nurseries in schools, after-school programs, tutors and mentors, civic pride demonstrations, tenant management of housing projects). In the early years, the "weed" portion was clearly favored; in the early 1990s, "seed" programs based on analysis of the specific needs of the individual community were developed and spread—about the time the crime rates began to plunge.

vention has to be the first and most important strategy for dealing with the new threats.

Two major approaches will evolve over the next few years. First, national and international partnerships will be necessary to cope with crimes without borders. In 2000, a task force of agents from 32 U.S. communities, the federal government, and 13 other nations conducted the largest-ever crackdown on child pornography exchanged internationally over the Internet. Coordinated by the U.S. Customs Service, the raid resulted in shutting down an international child-pornography ring that used secret Internet chat rooms and sophisticated encryption to exchange thousands of sexually explicit images of children as young as 18 months. It is this type of coordinated transnational effort that will be necessary to cope with infotech and biotech crime and terrorism.

Second, the focus of prevention must change from opportunity reduction to desire reduction. Crime-prevention specialists have long used the equation, Desire + Opportunity = Crime. Prevention programs have traditionally focused on reducing opportunity through target hardening. Locks, alarms, high-intensity lighting, key control, and other methods have been used, along with neighborhood crime watches and citizen patrols.

Little attention has been paid to desire reduction, in large part because of the atomistic approach to crime. Specifically, an offender's criminal behavior is viewed as a result of personal choice. Meanwhile, criminologists and other social scientists say crime is more likely to be a product of the conditions under which the criminal was reared and lived—yet there were no significant efforts to fix this root of the problem. Instead, the criminal-justice system stuck to target hardening, catching criminals, and exacting punishment.

Quashing conditions that lead to a desire to commit crime is especially necessary in light of the apparent reasons terrorists and international criminals attack: religious fervor heightened by seeing abject poverty, illiteracy, and often homelessness and hunger all around while also seeing others live in seeming splendor.

The opportunity to reduce crime and disorder is at hand. The strategies outlined above will go a long way toward that lofty goal, as will new technologies. A boom in high-tech development has brought about new surveillance and tracking gadgetry, security machines that see through clothing and skin, cameras and listening devices that see and hear through walls and ceilings, "bugs" that can be surreptitiously placed on individuals, and biometric scanners that can identify suspects in large crowds. On the other hand, these are also the technologies that could take away our freedom, particularly our freedom of speech and movement. Some in high government positions believe loss of privacy and presumption of innocence is the price we must pay for safety.

For many it is too high a price. One group that urges judicious use of technology within the limitations of civil liberties protected by the U.S. Constitution is the Society of Police Futurists International (PFI)—a collection primarily of police officials from all over the world dedicated to improving the professional field of policing by taking a professional futurist's approach to preparing for the times ahead. While definitely interested in staying on the cutting edge of technology and even helping to guide its development, PFI debates the promises and perils of each new innovation on pragmatic and ethical grounds. Citizens need to do the same.

About the Author Gene Stephens will be a featured guest speaker at the 2003 World Future Society annual conference in San Francisco. He is a distinguished professor emeritus of the Department of Criminology and Criminal Justice, University of South Carolina. He is also the criminal justice editor of THE FUTURIST. His address is 313 Lockner Court, Columbia, South Carolina 29212. Telephone 1-803-777-7315; e-mail stephens-gene@sc.edu; Web site www.thefuregene.com.

Originally published in the May/June 2003 issue of *The Futurist*. Used with permission from the World Future Society, 7910 Woodmont Avenue, Suite 450, Bethesda, MD 20814. Telephone: 301/656-8274; Fax: 301/951-0394; http://www.wfs.org. © 2003.

Reasonable Doubts

Crime's down but the system's broken:
The Monthly's *guide to criminal justice reform*

BY STEPHEN POMPER

CRIME MAY BE DOWN BUT THE CRIMINAL JUSTICE SYSTEM remains something of a mess. If you've ever spent time on a jury, if you've worked in a criminal court, or if you caught even 10 minutes of the O.J. trial on TV, you've seen some of the problems. The system has an Alice-in-Wonderland quality: The guilty are over-protected, the innocent are under-served, and much of the time the public interest simply fails to enter the picture. Jurors spend days in court dozing through endless delays and witnesses who dare come forward find their lives imperiled. When all is said and done, too many violent and dangerous felons wind up with Get-Out-of-Jail-Free cards and too many non-violent and just-plain-innocent people wind up doing time.

How do we make it better? Read on for the Monthly's guide to criminal justice reform.

Get the Truth Out

Courts are supposed to be finders of fact. Yet there's an awful lot about the criminal justice system that keeps them from ever getting to those facts. Some of the obstacles are straight-forwardly bad laws. Others are more a question of resources and oversight. We could help our courts get past some of these obstacles and here's how:

1. End "Two Wrongs Make a Right" Criminal Procedure:
The judicial system labors under rules crafted by the Warren Court, which protect defendants even if it's at the expense of the truth. In a 1997 law review article, University of Minnesota law professor Michael Stokes Paulsen casts this as the "Dirty Harry" problem. In the movie of the same name, Detective Harry Callaghan gets increasingly violent as he goes after a serial murderer named "Scorpio." He busts into his place without a warrant, nabs the murder rifle, and savages Scorpio until he spits out the location of a kidnap/rape/murder victim. But here's the kicker: Although Scorpio is a monster, and Harry does some monstrous things, neither of them is actually punished. Scorpio goes free because all the evidence against

him is tainted by Harry's antics, and Harry slides by because cops get away with stuff.

Decades later, this lose-lose approach is still at the heart of criminal procedure. To be sure, the failing has noble origins. Back in the Civil Rights era, the Supreme Court, concerned about segregationist states deploying policemen to harass and imprison minorities, developed a set of constitutional principles that stopped them from doing that: Ill-gotten evidence was treated like fruit from a poisoned tree and had to be discarded. If the police ransacked your car without a warrant, the resulting evidence could not be produced at trial.

But the days of officially-sponsored police racism are over. And while there's still racism and police abuse on a different scale, it's hard to see why they are best dealt with by excluding otherwise helpful evidence. It's one thing to say that forced confessions should not be considered: That protects innocent people who might be beaten into confessing crimes they did not commit. But what kind of protection does an innocent person get from an "exclusionary rule" that prevents a court from considering ill-gotten evidence? If Harry busts into an innocent person's apartment and doesn't find anything to seize, then there won't be any evidence for a court to exclude, and there won't be any negative consequence for the police. Not that exclusion is such a negative consequence anyway: when police are evaluated in cities like New York, the emphasis is on the number of arrests to their credit—not convictions. If Scorpio goes free because Harry trashes his place, Harry still may be eligible for a promotion.

Part of the problem with the exclusionary rule is that it assumes that the Bill of Rights is focused on protecting the guilty rather than the innocent. But some leading constitutional scholars have begun to suggest that this assumption is backwards—protecting the innocent is in fact the top priority. The correct way to control police abuse is not by tossing potentially useful evidence onto the compost pile. It is by punishing the policeman or the police department through a lawsuit or through criminal charges. But the court should, by all means, be allowed to consider Scorpio's rifle and any other relevant evidence that Harry has managed to dig up.

In 1995 Congress considered a bill that would have gone in this direction—by getting rid of the exclusionary rule and making it easier to sue delinquent cops—but it fizzled. Supporters of the status quo argue that it doesn't really matter: There are so many exceptions to the exclusionary rule that only a small percentage of arrests are lost as a result. They also argue that the rule is useful because it provides at least some check on police abuse—and that creating an alternate system of checks would be a real challenge. This, however, ignores the problems in the current system. Read the recent coverage about the Los Angeles and New York police departments and you will see that the exclusionary rule is not an especially effective mechanism for controlling police brutality. Meanwhile, courts and lawyers waste their time on motions to suppress evidence that can only undermine the truth-seeking process.

Getting to the truth should be the court's foremost objective. And this principle doesn't apply just to the exclusionary rule. For example, a majority of states have deadlines after which a convict cannot introduce new evidence to prove his innocence. In Virginia, the deadline is a scant 21 days after trial. The idea is to keep appeals from dragging out endlessly, but that's not a good rationale for keeping innocent people in jail. If a convict can present credible new evidence, then a court should review it. But if a case reopens for this reason and the state has come up with new evidence of guilt, the court should look at that too.

It's time to end the lose-lose cycle that we create by excluding evidence. A court must get the information it needs to send Scorpio to Alcatraz. If he can prove his innocence later, it must hear the evidence it needs to spring him. And the Harrys of this world must pay for their brutality through some mechanism that punishes them directly—rather than one that punishes the community by putting guilty people back on the street.

2. Create a Universal DNA Database. This is an idea that Rudy Giuliani has endorsed and the ACLU has said could usher in a "brave new world" of genetic discrimination—but looking past the rhetoric, it's a winner.

The idea is to take full advantage of the enormous power of DNA evidence. Because it's so much more reliable at identifying people than eyewitnessing, DNA evidence can keep innocent people from going to death row and guilty people from going free. And because it is such powerful proof, it can help shorten trials, relieve problems with witness intimidation, and generally lend itself to a more efficient and reliable criminal justice system. But in order to maximize its usefulness, you need to be able to check crime scene DNA samples against the biggest possible database. The government is already coordinating a database that will include mostly convicted

felons' DNA samples. That's a decent start: Convicted felons have a high probability of returning to their old ways when released from prison. Still, plenty of crime is committed by people who have never spent time behind bars. So why not do it right and create a database that includes everybody?

The idea is simple and non-discriminatory. Upon the birth of any child, a hospital would take a DNA sample using a simple procedure that involves swabbing cells off the inside of a cheek with a bit of cotton and then analyzing their genetic material for patterns at 13 separate points, called loci. The information recorded at these loci is referred to as "junk" by geneticists because it doesn't say anything interesting about whether a person is likely to be an insurance risk, is likely to win a Nobel Prize, is a cat or a dog person, or anything of the sort. Like a fingerprint, it would simply identify who a person is. This information would be sent to a federal database where it could be used only by law enforcement authorities when trying to establish the identity of a criminal.

Civil libertarians get hysterical over the privacy issues, but where's the beef? Given the restricted information that we're talking about, and the limited access that would be afforded, the main privacy right at stake is the right to commit crimes anonymously. It's also worth noting that millions of hospital patients leave blood and tissue samples when they come for treatment. Some hospitals keep these on file. So if your local homicide chief decides that he wants to get a DNA profile on you, he may very well be able to go down to City General, retrieve some old cells of yours, and do his own genetic analysis. This analysis could wind up furnishing information that is much more sensitive than the information that would be recorded in the national database. Wouldn't it be preferable to require the police to limit their DNA sleuthing to one tightly controlled source?

One more point on DNA evidence: It can help us correct past mistakes, and we should use it to do so. States should be required to take DNA samples from all convicts in all cases where it could prove their innocence and the prisoner wants it. Given that no fewer than 67 prisoners have already been found innocent using DNA testing, states should be working overtime to find other innocents who have been wrongly imprisoned. The flip side of this position is that states and courts should do whatever it takes to make certain that statutes of limitations don't stop victims and prosecutors from going after violent offenders where DNA technology for the first time allows guilt to be established.

3. Save the Witnesses. If you watch too many movies of the week, you can get a highly distorted view of what this country does to protect its witnesses. There is a romantic idea that once you agree to testify in a dangerous case, the FBI rushes in with a team of plastic surgeons, draws up new papers, and moves you to the furthest corner of the furthest possible state—where it continues to keep a watchful eye on you for the rest of your natural born days. But there's a problem: The FBI program is for federal witnesses—it was designed to help U.S. attorneys bust up organized crime. It doesn't do a thing to help out at the state and local levels where most crime, and most witness intimidation, occurs.

And a shocking amount of witness intimidation does occur at those levels. According to a 1995 report published by the National Institute of Justice (their latest on this subject), some prosecutors were able to identify gang-dominated neighborhoods where between 75 and 100 percent of violent crimes involved intimidation—from knee capping potential witnesses to staring them down in court to actually rubbing them out. That's an unsettling figure when you consider that a court's fact-finding machinery can grind to a halt without witnesses.

Consider the following example: A Baltimore jury recently acquitted three men who had been accused of shooting one Shawn L. Suggs in a street fight that spilled out into rush hour traffic. At first, the prosecution seemed to have a good case—but then the key witnesses started dropping out of the picture: The first was killed in his home. Another disappeared without a trace. And the third (Suggs' former girlfriend) claimed at the last moment to have lost her memory to heroin addiction. "I think she is afraid to tell the truth," Suggs' mother told the *Baltimore Sun*. "I think I would be afraid too."

How do you fight that kind of fear? Many states and communities have created their own witness protection programs that try to offer some measure of security—from posting police cars outside witnesses' homes to moving witnesses out of their old neighborhood until the trial is over. But the programs often lack adequate funding. And on top of that, it can be a lot tougher to protect state and local witnesses than it is to deal with mob rats. Street and gang crime witnesses are frequently reluctant to abandon their homes and neighborhoods. They get bored, lonely, and afraid when they're pulled away from their families. And even if they can be persuaded to move a short distance—say a few towns away—the temptation to look in on friends and relatives back in the old neighborhood can be both irresistible and dangerous.

More could be done. Improving funding and stiffening penalties would be a good start. When prosecutors can persuade a witness to cooperate, they should have the money they need to pay for motel bills, replace locks on doors, and pick up the tab for gas and groceries. Because it can be tough to come up with the scratch to do this on short notice, some states, like California, have set aside funds that communities can use to foot the bill. Other states should follow their lead, and the federal government should set up an emergency fund to help communities pick up the slack when there's a shortfall. And with regard to penalties, states should rank intimidation right up there with the gravest non-capital offenses. Under Washington, D.C. law, intimidators can get up to life imprisonment. That sounds about right.

4. Police the Prosecutors—As Well As the Police. Police and prosecutors are the gatekeepers of the criminal justice system. But although police brutality gets a lot of attention—as it has recently in New York and Los Angeles—prosecutors tend to escape scrutiny.

We should pay closer attention to the prosecutors. They, after all, are the ones who decide which cases go to trial and how they're presented. If they misrepresent the facts, they can wind up sending innocents to jail. And that's a problem for two reasons. First, there are a lot of powerful incentives that make prosecutors want to win—sometimes even at the expense of the truth. ("Winning has become more important than doing justice," complained Harvard Law School professor Alan Dershowitz in a 1999 *Chicago Tribune* interview. "Nobody runs for Senate saying 'I did justice.'") Second, when a prosecutor does step over the line, he rarely faces serious punishment.

How do we know? In 1999, *The Chicago Tribune* published a nationwide survey. They looked at all the murder cases in the past 40 years that had to be retried because a prosecutor hid evidence or permitted a witness to lie. They found 381 in all. What happened to the prosecutors in those cases? Almost nothing. About a dozen were investigated by state agencies, but only one was actually fired—and he was eventually reinstated. And not a single one of the offending prosecutors was ever convicted of either hiding or presenting false evidence. Indeed, not a single prosecutor in the history of the Republic has ever been convicted on those grounds—even though they're both felony offenses. As Pace University law professor Bennett Gershman told the *Tribune*: "There is no check on prosecutorial misconduct except for the prosecutor's own attitudes and beliefs and inner morality."

But isn't the defense bar a check on prosecutorial misconduct? Don't count on it. In December 1999, *The New York Times* noted that the number of legal aid lawyers in New York City's Criminal Court had dropped from 1,000 a decade ago to 500 today. And it quoted Manhattan defense attorney Ronald Kuby as saying that "No competent criminal defense lawyer zealously representing his clients can make a living on [legal aid rates]." This problem is obviously not limited to New York.

All this suggests that if we want to make certain prosecutors are doing the right thing, we have to police them more aggressively. That means creating well-muscled independent agencies that have strong incentives to find out when prosecutors misbehave—and to fine, press charges, and/or fire them when they do. Judges should help them out by publishing the names of prosecutors who commit misconduct in their orders and opinions (not a common practice)—and circulating them to the independent watchdogs. And while we're on the subject, states should also set up similar watchdogs to police the police—both for abuse and sheer incompetence. There should be independent civilian commissions that not only have responsibility for overseeing police departments, but that also have the power to impose discipline on the departments when they stray.

5. Abolish the Insanity Defense.   It is true that you have to be a bit crazy to shoot the President like John Hinckley, or to cut off your husband's penis like Lorena Bobbit—but should that affect the state's ability to keep you separated from the rest of society, where you might do further harm? If you are rich or high profile or just plain lucky enough to find a defense lawyer who can successfully argue the insanity defense on your behalf, it can.

Consider the case of Tomar Cooper Locker, who opened fire on a crowded D.C. hospital ward—killing a boxer named Ruben Bell and wounding five bystanders. The apparent motive for the shooting was that Locker had a vendetta against Bell, whom he thought had killed his girlfriend. But Locker pled insanity based on the claim that he was suffering from a momentary attack of post-traumatic stress disorder—a claim endorsed by the same psychiatrist who testified in the Lorena Bobbit incident. The jury bought it. Locker was then committed to St. Elizabeth's Hospital, where he was treated for two whole months until, earlier this spring, doctors declared him fit to reenter society.

Michael Lazas is another example of someone who slipped through the system as a result of the insanity defense. In 1993, Lazas was found not guilty by reason of insanity for strangling his infant son and sent to Maryland's Perkins Hospital Center. It was his second violent assault; two years earlier he had stabbed a picnic companion in the throat. In 1998, Perkins officials thought Lazas was ready for a group home, so they moved him to an essentially zero-security facility in Burtonsville, Maryland. In February of this year, Lazas simply walked away from the Burtonsville facility. He was reportedly gone for four days before anyone notified the authorities he was missing.

In both cases, the public would have been better served if there were no insanity defense. There is no dispute that Locker and Lazas did what they were accused of doing. As a society, we've made a judgment that people who do these things need to be separated from the rest of us for a certain amount of time. Locker and Lazas should each have been found guilty and served the requisite time for his offenses—in an appropriate treatment facility to the extent necessary. The law should not force chronic schizophrenics to do hard time in maximum-security prisons. But it should be adamant about finding ways to keep those who commit violent crimes at a safe distance from the rest of society.

Lock up the right people

Politicians who vote for mandatory minimum sentences stake a claim to being tough on crime. Politicians who vote against them run the risk of appearing weak. Of course in a perfect world, "toughness" would be assessed by whether you put the right (i.e., most dangerous) people in jail—rather than how many people you put in jail. But the world of sentencing statutes is far from perfect.

The political blindness that surrounds these laws can be partly traced to the death of Len Bias—a Maryland basketball star who had been the Celtics' first pick in the NBA draft. When Bias overdosed on cocaine in his college dorm room in 1986, he become an overnight poster child for the war on drugs. It was an election year and Beltway legislators, who were close enough to Maryland to be caught up in the public horror at Bias' death, wanted to make a statement. So they replaced a set of temporary federal sentencing guidelines that had been in place with permanent "mandatory minimum" sentencing requirements. States followed suit with their own iterations of these requirements. And in 1994, California and Washington added a new wrinkle when they passed so-called "three strikes laws" that require courts to give 25-year minimum sentences to any two-time felony offender who steps out of line a third time—even if to commit a misdemeanor offense.

These laws have generated some spectacularly unfair results. For example, a California court recently sentenced Michael Wayne Riggs, a homeless man, to 25 years in jail for stealing a bottle of vitamins. His most serious prior offense was snatching a purse.

But if Riggs' story is maddening at the individual level, the major concern at the policy level is what all this chest-thumping legislation is doing to our nation's prison system. There are roughly 2 million Americans behind bars, of whom more than half are there for non-violent (in most cases drug-related) crimes. The country spends $31 billion per year on corrections—twice what it spent 10 years ago. There is still not enough room in America's prisons.

Even looking past the overcrowding issues, however, sentencing laws have proven to be losers. Sending minor drug offenders to jail exposes them to hardened criminals and increases the risk of them committing more serious felonies when they get out. The Rand Corporation has found that mandatory minimums are the least cost-effective way to reduce drug use and crime—as compared to treatment programs and discretionary sentencing. Even White House Drug Czar Barry McCaffery has acknowledged that "we can't incarcerate our way out of the drug problem." It is therefore unsurprising that a dozen or so states have formed commissions to reconsider their rigid sentencing policies and several, like Michigan, have begun to repeal them. And on the progressive front, Arizona recently became the first state to offer the option of drug treatment, rather than prison to its non-violent offenders convicted on drug charges.

Arizona's program is both cost efficient and makes sense. A California study found that one dollar spent on drug treatment saves seven dollars in reduced hospital admissions and law enforcement costs. These savings can be put to better use elsewhere in the criminal justice system. For example, they can be used to help communities develop facilities to siphon off non-violent offenders from the heart of the system. Roughly two percent of the nation's drug offender traffic is processed in special "drug courts," which dole out a combination of light sentencing—such as short jail terms, community service, and probation—plus mandatory drug treatment. More drug courts would almost certainly be a good thing.

Communities also do themselves a service when they set up tough probation programs that actually help minor offenders steer away from trouble. Orange County, California has had substantial success with a program that involves 6 a.m. inspection visits to all participants from program officers, surprise drug testing, counseling, and monthly evaluations by the supervising judge. Anecdotal evidence suggests that in order to work these programs have to be ready to dish out real discipline to participants who fail to live up to their end of the bargain. Orange County participant Dale Wilson, who had been addicted to cocaine for three decades before joining the program, told the *Los Angeles Times* that he was sent to jail for nine days when he had a relapse. "It's a strict program," he said. "But I never would've gotten to the point to keep me sober if I hadn't been faced with these punishments."

Put More Order in the Courts

Finally, we shouldn't forget that the best laws and policies in the world aren't going to do a whole lot of good unless we have reliable, industrious, and smoothly administered courts. And while there are lots of hard-working judges with the same objective, there are also plenty of clunkers.

In a 1996 San Francisco case, for example, two municipal court judges batted a domestic violence case back and forth on an October Friday. According to *The Recorder*, a legal newspaper, Judge Wallace Douglass was supposed to hear the case—but he double-booked another trial for the same day. So he sent it across the hall to Judge Ellen Chaitin, who held a mid-day conference—and then sent it back to Douglass when it failed to settle by the early afternoon. Douglass then said that he couldn't find a jury to hear the case (it was Friday afternoon, after all) and, because a delay would have violated the defendant's speedy trial rights, he dismissed it. This calls to mind the story of the Manhattan judge who in 1971 adjourned a robbery trial to catch a flight to Europe. Another trial would have violated the defendant's constitutional rights, so he walked away scot-free.

The problem is two-fold. One is that judges don't always push themselves that hard. In 1989, *Manhattan Lawyer* correspondents observed that, on average, the judges in Manhattan's criminal court were in session about four and a half hours a day. Sixty-two percent spent less than five hours in session, and 42 percent started after 10 a.m.

In Baltimore, which has more than 300 homicides per year, you can sometimes walk through a criminal courthouse around 3:30 or 4:00 p.m. and find courtrooms that have adjourned for the day.

But the additional problem is that judges are too often inclined to schedule things first for their own convenience, second for the convenience of lawyers, and last of all for the convenience of the people the system should be bending over to accommodate—jurors and witnesses. One prosecutor said that there are days in D.C. Superior Court that unfold as follows: The jury is instructed to arrive at 10 a.m. and sits for hours while the judge kibbitzes with the lawyers over technical legal issues. Sometimes the kibbitzing runs right into lunch. Then everybody trundles off for a two hour break. The trial starts in earnest at 3 p.m. And court adjourns between 4:30 and 5 p.m.—sometimes earlier.

Lack of organization is another problem. Washington D.C.'s Superior Court has no central scheduling mechanism. Judges control their own dockets and are allowed to book two or three trials for the same day, anticipating that there will be pleas and continuances. Policemen who are supposed to testify wind up milling around the courthouse for days on end, waiting for their trials to be called, and—if they otherwise happen to be off-duty—collecting overtime.

It has to be possible to run a tighter ship because some judges already do. As noted in last month's "Tilting at Windmills," for example, a Tennessee judge named Duane Slone has adopted a policy that he won't hear plea bargains on the day a trial is scheduled to begin. This saves the jury from having to sit and wait while lawyers haggle over a plea and allows trials to start promptly at 9 a.m. Common sense courtesies like this could kill a lot of the inefficiencies that you see in courtrooms today. But more importantly, disciplinary panels need to keep better tabs on the courts and punish (by fines or demotions if necessary) those judges who fail to show up on time, stay all day, and run an orderly docket.

What Next?

Wholesale reform of the criminal justice system obviously isn't going to happen overnight. Some reforms can only be made by Supreme Court decision. Others will have to be effected through new laws and practices at the federal, state, and local levels. Still, it's a set of tasks well worth facing. It's great that crime is down but if we want it to stay there, and if we want to make sure that we're sending the right people to jail, then we need a system that we can really trust beyond a reasonable doubt.

Research assistance provided by Elisabeth Frater and Patrick Esposito

Reprinted with permission from *The Washington Monthly*, June 2000, pp. 21-26. © 2000 by The Washington Monthly Company, 1611 Connecticut Ave., NW, Washington, DC 20009. (202) 462-0128; www.washingtonmonthly.com.

CAUSES AND CONSEQUENCES OF WRONGFUL CONVICTION

HUGO ADAM BEDAU

While erroneous convictions are found throughout the criminal justice system, the consequences of these errors are especially serious in capital cases. The history of capital punishment—in this country and elsewhere, in the distant past as well as today—is a history of erroneous convictions and executions. The range and variety of irreversible errors in the death penalty system is sobering:

- The defendant was convicted of a murder, rape, or other capital crime that never occurred.
- A capital crime was committed, but the wrong person was tried, convicted, sentenced, and executed.
- The defendant did kill the victim but was insane, mentally retarded, or otherwise not fully responsible.
- The defendant did kill the victim but the killing was in self-defense.
- The defendant did kill the victim but the killing was accidental.
- The defendant did kill the victim but because of incompetent trial counsel or other error he was wrongly convicted of first-degree (capital) murder instead of another type of criminal homicide.
- It is not known whether the defendant was guilty because his guilt and punishment were settled by a lynch mob, not by trial in court.

Every jurisdiction in the United States that has used capital punishment has imposed it on one or more defendants in one or more of these erroneous ways. What is truly amazing is the extent to which advocates or America's current death penalty system have disregarded or otherwise downplayed the significance of these irrevocable errors—as though they were relics of a distant past. Recent events suggest that this tolerance and complacency is wearing thin, however, as legislatures, governors, trial and appellate judges—state and federal—are reeling from the impact of a wide variety of research and scholarly studies identifying wrongful convictions in capital cases.

Without a doubt the most remarkable response to this research so far is also the most recent: the decision this past July by Manhattan federal district court judge Jed S. Rakoff in *United States v. Alan Quinones*. Judge Rakoff ruled that the 1994 federal death penalty statute is unconstitutional because enforcing it poses "an undue risk of executing innocent people." On July 2, 2002, the *New York Times* quoted Harvard's constitutional-law scholar Laurence H. Tribe as saying: "I've been thinking about this issue in a serious way for at least 20 years, and this is the first fresh, new and convincing argument that I've seen." In that same issue, the *Times* editorial page observed that while the decision might be reversed on appeal, "it offers a cogent, powerful argument that all members of Congress—indeed, all Americans—should contemplate."

SCOPE OF THE PROBLEM

The issue of wrongful convictions, sentences, and executions in the United States has its terminus ad quem for the present in the release in April 2002 of Arizona death row prisoner Ray Milton Krone, the 100th capital defendant to be released on grounds of innocence in the past 30 years, that is, since the death penalty was re-introduced in the mid-1970s. The terminus a quo for research on this grim subject was the study "Miscarriages of Justice in Potentially Capital Cases" by Michael L. Radelet and me, published in the *Stanford Law Review* in November 1987. That article was the first extensive and documented report on the subject—expanded (with co-author Constance E. Putnam) in our book *In Spite of Innocence* (1992)—covering the entire nation for most of the 20th century.

We co-authors were most impressed with several findings that no prior research had uncovered:

- All but six of America's death penalty jurisdictions had at least one case of wrongful conviction in a capital case.
- The most frequent cause of error was perjury by prosecution witnesses.
- The discovery of error and its rectification was usually not achieved by official participants in the system of criminal justice but by others, in spite of the system.
- In some two dozen cases, reprieve or other form of clemency leading to eventual vindication came just days or even hours before the scheduled execution.
- In all but three dozen of the 350 cases reported in the initial research, the innocence of the convicted defendant was rec-

ognized by pardon, indemnity, acquittal or retrial, or some other official action.

Critics typically have ignored these findings and refused to acknowledge the scope of the problem revealed by this research. Instead, they have concentrated on disputing the finding that among the wrongful convictions were two dozen innocent men who had been executed. The critics were quick to respond with various objections, including these three: First, all but one of the innocent-executed cases were pre-*Furman* thus could be dismissed as ancient history, with no relevance to post-*Furman* statutory safeguards. Second, reexamination of several of the cases tended to confirm rather than disconfirm the trial court's verdict of guilty. Third, no government official in the years under study had ever gone on record admitting that he had been (an innocent) party to, or even knew of, a wrongful conviction that ended in the execution of an innocent defendant.

Perhaps the critics will reconsider their confidence that no innocent persons have been executed when they examine the findings in the recent re-investigation by James Acker and his associates of the eight New York cases in our list (one-third of the two dozen at issue). Acker et al., endorse our judgment that all eight were innocent. (See Acker, et al., "No Appeal From the Grave: Innocence, Capital Punishment, and the Lessons of History," in Westervelt and Humphrey, *Wrongly Convicted: Perspectives on Failed Justice* 154–173 (2001).

NEW RESEARCH

Since the work of Radelet, Bedau, and Putnam in 1992, important additional research has been undertaken by several different sets of authors, all of whom have published their results within the past three years. Heading the list by a wide margin is the well named study, *A Broken System: Error Rates in Capital Cases, 1973–1995,* by James S. Liebman, professor of law at Columbia University, and his associates. Part 1 of the Liebman report appeared in the summer of 2000; Part II became available in February 2002.... The same consideration applies to the second study, the report and recommendations (of April 2002) to Illinois Governor George Ryan by the special commission he created in March 2000....

At about the same time the Illinois Commission tendered its report, Harvard Law School was host to a conference on "Wrongful Convictions: A Call to Action." The full-day conference was co-sponsored by the Boston law firm of Testa, Hurwitz, and Thibault, and by the New England Innocence Project (an affiliate of the Innocence Project created at Cardozo Law School by Barry Scheck and Peter Neufeld). Although not presenting new research as such and not confined to wrongful convictions in capital cases, the conference proceedings (available on tape from the Criminal Justice Institute, Harvard Law School) amplified printed materials distributed to the participants in a volume of nearly 800 pages, reprinting 56 articles, documents, memoranda, and reports—a virtual omnium gatherum on all aspects of the topic.

DEATH PENALTY

Among the many books on the death penalty published in recent years (I discussed nine of them in my essay-review in *Boston Review* for April/May 2002), only two have much to offer by way of original research that bears on the problem before us, and neither is confined to death penalty cases. One is *Wrongly Convicted: Perspectives on Failed Justice,* edited by Saundra D. Westervelt and John A. Humphrey (2001). The 14 chapters, each by a different author or authors, are grouped into four parts: the causes of wrongful convictions, the social characteristics of wrongfully convicted prisoners, illustrative case studies, and prospects for the future. The other book is *Actual Innocence: Five Days to Execution, and Other Dispatches from the Wrongly Convicted* (2000, revised 2001), by attorneys Barry Scheck and Peter Neufeld and journalist Jim Dwyer. *Actual Innocence* is largely devoted to narratives of cases where DNA testing came to the rescue, including what the authors seem to believe was the first such case a decade ago (1992) in New York.

These books are particularly interesting due to their broadened scope. Since capital cases represent a small percentage of all criminal convictions, a reasonable inference can be drawn that large numbers of wrongful convictions occur in non-capital cases. Cases involving biological evidence, whether capital or not, are also a small percentage of all criminal cases, so the DNA exonerations examined in *Actual Innocence,* for example, may indicate a similar conclusion. That is, wrongful convictions likely occur in cases without evidence that can be tested as reliably as can biological evidence with DNA technology.

USE OF DNA

No doubt the salient factor in the public's interest in the problem of convicting the innocent is the discovery that DNA could be put to forensic uses and provide virtually unassailable evidence for or against the guilt of an accused—at least in those cases (as in rape or felony-murder-rape) where traces of DNA are available and relevant. Evidence of this sort was not available in 1987, but it was by 1994; the case of Kirk Bloodsworth (wrongly convicted of rape-murder in 1983 and released from Maryland's death row a decade later) pioneered the use of DNA results to free a prisoner on death row.

Forensic evidence from DNA testing has also had a powerful impact on courts and legislatures, and it is perhaps the dominant reform in the entire system of criminal justice currently sought by those who appreciate the impact such testing can have on the question of the guilt of the accused. As Scheck and Neufeld observed in their article in the Westervelt and Humphrey book, "Nothing comparable has ever happened in the history of American jurisprudence; indeed nothing like it has happened to any judicial system anywhere."

A COTTAGE INDUSTRY

Recounting stories by or about innocent men released from death row verges on becoming a cottage industry. Two among the many recent additions, not surprisingly, are accounts of Illinois cases. Thomas Frisbie and Randy Garrett, in *Victims of Justice* (1998), tell the story of Alejandro Hernandez and Rolando Cruz, who spent 14 years on death row. David Protess and Rob Warden, in *A Promise of Justice* (1998), tell the story of Dennis Williams (12 years in prison) and Verneal Jimerson (18 years on death row)....

In 1987, Bedau and Radelet reported that the most frequent causes of wrongful convictions in capital cases, in descending order of frequency, were: perjury by prosecution witnesses; mistaken eyewitness identification; coerced or otherwise false confession; inadequate consideration of alibi evidence; and suppression by the police or prosecution of exculpatory evidence. The two cases involving the four Illinois defendants mentioned above fall into this pattern. Jimerson was a victim of perjured testimony suborned by the prosecution. William's alibi testimony proved unpersuasive to the jury, and his attorney was incompetent by any reasonable standard. Cruz and his co-defendant were above all victims of perjury by prosecution witnesses, as well as of excessive prosecutorial zeal, erroneous expert testimony, and misleading physical evidence. In short, the causes of error in these cases were the usual ones.

Also in 1987, Bedau and Radelet reported what their data showed to be the most frequent scenarios of vindication, again in descending order of frequent: The defense attorney persists in post-trial efforts to establish his client's innocence; the real culprit confesses; a new witness comes forward; a journalist or other writer exposes the error; a private citizen discovers the error. Cruz and his co-defendant were rescued by the confession of the real murderer; the dogged efforts of a cadre of defense lawyers, and DNA evidence. Verneal Jimerson and his co-defendants were rescued by the detective work of Protess's journalism class at Northwestern University—a perfect illustration of the principle that vindication comes not because of but in spite of the system.

"LEGAL LYNCHING"

Thanks to the work of capital defense lawyers—several of whom (Stephan Bright, David Bruck, Bryan Stevenson, Ronald Tabak, Frank Zimring, and especially Anthony Amsterdam) are well known through their lectures and writing—other lawyers and the law-review reading public have been thoroughly educated in the woefully unsatisfactory practices by the defense, the prosecution, and the judiciary in their handling of capital cases at trial and on appeal. This mismanagement, plus the overwhelming evidence that the part of the nation where a death penalty culture is most entrenched is in the southern states of the Old Confederacy, has sparked interest in the connection between yesterday's unlawful lynchings and today's lawful executions. So far, however, to the best of my knowledge the only serious attempt to connect lynching and the death penalty was in passing references by James W. Marquart, Sheldon Ekland-Olson, and Jonathan R. Sorenson, in their monograph, *The Rope, the Chair, and the Needle: Capital Punishment in Texas, 1923–1990* (1994). Nowhere is the connection more provoca-

tively brought to public attention than in the title of the recent book, *Legal Lynching* (2001), by Jesse Jackson, his son, Jesse Jr., and journalist Bruce Shapiro.

Taken strictly, of course, "legal lynching" is an oxymoron, and it is tempting to dismiss the whole idea out of hand as a distorting exaggeration. But to do so would be a grave mistake. First, the mentality that once tolerated—indeed, demanded—lynching a century ago can be seen today in the mentality that tolerates—indeed, demands—continuation of our badly flawed death penalty system. Second, the states that historically were the sites of the most frequent lawless executions—lynchings—are also the states with the greatest frequency of lawful executions today. Third, the complete disregard for due process of law and the rule of law manifest in a lynching survives in the indifference and disrespect for law as the instrument of justice to be found in many (most?) capital cases. Fourth, just as the paradigm lynchings in American history were carried out by white mobs on helpless black men as a populist method of ruthless social control, so the death penalty is to a troubling extent a socially approved practice of white-on-black violence, especially where the crimes involved are black-on-white. Fifth, many of those who opposed lynching in the South relied on the argument that the death penalty could do under color of law what lynching did lawlessly—and the record of abandonment in capital cases of any but the thinnest pretence of due process proved the point. Sixth, in cases where a posse was formed to hunt down an accused with the intention of killing him on the spot, rather than merely taking him into custody, it is virtually impossible to tell whether the killing should be judged murder by a mob or a quasi-legal summary execution.

Finally, just as the defense of lynching a century ago was predicated on states' rights and vigorous resistance to federal interference with local self-government, the attack on federal habeas corpus for state capital defendants takes refuge today, to some extent, in the same hostility to judicial intervention from Washington, D.C. (This is obscured by the Supreme Court's own inconsistent attempts to regulate the nation's death penalty system, which often puts judicial restraint, respect for federalism, and deference to the legislatures ahead of substantive justice under the Bill of Rights.) One way to view the current moratorium movement, insofar as it is supported by those who seek to defend the death penalty, is to see it as the latest nationwide effort to erase the many disturbing parallels between the lynching practices of a century ago and the death penalty practices of our own day.

REFORMS

This naturally leads us to inquire about the proposed reforms aimed at reducing the likelihood of convicting the innocent. The subject is too large to address in this essay-review, nor do any of the books and articles under discussion have a monopoly on recommended reforms. Furthermore, the various voices being heard are too many to summarize and evaluate here. Frequently if not unanimously recommended are two reforms: Obtain DNA evidence wherever possible, and exempt the mentally retarded from liability to a death sentence. This latter recommendation in fact became law under the Supreme Court's ruling this past June in *Atkins v. Virginia.*

Liebman and his associates in *A Broken System* confined their 10 reform recommendations to death penalty jurisprudence. Although one of them—abolishing judicial override of the jury's sentencing decision—has become law, thanks to the Supreme Court's ruling this past June in *Ring v. Arizona,* some of their other recommendations may have a longer and rough road to adoption. These include: Requiring proof of guilt "beyond *any* doubt" in a capital case; insulating sentencing and appellate judges who deal with capital cases from "political pressure"; and increasing compensation for capital defense lawyers to provide incentives for "well-qualified lawyers" to do the work.

Mandatory Justice: Eighteen Reforms to the Death Penalty, was released last year by The Constitution Project, part of Georgetown University's Public Policy Institute. Among its recommendations are these four: Adopt a better standard for incompetence of defense counsel than is provided by *Strickland v. Washington;* enact LWOP (life in prison without possibility of parole) as the alternative to the death sentence; conduct proportionality review of all capital convictions and sentences; and treat the jury's "lingering doubt" over the defendant's guilt as a mitigating circumstance in the sentencing phase.

CONTROLLING EVIDENCE

Scheck, Neufeld, and Dwyer offer a list of 40 proposed reforms. Seven of them would restrict the admissibility of eyewitness testimony. Fourteen others are devoted to controlling the evidence tendered by jailhouse snitches. Another 14 would constrain forensic laboratories and the use of their findings. Two of their proposed reforms would be relatively easy to implement; Use sequential rather than simultaneous presentation of suspects in police lineups, and videotape all interrogations.

Governor Ryan's Commission on Capital Punishment has produced by far the greatest number of recommendations—no fewer than 85. Nineteen are addressed to police and pretrial practices; the Commission also joins with Scheck et al. in endorsing videotaping of interrogations and in favoring a sequential lineup. Seven of their recommendations address the role of forensic evidence, and of course they urge wider use of DNA testing. Prosecutorial selection of which homicide cases will be tried as capital cases—one of the most troubling and unregulated areas in capital punishment jurisprudence—is the subject of three proposed reforms.

Ten of the recommendations are aimed at overhauling pretrial proceedings, including use by the prosecution of testimony by informants in custody ("jailhouse snitches"). They would not bar such testimony; instead, the Commission would require that the defense be fully informed of the prosecution's intention to use such testimony, and that the "uncorroborated testimony" of such a witness "may not be the sole basis for imposition of a death penalty." The Commission agrees with Liebman et al. in favoring "adequate compensation" for trial counsel (although their Recommendation 80 is unfortunately unclear about comparable compensation for defense counsel in post-conviction litigation).

What are we to make of these 150 recommendations (some of which overlap with each other)? Could we imagine a conference devoted to achieving a consensus on reform in which, say, 15 or 20 of these proposals received unanimous endorsement? Could the Supreme Court be persuaded to adopt some if not all of these reforms, just as it has adopted two new rules in *Ring* and *Atkins* this past spring? Or could state legislatures take it upon themselves to introduce some of these reforms, without waiting for the Supreme Court to act? We should have answers to these questions within the next few years.

THE STRUGGLE CONTINUES

The Illinois Commission has done its work well and left us with a comprehensive set of model reforms. Taken together with the reforms proposed by Scheck and Liebman and their associates, lawyers, legislators, and the general public have a set of proposals that—if put into practice—would appreciably improve the system in both capital and non-capital cases. Moratorium study commissions in other states could provide re-inforcement on several proposed reforms as well. Yet everything turns on the willingness of legislatures to enact statutes that incorporate reforms. Friends of the death penalty can hardly complain if these reforms narrow the range of death-eligible defendants and increase the economic costs of the entire system, any more than its critics can complain if good-faith adoption of these reforms breathes new life into our current "broken" and deregulated death penalty system.

If the past three decades of struggle over the future of capital punishment in this country have taught us anything, it is this: The appellants in *Gregg v. Georgia* (1976) were right, and the Supreme Court was wrong. The reforms that emerged in the wake of *Furman* (1972) inspired by the Supreme Court's ruling have turned out, to a disturbing extent, to be merely "cosmetic." Astute observers of the system argued even then that it was impossible to design reforms that would be effective in bringing greater fairness into the death penalty system and still serve rational goals of deterrence, incapacitation, and retribution. Whether the death penalty system in this country that would be created if these reforms are enacted will prove to be otherwise cannot be foretold. What can be predicted is that pressure for complete abolition will not vanish or even subside. The struggle over the nation's soul will continue for some time to come.

Mr. Bedau is professor emeritus at Tufts University. From "Causes and Consequences of Wrongful Convictions: An Essay-Review," by Hugo Adam Bedau, Judicature. *September/October 2002, pages 115–119.*

On Patrol

The tough job of police officer gets more complicated every day

By Eli Lehrer

Bored after writing a few traffic tickets, throwing a foul-mouthed malingerer out of a hospital, and grabbing a bite to eat, Fort Myers patrol officer Rebecca Prince heads toward "the crack McDonald's. " That's what she calls a run-down heap of leaky garden apartments on Bramen Avenue, just off a commercial corridor cluttered with gas stations, rent-to-own furniture stores, and taco stands. Even on a January night just a few degrees above freezing, it takes Prince only five minutes to find a wrongdoer.

On a side street, Christine Bosewell, a prostitute whom Prince has arrested "20 or 30 times, minimum" makes an appearance. Bosewell, a computer check confirms, has a thick pile of warrants—enough for an arrest—for failing to pay the loitering tickets Prince writes. Prince calls another officer for backup and searches Bosewell thoroughly. She finds a crack pipe in Bosewell's bra, a can of mace in her pocket, and a knife in her purse. Prince smashes the pipe and tosses the knife down a sewer, then handcuffs Bosewell and takes her back to the city's police station for booking and lockup.

As the crackling police radio grows silent around 9 p.m., Prince answers a false burglar alarm, yells at a gas station owner who lets drug dealing go on in his parking lot, and takes time to chat with a storekeeper grown weary of his neighborhood addicts.

Around 11, Prince stops a dented maroon Cadillac running a red light. A cloud of marijuana smoke strong enough to make a visitor dizzy hits Prince's face as soon as she opens the door. The smoke provides probable cause for a search. Prince calls for other officers, and four more cruisers soon appear. The search turns up a bag of cocaine, some crack, and a package of marijuana. The drug-using driver goes back to the station.

The evening didn't include the violence or physical danger that cops on TV face nearly every episode. Indeed, because of the unusual cold the night brought less action than typical. But for a good cop like Prince it was a fairly normal turn at the office. And thanks to her efforts, the neighborhood immediately became a little less ugly and dangerous.

Last year marked the ninth consecutive year of declining crime in America, though the drop was the smallest since rates started falling, and in the South crime actually rose. Still, the last decade represents the longest sustained period of crime reduction since our nation started keeping systematic statistics in 1934. Increased imprisonment, successful campaigns against drug use, favorable demographic trends, improvements in urban design, a revival of civil society in some inner cities, the peaking of underclass illegitimacy, and the end of cash-entitlement welfare have all helped to reduce crime. But great strides in the way police operate have also helped.

With an eye toward documenting crime fighting today, *TAE* recently researched the twin cities of Fort Myers and Cape Coral, Florida. Located on opposite sides of the Caloosahatchee River in southwestern Florida, Fort Myers and Cape Coral reveal how American crime is evolving, and how police are responding.

Fort Myers is a fairly typical U.S. city—centralized around a downtown, racially diverse, a bit stressed and chaotic, but fairly prosperous. The town's population of around 48,000 is about 30 percent black and 8 percent Latino, with whites (many of them retirees) making up the balance. Around 15 percent of residents live in poverty.

Florida has the highest crime rate of any American state—about twice the national average. While crime fell in the state during the 1990s, Florida still has a long way to go. Several of its cities rank among America's most dangerous.

Fort Myers in particular is an extremely high-crime area by national standards. In 2000, it experienced 125 serious reported crimes per 1,000 residents. That makes it around three times more dangerous than New York City, about twice as dangerous as Chicago, about the same as St. Louis, the most crime ridden large city (over 100,000 population) in the country. Fort Myers' crime rates are about four times the national average.

Like some other southern cities, Fort Myers de-incorporated certain black areas during the 1950s in order to keep newly enfranchised African Americans out of city politics. The unincorporated areas—poor and crime-ridden—resemble numerous little islands floating deep in-

Yet, like most of Florida, Cape Coral has more crime than comparable communities in other parts of America. It reported 37 serious crimes per 1,000 residents in 2000 (compared to Fort Myers' 125). That puts Cape Coral just about at the national average—which is high for a low-poverty bedroom community. And while crime rates fell a bit last year in Fort Myers, they rose in Cape Coral.

Cape Coral and Fort Myers both have professional police departments with dynamic, well-respected chiefs at the top. Fort Myers Chief Larry Hart is known nationally for urging the use of big-city community policing strategies in mid-sized cities. Cape Coral Chief Arnold Gibbs takes great pride in his department's certification from the Commission on Accreditation for Law Enforcement Agencies. Neither department, however, does anything truly extraordinary. Each has about 160 sworn officers authorized to use weapons and make arrests.

Police work is a helping profession that sometimes involves the use of violence. Police arrest murderers, hunt down missing children, stop unsafe motorists, settle quarrels between neighbors, collar shoplifters, and scatter unruly crowds. They do these things better than other citizens because they are authorized to apply force if necessary. Police must walk a fine line between being gentle enough to inspire trust and confidence while being sturdy enough to deter crime by force if pushed into that. The police thus have a nearly impossible task: They must use fear to mitigate fear.

The latest and most promising attempt to manage this difficult assignment is something called "community policing," which aims to prevent crime by working with the community to keep order. As the twentieth century unfolded, the need for courtesy, pre-emptive problem-solving, and community partnerships tended to get lost in other police priorities. Responding quickly to emergency calls became the chief goal, and so rapid mobility in cars, new technologies, reactive investigations, and paramilitary command structures were emphasized.

Today, police departments again emphasize human skills, for even the most routine police activities can demand a good deal of interpersonal deftness. At 7:30 on a quiet Thursday night, Cape Coral patrol officer Steve Petrovich responds to a radio call about a car accident. A gray-haired man in a sweatshirt has crinkled the sheet metal of his Oldsmobile by pulling in front of a pickup truck. A Taurus, trying to avoid the pile up, has run off the road. Petrovich helps a colleague administer a series of field sobriety tests.

The Oldsmobile driver, obviously inebriated, goes through a long series of kindergarten-like exercises. Asked to count backwards from 76, he recites, "76, 78, 73, 72, 75." He misses several times when asked to touch his finger to his nose. "Those tests must look pretty silly" remarks Petrovich. "But if we don't do them, we don't get the people, or we don't make good arrests. It's that sim-

PBS STUDIO/SAM JOHNSON

Officer Rebecca Prince

side city boundaries. They present headaches for the police, because city officers cannot make arrests or conduct investigations in the unincorporated neighborhoods without calling in the Lee County Sheriff. Criminals know this and sometimes conduct their business on the jurisdictional boundaries, fleeing one way if a city cruiser pulls up, and another way if it's a sheriff's car.

Cape Coral is entirely different. It began one day in 1957 when Jack and Leonard Rosen—Baltimore cosmetics manufacturers turned hardball swampland salesmen—staked out a Florida field of dreams. Within ten years a community of 50,000 people grew up; the 100,000th resident moved in last year. Though in population it is now a bigger "city" than neighboring Fort Myers, Cape Coral remains mostly a sprawling bedroom community, with some commercial strip malls strung along the main highways—a classic suburbanized sunbelt creation, full of transplants and retirees occupying low-slung single-family houses that front a grid of numbered streets and canals. The city has little poverty. About 95 percent of residents are white, though an increasing number of blacks have purchased homes in recent years to escape Fort Myers' urban ills. There are no terrible neighborhoods, and the "bad" parts of town consist of short stretches of cheesy tract homes with unkempt lawns and trash in the yards.

ple." As he is being handcuffed, the man quietly admits to drunk driving.

Policing has become a very complex helping profession, as tricky and demanding as teaching or nursing.

While the procedures of DWI stops can be taught fairly easily, a failure to follow them can cause enormous problems and some aspects of patrol work require far more discretion. Later that evening, Petrovich is called to a subdivided ranch house on a barren lot. A woman and her live-in boyfriend have gotten into a serious fight over his failure to accompany their daughter to receive an award at school. Their well-furnished but messy home, littered with fast-food packages, empty beer cans, and Harlequin romances, smells heavily of alcohol. The woman seems drunker than her boyfriend. Petrovich and another officer who assists refer to everyone as "sir" and "ma'am" and are consistently respectful to the intoxicated couple.

The man and woman tell contradictory stories: She complains he sexually propositioned a neighbor, while he says she hit him in a rage. The officers' professional attitude calms the angry couple and wins the trust of their dark-haired, dark-eyed daughter. Standing a few feet away from her parents in the kitchen, the daughter quickly warms to Petrovich. He questions her gently, sounding more like a teacher than a cop as he gracefully mixes concern and sternness.

The 12-year-old tells Petrovich that her mother, drunk as usual, started the argument, although not the physical violence. Her father, whom she thinks has a criminal record, hits her mother a lot. After talking also with some neighbors, who frequently hear the couple arguing but aren't sure who threw the first punch this time, Petrovich hauls the man off to the police station. "It's often impossible to tell what happened for sure, but you always have to try to make a solid decision," he explains. "I just believed the girl. She's pretty mature." Petrovich's procedures show a good command of police ethics: He starts without any assumption of guilt or innocence, treats people with respect, and shows special deference toward children.

Many times, the most important part of police work is just to be quick. Around 6:30 one evening Fort Myers patrol officer Joseph Schwartz is called to an area behind a notoriously troublesome liquor store where men and women congregate to drink malt liquor. A fight has just occurred as our cruiser pulls up, in a lot littered with 40-ounce malt liquor bottles and cans. Two women eye each other threateningly. An older man lies on the ground twitching, obviously drunk or on drugs. Nobody in the crowd welcomes Schwartz's presence, and dark stares greet him. The crowd claims the man lying on the ground "hit his head on the sign." Schwartz orders people to clear

out. By showing the colors, he scatters the crowd and avoids a situation that could have turned ugly fast.

Even in a high-crime city like Fort Myers, officers often go an entire night without making an arrest. Their activities to prevent crime *before* it happens, and to collect problem-solving information about crimes that have taken place earlier, can be just as valuable as a collar, though. Police officers have a tremendous amount of latitude in many aspects of their work, and, in trying to squelch crime before and after the fact, professional training can take an officer only so far. The best ones have strong instincts for fixing problems.

Like other proactive cops, Rebecca Prince uses her powers of observation to fight crime. By paying careful attention to little infractions, she often uncovers big ones. The night after Prince arrested Christine Bosewell and the drug-using Cadillac driver, Fort Myers' police headquarters buzzes with news of a two-man burglary ring that broke into nearly 20 homes and businesses over New Year's weekend. During his roll call briefing, Scott Cain, Prince's watch supervisor, asks officers to look out for two African-American men, one taller than average and the other perhaps 6'7".

Thanks to the freakish cold, things remain slow for Prince on that night's patrol. Once again she cruises the area near the crack McDonald's. Soon she comes upon a hard-looking bleached-blonde woman with sun-leathered skin and missing teeth, clearly intoxicated or on drugs. Prince, who often works this area as a hooker decoy in undercover stings, knows her well, and reports she has a closetful of previous citations for prostitution. Unlike Bosewell, who was resigned to spending an evening in jail, this woman badly wants to stay out of lockup. Prince proves willing to deal. "What can you give me?" she asks, shuffling the prostitute into her patrol car. Prince listens to stories about drug dealing at well-known locations. "Give me something better!" she demands.

Finally, the hooker comes up with some street information Prince can use: a story of two men, one tall and one very tall, who are running a burglary ring out of a white house at the end of a cul de sac. The house backs up onto a wooded strip separating it from a parking lot on the other side. According to Prince's informant, the men unload their booty in the parking lot and use a shopping cart to transport it to the house. Thinking she's hit pay dirt, Prince gives the prostitute a lift to a sleazy bar (even promising to bring her back home at the end of the night), and heads for the dead-end street.

The house comes into view just as Prince's informant described it: a low-lying white residence with a junky yard, backing perfectly up against a strip of no-man's land that leads to the parking lot on the commercial strip. The driveway is empty late at night. But lights burn inside, and the bed sheets which hang over the windows ripple when Prince shines her patrol car's spotlight on the home's exterior.

Calling for backup, Prince decides to investigate. Another officer comes to wait in the street and Prince walks up to the door. When two young women answer the door, Prince launches into a convincing patter about a complaint from neighbors about a loud stereo. The women, who say they're "baby-sitting for a friend" stand firmly in the doorway, blush and fidget as Prince talks with them and looks over their shoulders. There's no noise from a stereo, yet the women apologize anyway. But they stand blocking her entrance to the house.

They must find crime before it finds them.

Convinced something suspicious is afoot, and hoping her imaginative approach may have broken a bothersome case, Prince calls her supervisor. He has an officer posted on the roof of a nearby building to lie in wait for the burglars to return and start unloading their loot. He also offers a gentle reprimand to Prince: Without knowing it, she had strayed into one of the islands of real estate in the middle of the city that is supposed to be under the sheriff's jurisdiction, not her department's.

In many quiet neighborhoods and towns across America, good policing may just mean carefully training officers, avoiding corruption, and showing up quickly when people call. But police need more creative strategies in areas with high levels of transience or neighborhood decay, areas experiencing cultural dashes between ethnic groups, places poisoned by replacement of the work ethic with a welfare culture, neighborhoods with weak community standards, or streets infested with gangs or drug dealing. In particular, police have learned they need to partner with the community to stop crime *before* it happens.

This is an important principle behind "community policing," which nearly every police department in the country now claims to practice. It involves getting to know local residents; searching for long-term solutions to problems like vagrancy, derelict housing, and unsupervised juveniles; and eventually, teaching neighborhoods to police themselves.

Michael Titmuss is a former restaurant and nightclub owner who decided he wanted to help people, became a cop, and eventually a Fort Myers Community Policing Coordinator. Titmuss epitomizes the new type of officer who fixes local problems that breed crime, rather than simply responding to emergency calls on the radio. While he has the same rank and about the same pay as a patrol officer, Titmuss has a far different way of working. He focuses on making allies among local residents and businesspeople, finding the sources of neighborhood crime spikes, and then formulating solutions.

Titmuss begins by keeping in close touch with the four-square-mile area he's assigned to police. The counterman in a deli greets him by name. When he passes a notorious problem property, he explains chapter and verse the owner's habit of trading sex for rent. Driving through a motel that once provided "offices" for many of the area's prostitutes but now features gurgling fountains, a bronze sculpture of dolphins, and a German-speaking staff catering to tourists, Titmuss launches into a five-minute discourse about an angel developer who has remade many of the worst areas on this beat.

PBS STUDIO/SAM JOHNSON

Officer Michael Titmuss

Titmuss doesn't spend all his time on community relations. When a puff of smoke materializes behind railroad tracks, he speeds off to investigate. The fire department takes care of the fire but Titmuss radios in a report on some suspicious-looking youths nearby. "Ultimately, I've got to work with the patrol force," Titmuss says. "If I go to a block-watch meeting and people feel that the police won't do anything, then I can run all the youth programs in the world and it won't make a difference. I've got to know everything a patrol officer does and more."

This philosophy has helped Titmuss mobilize a series of revitalization task forces in his neighborhood. He has spearheaded mass trash pick-ups, set up new programs for children, and gotten abandoned buildings harboring vagrants knocked down. He has spent hundreds of hours compiling lists of the owners and managers of problem properties in the area, many of them out-of-towners. He is currently working to convert a long-closed bowling alley in a commercially critical shopping center into a center for area youth. Inside the mildewed structure he sketches his vision of a police- and city-run activity center with a snack bar, homework rooms, and boxing rings. And with his long background in successful nightclub operations, Titmuss's plans are practical and hard-nosed, not pipe dreams. Describing the uses of high ceilings, he explains "I always liked to use bowling alleys for clubs: lots of floor space with no internal supports."

His approach draws raves from community leaders. "It's a professional effort that does what we need them to," says Tony Corsentino, a former diner owner who heads the Palm Beach Boulevard Development Corporation near Titmuss's home base. "I didn't believe it would work out, but when we got a police officer who could coordinate all the city agencies we really did something about crime. The neighborhood is a lot cleaner and a lot safer." Even ordinary citizens notice the local police seem a little more helpful. "I've had problems with the cops in the past," one woman told *TAE*. "But when I call them, they listen."

> Titmuss epitomizes the new type of officer who fixes local problems that breed crime, rather than simply responding to emergency calls on the radio.

Titmuss argues that this method of policing creates long-term crime solutions. "I can sometimes arrest someone and they're out on the street the next day. That isn't very efficient. Or I can work with property owners to get him evicted. That solves the problem for that one guy pretty much permanently." In a typical afternoon, Titmuss might spend an hour or so on paperwork, a few more working with area kids, a few minutes chatting with local business owners and landlords, and an hour or two helping some patrol officers plan a raid on a gas station where drug sales have surged. He'll also find time to back up his colleagues on a few calls, take four or five radio calls himself, and maybe even collar a vandal.

Most patrol officers seem to respect the community cops. Some have doubts, however. "A lot of them slack off," complained one patrol officer. "They don't need to do anything; so unless they're naturally energetic, they aren't *going* to do anything." Working against this skepticism, both Fort Myers and Cape Coral are now trying to make community policing a department-wide philosophy, not just the work of a few specialized officers.

If these efforts succeed, the benefits could extend to officers as well as the city. Titmuss says he finds his job satisfying on many levels. "I can go home every day knowing I've made a positive difference in somebody's life. You work patrol long enough, and you swear there's not a decent human being on the face of this earth," he sighs. "But I can do this job and be convinced people are basically good."

Many traditional patrol officers admit they know only a handful of people on their beats, most of them bad guys. This is particularly a problem in the anonymous residential suburbia of Cape Coral. Despite the generally excellent relations between residents and the police in Cape Coral, officers *TAE* spoke with struggled to come up with the name of even one citizen in the large swath of tract homes they patrolled each evening.

Poor architecture and city design can do that. The atomized, sidewalk-less world of Cape Coral tends to make casual contact difficult or impossible. Though residential Cape Coral has more neighborhood watches than Fort Myers, its sterile civic grid makes neighborliness difficult. "All over the city we identify neighborhood watches by the chair's home address, because the neighborhoods don't have names," explains Brad Johnson, president of Cape Coral's citywide neighborhood watch federation.

Of course, police-community partnerships can only go so far in preventing crime. When miscreants go on the prowl, the police will still need to respond to protect the population. Finding and eliminating such crimes can be done through conventional sting operations and busts, or through more creative "problem solving" approaches.

Problem-solving policing aims not just to solve individual crimes, but to eliminate conditions that underlie lawbreaking. The focus is not on massive social forces like poverty and racism, which would be fruitless for police to try to battle. Rather, problem-solving police teams attempt to fix localized problems of disorder, decay, idleness, and inadequate oversight. Usually this begins with insights gathered through simple patrol work.

On a quiet Fort Myers side street between an apartment complex and a park lies a small wooden house that has become a hangout for prostitutes. The local community policing coordinator has discovered that the resident owner is a retired New York City cop who is providing a haven in return for sexual favors and drugs. Local officers are keeping a close eye on the place.

When a crowd of cars outside the house attracts her attention during one evening patrol, Rebecca Prince decides to knock on the door and see what happens. The retired cop comes to the door in his bathrobe, trim and courteous. She asks to come in. He isn't obligated to let her in, but does anyway. Inside, a surreal scene greets the visitors: Perhaps eight women lie around the house, some of them in strange postures. The rooms are spic and span, but almost devoid of furniture. A couple snuggles under a blanket. Prince strolls around, politely but firmly giving the owner a piece of her mind. "You see those girls over there… they have AIDS!" she exclaims. "I know them to be prostitutes. Are you aware of that?" The man protests that the hookers are simply friends whom he rents rooms to. She berates him for a few more minutes for allowing his house to become a serious neighborhood nuisance, then leaves.

Prince knows that any girl she locked up that night for some minor drug or sex offense would likely return to the house within a few days. Frustrated, she brainstorms for a solution. Soon she radios an older, highly experienced officer, fiftyish, with a bit of a beer belly. Meeting him outside a dark building where he was making a burglary check, Prince explains the situation in her neighborhood, says she wants the owner out, and picks her colleague's brain for advice.

After kicking around some complex nuisance-abatement laws, Prince mentions that the proprietor of the cat house said he is renting rooms. The older officer lights up. "You can get him for that," he says. "If he's running a boarding house without a license you can close the place down this week. It ain't a prostitution or drug conviction, but it'll make the problem go away." Her eyes shining, Prince makes a note to start the paperwork the next day with city housing officials.

The new methods of policing ask a lot of officers. They must be less detached, and much more personally involved with individuals. They must find crime before it finds them. They must work in tandem with many other arms of government, as well as with private businesses and civic organizations. At times it can be like wrestling with jello.

Policing has become a very complex helping profession. It may not match the sophistication of heart surgery, but in its current day-to-day practice, policing is easily as tricky and demanding as teaching or nursing.

But if the police are to become more effective, there is probably no alternative. They must help strengthen the bonds that hold American society together. Healthy civilizations depend on people controlling those impulses that bring them momentary pleasure at the expense of the community's good. The police need to step in when that fails, sometimes with force. But the best cops today use their leverage to help communities heal themselves.

TAE *contributing writer Eli Lehrer, visiting fellow at the Heritage Foundation, has observed at roughly 40 different law enforcement agencies while writing a book on policing.*

Teaching Kids To Kill

Michael Carneal, the fourteen-year-old killer in the Paducah, Kentucky, school shootings, had never fired a real pistol in his life. He stole a .22 pistol, fired a few practice shots, and took it to school. He fired eight shots at a high school prayer group, hitting eight kids, five of them head shots and the other three upper torso (Grossman & DeGaetano, 1999).

Dave Grossman

I train numerous élite military and law enforcement organizations around the world. When I tell them of this "achievement," they are stunned. Nowhere in the annals of military or law enforcement history can we find an equivalent achievement.

Where does a fourteen-year-old boy who never fired a gun before get the skill and the will to kill? Video games and media violence.

A Virus of Violence

First we must understand the magnitude of the problem. The murder rate does not accurately represent our situation because it has been held down by the development of ever more sophisticated life-saving skills and techniques. A better indicator of the problem is the aggravated-assault rate—the rate at which human beings are attempting to kill one another. And that rate went up from around 60 per 100,000 in 1957, to over 440 per 100,000 by the mid-1990s (*Statistical Abstracts of the United States*, 1957–1997).

Even with small downturns recently, the violent-crime rate is still at a phenomenally high level, and this is true not just in America, but also worldwide. In Canada, per-capita assaults increased almost fivefold between 1964 and 1993. According to Interpol, between 1977 and 1993 the per-capita assault rate increased nearly fivefold in Norway and Greece, and in Australia and New Zealand it increased approximately fourfold. During the same period it tripled in Sweden and approximately doubled in Belgium, Denmark, England-Wales, France, Hungary, the Netherlands, and Scotland. In India during this period the per-capita murder rate doubled. In Mexico and Brazil violent crime is also skyrocketing, and in Japan juvenile violent crime went up 30 percent in 1997 alone.

This virus of violence is occurring worldwide, and the explanation for it has to be some new factor that is occurring in all of these countries (Grossman, 1999b). As in heart disease, there are many factors involved in the causation of violent crime, and we must never downplay any of them. But there is only one new variable that is present in each of these nations, bearing the same fruit in every case, and that is media violence being presented as "entertainment" for children.

Killing Unnaturally

I spent almost a quarter of a century as an Army infantry officer, a paratrooper, a Ranger, and a West Point psychology professor, learning and studying how we enable people to kill. Most soldiers have to be trained to kill.

Healthy members of most species have a powerful, natural resistance to killing their own kind. Animals with antlers and horns fight one another by butting heads while against other species they go to the side to gut and gore. Piranha turn their teeth on everything, but they fight one another with flicks of the tail. Rattlesnakes bite anything, but they wrestle one another.

When a young child sees somebody on television being shot, stabbed, raped, brutalized, degraded, or murdered, to them it is real, and some of them embrace violence and accept it as a normal and essential survival skill in a brutal new world.

When we human beings are overwhelmed with anger and fear, our thought processes become very primitive, and we slam head on into that hard-wired resistance against killing. During World War II, we discovered that only 15 to 20 percent of the individual riflemen would fire at an exposed enemy soldier (Marshall, 1998). You can observe this phenomenon in killing throughout history, as I have outlined in much greater detail in my book, *On Killing* (Grossman, 1996), in my three peer-reviewed encyclopedia entries (Grossman, 1999a, 1999b, Murray and Grossman, 1999), and in my entry in the *Oxford Companion to American Military History* (1999) (all posted at www.killology.com).

That was the reality of the battlefield. Only a small percentage of soldiers were willing and able to kill. When the military became aware of this, they systematically went about the process of "fixing" this "problem." And fix it they did. By Vietnam, the firing rate rose to over 90 percent (Grossman, 1999a).

The Methods in this Madness

The training methods that the military uses are brutalization, classical conditioning, operant conditioning, and role-modeling. Let us explain these and then observe how the media does the same thing to our children, but without the safeguards.

Brutalization

Brutalization, or "values inculcation," is what happens at boot camp. Your head is shaved, you are herded together naked, and you are dressed alike, losing all vestiges of individuality. You are trained relentlessly in a total immersion environment. In the end, you embrace violence and discipline and accept it as a normal and essential survival skill in your brutal new world.

Something very similar is happening to our children through violence in the media. It begins at the age of eighteen months, when a child can begin to understand and mimic what is on television. But up until they are six or seven years old they are developmentally, psychologically, and physically unable to discern the difference between fantasy and reality. Thus, when a young child sees somebody on television being shot, stabbed, raped, brutalized, degraded, or murdered, to them it is real, and some of them embrace violence and accept it as a normal and essential survival skill in a brutal new world (Grossman & DeGaetano, 1999).

On June 10, 1992, the *Journal of the American Medical Association (JAMA)* published a definitive study on the effect of television violence. In nations, regions, or cities where television appears there is an immediate explosion of violence on the playground, and within fifteen years there is a doubling of the murder rate. Why fifteen years? That is how long it takes for a brutalized toddler to reach the "prime crime" years. That is how long it takes before you begin to reap what you sow when you traumatize and desensitize children (Centerwall, 1992).

JAMA concluded, "the introduction of television in the 1950s caused a subsequent doubling of the homicide rate, i.e., long-term childhood exposure to television is a causal factor behind approximately one-half of the homicides committed in the United States, or approximately 10,000 homicides annually." The study went on to state," if, hypothetically, television technology had never been developed, there would today be 10,000 fewer homicides each year in the United States, 70,000 fewer rapes, and 700,000 fewer injurious assaults" (Centerwall, 1992).

Today the data linking violence in the media to violence in society is superior to that linking cancer and tobacco. The American Psychological Association (APA), the American Medical Association (AMA), the American Academy of Pediatrics (AAP), the Surgeon General, and the Attorney General have all made definitive statements about this. When I presented a paper to the American Psychiatric Association's (APA) annual convention in May, 2000 (Grossman, 2000), the statement was made: "The data is irrefutable. We have reached the point where we need to treat those who try to deny it, like we would treat Holocaust deniers."

Classical Conditioning

Classical conditioning is like Pavlov's dog in Psych 101. Remember the ringing bell, the food, and the dog that could not hear the bell without salivating?

After the Jonesboro shootings, one of the high school teachers told me about her students' reaction when she told them that someone had shot a bunch of their little brothers, sisters, and cousins in the middle school. "They laughed," she told me with dismay, "They laughed."

In World War II, the Japanese would make some of their young, unblooded soldiers bayonet innocent prisoners to death. Their friends would cheer them on. Afterwards, all these soldiers were treated to the best meal they had in months, sake, and the so-called "comfort girls." The result? They learned to associate violence with pleasure.

This technique is so morally reprehensible that there are very few examples of it in modern U.S. military training. But the media is doing it to our children. Kids watch vivid images of human death and suffering, and they learn to associate it with laughter, cheers, popcorn, soda, and their girlfriend's perfume (Grossman & DeGaetano, 1999).

After the Jonesboro shootings, one of the high school teachers told me about her students' reaction when she told them that someone had shot a bunch of their little brothers, sisters, and cousins in the middle school. "They laughed," she told me with dismay, "they laughed." We have raised a generation of barbarians who have learned to associate human death and suffering with pleasure (Grossman & DeGaetano, 1999).

Operant Conditioning

The third method the military uses is operant conditioning, a powerful procedure of stimulus-response train-

ing. We see this with pilots in flight simulators, or children in fire drills. When the fire alarm is set off, the children learn to file out in orderly fashion. One day there is a real fire and they're frightened out of their little wits, but they do exactly what they've been conditioned to do (Grossman & DeGaetano, 1999).

In World War II we taught our soldiers to fire at bullseye targets, but that training failed miserably because we had no known instances of any soldiers being attacked by bullseyes. Now soldiers learn to fire at realistic, man-shaped silhouettes that pop up in their field of view. That is the stimulus. The conditioned response is to shoot the target and then it drops. Stimulus-response, stimulus-response, repeated hundreds of times. Later, when they are in combat and somebody pops up with a gun, reflexively they will shoot and shoot to kill. Of the shooting on the modern battlefield, 75 to 80 percent is the result of this kind of training (Grossman & Siddle, 1999).

When children play violent video games, especially at a young age, they receive this same kind of operant conditioning in killing. In his national presidential radio address on April 24, 1999, shortly after the Littleton high school massacre, President Clinton stated, "A former lieutenant colonel and professor, David Grossman, has said that these games teach young people to kill with all the precision of a military training program, but none of the character training that goes along with it." The result is ever more homemade pseudo-sociopaths who kill reflexively and show no remorse. Our kids are learning to kill and learning to like it. The most remarkable example of this is Paducah, Kentucky. The killer who fired eight shots and got eight hits on eight different milling, scrambling, screaming kids. (Grossman & DeGaetano, 1999).

Where did he get this phenomenal skill? Well, there is a $130-million law suit against the video game manufac-

turers in that case, working itself through the appeals system, claiming that the violent video games, the murder simulators, gave that mass murderer the skill and the will to kill.

In July 2000, at a bipartisan, bicameral Capital Hill conference in Washington, D.C., the AMA, the APA, the AAP, and the American Academy of Child and Adolescent Psychiatry (AACAP) issued a joint statement saying that "viewing entertainment violence can lead to increases in aggressive attitudes, values and behavior, particularly in children. Its effects are measurable and long lasting. Moreover, prolonged viewing of media violence can lead to emotional desensitization toward violence in real life.... Although less research has been done on the impact of violent interactive entertainment [such as video games] on young people, preliminary studies indicate that the negative impact may be significantly more severe than that wrought by television, movies or music."

Role Models

In the military your role model is your drill sergeant. He personifies violence, aggression, and discipline. The discipline, and doing it to adults, is the safeguard (Grossman, 1996). The drill sergeant, and hero figures such as John Wayne, Audie Murphy, Sergeant York and Chesty Puller, have always been used as role models to influence young, impressionable teenagers.

Today the media are providing our children with role models, not just in the lawless sociopaths in movies and in television shows, but in the transformation of these schoolyard killers into media celebrities.

In the 1970s we learned about "cluster suicides," in which television reporting of teen suicides was directly responsible for numerous copycat suicides of other teenagers. Because of this, television stations today generally do not cover teen suicides. But when the pictures of teenage killers appear on television, the effect is tragically similar. If there are children willing to kill themselves to get on television, are there also children willing to kill your child to get on television?

Thus we get the effect of copycat, cluster murders that work their way across America like a virus spread by the six o'clock local news. No matter what someone has done, if you put his or her picture on television, you have made that person a celebrity whom someone, somewhere, may emulate them. This effect is greatly magnified when the role model is a teenager, and the effect on other teens can be profound.

In Japan, Canada, and other democracies around the world it is a punishable, criminal act to place the names and images of juvenile criminals in the media because they know that it will result in other tragic deaths. The media has every right and responsibility to tell the story, but do they have a "right" to turn the killers into celebrities?

Unlearning Violence

On the night of the Jonesboro shootings, clergy and counselors were working in small groups in the hospital waiting room, comforting the groups of relatives and friends of the fifteen shooting victims. Then they noticed one woman sitting alone.

A counselor went up to the woman and discovered that she was the mother of one of the girls who had been killed. She had no friends, no husband, no family with her as she sat in the hospital, alone. "I just came to find out how to get my little girl's body back," she said. But the body had been taken to the state capital, for an autopsy. "I just don't know how we're going to pay for the funeral. I don't know how we can afford it."

That little girl was all she had in all the world, and all she wanted to do was wrap her little girl's body in a blanket and take her home. Some people's solution to the problem of media violence is, "If you don't like it, just turn it off." If that is your only solution to this problem, then come to Jonesboro, and tell her how this would have kept her little girl safe.

All of us can keep our kids safe from this toxic, addictive substance, but it will not be enough if the neighbors are not doing the same. Perhaps the time has come to consider regulating what the violence industry is selling to kids, controlling the sale of violent, visual imagery to children, while still permitting free access to adults, just as we do with guns, pornography, alcohol, tobacco, sex, and cars.

Fighting Back: Education, Legislation, Litigation

We must work against child abuse, racism, poverty, and children's access to guns, and toward rebuilding our families, but we must also take on the producers of media violence. The solution strategy that I submit for consideration is, "education, legislation, litigation."

Simply put, we need to work toward legislation that outlaws violent video games for children. In July 2000, the city of Indianapolis passed just such an ordinance, and every other city, county or state in the United States has the right to do the same. There is no Constitutional right to teach children to blow people's heads off at the local video arcade. And we are very close to being able to do to the media, through litigation, what is being done to the tobacco industry, hitting them in the only place they understand—their wallets.

Most of all, the American people need to be informed. Every parent must be warned of the impact of violent visual media on children, as we would warn them of some rampant carcinogen. Violence is not a game, it is not fun, it is not something that we let children do for entertainment. Violence kills.

CBS President Leslie Moonves was asked if he thought the school massacre in Littleton, Colorado, had anything to do with the media. His answer was, "Anyone who thinks the media has nothing to do with it, is an idiot," (Reuters, 2000, March 19). That is what the networks are selling, but we do not have to buy it. An educated and informed society can and must find its way home from the dark and lonely place to which it has traveled.

References

Centerwall, B. (1992). "Television and violence: The scale of the problem and where to go from here." *Journal of the American Medical Association*, 267: 3059–3061.

Grossman, D. (1996). *On Killing: The Psychological Cost of Learning to Kill in War and Society*. New York: Little, Brown, and Company.

Grossman, D. (1999). "Aggression and Violence." In J. Chambers (Ed.). *Oxford Companion to American Military History*. New York: Oxford University Press (p. 10).

Grossman, D. (1999a). "Weaponry, Evolution of." In L. Curtis & J. Turpin (Eds.). *Academic Press Encyclopedia of Violence, Peace and Conflict*. San Diego, CA: Academic Press (p. 797).

Grossman, D. & Siddle, B. (1999b). "Psychological effects of combat." In L. Curtis & J. Turpin (Eds.). *Academic Press Encyclopedia of Violence, Peace, and Conflict*. San Diego, CA: Academic Press (pp. 144–145).

Grossman, D. (2000, May). "Teaching Kids to Kill, A Case Study: Paducah, Kentucky." Paper presented at the American Psychiatric Annual Meeting, Chicago, IL.

Interpol International Crime Statistics, Interpol, Lyons, France, vols. 1977 to 1994.

Marshall, S.L.A. (1978). *Men Against Fire*. Gloucester, Mass.: Peter Smith.

Murray, K. and D. Grossman(1999). "Behavioral Psychology." In L. Curtis & J. Turpin (Eds.). *Academic Press Encyclopedia of Violence, Peace, and Conflict*. San Diego, CA: Academic Press.

Reuters Wire Service (2000, March 29). "CBS airing mob drama deemed too violent a year ago." *The Washington Post. Statistical Abstracts of the United States, 1957–1997.*

Lt. Col. Dave Grossman is a retired Army Ranger and West Point psychology professor, and an expert on the psychology of killing. He has testified before the U.S. House and Senate, and his research was cited by the President of the United States in the wake of the Littleton school shootings. He is director of the Killology Research Group in Jonesboro, Arkansas, and is co-author of *Stop Teaching Our Kids to Kill: A Call to Action Against Television, Movie, and Video Game Violence* (Crown/Random, 1999) and author of *On Killing: The Psychological Cost of Learning to Kill in War and Society* (Little, Brown and Co., 1996).

The New Terrorism

Securing the Nation against a Messianic Foe

By Steven Simon

In the minds of the men who carried them out, the attacks of September 11 were acts of religious devotion—a form of worship, conducted in God's name and in accordance with his wishes. The enemy was the infidel; the opposing ideology, "Western culture." That religious motivation, colored by a messianism and in some cases an apocalyptic vision of the future, distinguishes al-Qaida and its affiliates from conventional terrorists groups such as the Irish Republican Army, the Red Brigades, or even the Palestine Liberation Organization. Although secular political interests help drive al-Qaida's struggle for power, these interests are understood and expressed in religious terms. Al-Qaida wants to purge the Middle East of American political, military, and economic influence, but only as part of a far more sweeping religious agenda: a "defensive jihad" to defeat a rival system portrayed as an existential threat to Islam.

The explicitly religious character of the "New Terrorism" poses a profound security challenge for the United States. The social, economic, and political conditions in the Arab and broader Islamic world that have helped give rise to al-Qaida will not be easily changed. The maximalist demands of the new terrorists obviate dialogue or negotiation. Traditional strategies of deterrence by retaliation are unlikely to work, because the jihadists have no territory to hold at risk, seek sacrifice, and court Western attacks that will validate their claims about Western hostility to Islam. The United States will instead need to pursue a strategy of containment, while seeking ways to redress, over the long run, underlying causes.

trality of sacrifice in their liturgical traditions establish the legitimacy of killing as an act of worship with redemptive qualities. In these narratives, the enemy must be eradicated, not merely suppressed.

In periods of deep cultural despair, eschatology—speculation in the form of apocalyptic stories about the end of history and dawn of the kingdom of God—can capture the thinking of a religious group. History is replete with instances in which religious communities—Jewish, Christian, Islamic—immolated themselves and perpetrated acts of intense violence to try to spur the onset of a messianic era. Each community believed it had reached the nadir of degradation and was on the brink of a resurgence that would lead to its final triumph over its enemies—a prospect that warranted and required violence on a massive scale.

Such episodes of messianic zeal are not restricted to the distant past. In the mid-1980s, a group of Israeli settlers plotted to destroy the Dome of the Rock, the 8th-century mosque atop the Haram al Sharif in Jerusalem. The settlers appeared to believe that destroying the mosque would spark an Arab invasion, which would trigger an Israeli nuclear response—the Armageddon said by the Bible to precede the kingdom of God. The plot was never carried out, because the conspirators could not get a rabbinical blessing. Analogous attempts have characterized Christian apocalypticists and even a Buddhist community whose doctrine was strongly influenced by Christian eschatology—Aum Shinrikyo.

The Fabric of New Terrorism

Religiously motivated terrorism, as Bruce Hoffman of the RAND Corporation first noted in 1997, is inextricably linked to pursuit of mass casualties. The connection is rooted in the sociology of biblical religion. Monotheistic faiths are characterized by exclusive claims to valid identity and access to salvation. The violent imagery embedded in their sacred texts and the cen-

The Doctrinal Potency of al-Qaida

Similar thinking can be detected in narrative trends that inform al-Qaida's ideology and actions. Apocalyptic tales circulating on the Web and within the Middle East in hard copy tell of cataclysmic battles between Islam and the United States, Israel, and sometimes Europe. Global battles seesaw between infidel and Muslim victory until some devastating act, often the destruction of New York by nuclear weapons, brings Armageddon to an end and leads the world's survivors to convert to Islam.

The theological roots of al-Qaida's leaders hark back to a medieval Muslim jurisconsult, Taqi al Din Ibn Taymiyya, two of whose teachings have greatly influenced Islamic revolutionary movements. The first was his elevation of jihad—not the spiritual struggle that many modern Muslims take it to be, but physical combat against unbelievers—to the rank of the canonical five pillars of Islam (declaration of faith, prayer, almsgiving, Ramadan fast, and pilgrimage to Mecca). The second was his legitimization of rebellion against Muslim rulers who do not enforce *sharia*, or Islamic law, in their domains.

Ibn Taymiyya's ideas were revived in the 1960s in Egypt, where they underpinned 25 years of violence, including the assassination of Anwar Sadat in 1981. When the Egyptian government vanquished the militants, survivors fled abroad, taking advantage of European laws regarding asylum or of the lawlessness of Yemen, Afghanistan, and Kashmir.

Ibn Taymiyya's teachings have even deeper roots in Saudi Arabia. They became part of the founding ideology of the Saudi state when Muhammad Ibn Abd al Wahhab formed an alliance with Ibn Saud in 1744.

Al-Qaida embodies both the Egyptian and the Saudi sides of the jihad movement, which came together in the 1960s when some Egyptian militants sought shelter in Saudi Arabia, which was locked in conflict with Nasserist Egypt. Osama bin Laden himself is a Saudi, and his second-in-command, Ayman al Zawahiri, is an Egyptian who served three years in prison for his role in Sadat's assassination.

The jihadist themes in Ibn Taymiyya's teachings are striking an increasingly popular chord in parts of the Muslim world.

Al-Qaida's Geopolitical Reach

Religiously motivated militants have now dispersed widely to multiple "fields of jihad." The social and economic problems that have fueled their discontent are well known—low economic growth, falling wages and increasing joblessness, poor schooling, relentless but unsustainable urban growth, and diminishing environmental resources, especially water. Political alienation and resentment over the plight of the Palestinians and the intrusion into traditional societies of offensive images and ideas compound these problems and help account for the religious voice given to these primarily secular grievances. The mobilization of religious imagery and terminology further transforms secular issues into substantively religious ones, putting otherwise negotiable political issues beyond the realm of bargaining and making violent outcomes more likely.

The political power of religious symbols has led some pivotal states—in particular, Egypt and Saudi Arabia—to use them to buttress their own legitimacy. In so doing they perversely confer authority on the very clerical opposition that threatens state power and impedes the modernization programs that might, over the long haul, materially improve quality of life. Although the jihadists are unable to challenge these states, Islamists nevertheless dominate public discourse and shape the

debate on foreign and domestic policy. For the jihadists, the "near enemy" at home once took precedence over the "far enemy," which now includes the United States and the West. Thanks to bin Laden's doctrinal creativity, in Egypt and Saudi Arabia, Islamists have inextricably intertwined the near and far enemies. The governments' need to cater to the sentiments aroused within mosques and on the Islamist airwaves to keep their regimes secure dictates their tolerance or even endorsement of anti-American views. At the same time, strategic circumstances compel both states to provide diplomatic or other practical support for U.S. policies that offend public sensitivities. It is small wonder that Egyptians and Saudis are the backbone of al-Qaida and that Saudi Arabia spawned most of the September 11 attackers.

The fields of jihad stretch far and wide. In the Middle East, al-Qaida developed ties in Lebanon and Jordan. In Southeast Asia, Indonesians, Malaysians, and Singaporeans trained in Afghanistan, or conspired with those who had, to engage in terror, most horrifically the bombing in Bali. In Central Asia, the Islamic Movement of Uzbekistan became a full-fledged jihadist group. In Pakistan, jihadists with apocalyptic instincts nearly provoked a nuclear exchange between India and Pakistan. East Africa remains a field of jihad four years after the bombings of U.S. embassies in Kenya and Tanzania. Videotapes of atrocities of the Algerian Armed Islamic Group circulate in Europe as recruitment propaganda for the global jihad.

Given its role as a springboard for the September 11 attacks, Europe may be the most crucial field of jihad. Lack of political representation and unequal access to education, jobs, housing, and social services have turned European Muslim youth against the states in which they live. In the United Kingdom, the Muslim prison population, a source of recruits for the radical cause, has doubled in the past decade. Close to a majority of young Muslims in Britain have told pollsters that they feel no obligation to bear arms for England but would fight for bin Laden.

The United States remains al-Qaida's prime target. Suleiman Abu Ghaith, the al-Qaida spokesman, has said that there can be no truce until the group has killed four million Americans, whereupon the rest can convert to Islam.

The Recalcitrance of the Jihadists

How should the United States respond to the jihadist threat? To the extent one can speak of the root causes of the new terrorism, they defy direct and immediate remedial action. Population in the Middle East is growing rapidly, and the median age is dropping. The correlation between youth and political instability highlights the potential for unrest and radicalization. In cities, social welfare programs, sanitation, transportation, housing, power, and the water supply are deteriorating. In much of the Muslim world, the only refuge from filth, noise, heat, and, occasionally, surveillance is the mosque. Economists agree that the way out of the morass is to develop institutions that facilitate the distribution of capital and create opportunity; how to do that, they are unsure. The West can offer aid but cannot as yet correct structural problems.

Improving public opinion toward the United States is also deeply problematic. Decades of official lies and controlled press have engendered an understandable skepticism toward the assertions of any government, especially one presumed hostile to Muslim interests. Trust is based on confidence in a chain of transmission whose individual links are known to be reliable. Official news outlets or government spokespersons do not qualify as such links. Nor, certainly, do Western news media.

Moreover, highly respected critics of the United States in Saudi Arabia demonstrate an ostensibly profound understanding of U.S. policies and society, while offering a powerful and internally consistent explanation for their country's descent from the all-powerful, rich supplier of oil to the West to a debt-ridden, faltering economy protected by Christian troops and kowtowing to Israel. These are difficult narratives to counter, especially in a society where few know much about the West.

The prominent role of clerics in shaping public opinion offers yet more obstacles. The people who represent the greatest threat of terrorist action against the United States follow the preaching and guidance of Salafi clerics—the Muslim equivalent of Christian "fundamentalists." Although some Salafi preachers have forbidden waging jihad as harmful to Muslim interests, their underlying assumptions are that jihad qua holy war against non-Muslims is fundamentally valid and that Islamic governments that do not enforce *sharia* must be opposed. No authoritative clerical voice offers a sympathetic view of the United States.

The prognosis regarding root causes, then, is poor. The world is becoming more religious; Islam is the fastest-growing faith; religious expression is generally becoming more assertive and apocalyptic thinking more prominent. Weapons of mass destruction, spectacularly suited to cosmic war, will become more widely available. Democratization is at a standstill. Governments in Egypt, Saudi Arabia, Pakistan, and Indonesia are unwilling or unable to oppose anti-Western religiously based popular feeling. Immigration, conversion, and inept social policies will intensify parallel trends in Europe.

At least for now, dialogue does not appear to be an option. Meanwhile, global market forces beyond the control of Western governments hasten Western cultural penetration and generate ever-greater resentment. Jihadists could conceivably argue that they have a negotiable program: cessation of U.S. support for Israel, withdrawal from Saudi Arabia, broader American disengagement from the Islamic world. But U.S. and allied conceptions of international security and strategic imperatives will make such demands difficult, if not impossible, to accommodate.

Reducing Vulnerability to New Terrorism

Facing a global adversary with maximal goals and lacking a bargaining option or means to redress severe conditions that may or may not motivate attackers, the United States is confined primarily to a strategy of defense, deterrence by denial, and, where possible and prudent, pre-emption. Deterrence through the promise of retaliation is impossible with an adversary that controls little or no territory and invites attack.

> The United States remains al-Qaida's prime target. Suleiman Abu Ghaith, the al-Qaida spokesman, has said that there can be no truce until the group has killed four million Americans.

Adjusting to the new threat entails disturbing conceptual twists for U.S. policymakers. After generations of effort to reduce the risk of surprise attack through technical means and negotiated transparency measures, surprise will be the natural order of things. The problem of warning will be further intensified by the creativity of this adversary, its recruitment of Europeans and Americans, and its ability to stage attacks from within the United States. Thinking carefully about the unlikely—"institutionalizing imaginativeness," as Dennis Gormley has put it—is by definition a paradox, but nonetheless essential for American planners.

With warning scarce and inevitably ambiguous, it will be necessary to probe the enemy both to put him off balance and to learn of his intentions. The United States has done so clandestinely against hostile intelligence agencies. Against al-Qaida, a more difficult target, the approach will take time to cohere. Probes could also take the form of military action against al-Qaida–affiliated cantonments, where they still exist. The greater the movement's virtuality, however, the fewer the targets available for U.S. action. Preemptive strikes could target sites that develop, produce, or harbor weapons of mass destruction.

A decade of al-Qaida activity within the United States has erased the customary distinction between the domestic and the foreign in intelligence and law enforcement. The relationship between the Central Intelligence Agency and the Federal Bureau of Investigation must change. Only a more integrated organization can adapt to the seamlessness of the transnational arenas in which the terrorists operate.

Civil liberties and security must be rebalanced. How sweeping the process turns out to be will depend largely on whether the nation suffers another attack or at least a convincing attempt. Americans will have to be convinced that curtailing civil liberties is unavoidable and limited to the need to deal with proximate threats. They will need to see bipartisan consensus in Congress and between Congress and the White House and be sure that politicians are committed to keeping the rebalancing to a minimum.

The distinction between public and private sector has also been blurred. Al-Qaida has targeted the American population and used our infrastructure against us. A perpetual state of heightened readiness would impose unacceptable opportunity costs on the civilian world, so vulnerabilities must be reduced. Civilian ownership of the infrastructure is a complication. What the U.S. government does not own, it cannot completely defend. Private owners do not necessarily share the government's perception of the terrorist threat and are often able to resist regulation. Where they accept the threat, they view it as a national security issue for which the federal government should bear the cost. The idea of public-private partnership is only now finding acceptance in the cybersecurity realm as concerns over litigation have brought about a focus on due diligence. The pursuit of public-private partnership will have to be extended to all potentially vulnerable critical infrastructures by a government that does not yet understand perfectly which infrastructures are truly critical and which apparently dispensable infrastructures interact to become critical.

> ## Governments in Egypt, Saudi Arabia, Pakistan, and Indonesia are unwilling or unable to oppose anti-Western religiously based popular feeling.

Defending these infrastructures will also present unprecedented challenges. The U.S. government is not on the lookout for military formations, but for a lone, unknown person in a visa line. Technology—biometrics, data mining, super-fast data processing, and ubiquitous video surveillance—will move this needle-in-the-haystack problem into the just-possible category by providing the means to collect and store detailed and unique characteristics of huge numbers of people and match them to the person in the visa line. The cost will be the need to archive personal information on a great mass of individuals.

The United States must also devise ways to block or intercept vehicles that deliver weapons of mass destruction. It cannot do that alone. The cruise missile threat, for instance, requires the cooperation of suppliers, which means an active American role in expanding the remit of the Missile Technology Control Regime (MTCR). Weapons components themselves must be kept out of terrorists' hands. The recent adoption of MTCR controls on cheap technologies for transforming small aircraft into cruise missiles shows what can be accomplished. Washington has been buying surplus fissile materials from Russia's large stock and helping Russians render them useless for weapons; it will be vital to continue generous funding for that effort.

Remote detection of weapons, especially nuclear ones, that have reached the United States is crucial. Emergency response teams will need to be able to pinpoint the location of a device, identify its type, and know in advance how to render it safe once it has been seized. Local authorities will have to detect and identify biological and chemical agents that have been released. Genetically engineered vaccines must be rapidly developed and produced to stop local attacks from becoming national, and ultimately global, epidemics. Special medical units must be on standby to relieve local health care personnel who become exhausted or die.

Offensive opportunities will be limited but not impossible. They do, however, require impeccable intelligence, which has been hard to come by. The Afghan nexus in which jihadis initially came together and the cohesion of the groups that constitute the al-Qaida movement have made penetration forbiddingly complicated. But as al-Qaida picks up converts to Islam and Muslims who have long resided in Western countries,

penetration may become easier. The more they look like us, the more we look like them.

Another source of potentially vital information is the jihadis picked up by local authorities abroad on the basis of U.S. intelligence and then shipped to their countries of origin for interrogation. Transfers of this sort were carried out frequently during the 1990s and sometimes produced life-saving intelligence on imminent terrorist attacks. In some cases, the authorities where a suspect resides will not wish to make an arrest, fearing terrorist retaliation, political problems, or diplomatic friction. The United States has asserted the authority to conduct these operations without the consent of the host government but has generally refrained from acting. In the wake of September 11, Washington may want to reassess the risks and benefits of these actions.

Without revoking the long-standing executive order prohibiting assassination, the United States should also consider targeted killing, to use the Israeli phrase, of jihadists known to be central to an evolving conspiracy to attack the United States or to obtain weapons of mass destruction. As a practical matter, the intelligence value of such a person alive would generally outweigh the disruptive benefits of his death, assuming that U.S. or friendly intelligence services could be relied on to keep him under surveillance. But this will not always be so. When it is not, from a legal standpoint, targeted killing falls reasonably under the right to self-defense. Such a policy departure is unsavory. But in a new strategic context, with jihadis intent on mass casualties, unsavory may not be a sensible threshold. The killing of al-Qaida operatives in Yemen by missiles fired from a CIA-controlled aerial drone suggests that this threshold may already have been crossed.

Allied Cooperation

As the al-Qaida movement dissolves into virtuality in 60 countries worldwide, international cooperation becomes ever more indispensable to countering the threat.

Many countries that host al-Qaida will cooperate with the United States out of self-interest; they do not want jihadis on their soil any more than Americans do on theirs. A durable and effective counterterrorism campaign, however, requires not just bare-bones cooperation, but political collaboration at a level that tells the bureaucracies that cooperation with their American counterparts is expected. Such a robust, wholesale working relationship is what produces vital large-scale initiatives—a common diplomatic approach toward problem states; a sustainable program of economic development for the Middle East; domestic policy reforms that lessen the appeal of jihadism to Muslim diaspora communities; improved border controls; and tightened bonds among the justice ministries, law enforcement, customs, and intelligence agencies, and special operations forces on the front lines.

Whether this level of burden sharing emerges, let alone endures, depends on the give-and-take among the players. Since September 11, the United States has fostered allied perceptions that Washington is indifferent to their priorities. The United

States has not yet paid a serious penalty in terms of allied cooperation. The scale of the attacks and the administration's blend of resolve and restraint in the war on terrorism have offset allies' disappointment in its go-it-alone posture. But as the war grinds on, good will is certain to wear thin. The United States would be wise to adopt a more flexible posture to ensure allied support in the crises that will inevitably come. Washington's willingness to seek a new Security Council resolution on Iraq was a good start.

Washington's interests would also be well served by modifying what appears at times to be a monolithic view of terrorist networks that equates the Arafats and Saddams of the world with bin Laden (or his successors). Several European partners regard Arafat and his ilk as considerably more controllable through diplomacy than bin Laden. Greater American flexibility may prove essential for ensuring European capitals' military, law-enforcement, and intelligence cooperation. And the fact remains that al-Qaida has killed more Americans than have Iraq, Iran, or Palestinian groups and would use weapons of mass destruction against the United States as soon as it acquired them. A good case can be made for a preventive war against Iraq to stave off the prospect of a nuclear-armed Saddam regime. We should recognize, though, that dealing with this strategic challenge may galvanize the equally dangerous threat of mass casualty attacks by Sunni terrorists.

Israel and the Palestinians

Since the heyday of the Middle East peace process under Ehud Barak's Labor government, jihadists have exploited the Israeli-Palestinian conflict to boost their popularity. The strategem has worked: jihadists are seen as sticking up for Palestinian rights, while Arab governments do nothing. Direct, energetic U.S. diplomatic intervention in the conflict would lessen the appeal of jihadi claims and make it marginally easier for regional governments to cooperate in the war on terrorism by demonstrating American commitment to resolving the Israeli-Palestinian conflict.

The Bush administration, for good reason, fears becoming entangled in a drawn-out, venomous negotiation between irreconcilable parties. They see it distracting them from higher priorities and embroiling them in domestic political disputes over whether Washington should pressure Israel. Still, the administration has been drawn in by degrees and has announced its support for creating a Palestinian state. If the war on terrorism is now the highest U.S. priority, then more vigorous—and admittedly risky—involvement in the Israeli-Palestinian conflict is required. The jihadi argument that the United States supports the murder of Palestinian Muslims must be countered.

Democratization in the Middle East

As it continues to engage with the authoritarian regimes in Cairo and Riyadh, Washington should try to renegotiate the implicit bargain that underpins its relations with both. The current bargain is structured something like this: Egypt sustains its commitment to peace with Israel, Saudi Arabia stabilizes oil prices, and both proffer varying degrees of diplomatic support for American objectives in the region, especially toward Iraq. In return, Washington defers to their domestic policies, even if these fuel the growth and export of Islamic militancy and deflect public discontent onto the United States and Israel. With jihadis now pursuing nuclear weapons, that bargain no longer looks sensible.

Under a new bargain, Cairo and Riyadh would begin to take measured risks to lead their publics gradually toward greater political participation by encouraging opposition parties of a more secular cast and allowing greater freedom of expression. Saudi Arabia would throttle back on its wahhabiization of the Islamic world by cutting its production and export of unemployable graduates in religious studies and reducing subsidies for foreign mosques and madrasahs that propagate a confrontational and intolerant form of Islam while crowding out alternative practices. Both countries would be pushed to reform their school curricula—and enforce standards—to ensure a better understanding of the non-Islamic world and encourage respect for other cultures. With increased financial and technical assistance from the West, regimes governing societies beset by economic problems that spur radicalism would focus more consistently on the welfare of their people. In this somewhat utopian conception, leaders in both countries would use their new legitimacy to challenge Islamist myths about America and Western hostility toward Islam. In sum, Cairo and Riyadh would challenge the culture of demonization across the board, with an eye toward laying the groundwork for liberal democracy.

In the framework of this new bargain, the United States would move more boldly to establish contacts with moderate opposition figures in Egypt, Saudi Arabia, and perhaps other countries. The benefit would be twofold. Washington would get a better sense of events on the ground and would also gain credibility and perhaps even understanding on the part of critics. For this effort to bear fruit, however, the United States would have to use regional media efficiently—something for which it has as yet no well-developed strategy. Washington would also have to engage in a measure of self-scrutiny, examining how its policies contribute—in avoidable ways—to Muslim anti-Americanism. "Re-branding" is not enough.

Change will be slow. The regimes in Cairo and Riyadh face largely self-inflicted problems they cannot readily surmount without serious risks to stability. Nor is the United States entirely free to insist on the new bargain: it will need Saudi cooperation on Iraq as long as Saddam Hussein is in power, if not longer, given the uncertainties surrounding Iraq's future after Saddam leaves the stage. Egyptian support for a broader Arab-Israeli peace will also remain essential. But change has to start sometime, somewhere. It will take steady U.S. pressure and persistent attempts to convince both regimes that a new bargain will serve their countries' long-term interests. The sooner the new deals are struck, the better.

Hazardous but Not Hopeless

Western democracies face a serious, possibly transgenerational terrorist threat whose causes are multidimensional and difficult to address. The situation is hazardous, but not hopeless. The United States possesses enormous wealth, has capable allies, and stands on the leading edge of technological development that will be key to survival. A strategy that takes into account the military, intelligence, law-enforcement, diplomatic, and economic pieces of the puzzle will see America through. For the next few years, the objective will be to contain the threat, in much the same way that the United States contained Soviet power throughout the Cold War. The adversary must be prevented from doing his worst, while Washington and its allies wear down its capabilities and undermine its appeal to fellow Muslims. Success will require broad domestic support and a strong coalition abroad.

Prospects are, in many respects, bleak. But the dangers are not disproportionate to those the nation faced in the 20th century. America's initial reaction to September 11 was and indeed had to be its own self-defense: bolstering homeland security, denying al-Qaida access to weapons of mass destruction, dismantling its networks, and developing a law-enforcement and intelligence capacity to cope with the new adversary. Not all vulnerabilities can be identified and even fewer remedied, and al-Qaida need launch only one attack with a weapon of mass destruction to throw the United States into a profound crisis. Washington and its partners must convince Muslim populations that they can prosper without either destroying the West or abandoning their own traditions to the West's alien culture. That is a long-term project. American and allied determination in a war against apocalyptic—and genocidal—religious fanatics must be coupled with a generous vision about postwar possibilities. Militant Islam cannot be expected to embrace the West in the foreseeable future. But the United States can lay the foundation for a lasting accommodation by deploying its considerable economic and political advantages. It is not too late to begin.

Steven Simon is a senior fellow at the International Institute for Strategic Studies and coauthor, with Daniel Benjamin, of The Age of Sacred Terror *(Random House, October 2002).*

From the *Brookings Review*, Winter 2003. © 2003 by the Brookings Institution Press, Washington, DC. Reprinted by permission.

UNIT 6

Problems of Population, Environment, Resources, and the Future

Unit Selections

Key Points to Consider

- What are the advantages of slowing world population growth? How can it be done?

- Why are people concerned about current immigration patterns? Do you think their fears are largely imaginary? Explain your answer.

- Are you optimistic or pessimistic about the long term results of genetic engineering of humans?

- What does your crystal ball say about the future of the world? Which of the assessments of the future that are reviewed in the readings do you find the most plausible?

 **Links: www.dushkin.com/online/**
These sites are annotated in the World Wide Web pages.

Communications for a Sustainable Future
http://csf.colorado.edu

Human Rights and Humanitarian Assistance
http://www.etown.edu/vl/humrts.html

The Hunger Project
http://www.thp.org

The previous units have wrestled with many knotty problems in American society. In this unit the focus is on problems of the future, mostly from a worldwide perspective. Any discussion of the future must begin with a look at population trends. The first subsection in this unit analyzes problems of overpopulation and immigration. The second subsection looks at the environment and the problems of new technologies. The final subsection assesses the prospects for the future in very broad terms.

Some scholars are very concerned about the population's impact on the environment, and others are confident that technological developments will solve most of these problems. Since the debate is about the future, neither view can be"proved." Nevertheless, it is important to understand the seriousness of the problem. Lester Brown, Gary Gardner, and Brian Halweil discuss 16 impacts of population growth. The way societies are providing for the present 6 billion people is badly damaging Earth's ecosystems and crowding or overshooting environmental limits. Many changes are needed in the next few decades to achieve sustainability, including stabilizing world population. The World Bank provides another alarming summary of the world environmental situation. Its report also presents a"state of the world" assessment which describes world poverty, inequality and conflict. This report is a clear call to arms against these problems.

The next subsection looks at technological problems, specifically with issues that have been opened up by DNA research. The beneficial possibilities are enormous; so are the potential dangers and moral questions. For example society must now decide whether to continue to leave the creation of humans to providence and/or evolution or to genetically engineer our offspring. In this article, Colin Tudge presents the issues, options, and debates.

The final subsection assesses the prospects for the future. In the first article, Richard Pells acknowledges that American culture has a considerable impact around the world, but challenges the thesis that the culture of America is Americanizing the world as many critics argue. He points out that much of American culture is imported."American culture has spread throughout the world because it has incorporated foreign styles and ideas." In the next article, Amitai Etzioni describes the trends toward greater inequality and diversity in the United States and asks whether these trends threaten the integration of American society. Since the 1960s, identity politics have succeeded in reducing past injustices but also "have divided the nation along group lines." Etzioni draws on sociological theory to propose ways to build community by reducing inequalities, increasing bonds, and generating stronger value commitments. In the last article, William Van Dusen Wishard, a leading world trends expert, describes many historical realities that have ended and some aspects of the new era that is beginning. Currently the world is in a transition period. Some of its key trends are an increasing awareness that "our existence is a single entity" (globalization), the advance of technology to the point that technological developments could permanently alter life on Earth, and the realization that "we are in the midst of a long-term spiritual and psychological reorientation that is increasingly generating uncertainty and instability… In a sense, religion is being privatized."

16 Impacts of Population Growth

Ongoing global population growth may be THE most critical issue of today. Here are 16 ways it affects human prospects.

By Lester R. Brown, Gary Gardner, and Brian Halweil

The world's population has doubled during the last half century, climbing from 2.5 billion in 1950 to 5.9 billion in 1998. This unprecedented surge in population, combined with rising individual consumption, is pushing our claims on the planet beyond its natural limits.

The United Nations projects that human population in 2050 will range between 7.7 billion and 11.2 billion people. We use the United Nation's middle-level projection of 9.4 billion (from *World Population Prospects: The 1996 Revision*) to give an idea of the strain this "most likely" outcome would place on ecosystems and governments in the future and of the urgent need to break from the business-as-usual scenario.

Our study looks at 16 dimensions or effects of population growth in order to gain a better perspective on how future population trends are likely to affect human prospects:

Impacts on Food and Agriculture

1. Grain Production

From 1950 to 1984, growth in the world grain harvest easily exceeded that of population. But since then, the growth in the grain harvest has fallen behind that of population, so per-person output has dropped by 7% (0.5% a year), according to the U.S. Department of Agriculture.

The slower growth in the world grain harvest since 1984 is due to the lack of new land and to slower growth in irrigation and fertilizer use because of the diminishing returns of these inputs.

Now that the frontiers of agricultural settlement have disappeared, future growth in grain production must come almost entirely from raising land productivity. Unfortu-

nately, this is becoming more difficult. The challenge for the world's farmers is to reverse this decline at a time when cropland area per person is shrinking, the amount of irrigation water per person is dropping, and the crop yield response to additional fertilizer use is falling.

2. Cropland

Since mid-century, grain area—which serves as a proxy for cropland in general—has increased by some 19%, but global population has grown by 132%. Population growth can degrade farmland, reducing its productivity or even eliminating it from production. As grain area per person falls, more and more nations risk losing the capacity to feed themselves.

The trend is illustrated starkly in the world's four fastest-growing

Shanty town life in Bangladesh. Countries that fail to reduce population growth will endure the breakdown of their economic and social systems, according to the authors.

large countries. Having already seen per capita grain area shrink by 40%–50% between 1960 and 1998, Pakistan, Nigeria, Ethiopia, and Iran can expect a further 60%–70% loss by 2050—a conservative projection that assumes no further losses of agricultural land. The result will be four countries with a combined population of more than 1 billion whose grain area per person will be only 300–600 square meters—less than a quarter of the area in 1950.

3. Fresh Water

Spreading water scarcity may be the most underrated resource issue in the world today. Wherever population is growing, the supply of fresh water per person is declining.

Evidence of water stress can be seen as rivers are drained dry and water tables fall. Rivers such as the Nile, the Yellow, and the Colorado have little water left when they reach the sea. Water tables are now falling on every continent, including in major food-producing regions. Aquifers are being depleted in the U.S. southern Great Plains, the North China Plain, and most of India.

The International Water Management Institute projects that a billion people will be living in countries facing absolute water scarcity by 2025. These countries will have to reduce water use in agriculture in order to satisfy residential and industrial water needs. In both China and India, the two countries that together dominate world irrigated agriculture, substantial cutbacks in irrigation water supplies lie ahead.

4. Oceanic Fish Catch

A fivefold growth in the human appetite for seafood since 1950 has pushed the catch of most oceanic fisheries to their sustainable limits or beyond. Marine biologists believe that the oceans cannot sustain an annual catch of much more than 93 million tons, the current take.

As we near the end of the twentieth century, overfishing has become the rule, not the exception. Of the 15 major oceanic fisheries, 11 are in decline. The catch of Atlantic cod—long a dietary mainstay for western Europeans—has fallen by 70% since peaking in 1968. Since 1970, bluefin tuna stocks in the West Atlantic have dropped by 80%.

With the oceans now pushed to their limits, future growth in the demand for seafood can be satisfied only by fish farming. But as the world turns to aquaculture to satisfy its needs, fish begin to compete with livestock and poultry for feedstuffs such as grain, soybean meal, and fish meal.

The next half century is likely to be marked by the disappearance of some species from markets, a decline in the quality of seafood caught, higher prices, and more conflicts among countries over access to fisheries. Each year, the future oceanic catch per person will decline by roughly the amount of population growth, dropping to 9.9 kilograms (22 pounds) per person in 2050, compared with the 1988 peak of 17.2 kilograms (37.8 pounds).

5. Meat Production

When incomes begin to rise in traditional low-income societies, one of the first things people do is diversify their diets, consuming more livestock products.

World meat production since 1950 has increased almost twice as fast as population. Growth in meat

©PHOTODISC, INC.

The demand for energy will grow faster than population and create even more pollution as developing countries try to become as affluent as industrialized nations.

production was originally concentrated in western industrial countries and Japan, but over the last two decades it has increased rapidly in East Asia, the Middle East, and Latin America. Beef, pork, and poultry account for the bulk of world consumption.

Of the world grain harvest of 1.87 billion tons in 1998, an estimated 37% will be used to feed livestock and poultry, producing milk and eggs as well as meat, according to the U.S. Department of Agriculture. Grain fed to livestock and poultry is now the principal food reserve in the event of a world food emergency.

Total meat consumption will rise from 211 million tons in 1997 to 513 million tons in 2050, increasing pressures on the supply of grain.

Environment and Resources

6. Natural Recreation Areas

From Buenos Aires to Bangkok, dramatic population growth in the world's major cities—and the sprawl and pollution they bring—threaten natural recreation areas that lie beyond city limits. On every continent, human encroachment has reduced both the size and the quality of natural recreation areas.

In nations where rapid population growth has outstripped the carrying capacity of local resources, protected areas become especially vulnerable. Although in industrial nations these areas are synonymous with camping, hiking, and picnics in the country, in Asia, Africa, and Latin America most national parks, forests, and preserves are inhabited or used for natural resources by local populations.

Migration-driven population growth also endangers natural recreation areas in many industrial nations. Everglades National Park, for example, faces collapse as millions of newcomers move into southern Florida.

Longer waiting lists and higher user fees for fewer secluded spots are likely to be the tip of the iceberg, as population growth threatens to eliminate the diversity of habitats and cultures in addition to the peace and quiet that protected areas currently offer.

7. Forests

Global losses of forest area have marched in step with population growth for much of human history, but an estimated 75% of the loss in global forests has occurred in the twentieth century.

In Latin America, ranching is the single largest cause of deforestation. In addition, overgrazing and overcollection of firewood—which are often a function of growing population—are degrading 14% of the world's remaining large areas of virgin forest.

Deforestation created by the demand for forest products tracks closely with rising per capita consumption in recent decades. Global use of paper and paperboard per person has doubled (or nearly tripled) since 1961.

The loss of forest areas leads to a decline of forest services. These include habitat for wildlife; carbon storage, which is a key to regulating climate; and erosion control, provision of water across rainy and dry seasons, and regulation of rainfall.

8. Biodiversity

We live amid the greatest extinction of plant and animal life since the dinosaurs disappeared 65 million years ago, at the end of the Cretaceous period, with species losses at 100 to 1,000 times the natural rate. The principal cause of species extinction is habitat loss, which tends to accelerate with an increase in a country's population density.

A particularly productive but vulnerable habitat is found in coastal areas, home to 60% of the world's population. Coastal wetlands nurture two-thirds of all commercially caught fish, for example. And coral reefs have the second-highest concentration of biodiversity in the world, after tropical rain forests. But human encroachment and pollution are degrading these areas: Roughly half of the world's salt marshes and mangrove swamps have been eliminated or radically altered, and two-thirds of the world's coral reefs have been degraded, 10% of them "beyond recognition." As coastal migration continues—coastal dwellers could account for 75% of world population within 30 years—the pressures on these productive habitats will likely increase.

9. Climate Change

Over the last half century, carbon emissions from fossil-fuel burning expanded at nearly twice the rate of population, boosting atmospheric concentrations of carbon dioxide, the principal greenhouse gas, by 30% over preindustrial levels.

The 20 Largest Countries Ranked According to Population Size (in millions)

1998 Rank	Country	Population	2050 Country	Population
1	China	1,255	India	1,533
2	India	976	China	1,517
3	United States	274	Pakistan	357
4	Indonesia	207	United States	348
5	Brazil	165	Nigeria	339
6	Pakistan	148	Indonesia	318
7	Russia	147	Brazil	243
8	Japan	126	Bangladesh	218
9	Bangladesh	124	Ethiopia	213
10	Nigeria	122	Iran	170
11	Mexico	96	The Congo	165
12	Germany	82	Mexico	154
13	Vietnam	78	Philippines	131
14	Iran	73	Vietnam	130
15	Philippines	72	Egypt	115
16	Egypt	66	Russia	114
17	Turkey	64	Japan	110
18	Ethiopia	62	Turkey	98
19	Thailand	60	South Africa	91
20	France	59	Tanzania	89

SOURCE: UNITED NATIONS, WORLD POPULATION PROSPECTS: THE 1996 REVISION.

Fossil-fuel use accounts for roughly three-quarters of world carbon emissions. As a result, regional growth in carbon emissions tend to occur where economic activity and related energy use is projected to grow most rapidly. Emissions in China are projected to grow over three times faster than population in the next 50 years due to a booming economy that is heavily reliant on coal and other carbon-rich energy sources.

Emissions from developing countries will nearly quadruple over the next half century, while those from industrial nations will increase by 30%, according to the Intergovernmental Panel on Climate Change and the U.S. Department of Energy. Although annual emissions from industrial countries are currently twice as high as from developing ones, the latter are on target to eclipse the industrial world by 2020.

10. Energy

The global demand for energy grew twice as fast as population over the last 50 years. By 2050, developing countries will be consuming much more energy as their populations increase and become more affluent.

When per capita energy consumption is high, even a low rate of population growth can have significant effects on total energy demand. In the United States, for example, the 75 million people projected to be added to the population by 2050 will boost energy demand to roughly the present energy consumption of Africa and Latin America.

World oil production per person reached a high in 1979 and has since declined by 23%. Estimates of when global oil production will peak range from 2011 to 2025, signaling future price shocks as long as oil remains the world's dominant fuel.

In the next 50 years, the greatest growth in energy demands will come where economic activity is projected to be highest: in Asia, where consumption is expected to

Demographic Fatigue

To assess the likelihood that the U.N. population projections will actually occur, it is useful to bear in mind the concept of the demographic transition, formulated by Princeton demographer Frank Notestein in 1945. Its three stages help to explain widely disparate population-growth rates.

The first stage describes pre-industrial societies: Birthrates and death rates are both high, offsetting each other and leading to little or no population growth. In stage two, countries reach an unsustainable state as they begin to modernize: Death rates fall to low levels while birthrates remain high. In the third state, modernization continues: Birth and death rates are again in balance, but at lower levels, and populations are essentially stable. All countries today are in either stage two or stage three.

One key question now facing the world is whether the 150 or so countries that are still in stage two, with continuing population growth, can make it into stage three by quickly reducing births. Governments of countries that have been in stage two for several decades are typically worn down and drained of financial resources by the consequences of rapid population growth, in effect suffering from "demographic fatigue." Such countries are losing the struggle to educate their children, create jobs, and cope with environmental problems such as erosion, deforestation, and aquifer depletion.

Demographic fatigue is perhaps most evident in the inability of many governments to combat the resurgence of traditional diseases, such as malaria or tuberculosis, and new diseases, such as AIDS. If these threats are not dealt with, they can force countries back into stage one. For several African countries with high HIV infection levels, this is no longer a hypothetical prospect. Although most industrialized nations have held infection levels under 1%, governments overwhelmed by population pressures have not.

Zimbabwe, for example, has a 26% adult HIV infection rate and cannot pay for the costly drugs needed to treat the disease. Zimbabwe is expected to reach population stability in 2002 as death rates from the HIV/AIDS epidemic climb to offset birthrates, essentially falling back into stage one. Other African countries that are likely to follow include Botswana, Namibia, Zambia, and Swaziland.

—Lester R. Brown, Gary Gardner, and Brian Halweil

grow 361%, though population will grow by just 50%. Energy consumption is also expected to increase in Latin America (by 340%) and Africa (by 326%). In all three regions, local pressures on energy sources, ranging from forests to fossil fuel reserves to waterways, will be significant.

11. Waste

Local and global environmental effects of waste disposal will likely worsen as 3.4 billion people are added to the world's population over the next half century. Prospects for providing access to sanitation are dismal in the near to medium term.

A growing population increases society's disposal headaches—the garbage, sewage, and industrial waste that must be gotten rid of. Even where population is largely stable—the case in many industrialized countries—the flow of waste products into landfills and waterways generally continues to increase. Where high rates of economic and population growth coincide in

coming decades, as they will in many developing countries, mountains of waste will likely pose difficult disposal challenges for municipal and national authorities.

Economic Impacts and Quality of Life

12. Jobs

Since 1950, the world's labor force has more than doubled—from 1.2 billion people to 2.7 billion—outstripping the growth in job creation. Over the next half century, the world will need to create more than 1.9 billion jobs in the developing world just to maintain current levels of employment.

While population growth may boost labor demand (through economic activity and demand for goods), it will most definitely boost labor supply. As the balance between the demand and supply of labor is tipped by population growth, wages tend to decrease. And in a situation of labor surplus, the quality of

jobs may not improve as fast, for workers will settle for longer hours, fewer benefits, and less control over work activities.

As the children of today represent the workers of tomorrow, the interaction between population growth and jobs is most acute in nations with young populations. Nations with more than half their population below the age of 25 (e.g., Peru, Mexico, Indonesia, and Zambia) will feel the burden of this labor flood. Employment is the key to obtaining food, housing, health services, and education, in addition to providing self-respect and self-fulfillment.

13. Income

Incomes have risen most rapidly in developing countries where population has slowed the most, including South Korea, Taiwan, China, Indonesia, and Malaysia. African countries, largely ignoring family planning, have been overwhelmed by the sheer numbers of young people who need to be educated and employed.

Small families are the key to stabilizing population. Convincing couples everywhere to restrict their childbearing to replacement-level fertility is important enough to warrant a worldwide campaign, according to the authors.

If the world cannot simultaneously convert the economy to one that is environmentally sustainable and move to a lower population trajectory, economic decline will be hard to avoid.

14. Housing

The ultimate manifestation of population growth outstripping the supply of housing is homelessness. The United Nations estimates that at least 100 million of the world's people—roughly equal to the population of Mexico—have no home; the number tops 1 billion if squatters and others with insecure or temporary accommodations are included.

Unless population growth can be checked worldwide, the ranks of the homeless are likely to swell dramatically.

15. Education

In nations that have increasing child-age populations, the base pressures on the educational system will be severe. In the world's 10 fastest-growing countries, most of which are in Africa and the Middle East, the child-age population will increase an average of 93% over the next 50 years. Africa as a whole will see its school-age population grow by 75% through 2040.

If national education systems begin to stress lifelong learning for a rapidly changing world of the twenty-first century, then extensive provision for adult education will be necessary, affecting even those countries with shrinking child-age populations.

Such a development means that countries which started population-stabilization programs earliest will be in the best position to educate their entire citizenry.

16. Urbanization

Today's cities are growing faster: It took London 130 years to get from 1 million to 8 million inhabitants; Mexico City made this jump in just 30 years. The world's urban population as a whole is growing by just over 1 million people each week. This urban growth is fed by the natural increase of urban populations, by net migration from the countryside, and by villages or towns expanding to the point where they become cities or they are absorbed by the spread of existing cities.

If recent trends continue, 6.5 billion people will live in cities by 2050, more than the world's total population today.

Actions for Slowing Growth

As we look to the future, the challenge for world leaders is to help countries maximize the prospects for achieving sustainability by keeping both birth and death rates low. In a world where both grain output and fish catch per person are falling, a strong case can be made on humanitarian grounds to stabilize world population.

What is needed is an all-out effort to lower fertility, particularly in the high-fertility countries, while there is still time. We see four key steps in doing this:

Assess carrying capacity. Every national government needs a carefully articulated and adequately supported population policy, one that takes into account the country's carrying capacity at whatever consumption level citizens decide on.

Without long-term estimates of available cropland, water for irrigation, and likely yields, governments are simply flying blind into the future, allowing their nations to drift into a world in which population growth and environmental degradation can lead to social disintegration.

Fill the family-planning gap. This is a high-payoff area. In a world where population pressures are mounting, the inability of 120 million of the world's women to get family-planning services is inexcusable. A stumbling block: At the International Conference on Population and Development in Cairo in 1994, the industrialized countries agreed to pay one-third of the costs for reproductive-health services in developing countries. So far they have failed to do so.

Educate young women. Educating girls is a key to accelerating the shift to smaller families. In every society for which data are available, the more education women have, the fewer children they have. Closely related to the need for education of young females is the need to provide equal opportunities for women in all phases of national life.

Have just two children. If we are facing a population emergency, it should be treated as such. It may be time for a campaign to convince couples everywhere to restrict their childbearing to replacement-level fertility.

About the Authors

Lester R. Brown is founder, president, and a senior researcher at the Worldwatch Institute, 1776 Massachusetts Avenue, N.W., Washington, D.C. 20036. Telephone 1-202-452-1999; Web site www.worldwatch.org.

Gary Gardner is a senior Worldwatch researcher and has written on agriculture, waste, and materials issues for *State of the World* and *World Watch* magazine.

Brian Halweil is a Worldwatch staff researcher and writes on issues related to food and agriculture, HIV/AIDS, cigarettes, and biotechnology.

This article is drawn from their report *Beyond Malthus: Sixteen Dimensions of the Population Problem*. Worldwatch Institute. 1998. 98 pages. Paperback. $5.

Achievements and Challenges

W*orld Development Report 2003* is about sustainable development. It is about people and how we deal with each other. It is about our home planet and its fabric of life. And it is about our aspirations for prosperity and posterity.

Any serious attempt at reducing poverty requires sustained economic growth in order to increase productivity and income in developing countries. But there is more to development than just economic growth—much more. This Report argues that ensuring sustainable development requires attention not just to economic growth but also to environmental and social issues. Unless the transformation of society and the management of the environment are addressed integrally along with economic growth, growth itself will be jeopardized over the longer term.

Environment and social issues, when not addressed, accumulate over time and have consequences that do not show up in the shorter time horizons typical of economic policymaking. That is why this Report adopts a longer time horizon of 20 to 50 years. Within this time frame it is possible to identify environmental and social problems—local, national, and global—that can have very costly or even irreversible consequences if not addressed immediately. For other problems, where the consequences are not irreversible, the longer time horizon provides the lead time to start changing attitudes and institutions and so make it possible to respond before the problems become crises.

In short, this Report takes a comprehensive, longer term, and dynamic view of sustainability, with a clear focus on poverty reduction.

The core development challenge

Most current estimates suggest that 2 billion people will be added to the world's population over the next 30 years and another billion in the following 20 years.[1] Virtually all of this increase will be in developing countries, the bulk of it in urban areas. In these same countries, 2.5 billion to 3 billion people now live on less than $2 a day.[2] The core challenge for development is to ensure productive work and a better quality of life for all these people. This will require substantial growth in productivity and incomes in developing countries.

The challenge may seem daunting—and it is. But over the past 30 years world population also rose by 2 billion.[3] And this growth was accompanied by considerable progress in improving human well-being, as measured by human development indicators. Average income per capita (population-weighted in 1995 dollars) in developing countries grew from $989 in 1980 to $1,354 in 2000.[4] Infant mortality was cut in half, from 107 per 1,000 live births to 58, as was adult illiteracy, from 47 to 25 percent.[5]

Looking back to the 1950s and 1960s, it was feared at the time that the developing countries—particularly China, India, and Indonesia—would not be able to feed their rapidly growing populations. Thanks to the green revolution in agriculture, the doomsday scenarios of famine and starvation did not materialize in these, the most populous, developing countries. In the 1960s and 1970s the Club of Rome and many other groups forecast that the Earth would rapidly run out of key natural resources. So far, this has not happened, again because changes in technology and in preferences have allowed the substitution of new resources for existing ones—for example, fiber optics in place of copper. Global action has also led to major strides in eliminating disease scourges (smallpox and river blindness), and in addressing new problems (ozone depletion).

But accompanying these achievements were some negative social and environmental patterns that must not be repeated in the next 50 years if development is to be sustained.

- *Poverty: declining, but still a challenge.* There has been a significant drop in the percentage of people living in extreme poverty (that is, living on less than $1 per day). Even the absolute number of very poor people declined between 1980 and 1998 by at least 200 million, to almost 1.2 billion in 1998.[6] The decrease was primarily due to the decline in the number of very poor people in China as a result of its strong growth from 1980 onward.[7] Since 1993, there have also been encouraging signs of renewed poverty reduction in India. Sub-Saharan Africa, by contrast, has seen its number of very poor people increase steadily. Yet in 1998, despite the decline in Asia and the increase in Sub-Saharan Africa, East Asia and South Asia still accounted for two-thirds of the world's very poor people, and Sub-Saharan Africa for one-quarter. Development strategies will need to do better in eliminating abject poverty. The estimated 1 billion very poor people is of the same order of magnitude as the independently generated figures on the number of people who are undernourished and underweight.[8]
- *Inequality: widening.* The average income in the richest 20 countries is now 37 times that in the poorest 20. This ratio has doubled in the past 40 years, mainly because of lack of growth in the poorest countries.[9] Similar increases in inequality are found within many (but not all) countries.
- *Conflict: devastating.* In the 1990s, 46 countries were involved in conflict, primarily civil.[10] This included more than half of the poorest countries (17 out of 33). These conflicts have very high costs, destroying past development gains and leaving a legacy of damaged assets and mistrust that impedes future gains.

The increased scale and reach of human activity have also put great pressure on local and global common property resources (water, soil, and fisheries), as well as on local and global sinks (the ability of the biosphere to absorb waste and regulate climate).

- *Air: polluted.* At the local level, hundreds of developing-country cities have unhealthy levels of air pollution (see chapter 3, figure 3.4). At the global level, the biosphere's capacity to absorb carbon dioxide without altering temperatures has been compromised because of heavy reliance on fossil fuels for energy. Global energy use traditionally has grown at the same rate as gross domestic product (GDP). Greenhouse gas (GHG) emissions will continue to grow unless a concerted effort is made to increase energy efficiency and move away from today's heavy reliance on fossil fuels.[11] In the past 50 years excess nitrogen—mainly from fertilizers, human sewage, and combustion of fossil fuels—has begun to overwhelm the global nitrogen cycle, giving rise to a variety of ill effects ranging from reduced soil fertility to excess nutrients in lakes, rivers, and coastal waters. On current trends, the amount of biologically available nitrogen will double in 25 years.[12]
- *Fresh water: increasingly scarce.* Fresh water consumption is rising quickly, and the availability of water in some regions is likely to become one of the most pressing issues of the 21st century. One-third of the world's people live in countries that are already experiencing moderate to high water shortages. That proportion could (at current population forecasts) rise to half or more in the next 30 years unless institutions change to ensure better conservation and allocation of water.[13] More than a billion people in low- and middle-income countries—and 50 million people in high-income countries—lacked access to safe water for drinking, personal hygiene, and domestic use in 1995.[14]
- *Soil: being degraded.* Nearly 2 billion hectares of land worldwide (23 percent of all cropland, pasture, forest, and woodland) have been degraded since the 1950s. About 39 percent of these lands are lightly degraded, 46 percent moderately degraded, and 16 percent so severely degraded that the change is too costly to reverse. Some areas face sharp losses in productivity. Grasslands do not fare much better: close to 54 percent show degradation, with 5 percent being strongly degraded.[15]
- *Forests: being destroyed.* Deforestation is proceeding at a significant rate. One-fifth of all tropical forests have been cleared since 1960.[16] According to the Food and Agriculture Organization of the United Nations (FAO), deforestation has been concentrated in the developing world, which lost nearly 200 million hectares between 1980 and 1995. In the Brazilian Amazon annual deforestation rates varied between 11,000 and 29,000 square kilometers a year in the 1990s. Deforestation in developing countries has several causes, including the conversion of forests to large-scale ranching and plantations and the expansion of subsistence farming. At the same time, forest cover in industrial countries is stable or even increasing slightly, although the forest ecosystem has been somewhat altered. According to a 1997 World Resources Institute (WRI) assessment, just one-fifth of the Earth's original forest remains in large, relatively natural ecosystems.[17]

- *Biodiversity: disappearing*. Through a series of local extinctions, the ranges of many plants and animals have been reduced from those at the beginning of the century. In addition, many plants and animals are unique to certain areas. One-third of terrestrial biodiversity, accounting for 1.4 percent of the Earth's surface, is in vulnerable "hot spots" and is threatened with complete loss in the event of natural disasters or further human encroachment.[18] Some statistics suggest that 20 percent of all endangered species are threatened by species, introduced by human activity, alien to the locality.[19]

- *Fisheries: declining*. The aquatic environment and its productivity are on the decline. About 58 percent of the world's coral reefs and 34 percent of all fish species are at risk from human activities.[20] Seventy percent of the world's commercial fisheries are fully exploited or overexploited and experiencing declining yields.[21]

None of these social and environmental patterns is consistent with sustained growth in an interdependent world over the long term. Given the social and environmental stresses caused by past development strategies, the goal of raising human well-being worldwide must be pursued through a development process that "does better"—a poverty-eliminating growth path that integrates social and environmental concerns in pursuit of the goal of sustained improvements in well-being.

Windows of opportunity

The development process is about change and transformation. Economies evolve. Societies and cultures evolve. Nature evolves. But they evolve at different speeds, creating stresses that need to be addressed and managed.[22] Moreover, in an era of globalization, the growing scale and speed of change in human activity are in some cases outpacing the rate at which natural processes and life-support systems can adapt.[23] Globalization and faster technological change are also altering the nature of social interaction and affecting the efficacy of existing institutions. Although globalization and technological change offer many benefits, they can have deleterious side effects if institutions at local, national, and international levels do not evolve fast enough to deal with the adverse spillovers. The consequences of previous patterns of development are also beginning to bind, restricting certain growth paths or making them more costly.[24]

But these processes, if managed well, can create new opportunities. Of the many interrelated drivers of change and transformation, four stand out: scientific and technological innovation, income growth, population growth, and urbanization. The first two are likely to continue changing preferences and providing new opportunities to satisfy these preferences. The demographic and urban transitions, by contrast, are one-time changes, and the opportunities they offer are perhaps less well recognized. These are discussed in the next section.

- *Scientific and technological innovation*. The flow of information and ideas, boosted greatly by the Internet, can enable developing countries to learn more rapidly from each other and from industrial countries. It can also facilitate the emergence of networks to monitor a wider array of development impacts. Other technological changes can enable developing countries to leapfrog stages in the development process that rely on inefficient uses of natural resources. Science and technology can help address major socioeconomic problems. As noted, the green revolution was critical in enabling many developing countries to avoid widespread starvation. To benefit from these opportunities, institutions are needed that can stimulate and diffuse technological innovations and avoid or mitigate any deleterious consequences.

- *Income growth*. A projected growth in global income of 3 percent a year over the next 50 years implies a fourfold increase in global GDP. Increasing income growth may place a strain on the environmental and social fabric if there is too little attention to shifting consumption and production patterns. But this future economic growth will also require major investments in new human-made capital to expand capacity and to replace existing capacity as it ages. Making these investments (many of which are long lived) more environmentally and socially responsible through appropriate investment criteria will go a long way toward putting development on a more sustainable path—an opportunity not to be missed.

Opportunities in the demographic transition

When today's industrial countries were themselves developing, their population densities and growth rates were much lower than those of developing countries today, and the pressure on their resources was consequently lower. They also had a more evenly distributed age structure and lower dependency rates, allowing social institutions to adapt gradually to the requirements of a changing population.

Populations in industrial countries as a group were fairly stable for most of the second half of the 20th century. As a result, the growth in world population in this period has been driven primarily by population growth in developing countries. The stresses and spillovers from this population growth are generally observed not, as was originally expected, at the aggregate level (for example, in large-scale famines and food shortages) but, rather, in more insidious ways—in many smaller interactions between population, poverty, and resources.[25] The outcomes are felt in greater pressures on fragile lands, in lower wages, and in persistent unemployment.

Figure 1.1
Global population approaching stability

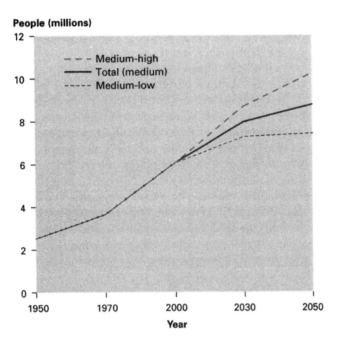

People (millions)

Note: Medium-high and medium-low variants based on U.N. projections of medium-high and medium-low scenarios scaled to World Bank aggregates.
Source: World Bank estimates.

It is now clear that a global demographic transition is well underway, even if it is not yet complete. This is a major historic opportunity. World population is expected to stabilize by the end of this century at 9 billion to 10 billion people, 20 to 30 percent lower than forecast in the 1960s and 1970s. Many factors have contributed to this slow-down:

- More educated, employed women and smaller families
- Greater off-farm opportunities, creating a need for more education for children
- Widespread dissemination of modern contraceptive technology, making it easier for people to plan childbearing.

Of the expected population increase, 85 percent (3 billion) will be born in the next 50 years (figure 1.1). But the speed of the transition, and the resulting population size and structure, will vary by region (figure 1.2) and by country. If fertility rates do not fall as rapidly as now projected, aggregate populations will be larger, putting greater pressures on natural resources and the social fabric. If they drop faster, many countries will have to deal sooner than expected with another problem—an aging population. This can have major consequences, especially for rural populations, for whom formal social safety nets

are either nonexistent or not well developed. For example, one consequence of China's one-child policy—which dramatically and successfully lowered aggregate population—may be that by 2030 as much as one-third of the population will be over age 65.[26]

Influencing the demographic processes in many countries is the growing incidence of HIV/AIDS, malaria, and tuberculosis. For example, current estimates and projections in Sub-Saharan Africa indicate increasingly large losses of working-age people to the AIDS epidemic. The economic impact of such high mortality is especially serious because enormous private and public investments have already been made in members of this age group. The loss of their productive lives leaves large and unpredictable gaps in the labor force. Malaria causes high levels of adult sickness rather than deaths, but this too inflicts heavy losses on labor productivity. Changes in the incidence of disease will have profound effects on health expenditures in these African countries.

Figure 1.2
Some regions growing fast, others stable

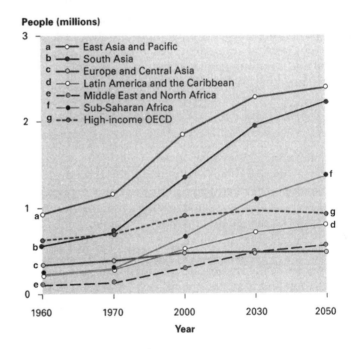

People (millions)

a — East Asia and Pacific
b — South Asia
c — Europe and Central Asia
d — Latin America and the Caribbean
e — Middle East and North Africa
f — Sub-Saharan Africa
g — High-income OECD

Source: WDI database and SIMA.

With declining fertility, the age structure of the population changes, opening a window of opportunity in developing countries for a few decades—a window they can use for catching up and raising welfare for all. As figure 1.3 shows, the proportion of the working-age population rises in relation to the proportions of children (those under 15) and the elderly (over 65), enabling societies to spend less on school construction and on old-age medical

Figure 1.3
Dependency ratios on the decline—for a while

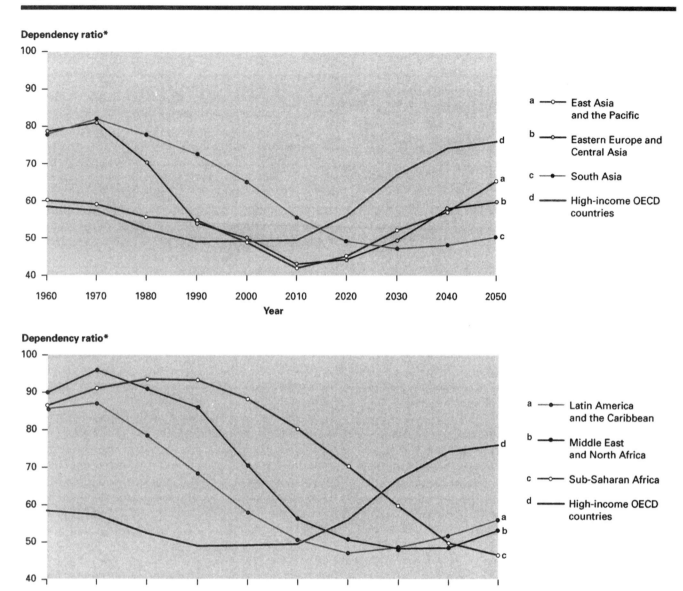

Dependency ratio*

a —○— East Asia and the Pacific

b —○— Eastern Europe and Central Asia

c —●— South Asia

d —— High-income OECD countries

Dependency ratio*

a —●— Latin America and the Caribbean

b —●— Middle East and North Africa

c —○— Sub-Saharan Africa

d —— High-income OECD countries

* The dependency ratio is the ratio of the non-working-age population (under 15 years old and over 64 years old) to the working-age population (ages 15 to 64).
Source: World Bank (2001g)

expenses and to invest the savings in generating economic growth. But such benefits will materialize only if the members of the working-age population are gainfully employed and have opportunities to expand their asset base. Eventually, dependency ratios rise again as these workers age, and the window of opportunity starts to close, as it will soon begin doing in East Asia and Eastern Europe (see figure 1.3).

Some regions, notably East Asia, have benefited substantially from the drop in the ratio of dependents to workers.[27] Investment in forming a skilled, healthy labor force, combined with policy and institutional settings conducive to using this labor force effectively, helped generate strong economic growth. Two keys to success were maintenance of an open economy and investment in sectors with high growth potential. Since most developing regions will continue to experience relatively low dependency ratios for some decades, careful preparation now can help make the most of their windows of opportunity.

Until now, populations have been growing too rapidly for fiscally constrained governments to expand the provision of jobs, infrastructure, and public services enough to keep pace with people's needs. This task will become easier now that the global population is approaching stability. Governments in both urban and rural areas can move from catching up with the quantitative need for services, to upgrading their quality. Much of the social tension and frustration arising from unemployment and poor public services can then be attenuated.

Lower rates of population growth will reduce pressure on natural resources, but this will be offset by the increase in per capita consumption. The latter trend makes it essential to adopt the technologies and growth paths for production and consumption that will ensure the sustainable use of natural resources. To benefit from the opportunities a stabilizing population provides, it is critical to anticipate problems and identify development strategies for getting through the transition period (the next 20 to 50 years) without creating conditions that generate further conflict or resource degradation.

Opportunities in the urban transition

As countries move from poverty to affluence, the required growth in productivity involves a shift from heavy dependence on agriculture as a primary source of employment and income to nonagricultural activities that do not make intensive use of land. This is generally accompanied by a major shift in population from rural to urban areas. Indeed, the most important socioeconomic and cultural transformation over the past 150 years has been the transformation of relatively closed, exclusive, custom-based rural societies into relatively open, inclusive, innovation-oriented urban societies.[28]

Rural communities, especially in less accessible areas, have long adapted to their circumstances, developing vibrant, self-sufficient communities. As long as risks could be absorbed locally, these communities continued to learn and adapt. Dependence on local ecosystems, however, imposed limits on risk taking and innovation. This autonomous development path changes as rural areas become drawn into larger markets and strengthen their links with urban areas, making trade networks and distance from market centers more critical features of development opportunities and local resource pressures.

Increasing densities in towns and cities, and the greater connectivity between cities, as well as between urban and rural areas, increases the catchment area of markets and the returns to economic endeavor. If managed well, this transformation enables the emergence of new activities and productive job opportunities. Towns, as market centers for a rural hinterland, start the process of creating economies of scale for nonagricultural activities.

Urban society also permits the spreading of risks over larger numbers of people and activities. Knowledge flows more readily, through increased opportunities for face-to-face contacts among various actors. And the need to accommodate diverse views and meet rapidly changing challenges stimulates innovation and new applications of technology. As a result, larger cities become incubators of new values—among them, risk taking and innovation.

Creativity, knowledge flow, the increasing scale of activities, and larger catchment areas are central to specialization and productivity growth. This is true not just for the production of goods but also for the provision of services. A village or neighborhood can support a primary school or basic clinic, and the local teacher or doctor can be a generalist. But providing higher, more sophisticated, and more differentiated education and health care requires more specialized skills. Because of the fixed costs of supporting these specialized skills, a larger catchment area (a town or a subsection of a city) is required. The higher population densities, lower transport costs, and lower communications costs in towns and cities make the more specialized operations possible. In moving further up the hierarchy of required specialization, the required catchment area also increases. So, the transition from villages to towns, and from cities to metropolitan areas, corresponds to the different functional capabilities of larger, higher-density conurbations. The potential benefits of higher densities and greater connectivity can be more easily realized if the investment climate is improved through better enabling rules and frameworks and better physical infrastructure. Stimulating and attracting investments—in particular, by the small and medium-size enterprises that provide most of the jobs for growing urban populations—is the key to accommodating the expected growth in urban populations and ensuring their ability to pay for needed urban services and amenities.

Seeing the socioeconomic transformations in spatial terms

Economists and engineers focus on the sectoral changes that accompany economic growth and technological innovations. This is understandable when focusing on GDP and the emergence or obsolescence of industries, but it is not very helpful for understanding the impact of these changes on society and nature. The most fundamental social and economic transformation—from traditional rural to modern urban—is manifested spatially. Except in the most populous countries, such as China and India, rural societies are relatively low in density and heavily dependent on agriculture as the primary source of employment and output. Modern urban societies are generally higher in density and dependent on activities that benefit from proximity and do not require a great deal of land, such as manufacturing and services. These activities and land use patterns generate different types of sociocultural and environmental problems.

Most ecosystems, too, are defined spatially. Much flora and fauna is locally unique and adapts gradually to changes in local circumstances. Local problems and stresses appear earliest, whether in the form of local extinctions, the reduction of the ranges of many plants and animals, or soil, air, and water pollution. These changes, the result of local development pressures, do not show up at national and global levels until they accumulate, but they provide early warning of problematic consequences of current development patterns.

The jurisdictions of many institutions that make or implement rules and laws (legislatures, constitutions, and government agencies) are also defined spatially. Often, the spatial jurisdiction of institutions does not match the spatial nature of the social and environmental problems generated by economic activity—one reason for the persistence of these problems.

Given our interest in people, where they live, and how they interact with each other and with nature, it is important to look at where people are now and where they are likely to be in the future. The world's population increased by more than 3.5 billion people in the past 50 years, and 85 percent of these added people were in developing and transition countries (see Figure 1 in the Roadmap). The number of people living in fragile rural areas in developing countries doubled, in stark contrast to the declining numbers in this category in high-income countries. The number of cities with a population of more than 10 million people went from 0 to 15 in developing countries but only from 1 to 4 in high-income countries.

In the next 30 to 50 years the 2 billion to 3 billion increase in the world's population will be almost exclusively (97 percent) in developing and transition countries, and virtually all of it will be in urban areas. The growth of the urban population is driven by natural increase, rural-to-urban migration, and the incorporation of high-density rural areas on the urban fringe. The number of megacities in developing countries is likely to increase to 54, while it will stabilize at 5 in high-income countries. It is not yet clear whether the number of people living in fragile areas will continue to increase, but it probably will unless migration opportunities change. As many as 2 billion people will live in two areas that are difficult to manage: fragile rural areas and megacities.[29] Dealing with these people's needs will be a major challenge, since there is not much experience in industrial countries that can be adapted to their needs.

The following are some of the key questions with local and global implications that will face the world's population over the next two to five decades:

- Will rural populations—especially those on fragile lands, in more commercially active areas, and on agricultural frontiers—be able to overcome poverty, improve their livelihoods, and adapt to new opportunities, including opportunities in towns and cities?
- Will the rapidly growing cities of the developing world live up to their potential as dynamic engines of growth and social modernization, or will they get mired in poverty, pollution, congestion, and crime?
- Will renewable resources—particularly forests, soil, water, biodiversity, and fisheries—be depleted, or will they be managed as indefinitely sustained sources of livelihood and well-being?
- Will societies be sufficiently creative, resilient, and forward-looking as they undergo sweeping transformations in patterns of growth and migration? Will they be able to promote more equitable development and cope with unexpected shocks?
- Will poor countries be able to accelerate their growth without destabilizing social and environmental stresses? Will the prospective $140 trillion world GDP at mid-century generate fewer environmental and social stresses than the much smaller global economy today?

These are difficult but important questions, which this Report cannot answer definitely. However, it identifies an approach and process that should generate more dialogue and creativity in finding answers.

The interactions among society, economy, and nature vary in the different spatial arenas, although problems across locations are linked. Productivity increases in agriculture help feed the cities. Innovation and productivity increases in the cities help raise productivity and the quality of life in rural areas. Geography matters because of the characteristics of local ecosystems, such as the cost of overcoming local diseases.[30] Geography also matters because of geometry in the form of connectivity and distance to central nodes and markets; the cost of transport is more important here than that of communication.[31] Indeed, the strong association between rural poverty in remote and fragile ecosystems becomes more apparent when the problem is viewed through a spatial lens.

For this reason, the Report is organized by spatial areas that have different characteristics and require correspondingly different approaches to their development.

Fragile lands. The estimated 1.3 billion people living on fragile lands have modest assets that can help bring them out of extreme poverty, but these assets are seldom nurtured by local or national institutions. The people have land that is subject to many constraints, making it vulnerable to degradation, erosion, floods, and landslides. They possess human capital, which is handicapped by restrictive traditions, limited mobility, lack of voice, and poor access to services. This is even more true for women, who are thus the most marginal group. The mainly poor people on fragile lands also face circumstances vastly different from their counterparts on Europe's rural periphery

50 to 100 years ago. Today, international migration is highly restricted, and while rural-to-urban migration is important for them, there are limited numbers of jobs at above-subsistence wages for unskilled workers, especially in the low-growth economies. As a result, as noted above, instead of declining sharply, the number of people living on fragile lands is estimated to have doubled in the past 50 years—despite some outmigration.

Rural areas with potential for commercial crops. The problem of feeding a growing and more urban population calls for better management of the interaction with nature, particularly with respect to land and water (extensification versus intensification of agriculture). Whether or not rural families have land, water, and education is critical to their current livelihood, as well as to their ability to move to cities in the future. More egalitarian access to these assets is also crucial for determining the quality of society's institutions. A successful rural-urban transition requires the elimination of poverty for those who stay in the countryside and better preparation of those who move to the cities. It also demands protection of remaining natural ecosystems and habitats, given their central role in maintaining life-support systems and biodiversity. This latter requirement is one reason to intensify agricultural production in areas already under commercial crops and pasture. Intensification in such areas not only minimizes pressure on biodiversity and on marginal agricultural areas but also increases the food available to cities and leads to dynamic rural-urban linkages. Higher population density in these rural areas would also make investments in health and education more cost-effective and would increase the potential for off-farm employment and help farmers accept risk and innovate.

Urban areas. Cities of the developing world face a formidable undertaking, given the expected rapid rate of growth and sheer numbers of urban residents to be employed, housed, and serviced. The characteristics of periurban settlements, towns, cities, and megacities—higher density, large scale of settlement, and greater social diversity—facilitate the creation of productive employment opportunities, efficient provision of services, and access to ideas and learning. But having many people at close quarters also creates the potential for social problems—crime and social dislocation—and for environmental spillovers that pose health and safety hazards, especially for those living in neighborhoods without sanitation or drainage and in potential disaster zones. The long life of urban physical capital stock can lock in certain development paths, making changes costly. If managed well, urban areas can be the future engines of growth. If not, their environmental and social problems will be concentrated and difficult to fix.

The discussion of problems affecting fragile lands, rural commercial areas, and urban settings, and of possible solutions, is important because many public goods and externalities are local in nature and are, in principle, amenable to action at the local level. An enabling framework for local action and the principle of subsidiarity require that public goods and externalities that affect wider catchments be addressed, at higher levels—national and global.

At the national level. The political, legal, and market domain for coordinating many activities is frequently the nation. Many externalities spill over beyond local communities and municipalities, and even across regional boundaries. The nation is thus often the level at which interests can be balanced, either directly or by facilitating negotiation among localities. National actors may be better placed to organize the provision of public goods and to take advantage of scale economies when the beneficiaries extend beyond subnational regions. Generating a strong investment climate, including sound macroeconomic fundamentals, good governance, and basic infrastructure, requires a framework that is typically national in scope. Dismantling perverse subsidies, husbanding forests and fisheries, and curbing water and air pollution in river basins and airsheds are major national challenges. Managing foreign aid and avoiding civil conflict are other key national concerns that determine whether development is sustainable.

At the global level. Many economic, environmental, and social processes—knowledge, conflict, disease, pollution, migration, and finance—spill over national boundaries. A few of these processes generate problems that are purely global: depletion of the stratospheric ozone layer is an example. But most global problems and opportunities are experienced at the local level as well. Automobiles that pollute local airsheds also generate greenhouse gases; wetland destruction that disrupts local water resources also undermines biodiversity of global significance; new ideas that are generated in one place can benefit people in other places, near and far. The public goods nature of many of these issues and the need to address the negative externalities requires coordination across boundaries. The distinctive challenge for global issues is to balance interests and commit to solutions in the absence of a global authority.

Act now—for long-term problems

Before proceeding to a discussion of local, national, and global issues, this Report sets forth a framework which argues that social and environmental outcomes have a bearing on human well-being both directly and through their effect on growth. When social and environmental issues are systematically neglected for long periods, economic growth will be affected. That is why improving the quality of life for those living in poverty today—and for the 2 billion to 3 billion people who will be added to the world's population over the next 50 years—will require a growth path that integrates environmental and social concerns more explicitly.

Some problems of sustainability are already urgent and require immediate action; examples are local ecosystems where population is pressing on deeply degraded soils, and forests and water stocks that have been nearly depleted. In such cases productivity is already on the decline and opportunities for correction or mitigation may even have been lost; abandonment of existing practices and outmigration may be necessary. The urgency of some of these problems has been overlooked because the people most affected are physically remote from centers of power, or because their voices are not heard, or both.

Some issues call for immediate action because there are good prospects for reversing the damage to the environment at relatively low cost, as in taking measures against air and water pollution. Even then, undoing some of the damage to the affected population (such as the respiratory damage caused by breathing air laden with particulates) may not be fully possible. But knowing the health impacts does create a moral imperative to protect those affected from further exposure, to compensate them to the extent possible, and to prevent others from becoming victims.

Another category of issues unfolds over a longer time horizon. The problems may not yet be urgent, but the direction of change is unmistakable. For these, it is essential to get ahead of the curve and prevent a worsening crisis before it is too costly. Biodiversity loss and climate change are in this category: there is already a need to adapt to the consequences of past and current behavior, but there is also still scope for mitigation, though not for complacency. Similarly, the need to anticipate urban growth by facilitating low-income settlements in safe areas and by setting aside major rights-of-way and spaces for public amenities makes it necessary to act now to avoid greater costs and regrets later.

What is clear is that almost all of the challenges of sustainable development require that action be initiated in the near term, whether to confront immediate crises, such as the health risks to children from unsanitary living conditions in existing slums, or to stem the tide of crises where concerted action in the near term could avert much greater costs and disruption to human development in the longer term.

In looking back over past successes and failures in solving development problems, it is clear that there have been more successes where markets function well (for example, in providing food to people with effective demand), even where the problems that markets have to solve (such as transport and communications) are relatively complex. The major problems that remain (inclusion, poverty reduction, deforestation, biodiversity, and global warming) are, however, generally not amenable to standard market solutions, although markets can help solve subsets of these problems.

One difficulty is that environmental and social assets suffer from underinvestment and overuse because they have the characteristics of public goods:

- Sometimes, ignorance of the consequences of action leads to overuse or underprovision. The ignorance is in part due to underinvestment in knowledge and understanding—itself a public good.[32]
- In other cases there are no mechanisms for facilitating cooperation among individuals, communities, or countries even when it is clear to those involved that the returns to cooperation (especially in the long run), exceed the returns to unilateral action (especially in the short run).
- In still other cases the gains from acting in the broader interests of society fail to be realized because correcting a spillover has distributional consequences and the potential losers resist change.
- Sometimes underprovision is a response to perceived tradeoffs between growth and the costs of correcting externalities. These tradeoffs may be the unfortunate outcome of having been boxed into a corner through a past failure of foresight. Or there may be genuinely difficult choices in balancing legitimate interests and assessing the value of nonmarket benefits and risk reduction, especially if those who would benefit are dispersed over current and future generations.

Environmental and social stresses reflect the failure of institutions to manage and provide public goods, to correct spillovers, and to broker differing interests. Because the spatial extent of spillovers varies by problem, appropriate institutions are needed at different levels, from local through national to global. Getting to socially preferred outcomes requires institutions that can identify who bears the burden of social and environmental neglect and who benefits—and who can balance these diverse interests within society. This perspective helps in understanding why technically sound policy advice (for instance, "eliminate perverse incentives" or "impose charges on environmental damages") is so seldom taken up.

The emphasis of this Report is not on identifying a specific set of policies or outcomes considered advantageous but on the processes by which such policies and outcomes are selected. Outcomes emerging from strong processes are more robust. In many cases, and increasingly, institutions respond too late or too poorly—or without the capacity to commit to a course of action. In today's world the lag between the emergence of a problem and the emergence of institutions that can respond to it is too long. We need to see farther down the road. Why? Because institutions that facilitate and manage national economic growth, and even globalization, are still inadequate, yet where such institutions are in fact emerging, they are developing faster than complementary institutions that might be able to avoid or cope with the deleterious environmental and social consequences of economic change.

Endnotes

1. World Bank 2001h CD Rom (SIMA 349).

2. Chen and Ravallion (2000).

3. World Bank 2001h CD Rom (SIMA 349).

4. World Bank 2001h CD Rom (SIMA 349).

5. World Bank 2001h CD Rom (SIMA 349).

6. The quality and coverage of the household survey data used to measure poverty have improved dramatically in the past 10 to 15 years, and the World Bank has played an important role in facilitating this improvement. Since 1990, the Bank's $1 per day poverty estimates have drawn fully on these new data. However, the paucity of adequate survey data for the past naturally makes estimation over longer periods more hazardous. In *Globalization, Growth and Poverty* (World Bank 2002g), it was estimated that the number of people living below $1 per day had fallen by 200 million between 1980 and 1998. As noted in the Report, that estimate had to draw on two different sources that used different methods. Further checks using more consistent methods corroborate the earlier estimate. These estimates also suggest that if China were excluded, there would have been little or no net decline in the total number of poor people.

7. In 1978 China abandoned its reliance on collective agriculture, sharply increased the prices paid for agricultural goods, and dramatically increased the role of market signals and foreign investment.

8. Brown and others (2001). World Watch Institute's estimates based on national-level surveys of body weight by the United Nations (U.N.) and the World Health Organization (WHO).

9. World Bank 2001i.

10. World Bank 2001h; Sambanis (2000, p. 13).

11. UNDP, UNEP, and others (1999).

12. UNDP, UNEP, and others (1999).

13. UNDP, UNEP, and others (1999).

14. Available at World Bank Group, "Access to Safe Water," (2000).

15. UNEP (1997b); Scherr (1999); Scherr and Yadav (1996); White, Murray and others (2002); Cosgrove and Rijsberman (2000).

16. World Bank (2001c).

17. UNDP, UNEP, and others (1999).

18. Myers, Mittermeier, and others (2000).

19. UNDP, UNEP, and others (1999).

20. UNDP, UNEP, and others (1999).

21. World Bank (2001c).

22. Social change and cultural evolution have also been speeding up, but not uniformly within or across societies. Some cultures are less able to adapt to speed of change even if they wanted to, while others may not even want to.

23. Inconsistencies between human and natural processes manifest themselves spatially (location-specific sources and sinks) and at different scales.

24. Until recently, the carbon emissions generated by energy-intensive activities (that rely on fossil fuels, such as coal) did not affect global temperatures because they had not exceeded the biosphere's absorptive capacity. Now more expensive alternatives are needed to avoid further damage.

25. Dasgupta (2002).

26. Yi (2002).

27. Bloom and Williamson (1997).

28. Much like the dynamics by which teams become more creative, populations moving to cities go through stages of forming, storming, norming, and performing. *Forming* occurs when individuals with different backgrounds come together; *storming*, when their different perspectives clash; *norming*, when more inclusive norms evolve; and *performing*, when constructive behavior replaces destructive behavior. The result is that cities, in the best cases, become centers where different cultural values come together and jointly develop more inclusive values to accommodate different perspectives and provide space for different subgroups to specialize and innovate.

29. The complete series for developing and for highincome countries for 1950–2050 were created using various interpolations and extrapolations of existing data while maintaining consistency with available World Bank and U.N. control totals. Estimates for size classes of 100,000 population and more were made using the following sources: U.N. and World Bank control totals for urban population in developing and high-income countries; U.N., *World Urbanization Prospects, 1999 Revision*, digital files from the U.N. Population Division; and the database of cities above 100,000 population compiled for the U.N.-HABITAT Successful Cities project. (World Bank projections for urban population are lower than those of the U.N. and closer to those of the International Institute for Applied Systems Analysis, as they assume a slower growth rate for most countries.) The populations of smaller towns (those with populations of less than 100,000) were calculated as the residual of total urban population as indicated by U.N. and

World Bank sources minus the total estimated population of cities larger than 100,000.

30. Krugman (1998); Gallup and Sachs (1998).

31. Henderson, Shalizi, and Venables (2001).

32. Meaningfully evaluating the consequences or probabilities of outcomes, tradeoffs, and priorities becomes difficult, if not impossible, without the appropriate data and informa-

tion. For environmental and social variables, there may be some time-series data at the local level, but there are rarely equivalent disaggregated data for GDP variables. At the national level, the situation is often reversed. This obstructs any attempt to quantitatively model or assess changes over time or their determinants. This Report relies heavily on case studies that are thought to be representative.

From *The World Development Report,* 2003. Reprinted by permission.

The future of humanity

"How beauteous mankind is!" said Miranda in *The Tempest*.
But can natural evolution or our own genetic engineering
improve on the present model?

By **Colin Tudge**

Are we it? Have we already seen the best of humanity? Was Plato or Shakespeare or Einstein or Buddha or Lao Tzu or the prophet Mohammed as clever as any human being is ever likely to be? Modern athletes with their minutely cultured hearts and limbs don't run the 100 metres significantly faster than Jesse Owens did in 1936. So is this as fast as people can ever be? In short: has our evolution stopped: and if so, why, and if not, what lies in store? Or might genetic engineering allow us to breed our own superspecies, if not in God's image, at least according to the demands of market forces?

To begin at the beginning. Darwin's great contribution in *The Origin of Species* was to propose not simply evolution, but a plausible mechanism: it happens, he said, "by means of natural selection". The individuals best able to cope at any one time are those most likely to survive and leave offspring. So as the generations pass, each lineage of creatures becomes more and more closely adapted ("fitted") to its particualr surroundings. Natural selection requires an appropriate mechanism of inheritance—one that ensures "like begets like" (that cats have kittens, and horses give birth to foals), but also provides variation, so that not all kittens and foals are identical. Darwin's near contemporary, Gregor Mendel, working in what was then Moravia and is now the Czech Republic, provided just what was needed: he showed that inheritance works by transmitting units of information, now known as genes. Genes encapsulate the characters

of the parents, but they are recombined in the offspring through the machinations of sex and and are also prone to random change, of the kind known as mutation. So they provide all the variation that is required.

Darwin did not know of Mendel's work (he had Mendel's account on his desk, but failed to cut the pages), but 20th-century biologists put the two together and, by the 1940s, generated "neo-Darwinism". Creatures that reproduce through sex continually swap and recombine their genes, so all the genes in all the individuals in a sexually breeding population form one great "gene pool". Natural selection operates on the pool as a whole (these neo-Darwinists said). It knocks out individuals who contain less helpful genes, but favours those whose genes are especially advantageous. Thus the "bad" genes tend to be lost as time goes by, while the ones that promote survival and reproduction spread through the pool. Over time, the composition of the gene pool changes and so the creatures change as well. The neo-Darwinian model has been modified somewhat, but that general picture obtains.

There is no destiny in evolution, Darwinian or neo-Darwinian. Natural selection is opportunist and answers to the here and now; it has no mind for the distant future. The fossils tell us that our ancestors grew taller over the past five million years, from about a metre to nearly two, while our brains have puffed up from an apish 400ml or so to 1,400ml—easily the biggest in proportion to body weight of any animal. Perhaps this has made us more like God. But there is nothing in natural selection to suggest that our ancestors did more than adapt to whatever their surroundings threw at them, or to imply that we will grow more godlike as the future unfolds.

Neither will we go the way of *The Eagle*'s Mekon, arch-enemy of Dan Dare: a green homunculus with a head as big as a dustbin and legs like cribbage pegs. Before Darwin, the Frenchman Jean-Baptiste Lamarck proposed a different mechanism of evolution, through "inheritance of acquired characteristics". He observed rightly enough that bodies adapt to whatever is demanded of them, so that blacksmiths, say, acquire bigger muscles. But he was wrong to propose that a blacksmith passes on his hard-earned biceps to his children. If the children want to be tough, they have to do their own smithying. By the same token, thinking won't make our brains grow bigger, in any heritable way, and physical indolence will not shrink our descendants' legs. So our evolution is not shaped by destiny, nor by our own endeavours, nor by our self-indulgence. Neo-Darwinian mutation and selection (plus large slices of chance) are all there is.

The same techniques that made wheat from wild grasses could transform humanity, too

---

But in us, the neo-Darwinian mechanism seems logjammed. Some genetic variants are being lost, as small tribal groups continue to die out; and others are constantly gained by mutations, some of which persist. There are fluctuations: genes that confer resistance to Aids are gaining ground in Africa, for instance, while Kenyans are currently breeding faster than Italians, so any genetic variants that are peculiar to either group must be increasing or falling. But the permanent losses of genes through extinction of minorities are small compared to the whole pool, and while the particular genes of Kenyans may wax in one century, they may wane in another. Most importantly, there is no consistent pressure to push our gene pool in any particular direction. Nobel prize-winners and professional basketball players are lauded, but do not typically leave more offspring than the ordinary Joe. Infant mortality is still high in some societies but, in genetic terms, it strikes randomly because the poor are not genetically distinct.

Genetic logjams certainly happen, as is clear from the fossils. Some lineages of clams remained virtually unchanged for tens or even hundreds of millions of years. Today's leopards and impala are more agile and brainy than their ancestors of 50 million years ago, but they have not changed much in the past three million years. People anatomically undistinguishable from us were living in Africa at least 100,000 years ago.

Yet the deadlock could be broken. Through global war or some other ecological disaster, human beings could again become isolated into island groups, and natural selection could then go to work on each of them separately to produce a range of neo-humans, each adapted to its own island. We should not assume that any of the islands would especially favour brains, which require a great deal of nourishment. Agile climbers of fruit trees might fare best, and so we might again become more simian.

Or human beings might take their own genetic future in hand—which, in principle, has long been within our gift. The same techniques that made wheat from wild grasses and Aberdeen Angus from aurochs could transform humanity, too, in any direction we might care to prescribe—albeit over longer periods, given that we have such an extended generation interval, and many of the characters we might be most interested in undoubtedly have a complex genetic basis. Eugenics, the deliberate transformation of the human gene pool, was popular 100 years ago through most of Europe, and *de rigueur* in the US. Only the Catholics spoke out consistently against it, and the socialists H G Wells, George Bernard Shaw and Sidney and Beatrice Webb were among its most incongruous advocates. Up-to-date Edwardian matrons spoke approvingly of "eugenic" marriages.

The eugenicists were interested not so much in breeding super-people as in preventing the "decline" of the species through the perceived reproductive prodigality of the "feeble minded" (who were taken to include a great many foreigners and a large section of the working class). Hitler revealed the political perils, however, as he wiped out the people who did not meet his own particular criteria and matched blonds with blondes like prize porkers. So eugenics has gone out of fashion and now is virtually taboo. But in various ways, the new biotechnologies seem to open new possibilities and have concentrated minds afresh: cloning, genomics, genetic engineering.

Genetic engineering is the biggie: the transfer of particular stretches of DNA from one individual to another. The first phase of the Human Genome Project was completed last year, and it is already beginning to show which pieces of DNA correspond to which particular genes and which, therefore, are worth transferring. Cloning *qua* cloning is not directly pertinent, but it does provide techniques that will generally be necessary if genetic engineering is ever to progress beyond its simplest stages. Genetic engineering is already commonplace in bacteria, increasingly in food crops (GMOs), and in laboratory mice. It has at least been essayed in farm livestock and, in principle, is certainly applicable to humans. So where might it lead?

Most simply, doctors already try to repair the affected tissues in people with particular diseases: for example, to correct the damaged genes in the lungs of patients with cystic fibrosis (CF). Genetic changes made to the lungs (if and when this becomes possible) would not be reflected in the eggs and sperm, and so would not be passed on to future generations. Some argue that genetically transformed lung cells could escape, to be breathed in by the rest of us. But apart from this hypothetical hazard, no third parties are involved. The ethical problems therefore seem minimal.

More radical would be to repair the CF gene in a very young embryo, so that the whole person who subsequently develops would be genetically changed. His or her sperms or eggs would develop from cells that were already transformed, so the genetic alteration would be passed down the generations. Biologically and ethically, this is far more heavy-duty than *ad hoc* tissue repair.

Whether CF cells are repaired *ad hoc*, or in a young embryo and so passed on, such procedures are clearly in the realms of therapy. CF is a disease that causes suffering: to correct the gene is to attempt a cure. Western medicine is rooted in the belief that therapy, to correct unmistakable illness, is good.

But some already speak not simply of repairing what is obviously damaged, but of improving (according to their own or their clients' judgement) on what already works well enough. By analogy with traditional medicine, this would move us from physic to tonic—a distinction clearly spelled out by controllers of sports, who allow insulin to correct diabetes (some of the greatest athletes have had diabetes) but forbid steroids to pump up muscles that are already perfectly functional. At the end of the line lies the "designer baby", built to a specification in the way that Ferrari builds motor cars. In *Remaking Eden,* Professor Lee Silver of Princeton University in effect advocates such a course, proposing that "GenRich" (genetically enhanced) individuals, primed to gain honours at Princeton and/or to outreach Michael Jordan at the basketball hoop, will be tomorrow's elite. There are plenty of people with cash to spare for such indulgences, says Silver, and plenty of molecular biologists anxious to oblige; and, he says, where the market presses, reality should and indeed must follow.

Yet for all the hype and hand-wringing, the evolutionary impact of these new technologies will surely be virtually zero. The genetic repair of damaged embryos would affect the future, at least in a few families, but it is very difficult to see why anybody should ever want to do such a thing. A person may carry the CF gene (say) yet half of his or her sperm or eggs will be free of it. Even if a carrier marries another carrier, one in four of their embryos will be totally free of the damaged gene. It would be far easier in principle to induce superovulation, fertilise the eggs in vitro to produce a batch of embryos (as is already standard practice for IVF births), and then select the ones that do not contain the mutant gene at all. Only these healthy embryos would then be implanted into the mother. Techniques of the kind that have been developed largely in the context of genetic engineering are employed for diagnosis, but no actual genetic transformation takes place.

Critics, though, have perceived indirect evolutionary consequences if we contrive to rescue babies with damaged genes who would otherwise have died. Those damaged genes, they argue, would once have been purged from the human lineage, but now they survive, and surely this will weaken the pool as a whole. This argument is similar to that of the old eugenicists

who feared the genes of the "feeble minded", and is at least equally misguided.

Most of the genes that cause "single-gene disorders", including CF, have no adverse effects unless they are inherited from both parents. The unfortunate individuals with a double dose are called "homozygotes". The "heterozygotes"—those who inherit the "bad" gene from only one parent—carry that gene and may pass it on to their offspring, but they are not diseased themselves.

Most "bad" genes are rare, but a few are common. The genes that cause sickle-cell anemia occur frequently in people of African descent, while an astonishing one in 20 Caucasians carries the CF mutant. But assuming random mating (as biologists say), each CF carrier has only a one-in-20 chance of mating with another CF carrier; so only one in 400 Caucasian marriages will bring two carriers together. Only one in four of their offspring will inherit the bad gene from both parents, and so be homozygous for CF; so only one in 1,600 children in a Caucasian population will actually manifest the disease. It would be possible to sterilise those children (as if they did not have problems enough already) or to let them die, as they would do if neglected. But it makes no genetic sense to eliminate one in 1,600 children while leaving the carriers, who are so much more common, intact. Indeed, before modern medicine came along, nature had been assiduously eliminating the unfortunate homozygotes for many thousands of years (ever since the CF mutation first occurred) and yet it is still with us.

To eliminate all "bad" genes, we would need to wipe out the entire human species

Some eugenic zealots could track down all the carriers, and eliminate them: although, if such zealots were Caucasian, they might well find that they themselves were carriers. It's easy to see intuitively, too, that the rarer the gene—and most are far rarer than CF—the more dramatically the heterozygous carriers outnumber the homozygous sufferers. Besides, at least 5,000 different syndromes have been described that are caused by mutations in single genes, and there must in reality be many more, because all our genes are prone to mutation. Thus it is estimated that every one of us is liable to carry an average of five damaged genes that would cause disease if we had children by some similar carrier. To eliminate all "bad genes", we would need to wipe out the entire human species. In short, genetic zealotry is born of nonsense. Humane, sensible medicine implies no genetic risk for our species as a whole.

The designer baby, however, the child conceived like a custom car, is metaphorical pornography that, we may note in passing, is perpetrated not by the much-maligned "press", but by the scientists themselves, many of whom have their eyes on megabucks and argue the market mantra that what people are prepared to pay for is by definition good. Fortunately, it is also ludicrous. This listing of genes through the Human Genome Project does not "open the book of life" as some idle geneticists (not the Cambridge scientists who actually did the work) have claimed.

If we think of genes as words, then what we have is an incomplete lexicon. An individual's apportionment of genes—the genome—should be construed as an arcane work of literature with its own syntax, puns, allusions, redundancies, colloquialisms and overall "meaning" of which we have almost no inkling, and may never understand exhaustively. On present knowledge, or even with what we are likely to know in the next two centuries, it would be as presumptuous to try to improve on the genes of a healthy human baby as it would be to edit sacred verse in medieval Chinese if all we had to go on was a bad dictionary.

So all in all, human beings seem likely to remain as they are, genetically speaking, barring some ecological disaster; and there doesn't seem to be much that meddling human beings can do about it. This, surely, is a mercy. We may have been shaped blindly by evolution. We may have been guided on our way by God. Whichever it was, or both, the job has been done a million times better than we are ever likely to do. Natural selection is far more subtle than human invention. "What a piece of work is a man!" said Hamlet. "How beauteous mankind is!" said Miranda. Both of them were absolutely right.

From *New Statesman*, April 8, 2002, pp. 25-27. © 2002 by New Statesman Ltd. Reprinted by permission.

American Culture Goes Global, or Does It?

By RICHARD PELLS

Since september 11, newspaper and magazine columnists and television pundits have told us that it is not only the economic power of the United States or the Bush administration's "unilateralist" foreign policy that breeds global anti-Americanism. Dislike for the United States stems also, they say, from its "cultural imperialism." We have been hearing a good deal about how American mass culture inspires resentment and sometimes violent reactions, not just in the Middle East but all over the world.

Yet the discomfort with American cultural dominance is not new. In 1901, the British writer William Stead published a book called, ominously, *The Americanization of the World*. The title captured a set of apprehensions—about the disappearance of national languages and traditions, and the obliteration of the unique identities of countries under the weight of American habits and states of mind—that persists today.

More recently, globalization has become the main enemy for academics, journalists, and political activists who loathe what they see as a trend toward cultural uniformity. Still, they usually regard global culture and American culture as synonymous. And they continue to insist that Hollywood, McDonald's, and Disneyland are eradicating regional and local eccentricities—disseminating images and subliminal messages so beguiling as to drown out competing voices in other lands.

Despite those allegations, the cultural relationship between the United States and the rest of the world over the past 100 years has never been one-sided. On the contrary, the United States was, and continues to be, as much a consumer of foreign intellectual and artistic influences as it has been a shaper of the world's entertainment and tastes.

That is not an argument with which many foreigners (or even many Americans) would readily agree. The clichés about America's cultural "hegemony" make it difficult for most people to recognize that modern global culture is hardly a monolithic entity foisted on the world by the American media.

Neither is it easy for critics of Microsoft or AOL Time Warner to acknowledge that the conception of a harmonious and distinctively American culture—encircling the globe, implanting its values in foreign minds—is a myth.

In fact, as a nation of immigrants from the 19th to the 21st centuries, and as a haven in the 1930s and '40s for refugee scholars and artists, the United States has been a recipient as much as an exporter of global culture. Indeed, the influence of immigrants and African-Americans on the United States explains why its culture has been so popular for so long in so many places. American culture has spread throughout the world because it has incorporated foreign styles and ideas. What Americans have done more brilliantly than their competitors overseas is repackage the cultural products we receive from abroad and then retransmit them to the rest of the planet. In effect, Americans have specialized in selling the dreams, fears, and folklore of other people back to them. That is why a global mass culture has come to be identified, however simplistically, with the United States.

Americans, after all, did not invent fast food, amusement parks, or the movies. Before the Big Mac, there were fish and chips. Before Disneyland, there was Copenhagen's Tivoli Gardens (which Walt Disney used as a prototype for his first theme park, in Anaheim, a model later re-exported to Tokyo and Paris).

Nor can the origins of today's international entertainment be traced only to P.T. Barnum or Buffalo Bill. The roots of the new global culture lie as well in the European modernist assault, in the early 20th century, on 19th-century literature, music, painting, and architecture—particularly in the modernist refusal to honor the traditional boundaries between high and low culture. Modernism in the arts was improvisational, eclectic, and irreverent. Those traits have also been characteristic of, but not peculiar to, mass culture.

The hallmark of 19th-century culture, in Europe and also in Asia, was its insistence on defending the purity of literature, classical music, and representational painting against the intrusions of folklore and popular amusements. No one confused Tolstoy with dime novels, opera with Wild West shows, the Louvre with Coney Island. High culture was supposed to be educational, contemplative, and uplifting—a way of preserving the best in human civilization.

Such beliefs didn't mean that a Dickens never indulged in melodrama, or that a Brahms disdained the use of popular songs. Nor did Chinese or Japanese authors and painters refuse to draw on oral or folkloric traditions. But the 19th-century barriers between high and low culture were resolutely, if imperfectly, maintained.

The artists of the early 20th century shattered what seemed to them the artificial demarcations between different cultural forms. They also challenged the notion that culture was a means of intellectual or moral improvement. They did so by emphasizing style and craftsmanship at the expense of philosophy, religion, or ideology. They deliberately called attention to language in their novels, to optics in their paintings, to the materials in and function of their architecture, to the structure of music instead of its melodies.

And they wanted to shock their audiences. Which they succeeded in doing. Modern painting and literature—with its emphasis on visually distorted nudes, overt sexuality, and meditations on violence—was attacked for being degrading and obscene, and for appealing to the baser instincts of humanity. In much the same way, critics would later denounce the vulgarity of popular culture.

Although modernism assaulted the conventions of 19th-century high culture in Europe and Asia, it inadvertently accelerated the growth of mass culture in the United States. Indeed, Americans were already receptive to the blurring of cultural boundaries. In the 19th century, symphony orchestras in the United States often included band music in their programs, and opera singers were asked to perform both Mozart and Stephen Foster.

So, for Americans in the 20th century, Surrealism, with its dreamlike associations, easily lent itself to the wordplay and psychological symbolism of advertising, cartoons, and theme parks. Dadaism ridiculed the snobbery of elite cultural institutions and reinforced, instead, an existing appetite (especially among the immigrant audiences in the United States) for low-class, anti-bourgeois nickelodeons and vaudeville shows. Stravinsky's experiments with atonal (and thus unconventional and unmelodic) music validated the rhythmic innovations of American jazz. Writers like Hemingway, detesting the rhetorical embellishments of 19th-century prose, invented a terse, hard-boiled language, devoted to reproducing as authentically as possible the elemental qualities of personal experience. That laconic style became a model for modern journalism, detective fiction, and movie dialogue.

All of those trends provided the foundations for a genuinely new culture. But the new culture turned out to be neither modernist nor European. Instead, the United States transformed what was still a parochial culture, appealing largely to the young and the rebellious in Western society, into a global phenomenon.

The propensity of Americans to borrow modernist ideas, and to transform them into a global culture, is clearly visible in the commercial uses of modern architecture. The European Bauhaus movement—intended in the 1920s as a socialist experiment in working-class housing—eventually provided the theories and techniques for the construction of skyscrapers and vacation homes in the United States. But the same architectural ideas were then sent back to Europe after World War II as a model for the reconstruction of bombed-out cities like Rotterdam, Cologne, and Frankfurt. Thus, the United States converted what had once been a distinctive, if localized, rebellion by Dutch and German architects into a generic "international style."

But it is in popular culture that the reciprocal relationship between America and the rest of the world can best be seen. There are many reasons for the ascendancy of American mass culture. Certainly, the ability of American-based media conglomerates to control the production and distribution of their products has been a major stimulus to the worldwide spread of American entertainment. But the power of American capitalism is not the only, or even the most important, explanation for the global popularity of America's movies and television shows.

The effectiveness of English as a language of mass communications has been essential to the acceptance of American culture. Unlike, for example, German, Russian, or Chinese, the simple structure and grammar of English, along with its tendency to use shorter, less-abstract words and more-concise sentences, are all advantageous for the composers of song lyrics, ad slogans, cartoon captions, newspaper headlines, and movie and TV dialogue. English is thus a language exceptionally well-suited to the demands and spread of American mass culture.

American musicians and entertainers have followed modernist artists like Picasso and Braque in drawing on elements from high and low culture.

Another factor is the size of the American audience. A huge domestic market has made it possible for many American filmmakers and TV executives to retrieve most of their production costs and make a profit within the borders of the United States. That economic cushion has enabled them to spend more money on stars, sets, special effects, location shooting, and merchandising—the very ingredients that attract international audiences as well.

Yet even with such advantages, America's mass culture may not be all that American. The American audience is not only large; because of the influx of immigrants and refugees, it is also international in its complexion. The heterogeneity of America's population—its regional, ethnic, religious, and racial diversity—has forced the media, since the early years of the 20th century, to experiment with messages, images, and story lines that have a broad multicultural appeal. The Hollywood studios, mass-circulation magazines, and television networks have had to learn how to speak to a variety of groups and classes at home. That has given them the techniques to appeal to an equally diverse audience abroad. The American domestic market has, in essence, been a laboratory, a place to develop cultural products that can then be adapted to the world market.

An important way that the American media have succeeded in transcending internal social divisions, national borders, and language barriers is by mixing up cultural styles. American musicians and entertainers have followed the example of modernist artists like Picasso and Braque in drawing on elements from high and low culture, combining the sacred and the profane. Advertisers have adapted the techniques of Surrealism and Abstract Expressionism to make their products more intriguing. Composers like Aaron Copland, George Gershwin, and Leonard Bernstein incorporated folk melodies, religious hymns, blues, gospel songs, and jazz into their symphonies, concertos, operas, and ballets. Indeed, an art form as quintessentially American as jazz evolved during the 20th century into an amalgam of African, Caribbean, Latin American, and modernist European music. That blending of forms in America's mass culture has enhanced its appeal to multiethnic domestic and international audiences by capturing their varied experiences and tastes.

NOWHERE ARE FOREIGN INFLUENCES more evident than in the American movie industry. For better or worse, Hollywood became, in the 20th century, the cultural capital of the modern world. But it was never an exclusively American capital. Like past cultural centers—Florence, Paris, Vienna—Hollywood has functioned as an international community, built by immigrant entrepreneurs and drawing on the talents of actors, directors, writers, cinematographers, editors, and costume and set designers from all over the world. The first American movie star, after all, was Charlie Chaplin, whose comic skills were honed in British music halls.

Moreover, during much of the 20th century, American moviemakers thought of themselves as acolytes, entranced by the superior works of foreign directors. In the 1920s, few American directors could gain admittance to a European pantheon that included Sergei Eisenstein, F.W. Murnau, G.W. Pabst, Fritz Lang, and Carl Dreyer. The postwar years, from the 1940s to the mid-'60s, were once again a golden age of filmmaking in Britain, Sweden, France, Italy, Japan, and India. An extraordinary generation of foreign directors—Ingmar Bergman, Federico Fellini, Michelangelo Antonioni, François Truffaut, Jean-Luc Godard, Akira Kurosawa, Satyajit Ray—were the world's most celebrated auteurs.

Nevertheless, it is one of the paradoxes of the European and Asian cinemas that their greatest success was in spawning American imitations. After the release, in 1967, of *Bonnie and Clyde* (originally to have been directed by Truffaut or Godard), the newest geniuses—Francis Ford Coppola, Martin Scorsese, Robert Altman, Steven Spielberg, Woody Allen—were American. They may have owed their improvisational methods and autobiographical preoccupations to Italian neo-Realism and the French New Wave. But who, in any country, needed to see another *La Dolce Vita* when you could enjoy *Nashville*? Why try to decipher *Jules and Jim* or *L'Avventura* when you could see *Annie Hall* or *The Godfather*? Wasn't it conceivable that *The Seven Samurai* might not be as powerful or as disturbing a movie as *The Wild Bunch*?

It turned out that foreign filmmakers had been too influential for their own good. They helped revolutionize the American cinema, so that, after the 1960s and '70s, it became hard for any other continent's film industry to match the worldwide popularity of American movies.

Once again, however, we need to remember that Hollywood movies have never been just American. To take another example, American directors, in all eras, have emulated foreign artists and filmmakers by paying close attention to the style and formal qualities of a movie, and to the need to tell a story visually. Early-20th-century European painters wanted viewers to recognize that they were looking at lines and color on a canvas rather than at a reproduction of the natural world. Similarly, many American films—from the multiple narrators in *Citizen Kane*, to the split-screen portrait of how two lovers imagine their relationship in *Annie Hall*, to the flashbacks and flash-forwards in *Pulp Fiction*, to the roses blooming from the navel of Kevin Spacey's fantasy dream girl in *American Beauty*—deliberately remind the audience that it is watching a movie instead of a play or a photographed version of reality. American filmmakers (not only in the movies but also on MTV) have been willing to use the most sophisticated techniques of editing and camera work, much of it inspired by European directors, to create a modernist collage of images that captures the speed and seductiveness of life in the contemporary world.

Hollywood's addiction to modernist visual pyrotechnics is especially evident in the largely nonverbal style of many of its contemporary performers. The tendency to mumble was not always in vogue. In the 1930s and '40s, the sound and meaning of words were important not only in movies but also on records and the radio. Even though some homegrown stars, like John Wayne and Gary Cooper, were famously terse, audiences could at least hear and understand what they were saying. But the centrality of language in the films of the 1930s led, more often, to a dependence in Hollywood on British actors (like Cary Grant), or on Americans who sounded vaguely British (like Katharine Hepburn and Bette Davis). It is illustrative of how important foreign (especially British) talent was to Hollywood in an earlier era that the two most famous Southern belles in American fiction and drama—Scarlett O'Hara and Blanche DuBois—were played in the movies by Vivien Leigh.

The verbal eloquence of pre-World War II acting, in both movies and the theater, disappeared after 1945. After Marlon Brando's revolutionary performance in *A Streetcar Named Desire*, in the 1947 stage version and the 1951 screen version, the model of American acting became inarticulateness—a brooding and halting introspection that one doesn't find in the glib and clever heroes or heroines of the screwball comedies and gangster films of the '30s. Brando was trained in the Method, an acting technique originally developed in Stanislavsky's Moscow Art Theater in prerevolutionary Russia, then imported to New York by members of the Group Theater during the 1930s. Where British actors, trained in Shakespeare, were taught to subordinate their personalities to the role as written, the Method encouraged actors to improvise, to summon up childhood memories, and to explore their inner feelings, often at the expense of what the playwright or screenwriter intended. Norman Mailer once said that Brando, in his pauses and his gazes into the middle distance, always seemed to be searching for a better line than the one the writer had composed. In effect, what Brando did (along with his successors and imitators, from James Dean to Warren Beatty to Robert De Niro) was to lead a revolt against the British school of acting, with its reverence for the script and the written (and spoken) word.

Thus, after World War II, the emotional power of American acting lay more in what was not said, in what could not even be communicated in words. The Method actor's reliance on physical mannerisms and even silence in interpreting a role has been especially appropriate for a cinema that puts a premium on the inexpressible. Indeed, the influence of the Method, not only in the United States but also abroad (where it was reflected in the acting styles of Jean-Paul Belmondo and Marcello Mastroianni), is a classic example of how a foreign idea, originally meant for the stage, was adapted in postwar America to the movies, and then conveyed to the rest of the world as a paradigm for both cinematic and social behavior. More important, the Method's disregard for language permitted global audiences—even those not well-versed in English—to understand and appreciate what they were watching in American films.

FINALLY, American culture has imitated not only the modernists' visual flamboyance, but also their emphasis on personal expression and their tendency to be apolitical and anti-ideological. The refusal to browbeat an audience with a social message has accounted, more than any other factor, for the worldwide popularity of American entertainment. American movies, in particular, have customarily focused on human relationships and private feelings, not on the problems of a particular time and place. They tell tales about romance, intrigue, success, failure, moral conflicts, and survival. The most memorable movies of the 1930s (with the exception of *The Grapes of Wrath*) were comedies and musicals about mismatched people falling in love, not socially conscious films dealing with issues of poverty and unemployment. Similarly, the finest movies about World War II (like *Casablanca*) or the Vietnam War (like *The Deer Hunter*) linger in the mind long after those conflicts have ended because they explore their characters' intimate emotions rather than dwelling on headline events.

Such intensely personal dilemmas are what people everywhere wrestle with. So Europeans, Asians, and Latin Americans flocked to *Titanic* (as they once did to *Gone With the Wind*) not because it celebrated American values, but because people all over the world could see some part of their own lives reflected in the story of love and loss.

America's mass culture has often been crude and intrusive, as its critics—from American academics like Benjamin Barber to German directors like Wim Wenders—have always complained. In their eyes, American culture is "colonizing" everyone else's subconscious, reducing us all to passive residents of "McWorld."

But American culture has never felt all that foreign to foreigners. And, at its best, it has transformed what it received from others into a culture that everyone, everywhere, can embrace, a culture that is both emotionally and, on occasion, artistically compelling for millions of people throughout the world.

So, despite the current hostility to America's policies and values—in Europe and Latin America as well as in the Middle East and Asia—it is important to recognize how familiar much of American culture seems to people abroad. If anything, our movies, television shows, and theme parks have been less "imperialistic" than cosmopolitan. In the end, American mass culture has not transformed the world into a replica of the United States. Instead, America's dependence on foreign cultures has made the United States a replica of the world.

Richard Pells is a professor of history at the University of Texas at Austin. His books include Not Like Us: How Europeans Have Loved, Hated, and Transformed American Culture Since World War II (*Basic Books, 1997*).

Originally published in *The Chronicle of Higher Education*, April 12, 2002, pp. B7, B9. © 2002 by Richard Pells. Reprinted by permission.

COMMUNITY BUILDING
STEPS TOWARD A GOOD SOCIETY

AMITAI ETZIONI

Well-formed national societies are not composed of millions of individuals but are constituted as communities of communities. These societies provide a framework within which diverse social groups as well as various subcultures find shared bonds and values. When this framework falls apart, we find communities at each other's throats or even in vicious civil war, as we sadly see in many parts of the world. (Arthur Schlesinger Jr. provides an alarming picture of such a future for our society in his book, *The Disuniting of America*.)

Our community of communities is particularly threatened in two ways that ought to command more of our attention in the next years. First, our society has been growing more diverse by leaps and bounds over recent decades, as immigration has increased and Americans have become more aware of their social and cultural differences. Many on the left celebrate diversity because they see it as ending white European hegemony in our society. Many on the right call for "bleaching out" ethnic differences to ensure a united, homogenous America.

A second challenge to the community of communities emanates from the fact that economic and social inequality has long been rising. Some see a whole new divide caused by the new digital technologies, although others believe that the Internet will bridge these differences. It is time to ask how much inequality the community of communities can tolerate while still flourishing. If we are exceeding these limits, what centrist corrections are available to us?

DIVERSITY WITHIN UNITY

As a multiethnic society, America has long debated the merit of unity versus pluralism, of national identity versus identity politics, of assimilation of immigrants into mainstream culture versus maintaining their national heritages. All of these choices are incompatible with a centrist, communitarian approach to a good society. Assimilation is unnecessarily homogenizing, forcing people to give up important parts of their selves; unbounded racial, ethnic, and cultural diversity is too conflict-prone for a society in which all are fully respected. The concept of a community of communities provides a third model.

The community of communities builds on the observation that loyalty to one's group, to its particular culture and heritage, is compatible with sustaining national unity as long as the society is perceived not as an arena of conflict but as a society that has some community-like features. (Some refer to a community of communities as an imagined community.) Members of such a society maintain layered loyalties. "Lower" commitments are to one's immediate community, often an ethnic group; "higher" ones are to the community of communities, to the nation as a whole. These include a commitment to a democratic way of life, to a constitution and more generally to a government by law, and above all to treating others—not merely the members of one's group—as ends in themselves and not merely as instruments. Approached this way, one realizes that up to a point, *diversity can avoid being the opposite of unity and can exist within it.*

Moreover, sustaining a particular community of communities does not contradict the gradual development of still more encompassing communities, such as the European Union, a North American community including Canada and Mexico, or, one day, a world community.

During the last decades of the 20th century, the U.S. was racked by identity politics that, in part, have served to partially correct past injustices committed against women and minorities, but have also divided the nation along group lines. Other sharp divisions have appeared between the religious right and much of the rest of the country. One of the merits of the centrist, communitarian approach has been that it has combined efforts to expand the common ground and to cool intergroup rhetoric. Thus communitarians helped call off the "war" between the genders, as Betty Friedan—who was one of the original endorsers of the Communitarian Platform—did in 1997.

New flexibility in involving faith-based groups in the provision of welfare, health care, and other social services, and even allowing some forms of religious activities in public schools, has defused some of the tension between the religious right and the rest of society. The national guidelines on religious expression in public schools, first released by the U.S. Department of Education on the directive of President Clinton in August of 1995, worked to this end. For example, in July of 1996, these guidelines spurred the St. Louis School Board to implement a clearly defined, districtwide policy on school prayer. This policy helped allay the confusion—and litigation—that had previously plagued the role of religion in this school district.

The tendency of blacks and whites not to dialogue openly about racial issues, highlighted by Andrew Hacker, has to some degree been overcome. The main, albeit far from successful, effort in this direction has been made by President Clinton's Advisory Board on Race. And for the first time in U.S. history, a Jew was nominated by a major political party for the post of vice president.

In the next years, intensified efforts are called for to balance the legitimate concerns and needs of various communities that constitute the American society on one hand, and the need to shore up our society as a community of communities on the other. Prayers truly initiated by students might be allowed in public schools as long as sufficient arrangements are made for students who do not wish to participate to spend time in other organized activities. There are no compelling reasons to oppose "after hours" religious clubs establishing themselves in the midst of numerous secular programs. Renewed efforts for honest dialogues among the races are particularly difficult and needed. None of these steps will cause the differences among various communities—many of which serve to enrich our culture and social life—to disappear. But they may go a long way toward reinforcing the framework that keeps American society together while it is being recast.

UNIFYING INEQUALITY

Society cannot long sustain its status as a community of communities if general increases in well-being, even including those that trickle down to the poorest segments of the society, keep increasing the economic distance between the elites and the common people. Fortunately, it seems that at least by some measures, economic inequality has not increased in the United States between 1996 and 2000. And by several measures, the federal income tax has grown surprisingly progressive. (The opposite must be said about rising payroll taxes.) About a third of those who filed income tax returns in 2000 paid no taxes or even got a net refund from the Internal Revenue Service (IRS). However, the level of inequality in income at the end of the 20th century was substantially higher than it was in earlier periods. Between 1977 and 1999, the after-tax income of the top 1 percent of the U.S. population increased by 115 percent, whereas the after-tax income of the U.S. population's lowest fifth decreased by 9 per-

cent. There is little reason to expect that this trend will not continue.

SOCIAL JUSTICE

We may debate what social justice calls for; however, there is little doubt about what community requires. If some members of a community are increasingly distanced from the standard of living of most other members, they will lose contact with the rest of the community. The more those in charge of private and public institutions lead lives of hyper-affluence—replete with gated communities and estates, chauffeured limousines, servants and personal trainers—the less in touch they are with other community members. Such isolation not only frays social bonds and insulates privileged people from the moral cultures of the community, but it also blinds them to the realities of the lives of their fellow citizens. This, in turn, tends to cause them to favor unrealistic policies ("let them eat cake") that backfire and undermine the trust of the members of the society in those who lead and in the institutions they head.

The argument has been made that for the state to provide equality of outcomes undermines the motivation to achieve and to work, stymies creativity and excellence, and is unfair to those who do apply themselves. It is also said that equality of outcomes would raise labor costs so high that a society would be rendered uncompetitive in the new age of global competition. Equality of opportunity has been extolled as a substitute. However, to ensure equality of opportunity, some equality of outcome must be provided. As has often been pointed out, for all to have similar opportunities, they must have similar starting points. These can be reached only if all are accorded certain basics. Special education efforts such as Head Start, created to bring children from disadvantaged backgrounds up to par, and training for workers released from obsolescent industries are examples of programs that provide some equality of results to make equality of opportunity possible.

Additional policies to further curb inequality can be made to work at both ends of the scale. Policies that ensure a rich basic minimum serve this goal by lifting those at the lower levels of the economic pyramid. Reference is often made to education and training programs that focus on those most in need of catching up. However, these work very slowly. Therefore, in the short run more effects will be achieved by raising the Earned Income Tax Credit and the minimum wage, and by implementing new inter-community sharing initiatives.

The poor will remain poor no matter how much they work as long as they own no assets. This is especially damaging because people who own assets, especially a place of residence (even if only an apartment), are most likely to "buy" into a society—to feel and be part of a community. By numerous measures, homeowners are more involved in the life of their communities, and their children are less likely to drop out of school. Roughly one-third of Americans do not own their residence; 73 percent of whites do, compared to 47 percent of African Americans and Hispanics.

MORTGAGES

Various provisions allowing those with limited resources to get mortgages through federally chartered corporations like Fannie Mae, which helps finance mortgages for many lower-income people, have been helpful in increasing ownership. More needs to be done on this front, especially for those of little means. This might be achieved by following the same model used in the Earned Income Tax Credit in the U.S. and the Working Families Tax Credit in the United Kingdom: providing people who earn below a defined income level with "earned interest on mortgages," effectively granting them two dollars for every dollar set aside to provide seed money for a mortgage. And sweat equity might be used as the future owner's contribution—for instance, if they work on their own housing site. (Those who benefit from the houses that Habitat for Humanity builds are required to either make some kind of a financial contribution themselves or help in the construction of their homes.) Far from implausible, various ideas along these lines were offered by both George W. Bush and Al Gore during the 2000 election campaign, as well as by various policy researchers.

Reducing hard core unemployment by trying to bring jobs to poor neighborhoods (through "enterprise zones") or by training the long-unemployed in entrepreneurial skills is often expensive and slow, and is frequently unsuccessful. The opposite approach, moving people from poor areas to places where jobs are, often encounters objections by the neighborhoods into which they are moved, as well as by those poor who feel more comfortable living in their home communities. A third approach should be tried much more extensively: providing ready transportation to and from places of employment.

Measures to cap the higher levels of wealth include progressive income taxes, some forms of inheritance tax, closing numerous loopholes in the tax codes, and ensuring that tax on capital is paid as it is on labor. Given that several of these inequality curbing measures cannot be adopted on a significant scale if they seriously endanger the competitive state of a country, steps to introduce many of them should be undertaken jointly with other Organization for Economic Cooperation and Development (OECD) countries, or better yet, among all the nations that are our major competitors and trade partners.

One need not be a liberal—one can be a solid communitarian—and still be quite dismayed to learn that the IRS audits the poor (defined as income below $25,000) more than the rich (defined as income above $100,000). In 1999, the IRS audited 1.36 percent of poor taxpayers, compared to 1.15 percent of rich taxpayers. In 1988, the percentage for the rich was 11.4. In one decade, there was thus a decline of about 90 percent in auditing the rich. This oc-

curred because Congress did not authorize the necessary funds, despite the General Accounting Office's finding that the rich are more likely to evade taxes than are the poor. This change in audit patterns also reflects the concern of Republican members of Congress that the poor will abuse the Earned Income Tax Credit that the Clinton administration has introduced. It should not take a decade to correct this imbalance.

Ultimately, this matter and many others will not be properly attended to until there is a basic change in the moral culture of the society and in the purposes that animate it. Without such a change, a major reallocation of wealth can be achieved only by force, which is incompatible with a democratic society and will cause a wealth flight and other damage to the economy. In contrast, history from early Christianity to Fabian socialism teaches us that people who share progressive values will be inclined to share their wealth voluntarily. A good society seeks to promote such values through a grand dialogue rather than by dictates.

THE NEW GRAND DIALOGUE

The great success of the economy in the 1990s made Americans pay more attention to the fact that there are numerous moral and social questions of concern to the good society that capitalism has never aspired to answer and that the state should not promote. These include moral questions such as what we owe our children, our parents, our friends, and our neighbors, as well as people from other communities, including those in far away places. Most important, we must address this question: What is the ultimate purpose our personal and collective endeavors? Is ever greater material affluence our ultimate goal and the source of meaning? When is enough—enough? What are we considering the good life? *Can a good society be built on ever increasing levels of affluence? Or should we strive to center it around other values, those of mutuality and spirituality?*

The journey to the good society can benefit greatly from the observation, supported by a great deal of social science data, that ever increasing levels of material goods are not a reliable source of human well-being or contentment—let alone the basis for a morally sound society. To cite but a few studies of a large body of findings: Frank M. Andrews and Stephen B. Withey found that the level of one's socioeconomic status had meager effects on one's "sense of well-being" and no significant effect on "satisfaction with life-as-a-whole." Jonathan L. Freedman discovered that levels of reported happiness did not vary greatly among the members of different economic classes, with the exception of the very poor, who tended to be less happy than others. David G. Myers reported that although per capita disposable (after-tax) income in inflation-adjusted dollars almost exactly doubled between 1960 and 1990, 32 percent of Americans reported that they were "very happy" in 1993, almost the same proportion as did in 1957 (35 percent). Although economic growth slowed after the mid-1970s, Americans' reported happiness was remarkably stable (nearly always between 30 and 35 percent) across both high-growth and low-growth periods.

HAPPINESS

These and other such data help us realize that the pursuit of well-being through ever higher levels of consumption is Sisyphean. When it comes to material goods, enough is never enough. This is not an argument in favor of a life of sackcloth and ashes, of poverty and self-denial. The argument is that once basic material needs (what Abraham Maslow called "creature comforts") are well sated and securely provided for, additional income does not add to happiness. On the contrary, hard evidence—not some hippie, touchy-feely, LSD-induced hallucination—shows that profound contentment is found in nourishing ends-based relationships, in bonding with others, in community building and public service, and in cultural and spiritual pursuits. Capitalism, the engine of affluence, has never aspired to address the whole person; typically it treats the person as *Homo economicus.* And of course, statist socialism subjugated rather than inspired. It is left to the evolving values and cultures of centrist societies to fill the void.

Nobel laureate Robert Fogel showed that periods of great affluence are regularly followed by what he calls Great Awakenings, and that we are due for one in the near future. Although it is quite evident that there is a growing thirst for a purpose deeper than conspicuous consumption, we may not have the ability to predict which specific form this yearning for spiritual fulfillment will take.

There are some who hold firmly that the form must be a religious one because no other speaks to the most profound matters that trouble the human soul, nor do others provide sound moral guidance. These believers find good support in numerous indicators that there was a considerable measure of religious revival in practically all forms of American religion over the last decades of the 20th century. The revival is said to be evident not merely in the number of people who participate in religious activities and the frequency of their participation in these activities, but also in the stronger, more involving, and stricter kinds of commitments many are making to religion. (Margaret Talbot has argued effectively that conservative Christians, especially fundamentalists, constitute the true counterculture of our age; they know and live a life rich in fulfillment, not centered around consumer goods.) Others see the spiritual revival as taking more secular forms, ranging from New Age cults to a growing interest in applied ethics.

PRIORITIES

Aside from making people more profoundly and truly content individuals, a major and broadly based upward shift on the Maslovian scale is a prerequisite for being able to better address some of the most tantalizing problems plaguing modern societies, whatever form such a shift may take. That is what is required before we can come into harmony with our environment, because these higher priorities put much less demand on scarce resources than do lower ones. And such a new set of priorities may well be the only conditions under which those who are well endowed would be willing to support serious reallocation of wealth and power, as their personal fortunes would no longer be based on amassing ever larger amounts of consumer goods. In addition, transitioning to a knowledge-based economy would free millions of people (one hopes all of them, gradually) to relate to each other mainly as members of families and communities, thus laying the social foundations for a society in which ends-based relationships dominate while instrumental ones are well contained.

The upward shift in priorities, a return to a sort of moderate counterculture, a turn toward voluntary simplicity—these require a grand dialogue about our personal and shared goals. (A return to a counterculture is not a recommendation for more abuse of controlled substances, promiscuity, and self-indulgence—which is about the last thing America needs—but the realization that one can find profound contentment in reflection, friendship, love, sunsets, and walks on the beach rather than in the pursuit of ever more control over ever more goods.) Intellectuals and the media can help launch such a dialogue and model the new forms of behavior. Public leaders can nurse the recognition of these values by moderating consumption at public events and ceremonies, and by celebrating those whose achievements are compatible with a good society rather than with a merely affluent one.

But ultimately, such a shift lies in changes in our hearts and minds, in our values and conduct—what Robert Bellah called the "habits of the heart." We shall not travel far toward a good society unless such a dialogue is soon launched and advanced to a good, spiritually uplifting conclusion.

Mr. Etzioni is editor of The Responsive Community. *From "Next: Three Steps Towards A Good Society," by Amitai Etzioni,* The Responsive Community, *Winter 2000–01, pages 49–58.*

Reprinted from *Current,* January 2001, pp. 29-33. Originally printed in *The Responsive Community,* Vol. II, No. 1, Winter 2000/01, pp. 49-58, which was adapted from the author's book *Next: The Road to the Good Society* (New York: Basic Books, 2001).

A New Era Of History:

YOU HAVE ENTERED THE MOST DECISIVE THREE DECADES IN HISTORY

Address by WM. VAN DUSEN WISHARD, *President, World Trends Research*
Delivered to the Emery Reves Memorial Lecture, Reves Center for International Studies, Delivered to
The College of William & Mary, Williamsburg, Virginia, November 13, 2000

It is a singular honor to give the inaugural Reves Memorial Lecture, and I want to thank Dean Reiss for the invitation.

Emery Reves was a remarkable man. Let me put it this way. If any of you are aspiring biographers or movie script writers, the story of Emery and Wendy Reves is your ticket to fame and fortune. As far as I can tell, it's a story that's never been told to the general public, even though Google gave me over 400 hits on Emery Reves' name.

Reves was born in Hungary in 1904, and grew up in the Europe of World War I and the League of Nations. Emery studied to become a concert pianist, had perfect pitch, and could whistle an entire Beethoven symphony. He earned his doctorate of political economy at the University of Zurich where his two best friends were fellow Hungarians John von Neumann, later to become one of the fathers of the computer, and William Fellner, eventually to be known as one of America's premier economists.

After university, Reves, who was fluent in nine languages, worked in Berlin as a writer, but had to flee—in his tuxedo, no less—just as Nazi Storm Troopers were about to seize him. He went to Paris in 1930 and founded the Cooperation Press Service, the first international media company, which eventually serviced 400 newspapers in 70 countries.

Reves helped Winston Churchill rise from the political ash heap in the 1930s after everyone thought Churchill was finished as a serious politician. All through the 1930s Reves responded to Hitler's bombastic speeches by getting Churchill to write replies, which Reves would publish in the newspapers of Europe the next day. Finally, as the German tanks rolled into Paris, Reves went to London, where Churchill asked him to revamp the British intelligence service.

Churchill then sent Reves to New York to help with the public relations campaign designed to urge America to support Britain. While in New York, Reves met the beautiful fashion model, Wendy Russell, a successful entrepreneur in her own right. After the war, they traveled all over Europe together, eventually buying the Riviera home of Coco Chanel, founder of the Chanel Perfume empire. During the 1950s and '60s, they entertained everyone from Churchill to Greta Garbo to Somerset Maugham to Albert Einstein. Emery became a major publisher, ultimately publishing Churchill's war memoirs. In the midst of this whirlwind life, Emery and Wendy amassed a $40 million art collection, comprised of some 1,400 works of art, which is now housed in the Dallas Museum of Art.

Reves had a remarkable sense of the movement of history. This is the way he put it: "Looking back five thousand years, it can be seen that every decade, every year, every day, has always been a 'transitional period.' Human history is nothing but an endless chain of 'transitions.' Transition is the only permanent thing on this earth."

Reves believed the world needs a new level of universal law. He recognized the different legal jurisdictions that exist within nations. But he said the time has come for all nations to be subject to a higher legal authority, just as a citizen of Williamsburg is subject to the higher legal authority of the state of Virginia as well as the United States. He believed such a universal legal authority is the only way to ensure world peace.

In 1945 Reves published his views in The Anatomy of Peace, a book described by Einstein as "the answer" to the political problems of the world and to the challenges posed by atomic energy. It sold nearly a million copies in America, and was translated into 25 languages in over 30 editions.

In The Anatomy of Peace, Reves made a comment I want to take as the basis of my remarks tonight: The great majority of the living never realizes the fundamental changes taking place during their lifetime.

Today, talk about "change" is commonplace. We all know that genetics, the computer and Internet are reshaping the global landscape.

But do we understand the "fundamental" changes as Reves says? Given our thrashing about trying to define the so-called "post Cold War era," or the "information age" or the "biological era," I'm not so sure.

From any standpoint, it's clear the world is at something of a historical dividing line—the end of the modern era that began in the 1500s; the end of the Industrial Age; the end of America's population and culture being drawn primarily from Europe; the end of the monopoly of the printed word as the dominant mode of communication; the end of the Atlantic-based economic, political and military global hegemony; the end of the colonial period; the end of the nation-state as the outer limits of a people's identity; the end of the masculine, hierarchical epoch; and, as some have suggested, perhaps the end of the Christian eon. We're in what the ancient Greeks called kairos—the "right moment" for a fundamental change in principles and symbols.

Exactly what kind of era is opening up is far from clear. The only obvious fact is that it's going to be global, whatever else it is. Obviously, one epoch doesn't stop one day and a new one start the next week. Years—even generations or centuries—of overlap sometimes take place.

So in this sense, we re in an "in-between period"—between two ages, two ways of organizing our affairs; two ways of viewing our relationships to each other as individuals and nations; and two ways of understanding our relationship to earth and the universe. I call this in between period an "Interregnum," which Webster defines as an "interval, a break in continuity." How long this Interregnum will last is anyone's guess, but I suspect it will be the defining framework of world affairs for at least the next half-century.

Tonight I want to comment on three trends, which are part of this Interregnum. Let me start by stating my bias: I am bullish on the future. We've got huge challenges ahead. But I believe in the capacity of the human spirit to surmount any challenge if given the vision, the will and the leadership. With this in mind, let's look at three trends that are affecting all of us.

First trend: For the first time in human history, the world is forging an awareness of our existence as a single entity. Thus nations are incorporating the planetary dimensions of life into the fabric of our economics, politics, culture and international relations. The shorthand for this is "Globalization."

We all have some idea of what globalization means. We've all probably read Tom Friedman's book, and discussed the issues focused by the WTO and IMF conferences.

But globalization is far more than just non-Western nations adopting free markets and democratic political systems. In my judgment, globalization is the most ambitious collective experiment ever undertaken by the human race. If it succeeds, a new phase of well being may open up for most of the human race. If it fails, it could retard progress for generations.

At its core, globalization means that Western ideas are gradually seeping into the social and political fabric of the world. And even deeper than that, globalization is about culture, tradition, historic relationships and modes of interaction; it's about existing institutions and why and how they evolved. In short, globalization goes to the psychic foundation of a people.

Look at what's happening. Nations are adopting such ideas as the sanctity of the individual, due process of law, universal education, the equality of women, human rights, private property, legal safeguards governing business and finance, science as the engine of social growth, concepts of civil society, and perhaps most importantly, the ability of people to take charge of their destiny and not simply accept the hand dealt them in life. For millions of people these concepts are new modes of thought. In India, for example, the idea of not accepting the hand dealt in life directly challenges the essence of the Hindu religion.

Sometimes it's hard for us Americans to appreciate the underlying differences between Western ideas and the foundations of other nations. Take some of the basic contrasts between Asia and the West. The West prizes individuality, while the East emphasizes relationships and community. The West sees people dominating nature, while the East sees people as part of nature. In the West there is a division between mind and heart. In the East mind and heart are unified. The West sees a split between mind and body, while for the East, mind and body are simply the harmony and interconnectedness between opposites. The West tends to be extraverted, while the East is inclined to be introverted. The West prizes knowledge, the East seeks wisdom.

Or take Africa. In many parts of Africa, the African is far from the glorification of the rational, materialist, secular attitude that characterizes the Westerner. The African doesn't dream of regarding himself as the master of nature as does the Western scientific attitude. For the African, he is a part of nature, and it never occurs to him that he might dominate it. It's only the Westerner who devotes his greatest energies to the discovery of natural causes, whereas the African is inclined to rely more on the unknown power of chance.

One could go on and on. But my point is to illustrate the deep psychological trauma nations are experiencing as they confront the effects of globalization. For example, what's happening in the Middle East is not solely the result of hatred between the Arabs and Jews. It's also partially a result of the disorienting effects of what is seen as an American secular steamroller that's crushing established traditions, relationships and ways of doing things.

We must remember it took centuries for Western political, social and economic concepts to evolve. They are the product of a unique Western psychology and experience. We cannot expect nations to graft alien social attitudes onto an indigenous societal structure and psychological outlook overnight. So we Americans must be sensitive to the profound human and psychological upheaval people are experiencing as globalization reorients their lives. Above all, we must not become psychologically or emotionally isolated from the rest of the world. And there's a danger of that happening.

Second trend: We may have entered an unforeseen stage of technology development, a stage without precedent in the history of science and technology.

At least since Francis Bacon (1561–1628) we have viewed the purpose of science and technology as being the improvement of the human condition. As Bacon put it, the "true and lawful end of the sciences is that human life [his emphasis] be enriched by new discoveries and powers."

And indeed it has. Take America. In 1900, one child in 10 died before age one. Today it's one in 150. During the last century, the real GDP, in constant dollars, increased by $48 trillion. In 1900, all the greatest mathematicians in the world together didn't have the problem-solving resources of today's fourth grader with a $20 pocket calculator. With mapping the human genome, we may soon see cures for some of our most agonizing diseases. On and on the marvels of science and technology go.

But along with these wonders, uncertainties arise. The question today is whether certain technologies exist not to improve the human condition, but for themselves, under their own laws, and for purposes that seem to be to supplant human meaning and significance altogether.

Consider a remark by the co-founder of MIT's Artificial Intelligence Lab and one of the world's leading authorities on artificial intelligence: "Suppose that the robot had all of the virtues of people and was smarter and understood things better. Then why would we want to prefer those grubby, old people? I don't see anything wrong with human life being devalued if we have something better." Now just absorb that thought for a moment. One of the world's leading scientists ready to "devalue human life" if we can create something he thinks is better. Setting aside the question of who decides what "better" is, in my view, intentionally devaluing human life is an organized form of self-destruction. And it's being promoted as "progress" by some of our most distinguished citizens and institutions.

The editor of Wired magazine says we're in the process of the "wiring of human and artificial minds into one planetary soul." Thus, he believes, we'll be the first species "to create our own successors." The co-founder of the Electronic Frontier Foundation says that the overriding flavor of being human ultimately will be "the disappearance of the self altogether, right into the collective organism of the mind."

Some computer scientists talk of artificial life creating its own civilization. Reports come of some scientists reconfiguring machines as psychological objects and reconfiguring people as living machines. We now use computers to psychoanalyze people. It's as if some scientists no longer see "people as human being," but rather "people as machine" and "machine as human being."

Finally, consider a report issued by The United States Commission on National Security/21st Century, headed by former senators Gary Hart and Warren Rudman. The report addresses a number of conventional security issues, but then it looks at some of the potential consequences of advancing technology. For example, it discusses the significance of genetic engineering altering the human genome, mixing the organic with the inorganic, and changing the very composition of a human being. It then offers this paragraph: "The implications of such developments should not be underestimated. Our understanding of all human social arrangements is based, ultimately, on an understanding of human nature. If that nature becomes subject to significant alteration through human artifice, then all such arrangements are thrown into doubt." The report concludes by saying, "there is a growing unease that we are upping the ante to the point that a single mistake or a single act of sheer evil could leave a potentially fatal wound."

In sum, we are creating technology that forces us to ask what are humans for once we've created super intelligent robots that can do anything humans can do, only do it a thousand times faster? Do we really want to be able to make genetic-based choices about a baby's intelligence or characteristics? What will it mean to be able to change the genetic structure not just of an individual child, but also of all future generations? In an age when information overwhelms us and power is unlimited, what gives purpose to our capacities and restraint to our power?

An equally difficult question is: What is the moral justification for permitting a miniscule proportion of the world's population, i.e., the scientific-technological visionaries, to determine the fate of earth and its six billion inhabitants when that fate could possibly include extinction? The flip side of this question is this: Despite the widespread talk of spirituality and fundamentalism, has technology, in actual fact, become America's god? These are some of the questions that will be answered one way or the other during your lifetime.

Some people within the scientific-technological community itself are already seeking to answer such questions. Bill Joy, cofounder and chief scientist of Sun Microsystems, suggests we've reached the point where we must "limit development of technologies that are too dangerous, by limiting our pursuit of certain kinds of knowledge." Joy acknowledges the pursuit of knowledge as one of the primary human goals at least since Aristotle. But, he says, "If open access to, and unlimited development of, knowledge henceforth puts us all in clear danger of extinction, then common sense demands that we reexamine even these basic, long-held beliefs."

Third trend: We are in the midst of a long-term spiritual and psychological reorientation that is increasingly generating uncertainty and instability.

This trend affects all of us, for we're all part of America's collective psychology, whether we realize it or not. The best measure of America's psychological and spiritual life is not public opinion polls telling us what percentage of the population believes in God. Rather, it's the content and quality of our culture. For culture is to a nation what dreams are to an individual—an indication of what's going on in the inner life.

When we look at the religions of the world, what's happening? Massive fragmentation. In America alone, there are over 1,500 religions, including such contradictions as "Catholic Buddhists." In a sense, religion is being privatized.

In my judgment, the world is experiencing a long-term reorientation of the spiritual expressions that came into existence roughly in the 1,000-year period between 800 B.C. and A.D. 700. These are the religions that have given the world its moral base, its psychological stability and its culture. Granted, this refocusing is proceeding at an uneven pace depending on local culture and circumstances.

Certainly in the West, this spiritual impulse has been steadily eroding as the formative dynamic of our culture, especially among the "creative minority." One need only look at the changing relationship between the roles of the priest and the psychologist to see what has been happening. Early in the 20th century, if someone had personal problems he or she went to the priest for advice. Gradually that changed, and people started going to their psychologist. According to psychologist Rollo May, between 1918 and 1981, the population of the U.S. increased 122 percent, but membership in the American Psychological Association grew by more than 14,000 percent. In England, the Anglican Church has apparently declined to the point where the government is considering training civil servants in family counseling in order to fill the gap left by the diminishing number of priests. Even more, in another two years, practicing Muslims will outnumber practicing Anglicans in England.

As the collective spiritual impulse that originally shaped America and Europe fragments, people seek alternatives. Such a search is seen in New Age spirituality; in the rise of cults such as "Heaven's Gate"; in exploration of the paranormal; in extremist movements such as Germany's "skinheads"; in interest in mysticism, occultism, Buddhism and Eastern philosophy; in the rise of fundamentalism, which is taking place in all the world's religions; in the search for ancient wisdom as seen in The Celestine Prophecy; in the emergence of countless new schools of psychology; in the belief that extraterrestrial life has come to save us from ourselves; and last but certainly not least, in terrorism, which, at its core, is a demonic hatred expressed in spiritual terms.

Part of the psychological reorientation taking place is the breakup of our collective inner images of wholeness. For example, we used to talk about "Heaven," which denoted the transcendent realm, eternity, the dwelling place of the gods. Now we just speak of "space," which has no spiritual connotation. It used to be that when we looked up in the sky at nighttime, we saw the moon in heaven. Now, when we stand on the moon, we see the earth in heaven. In a sense, heaven and earth have become one, and so our whole symbolic system has been jumbled. We used to talk of "Mother Earth," which had a vital emotional association. From time immemorial, nature was filled with spirit. Now we just speak of "matter," a lifeless nature bereft of gods. Thus the transcendent meaning is diminished.

The function of symbolic language—such as "Heaven" and "Mother Earth"—is to link our consciousness to the roots of our being, to connect our consciousness to its base in the unconscious. When that link is devalued or discarded, there is little left to sustain the inner life of the individual. Few people are inwardly fed by any primal source of wholeness. In effect, our symbolic life and language have been displaced by a vocabulary of technology, a vocabulary that's increasingly devoid of transcendent meaning.

Another aspect of the psychological reorientation is the question of what is happening collectively to our unconscious life. By definition, the unconscious life is unknowable, and thus most of us never think about it. In fact, with all the scientific emphasis on investigating consciousness, science appears reluctant to approach the question of the unconscious. Yet the unconscious may be a greater influence on our lives than is consciousness. For the unconscious can produce psychic epidemics that erupt into contemporary events, and even become a collective madness, as was the origin of World War II.

We can see a reflection of what's happening to our unconscious in both art and our spiritual expressions. Take the difference one sees between Rembrandt and Picasso, and I'm not talking about aesthetic preference, but rather the psychic content of their art. Rembrandt painted during a time of psychological integration and wholeness, and thus his art is objective. Picasso painted during an era of psychological fracture and dissociation. Thus his paintings, like most modern art, are subjective. Picasso and modern art give us a sense of what's happening to our common unconscious life, for, as Shakespeare told us, art holds the mirror up to nature, and the unconscious is pure nature.

In a sense, the soul of America—indeed, of the world—is in a giant search for some greater expression of life. Despite the benefits of modernization, technological society offers no underlying meaning to life. Thus the search taking place is both healthy and normal—given the seminal shift to an entirely new epoch that is occurring as we speak.

What we're talking about is at the core of the crisis of meaning that afflicts not only America, but Europe and Asia as well. It's a global crisis of meaning. For example, John Pomfret writes in the International Herald Tribune from Beijing, "Across China people are struggling to redefine notions of success and failure, right and wrong. The quest for something to believe in is one of the unifying characteristics of China today." Wimal Dissanayake of the East/West Center in Hawaii notes that with increased technology and modernization, "the loss of self is an acute problem in Eastern societies." He notes the decline in family and authority, and concludes by saying, "Eastern religion no longer is the binding force in [Asian] society."

The late Joseph Campbell, one of the world's leading authorities on the function of myth and religious symbols, noted that the great spiritual myths of the world have historically fulfilled four functions: (1) To give the individual a sense of awe and wonder before the mystery of being; (2) to offer an awareness of the order of the universe that will maintain that wonder and awe; (3) to relate the individual to society, and to provide and validate a collective moral order; and (4) to regulate the psyche, to coordinate the individual's conscious life with his unconscious life or his instinct system. That's the function of religion.

But science has changed our understanding of the universe; travel and communications technology have enabled us to comprehend all religious systems and mythology in relation to our own and see their similarities; historical research suggests that the world's religious scriptures should be approached symbolically rather than literally; and psychology has given us new insights into the possible transpersonal dimension of the psyche. Thus the great religious myths, which used to operate in a globe where people lacked contemporary scientific understanding and were isolated from each other, are now unable to fulfill their primary functions in the same manner as in an earlier period. We have reached a point of increasing "mythlessness," which is the core of today's crisis of meaning. For all people need a "story" to live by, a story which gives meaning and coherence to their collective association.

Let me quickly summarize what we've been discussing. (1) Globalization—possibly the most ambitious collective human experiment in history; (2) a new stage of technology operating in its own right, under its own laws and for its own purposes; and (3) a long-term psychological and spiritual reorientation. These are only three of the trends shaping our future. And it's because of the magnitude and significance of such trends that I suggest the next three decades will be the most decisive thirty-year period in human history.

How do we respond to such a challenge? We're already responding in the most sweeping redefinition of life America has ever known. We're redefining and restructuring all our institutions. Corporations are redefining their mission, structure and modus operandi. In education, we're trying countless new experiments from vouchers to charter schools to home schooling. Alternative Dispute Resolution (ADR) is helping lift the burden off the back of our legal system. Civic and charitable organizations are assuming functions formerly undertaken by local governments. Some local functions, such as firefighting and neighborhood security are being privatized. More people are involved in efforts to help the elderly and those in poverty. In fact, it's estimated that well over fifty percent of all adult Americans donate a portion of their time to non-profit social efforts.

Against the background of the three trends I mentioned, perhaps this is a modest start, but at least it's a start. Clearly, there's another level of effort to move to. As Bill Joy suggests, such efforts must include an examination of the potential downsides of certain technologies, and deciding whether we should continue research and development of technologies that could, in Joy's words, bring the world to the edge of extinction. Obviously, such an examination must be done in a global context if it's to be valid.

But another question is, how are you and I to live in a world experiencing such upheaval? What gives meaning to our daily efforts in a world that's changing faster than individuals and institutions can assimilate?

I believe the starting place is Understanding; simply to understand, as Emery Reves put it, the fundamental changes taking place. And I suggest that the Reves Center for International Studies is the perfect place to begin to gain such understanding. This is where you can learn to see the world "whole"—see the interplay of national interests, culture, history, economics, technology, demographics, and our relationship to earth and the natural world. This is where you can build the life-long friendships with people from other nations and ethnic backgrounds, friendships that will form part of the fabric of a new era.

Most importantly, the Reves Center is where you can gain the understanding of people and what makes us tick. For the individual is the carrier of civilization—not technology, not government, but people like you and me. If we're to understand why history has unfolded as it has, and what is behind the changes taking place today, we need to understand people and why we do what we do.

An understanding of people. Where does it start? We've all heard Socrates' phrase "Know thyself" so often that we dismiss it as just another Athenian sound bite. But how well do we know ourselves? Do we really know the opposites of good and evil that dwell within each of us? Do we know how we project our own inferior qualities onto other people and nations, thus creating division in the world? Do we know what our reactions to other people and nations signify about ourselves? Do we know what we love and what we hate, and what that tells us about ourselves? Do we know how to turn our weaknesses into strengths? Or how to find wholeness and completeness in life? That's what "Know thyself" is all about.

Equally important is the question of security. Great change creates new challenges and opportunities. It also generates insecurity, and both change and insecurity will increase in the coming years. So what provides security in a time of upheaval? A fat 401(K)? An ever-rising Dow? The family, friends? The social structure? Military might? All these obviously provide a certain measure of security.

But all these can change very quickly. Even disappear. What then?

Let me suggest one source of security that I have found helpful. It is this: knowing who I am, why I am here, and what the meaning of my life is. If I know that, then I am connected to the deepest roots of my being, to the depths of my soul. That is a source of security that every person has to find for him or herself. There's no formula, only an inner journey that each of us can make. And that journey is important for this reason. We are all part of the same larger reality, of some common psychological fabric. And the way I live my life, the choices I make, either enhance or degrade that common fabric. The journey we make not only deepens our own inner life, but it also affects the collective soul of America.

Issues like these we've been talking about are important for many reasons, but I'll mention just one, and with this I'll close. An integrated world can only be built by integrated personalities. There's an impulse in the soul of humanity toward a unity, toward a worldwide consciousness. But it can only be made a reality by people who have bridged the divisions within themselves. Nelson Mandela is the example of this, an integrated personality who was able to rise above parochial divisions and create a new climate of peace for his nation.

Somehow I think Mandela and Emery Reves would have been kindred spirits had they ever met. Both had a world perspective, and both understood the unfolding of a new era of history.

So I guess the test for us is, each in our own unique way, in our own sphere of activity however limited we may feel it to be, to be the Mandelas for the future, the Sister Teresas for a new era, the John and Jane Does who make a difference. And above all, to reach for that future with all the zest, determination and joy of living that so characterized Emery and Wendy Reves.

Thank you.

From *Vital Speeches of the Day,* December 1, 2000, pp. 470-474. © 2000 by City News Publishing Company, Inc.

Index

Index

multinational corporations, weaknesses of, 39–41

Muncie, Indiana, 116

N

Namibia, AIDS in, 153

National Automobile Dealers Association, 3

National Practitioner Data Bank (NPDB), 147

National Salvage Motor Vehicle Consumer Protection Act, 37

natural resources, 196, 197–198

natural selection, 212–213

Negro Family: The Case for National Action, The (Moynihan), 18

Netherlands, prostitution in, 92

Nevada, malpractice insurance and, 146

New Deal, income inequality and, 54

New Jersey, malpractice insurance and, 146

Nietzsche, Friedrich, 21–22

Novak, Robert, 55

O

O'Connor, Sandra Day, 80

obstetricians, cost of malpractice insurance and, 142, 145, 148

oceanic fish catch, 195, 202

offshore outsourcing, 42–44

oil, 196–198

Omnibus Consolidated and Emergency Appropriations Act of 1998, 37

operant conditioning, media violence and, 183–184

orphans, AIDS and, 155

out-of-wedlock childbearing. *See* unmarried mothers

P

Palestinians, conflict of, with Israel and terrorism, 190

patent life extension, 37

Pennsylvania, malpractice insurance and, 146

Personal Responsibility and Work Opportunity Act, 70–75

Petrovich, Steve, 177–178

pharmaceutical industry, 37

physicians, cost of malpractice insurance and, 142–150

pluralism, 27–28

police: in Fort Myers, Florida, 176–181; reform of criminal justice system and, 169–170

population growth, 194–200, 203–206

poverty, sustainable development and, 202

power: class and, in America, 26–29; political contributions and, 36–38

prejudices, 84–87

Prince, Rebecca, 176, 178–179, 180–181

problem-oriented policing (POP), 162, 163, 180–181

Promise of Justice, A (Protess and Warden), 174

propaedeutic function, of public schools, 139–140

prosecutors, reform of criminal justice system and, 169

prostitution, 88–93; AIDS in Africa and, 155–157

Prostitution of Sexuality, The (Barry), 92–93

Protess, David, 174

Prussia, public school education and, 138–139

public school education, 137–141

R

racial issues: capital punishment and, 174; the fragmentation of social life and, 15

Rakoff, Jed S., 172

rape, global trends in, 162

Raymond, Janice, 89, 91–92

recreation areas, population growth and, 196

Reeves, Emery, 224

religion: community building and, 220–221, 223; the fragmentation of social life and, 15; re-moralizing America and, 21–23; spiritual reorientation and, 226–228; terrorism and, 186–191

Republican Party, 57, 70

rights: civil liberties and, and terrorism, 30–35; conflicts between, 8

Ritalin, 104

robbery, global trends in, 162

role models, media violence and, 184

Rowley, Coleen, 31–33

Ruranga, Rubaramira, 159

S

Saudi Arabia, 190

saving and loan (S&L) crisis, 37

Scalia, Antonin, 95

Schwartz, Joseph, 178

searches, balance rights and civil liberties and, 31

Section 6001: Superfund Recycling Equity, 36

security, balance between rights and civil liberties and, 30–35

selective function, of public schools, 139

service industries: offshore outsourcing and, 42–44; weaknesses of globalization and, 40

sex tourism, 89

sex trafficking, 88–93

sex, married couples and, 119–123

sexual orientation, the fragmentation of social life and, 15. *See also* homosexuality

shipping costs, weaknesses of globalization and, 40

single-parent families. *See* unmarried mothers

slavery, cultural attitudes toward marriage and, 127–128

small towns, the decline of, in the Great Plains, 45–47

smart houses, 109

Smith, Adam, 22

smoking, social conflict and, 9

social identity theory, 85

soil degradation, 202

Sosenko, Alexander, 142–146, 148–150

South Africa, AIDS in, 152, 153, 157–158

spousal rape, 115

Staal, Stephanie, 129, 131

"superstar" hypothesis, income inequality and, 53, 54

Supreme Court, U.S., right to privacy of homosexuals and, 94–96

Surrealism, 217

surveillance, balance rights and civil liberties and, 31

sustainable development, 201–211

Swaziland, AIDS in, 153

sweat equity, housing and, 222

Sweden: income distribution in, 57; unmarried mothers in, 124

symbolic interactionism, 5–6

T

Tajfel, Henri, 85

taxes, income inequality and, 57–58

technological development, 226; genetic engineering, 212–215; income inequality and, 53, 54; sustainable development and, 202

Temporary Assistance to Needy Families (TANF), 70–75

terrorism: al-Qaida and, 186–191; balance between rights and civil liberties and, 30–35

Test Your Knowledge Form

We encourage you to photocopy and use this page as a tool to assess how the articles in *Annual Editions* expand on the information in your textbook. By reflecting on the articles you will gain enhanced text information. You can also access this useful form on a product's book support Web site at *http://www.dushkin.com/online/*.

NAME: DATE:

_____

TITLE AND NUMBER OF ARTICLE:

_____

BRIEFLY STATE THE MAIN IDEA OF THIS ARTICLE:

_____

LIST THREE IMPORTANT FACTS THAT THE AUTHOR USES TO SUPPORT THE MAIN IDEA:

_____

WHAT INFORMATION OR IDEAS DISCUSSED IN THIS ARTICLE ARE ALSO DISCUSSED IN YOUR TEXTBOOK OR OTHER READINGS THAT YOU HAVE DONE? LIST THE TEXTBOOK CHAPTERS AND PAGE NUMBERS:

_____

LIST ANY EXAMPLES OF BIAS OR FAULTY REASONING THAT YOU FOUND IN THE ARTICLE:

_____

LIST ANY NEW TERMS/CONCEPTS THAT WERE DISCUSSED IN THE ARTICLE, AND WRITE A SHORT DEFINITION:

We Want Your Advice

ANNUAL EDITIONS revisions depend on two major opinion sources: one is our Advisory Board, listed in the front of this volume, which works with us in scanning the thousands of articles published in the public press each year; the other is you—the person actually using the book. Please help us and the users of the next edition by completing the prepaid article rating form on this page and returning it to us. Thank you for your help!

ANNUAL EDITIONS: Social Problems 04/05

ARTICLE RATING FORM

Here is an opportunity for you to have direct input into the next revision of this volume.
We would like you to rate each of the articles listed below, using the following scale:

1. **Excellent: should definitely be retained**
2. **Above average: should probably be retained**
3. **Below average: should probably be deleted**
4. **Poor: should definitely be deleted**

Your ratings will play a vital part in the next revision.
Please mail this prepaid form to us as soon as possible.
Thanks for your help!

RATING	ARTICLE
	1. Social Problems: Definitions, Theories, and Analysis
	2. The Fragmentation of Social Life
	3. How to Re-Moralize America
	4. Who Rules America?
	5. Rights, Liberties, and Security: Recalibrating the Balance After September 11
	6. How the Little Guy Gets Crunched
	7. The End of Globalization
	8. Where the Good Jobs Are Going
	9. A Broken Heartland
	10. For Richer: How the Permissive Capitalism of the Boom Destroyed American Equality
	11. The Real Face of Homelessness
	12. In Harm's Way: The Working Class on the War Front and the Home Front
	13. Corporate Welfare
	14. Requiem for Welfare
	15. What's At Stake
	16. Why We Hate
	17. Human Rights, Sex Trafficking, and Prostitution
	18. The War Over Gay Marriage
	19. The New Gender Gap
	20. When Baby Boomers Grow Old
	21. The American Family
	22. We're Not in the Mood
	23. Divorce and Cohabitation: Why We Don't Marry
	24. Should You Stay Together for the Kids?
	25. Against School: How Public Education Cripples Our Kids, and Why
	26. The Doctor Won't See You Now
	27. Death Stalks a Continent
	28. Global Trends in Crime
	29. Reasonable Doubts
	30. Causes and Consequences of Wrongful Convictions
	31. On Patrol
	32. Teaching Kids to Kill
	33. The New Terrorism: Securing the Nation Against a Messianic Foe
	34. Sixteen Impacts of Population Growth

RATING	ARTICLE
	35. Achievements and Challenges
	36. The Future of Humanity
	37. American Culture Goes Global, or Does It?
	38. Community Building: Steps Toward a Good Society
	39. A New Era of History

(Continued on next page)

BUSINESS REPLY MAIL
FIRST CLASS MAIL PERMIT NO. 551 DUBUQUE IA

POSTAGE WILL BE PAID BY ADDRESEE

McGraw-Hill/Dushkin
2460 KERPER BLVD
DUBUQUE, IA 52001-9902

ABOUT YOU

Name   Date

Are you a teacher? ❏   A student? ❏
Your school's name

Department

Address   City   State   Zip

School telephone #

YOUR COMMENTS ARE IMPORTANT TO US!

Please fill in the following information:
For which course did you use this book?

Did you use a text with this ANNUAL EDITION?   ❏ yes ❏ no
What was the title of the text?

What are your general reactions to the *Annual Editions* concept?

Have you read any pertinent articles recently that you think should be included in the next edition? Explain.

Are there any articles that you feel should be replaced in the next edition? Why?

Are there any World Wide Web sites that you feel should be included in the next edition? Please annotate.

May we contact you for editorial input?   ❏ yes ❏ no
May we quote your comments?   ❏ yes ❏ no